THE MAMMOTH BOOK OF

STORMS,
SHIPWRECKS AND
SEA DISASTERS

Also available

The Mammoth Book of Awesome Comic Fantasy
The Mammoth Book of Battles
The Mammoth Book of Best New Horror 2003
The Mammoth Book of Best New Science Fiction 16
The Mammoth Book of Comic Crime
The Mammoth Book of Comic Fantasy
The Mammoth Book of SAS & Elite Forces
The Mammoth Book of Endurance and Adventure
The Mammoth Book of Fighter Pilots
The Mammoth Book of Future Cops
The Mammoth Book of Great Detectives
The Mammoth Book of Haunted House Stories
The Mammoth Book of Heroes
The Mammoth Book of Heroic and Outrageous Women
The Mammoth Book of How It Happened: Battles
The Mammoth Book of How It Happened: Naval Battles
The Mammoth Book of How It Happened World War I
The Mammoth Book of How It Happened World War II
The Mammoth Book of Jack the Ripper
The Mammoth Book of Legal Thrillers
The Mammoth Book of Life Before the Mast
The Mammoth Book of Maneaters
The Mammoth Book of Men O'War
The Mammoth Book of Murder
The Mammoth Book of Murder and Science
The Mammoth Book of Oddballs and Eccentrics
The Mammoth Book of Pulp Action
The Mammoth Book of Puzzles
The Mammoth Book of Roman Whodunnits
The Mammoth Book of Secrets of the SAS and Elite Forces
The Mammoth Book of Seriously Comic Fantasy
The Mammoth Book of Soldiers at War
The Mammoth Book of Sword & Honour
The Mammoth Book of The Edge
The Mammoth Book of Travel in Dangerous Places
The Mammoth Book of True Crime (New Edition)
The Mammoth Book of True War Stories
The Mammoth Book of Unsolved Crimes
The Mammoth Book of Unsolved Mysteries
The Mammoth Book of Vampires
The Mammoth Book of Vampire Stories by Women
The Mammoth Book of War Correspondents
The Mammoth Book of Women who Kill

THE MAMMOTH BOOK OF
STORMS, SHIPWRECKS AND SEA DISASTERS

Edited by

Richard Russell Lawrence

CARROLL & GRAF PUBLISHERS
New York

Carroll & Graf Publishers
An imprint of Avalon Publishing Group, Inc.
245 W. 17th Street
NY 10011
www.carrollandgraf.com

AVALON
publishing group incorporated

First published in the UK by Robinson,
an imprint of Constable & Robinson Ltd 2004

First Carroll & Graf edition 2004

ISBN 0-7867-1468-9

Printed and bound in the EU

CONTENTS

Introduction   **1**

Natural   **5**

Acts, 27 St Paul's Shipwreck (1st century AD)   7
Shipwrecks of the Spanish Armada (1588)   11
Armada map   20
Portuguese Maritime Disasters 1550–1650   22
Map of Portuguese Maritime Disasters 1550–1650   23
Wrecked off New England (1635)   37
The Wreck of HMS *Proserpine* (1799)   44
HMS *Banterer* (1808)   55
The Loss of HMS *St George* and HMS *Defence* (1811)   61
The Wreck of HMS *Penelope* (1815)   68
The Wreck of HMS *Medusa* (1816)   73
The Wreck of HMS *Alceste* (1817)   77
Stove in by a whale (1820)   93
The *Royal Charter* Storm (1859)   147
Royal Charter map   148
The Wreck of the *Serica* (1868)   160
The Sinking of the *Titanic* (1912)   183
Cross-section of SS *Titanic*   186
The Last of the Windjammers (1920)   215
Schooner *Rosamund* (illustration)   216
Storm at Sea (1941)   246

Plymouth to Sydney in One Stage (1966)   250
Gipsy Moth IV (illustration)   251
Nightmare in the Southern Ocean (1967)   269
Adrift for 117 Days (1973)   291
(Map of) Outward track of Maurice &
   Maralyn Bailey's yacht *Auralyn*   292
Adrift for 117 days map   293
Capsized off Kodiak (1989)   342
Capsized off Kodiak map   343
Hurricane Roxanne (1995)   356
Hurricane Roxanne map   357
Vessels hit by Hurricane Roxanne   358
The Dismasting of *Kingfisher 2* (2003)   384
Kingfisher 2 map   385

Manmade   **389**

Victims of War

Wreck of HMS *Amazon* and
   Les Droits de l'Homme (1797)   391
Victims of War map   392
The Sinking of HMS *Audacious* (1914)   400
The Sinking of HMS *Hampshire* (1916)   402
The Sinking of the Hospital Ship, *Britannic* (1916)   405
The Sinking of the SS *Athenia* (1939)   414

Fire

The Burning of the *Elizabeth* (c.1762)   426
HMS *Boyne* (1795)   427
The Blowing Up of HMS *Amphion* (1796)   428
HMS *Resistance* is Struck by Lightning (1798)   431

Error

The Sinking of HMS *Victoria* (1893)   433
The *Torrey Canyon* (1967)   435
Torrey Canyon map   436
Exxon Valdez (1989)   454

Exxon Valdez map   455
The *Kursk* Disaster (2000)   467
SSGN *Kursk* diagram   468
Kursk map   469
The *Prestige* Disaster (2002)   475
Prestige and *Erika* map   476
The *Tricolor* (2002)   478

Unexplained   483

Jonah   485
Unexplained Events map   487
The Flying Dutchman (1821)   489
The Mystery of the *Mary Celeste* (1872)   492
Mary Celeste map   493
The Bermuda Triangle (1945)   495

Bibliography and Sources   499

Introduction

"Worse things have happened at sea" was a well-known phrase which was offered as a form of consolation. This book is a collection of some of the worst things that have happened – at sea. As historians are more likely to belong to the category of armchair sailors, it is appropriate to introduce this collection with the words of real sailors.

Samuel Kelly, an 18th-century seaman, wrote:

Seamen are neither reckoned among the living nor the dead, their whole lives being spent in jeopardy. No sooner is one peril over, but another comes rolling on, like the waves of a fullgrown sea.

Even among seamen some claimed that they faced more "danger and hardship" than others. Owen Chase did so on the basis of his experience of "being stove in by a whale" in 1821. This incident may have been the inspiration for Herman Melville's *Moby Dick*. Describing an earlier incident, Chase wrote:

Strange to tell, not a man was injured by this accident. Thus it happens very frequently in the whaling business, that boats are stove; oars, harpoons, and lines broken; hands and wrists sprained; boats upset, and whole crews left for hours in the water, without any of these accidents extending to the loss of life. We are so much accustomed to the continual recurrence of such scenes as these, that we become familiarized to them, and consequently always feel that confidence and self-possession, which teaches us every expedient in danger, and inures the body, as well as the mind, to fatigue, privation, and peril, in frequent cases exceeding belief. It is this danger and hardship that makes the sailor; indeed it is the distinguishing qualification amongst us; and it is a common boast of the whaleman, that he has escaped from sudden and apparently inevitable destruction oftener than his fellow. He is accordingly valued on this account, without much reference to other qualities.

Another incident which was caused by a yacht being "stove in by a whale" happened in 1973. It resulted in a married couple, Maurice and Maralyn Bailey, being cast adrift for 117 days in the Pacific.

In the 16th century, Simao Ferreira Paes described the lives of the pioneering Portuguese seamen:

Sleeping ordinarily with death in their arms, and fighting against the four elements, driving their wretched bodies until they lose their precious lives, and wrapped in rags and tatters, and thrown to the fishes for their miserable graves, they scorn all these misfortunes and endure all these dangers. . . They sail the most distant seas, suffer the most unhealthy climates, face misery so vile that it is impossible to conceive of it.

The rest of us can only agree with the Danish Major General Tellequist. In 1811 he wrote of the wreck of HMS *St George* and HMS *Defence* on the coast of Jutland:

I am very sorry, Sir, that I cannot give your Excellency of this accident an account less sorrowful.

Some of these accounts are so remarkable that one can only

marvel at them. For instance, Violet Jessop, who was involved in no less than four disasters at sea, including the sinking of the *Titanic* and her sister-ship the *Britannic*. Before the *Titanic* disaster she had been aboard the first Titanic class ship, the *Olympic*, when it was rammed by the cruiser HMS *Hawke*. She was still on board the *Olympic* in October, 1914 when it attempted to assist the sinking battleship HMS *Audacious*.

This collection is divided into three sections: Natural, Manmade and Unexplained. The Natural section consists of accounts involving ice, storm and wreck. The Manmade section consists of accounts involving Victims of War and disasters caused by Fire and by Error. It is interesting that the majority of the older accounts fall into the categories of Storm and Wreck but many of the more recent accounts fall into the category of Error. The Unexplained section includes mysteries like the *Mary Celeste* and the Bermuda Triangle. In each section the accounts are listed chronologically.

Richard Russell Lawrence

Natural

St Paul's Shipwreck

The apostle, Paul, was frequently accused of causing trouble by the Jewish religious authorities. Finally, in his own defence, he appealed to Caesar (in Acts chapter 25, verse 10). He was able to do this because he was a Roman citizen. Although the Roman authorities considered him innocent, once he had appealed to Caesar he had to go to Rome. On the way he was shipwrecked. Luke accompanied him on the journey and was an eyewitness. Luke was the author of the book of Acts. In chapter 27 he wrote:

1. And when it was determined that we should sail into Italy, they delivered Paul and certain other prisoners unto one named Julius, a centurion of Augustus' band.
2. And entering into a ship of Adramyttium, we launched, meaning to sail by the coasts of Asia; one Aristarchos, a Macedonian of Thessalonica, being with us.
3. And the next day we touched at Sidon. And Julius courteously entreated Paul, and but gave him liberty to go unto his friends to refresh himself.
4. And when we had launched from thence, we sailed under Cyprus, because the winds were contrary.
5. And when we had sailed over the sea of Cilicia and Pamphyila, we came to Myra, a city of Lycia.

6. And there the centurion found a ship of Alexandria sailing into Italy; and he put us therein.

7. And when we had sailed slowly many days, and scarce were come over against Cnidus, the wind not suffering us, we sailed under Crete, over against Salmone.

8. And, hardly passing it, came unto a place which is called the fair havens: nigh whereunto was the city of Lasea.

9. Now when much time was spent, and when sailing was now dangerous, because the fast was now already past, Paul admonished them,

10. And said unto them, Sirs, I perceive that this voyage will be with hurt and much damage, not only of the lading and ship, but also of our lives.

11. Nevertheless the centurion believed the master and the owner of the ship more than those things which were spoken by Paul.

12. And because the haven was not commodious to winter in, the more part advised to depart thence also, if by any means they might attain to Phenice, and there to winter; which is an haven of Crete, and lieth toward the south west and north west.

13. And when the south wind blew softly, supposing that they had obtained their purpose, loosing thence, they sailed close by Crete.

14. But not long after there arose against it a tempestuous wind, called Euroclydon.

15. And when the ship was caught, and could not bear up into the wind, we let her drive.

16. And running under a certain island which is called Clauda, we had much work to come by the boat:

17. Which when they had taken up, they used helps, undergirding the ship; and, fearing lest they should fall into the quicksands, strake sail, and so were driven.

18. And we being exceedingly tossed with a tempest, the next day they lightened the ship;

19. And the third day we cast out with our own hands the tackling of the ship.

20. And when neither sun nor stars in many days appeared, and no small tempest lay on us, all hope that we should be saved was then taken away.

21. But after long abstinence Paul stood forth in the midst of them, and said, Sirs, ye should have hearkened unto me, and not have loosed from Crete, and to have gained this harm and loss.

22. And now I exhort you to be of good cheer: for there shall be no loss of any man's life among you, but of the ship.

23. For there stood by me this night the angel of God, whose I am, and whom I serve;

24. Saying, fear not Paul thou must be brought before Caesar: and, lo, God hath given thee all them that sail with thee.

25. Wherefore, sirs, be of good cheer: for I believe God, that it shall be even as it was told me.

26. How be it we must be cast upon a certain island.

27. But when the fourteenth night was come, as we were driven up and down in Adria, about midnight the shipmen deemed that they drew near to some country;

28. And sounded, and found it twenty fathoms: and when they had gone a little further they sounded again, and found it fifteen fathoms.

29. Then fearing lest they should have fallen upon rocks, they cast four anchors out of the stern, and wished for the day.

30. And as the shipmen were about to flee out of the ship, when they had let down the boat into the sea, under colour as though they would have cast anchors out of the foreship,

31. Paul said to the centurion and to the soldiers, Except these abide in the ship, ye cannot be saved.

32. Then the soldiers cut off the ropes of the boat, and let her fall off.

33. And while the day was coming on, Paul besought them all to take meat, saying, This day is the fourteenth day that ye have tarried and continued fasting, having taken nothing.

34. Wherefore I pray you to take some meat: for this is for your health: for there shall not an hair fall from the head of any of you.

35. And when he had thus spoken, he took bread, and gave thanks to God in presence of them all: and when he had broken it, he began to eat.

36. Then were they all of good cheer, and they also took some meat.

37. And we were in all in the ship two hundred threescore and sixteen souls.

38. And when they had eaten enough, they lightened the ship, and cast out the wheat into the sea.

39. And when it was day, they knew not the land: but they discovered a certain creek with a shore, into the which they were minded, if it were possible, to thrust in the ship.

40. And when they had taken up the anchors, they committed themselves unto the sea, and loosed the rudder bands, and hoisted up the mainsail to the wind, and made toward shore.

41. And falling into a place here two seas met, they ran the ship aground; and the forepart stuck fast, and remained unmoveable, but the hinder part was broken with the violence of the waves.

42. And the soldiers' counsel was to kill the prisoners, lest any of them should swim out, and escape.

43. But the centurion, willing to save Paul, kept them from their purpose; and commanded that they which could swim should cast themselves first into the sea, and get to land:

44. And the rest, some on boards, and some on broken pieces of the ship. And so it came to pass, that they escaped all safe to land.

They had landed on Malta. They continued their journey in another ship, three months later.

Shipwrecks of the Spanish Armada

In 1588 King Philip II of Spain attempted to invade England. His fleet was known as the Armada. One hundred and forty-one ships sailed from Lisbon and fought their way through the English Channel to Calais. At Calais they were to embark the army of the Duke of Parma. The English attacked with fireships. The ships of the Armada set sail without any defensive formation. The Armada sailed north, pursued by the English as far as the Firth of Forth. The Armada began to disperse, seeking shelter from the bad weather and attacks. The remaining ships continued in a homeward direction, around the northern coast of Scotland and Ireland. Many of them were wrecked on the Scottish and Irish coasts.

Only 67 ships reached Spain. Many of those ships were badly damaged, their men dead or dying of disease and thirst. One third of all the men who sailed from Spain did not return. There exists approximately ten days difference between the dates given in English and Spanish accounts.

By 21 August the remaining ships of the Spanish Armada were straggling north of Ireland and Scotland. On 21 August the Duke of Medina Sidonia wrote:

After this long-continued bad and contrary weather . . . on four separate nights heavy gales with strong winds, thick fogs and rain . . . By God's mercy, yesterday at noon, the wind shifted to the west, somewhat more in our favour: We are therefore able to sail in a southerly direction . . . The wind has now veered to the West North West . . . Pray consider the distress of the Armada after so terrible a voyage.

Pedro Coco Calderon was purser-in-chief of the Armada:

From 24 (August) to 4 September we sailed without knowing whither, through constant storms, fogs and squalls. As this hulk could not beat to windward it was necessary to keep out at sea, and we were unable to discover the main body of the Armada until the 4th . . . when we joined it.

Pedro Coco Calderon continued:

From 5–10 [September], [having sighted some Armada ships which the heavy sea prevented them from joining] we continued to make Cape Clear, always working to windward, breaking our tackle, and taking a great deal of water . . . On the west coast of Ireland this hulk found herself near an island . . . the sea running strongly towards the land, to the great danger of the hulk. The purser [Calderon] ordered her to tack to the north-west, which took her 30 leagues distant, and it is believed that the rest of the Armada will have done the same. If not they will certainly have lost some of the ships, as the coast is rough, the sea heavy, and the winds strong from the seaward.

Pedro Coco Calderon's prediction was correct.

Captain Francisco de Cuellar had been in command of the San Pedro. *This ship was a Spanish galleon of 530 tons and 24 guns. It had a complement of 90 sailors and 184 soldiers. The* San Pedro *belonged to the Levantine squadron. The* San Pedro *was heavily involved in the fighting off Calais. A year later de Cuellar wrote from Antwerp:*

I believe you will be amazed to see this letter, for you can have had but little confidence in my being alive. It is to assure you of this fact that I am now writing, and at some length, as I have been given cause enough by the very great tribulations and misfortunes I have suffered since the day the Armada left Lisbon for England, from all of which our Lord in His infinite mercy delivered me. I have had no opportunity to write to you for over a year, nor could I do so before God brought me to these States of Flanders, whither I came twelve days ago with all those Spaniards who had escaped from the ships wrecked in Ireland, Scotland and Shetland, being more than twenty of the largest in the Armada. In them came a great army of splendid infantrymen, many captains, ensigns, camp-masters and other officers of war, as well as many gentlemen and scions of the nobility; yet out of all these [the latter] numbering more than two hundred, not five escaped, and all the rest died by drowning, or having succeeded in swimming ashore were hacked to pieces by the English garrisons maintained by the Queen in the kingdom of Ireland.

Having most earnestly commended my soul to our Lord and the Most Holy Virgin His Mother, I was delivered from the sea and my enemies, in company with more than three hundred soldiers who had managed to save themselves and swim to land. With them I endured great hardships, living for more than seven months of that winter naked and barefoot in the mountains and forests, among the savages that inhabit those regions of Ireland where we were wrecked.

As the Armada sailed north, De Cuellar had been summoned aboard La Lavia *(or* Labia*), Vice-Flagship of the Levantine squadron. When he came aboard he was accused of disobeying orders. He was sentenced to death by his Admiral.*

I remained on board his ship, where we were all soon in imminent danger of death from a storm which arose, opening her seams so that the water flooded in hour by hour and we could not keep her drained with the pumps. We had no hope of safety nor remedy unless it came from God, for the Duke still failed to make an appearance and the whole Armada was so scattered by the storm that some ships were heading for Germany, others for the islands of Holland and Zealand where they fell into enemy hands, others for Shetland, and yet others for Scotland where they sank or were set on fire. More than twenty were lost on the

shores of the kingdom of Ireland with all that was bravest
and best of the Armada.

I was on board one of the Levantine ships, as I have said,
and two other very large ships came to sail beside us, to help
us if they could. On board one of these was the camp-master
Don Diego the hunchback, and being unable to round Cape
Clear in Ireland because of strong head winds, he was forced
to make for land with these three ships, which were very large
as I have said, and anchor a little more than half a league
from the shore, where we remained four days without provisions nor means of getting any. On the fifth day such a great
gale arose on our beam, with a sea running as high as heaven,
that the cables could not stand the strain nor the sails be of
any avail, and all three ships were driven onto a beach of fine
sand with high cliffs on each side. I never saw the like, for in
the space of one hour all three ships were broken to pieces
and less than three hundred men escaped, more than a
thousand being drowned, among them many persons of
importance, captains, gentlemen and others.

Don Diego Enriquez met his death in this place in the most
miserable manner that ever was seen; out of fear of the huge
seas which were breaking over the ships, he and the son of the
Conde de Villafranca and two other Portuguese gentlemen,
carrying with them more than 16,000 ducats' worth of jewels
and coin took to the ship's tender which had a covered deck,
and went below, giving orders for the hatch to be battened
down and caulked behind them. Thereupon some seventy
survivors from the ship threw themselves onto the boat,
hoping to reach land in this way, but a great wave
overwhelmed and sank her and swept them all away.
Afterwards she drifted to and fro in the sea until she was cast
ashore keel upwards, by which misfortune the gentlemen
who had taken refuge under the deck died where they were.
A day and a half after she had been driven ashore some
savages found the boat, turned her over to get out the nails
and iron fittings, and breaking open the hatch took out the
dead men from inside. Don Diego breathed his last in their

hands, whereupon they stripped him of his clothes, took all the jewels and money they had with them, and threw the bodies on the ground unburied. Because the circumstances are both extraordinary and undoubtedly true, I wished to relate them to you, so that you might know the manner of this gentleman's death; but as it is right also that I should describe my own good fortune and how I came to reach land, I must tell you that I climbed to the highest part of the poop of my ship, and commending my soul to God and Our Lady gazed down at the great and terrible scene before me. Many were drowning inside their ships; others threw themselves into the sea and sank to the bottom never to reappear; others clutched rafts, barrels or floating timbers; others cried aloud from their ships imploring God to help them; captains threw their chains and money into the sea; others were swept away by the waves, even from inside their ships. I gazed my fill of this fiesta, not knowing what to do, nor what means of escape to try, for I cannot swim and the sea and wind were very great. Moreover the land and beach were full of enemies dancing and leaping with delight at our misfortunes, and whenever one of us set foot on the shore two hundred savages and other enemies surrounded him and stripped him stark naked, handling him roughly and wounding him without pity.

All this could be plainly seen from the wrecked ships, and the danger on one side seemed to me as great as that on the other.

I went to the Judge Advocate, God forgive him, who was very woebegone and miserable, and I told him to try and save his life before the ship went quite to pieces, and that she could not last more than a few minutes more – as in fact she did not. Most of her crew were already drowned or dead, including all the captains and officers, when I determined to seek my own safety and climbed onto a piece of the hull that had broken away; the Judge Advocate followed me, weighed down with the crown-pieces he carried sewn into his doublet and hose. But we could find no way of detaching the piece of the ship's side, as it was held fast by thick iron chains, and the

waves and the loose timbers beating against it hurt us cruelly.
I tried therefore to find another way to safety, which was to
take hold of a hatch-door as big as a good-sized table which
God in His mercy brought within my reach; but when I tried
to climb onto it I sank some six fathoms under the water and
swallowed so much that I came near to drowning. When I
rose to the surface again I called to the Judge Advocate and
helped him clamber on the hatch with me, but just as we
were pushing off from the ship such a great sea broke over us
that the Judge Advocate could hold on no longer and was
swept away and drowned. He cried aloud to God as he
drowned. I was unable to help him because now that the
hatch had no weight on one side it began to overturn, and at
the same instant a timber crushed my legs, but with a great
effort I succeeded in keeping my place on my hatch, calling
upon Our Lady of Ontanar to save me. There came four
great waves one after the other, and without knowing how I
got there nor yet being able to swim I was cast onto the shore,
where I arrived too weak to stand, covered with blood and
grievously injured.

The enemies and savages on the beach, who were stripping
any man who swam to shore, did not touch me nor come up
to me, seeing me as I have said with my legs and my hands
and my linen breeches smothered in blood; so I dragged
myself away as best I could little by little, passing many stark
naked Spaniards who had been left without a single garment
and were shivering with the cold, which was bitter at the
time. And so when night fell I threw myself down in a
deserted place upon some rushes on the ground, for I was
suffering greatly from pain. Soon afterwards a handsome
young man came up to me, mother-naked and in such a state
of terror that he could not speak or even tell me his name. It
must have been nine o'clock at night, the wind had dropped
and the sea was becoming calmer. I was soaked to the skin
and half dead with pain and hunger, when presently there
came by two men, one armed and the other with a great iron
axe in his hands; when they reached the place where I and my

companion were we held our peace as if nothing were the matter, and they were grieved at the sight of us, and without saying a word cut a great many rushes and some grass and covered us well. Then they went away to the shore to break open chests and anything else they could find, in company with more than two thousand savages and Englishmen from the neighbouring garrisons.

I tried to take a little rest and did indeed fall asleep, but about one o'clock I was wakened from deep slumber by a great noise of horsemen, more than two hundred of them, hurrying to pillage and destroy the ships. I turned and spoke to my companion to see if he were asleep, and I found him dead to my great affliction and sorrow. I learned afterwards that he was a person of some consequence. There he lay on the ground among more than six hundred other dead bodies cast up by the sea, and the ravens and wolves devoured them, for there was no one to bury any of them, not even poor Don Diego Enriquez.

When day dawned I began to make my way very slowly in search of a monastery where I could recover from my injuries as well as might be; after great tribulation and suffering I reached it, but I found it deserted, the church and its images of saints burned, everything destroyed, and inside the church twelve Spaniards hanged there by the English Lutherans, who were prowling about searching for us and bent on making an end of all those who had escaped from the sea. All the monks had fled into the mountains in terror of their enemies, who would have put them to death also if they caught them, for this was their custom, as it was also to leave no shrine nor hermitage standing, but demolish them all or make them into drinking-troughs for cows and pigs. I am writing at such great length so that you may imagine the hazards and misfortunes that befell me, and so pass the time after dinner in the entertainment of reading this letter, which may well seem to have been taken from some book of knight-errantry.

When I found no one in this monastery except the

Spaniards hanging from the iron grilles of the church, I hastened outside and took a path that ran through a great wood, and going along it for about a mile I met with a rough savage woman, more than eighty years of age, who was driving five or six cows into the wood to hide them, so that the English quartered in her village should not take them. When she saw me she stood still, and realizing who I must be said to me: "Thou Spain?" I made signs to her that this was so, and that I was one of those wrecked in the ships. She began to lament and weep much, indicating by signs that her house was hard by, but that I must not go there as there were many of the enemy in it who had been cutting the throats of many Spaniards. All this was terrible and afflicting news to me, alone as I was and suffering from my legs having been almost broken by a floating timber. But as a result of what the old woman told me, I decided at last to make for the shore, where the ships wrecked three days ago were lying, and whither of people were now hastening to cart away all our belongings to their huts. I did not dare show myself nor yet approach them, lest they should take the wretched linen garment from my back or even kill me, but presently I saw two poor Spanish soldiers coming towards me, as naked as the day they were born, crying aloud and calling on God to help them. One of them had a deep wound in the head, given him by those who stripped him naked. I called to them from my hiding-place, and they came to me and told me of the cruel murders and other punishments inflicted by the English on more than a hundred Spaniards they had taken prisoner. This was grievous news enough; but God gave me strength, and after commending myself to Him and His Blessed Mother I said to these two soldiers: "Let us go to the ships that are being plundered by these people; perhaps we may find something to eat or drink there." For I was in truth dying of hunger.

On our way thither we began to find dead bodies, a sad and pitiful sight; they were still being cast up by the sea, and more than four hundred of them were lying stretched on the beach.

We recognized some of them, among others the unlucky Don Diego Enriquez, and even in the sorry state I was in I could not pass him by without burying him in a hole which we dug in the sand at the water's edge; we placed him in it beside another worthy captain, a great friend of mine, and before we had finished burying them two hundred savages came up to see what we were doing. We told them by signs that we were burying these men because they were our brothers, and so that the ravens should not devour them; after which we went away and searched for something to eat on the shore, such as biscuits thrown up by the sea. Just then four savages came up to me, intending to strip the clothes from my back, but there was another of them who was sorry for me and made them go away when he saw them begin to ill-treat me; he must have been their leader, for they obeyed him. This man, by God's grace, protected me and my two companions; he took us away and remained in our company for some time, until he had set us on a road leading away from the shore to the village where he lived, telling us to wait for him there, and that he would return soon and direct us to a safe place.

De Cuellar and eighteen other survivors of Armada wrecks sailed across to Scotland in a "wretched boat". His troubles continued in Scotland. On 22 October 1589 he reached Dunkirk "once more reduced to nakedness". De Cuellar:

There was a Scottish merchant living at this time in Flanders, who offered his services and arranged with His Highness to come to Scotland for us and ship us on four vessels with all necessary provisions and bring us to Flanders, His Highness paying five ducats for every Spaniard conveyed to Flanders.

His Highness was the Duke of Parma, the Spanish Governor General in the Netherlands. The Spanish had reconquered the southern Netherlands, including Antwerp. At that time they also held Dunkirk. De Cuellar:

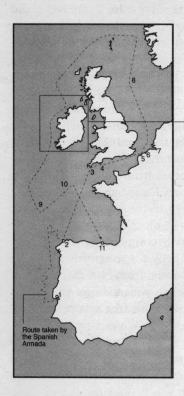

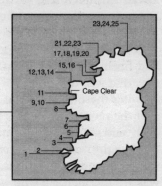

Detail of Armada Shipwrecks off the
Irish coast– Key

1　*Nuestra Senora de la Rosa*
2　*San Juan de Fernando Narra*
3　Biscayan ship
4　*A Zabra*
5　*San Marcos*
6　*Ship of San Sebastian*
7　*Ship of Flanders*
8　Unnamed
9　Unnamed
10　*El Gran Grin*
11　Unnamed
12　*La Rata Encoronada*
13　Unnamed
14　Unnamed
15　*Labia*
16　*San Juan*
17　Unnamed
18　Unnamed
19　Unnamed
20　Unnamed
21　*Duquese Santa Anna*
22　Unnamed
23　*Juliana*
24　*La Trinidad Valencare*
25　*Gerona*

Course of the Spanish Armada
(dates according to Spanish accounts)

Key

1　28 May 141 ships sail from Lisbon
2　19 June – 21 July Corunna
3　22 July 127 ships off the Lizard
4　31 July off Plymouth
5　7-8 August anchored at Calais
6　Dunkirk
7　Antwerp
8　12 August English gave up pursuit
9　17 September
10　20 September
11　23 September First Spanish ship
　　returned to Santander

The agreement was concluded and he came to fetch us, and embarked us unarmed and naked as he found us, and conveyed us by way of the ports of the Queen of England, which promised us safe conduct through all the fleets and ships of her kingdom. This was all treachery, for a treaty had been made with the ships of Holland and Zealand, by which it was agreed that they should put to sea and lie in wait for us off the bar of Dunkirk and put us all to the sword to the last man. The Dutch carried out this order and waited for us for a month-and-a-half at the said port of Dunkirk, and there they would have caught us all but for God's help. By God's grace, out of the four vessels in which we sailed two got away and ran ashore, where they went to pieces. Then the enemy, seeing our efforts to escape, put us under heavy artillery fire, so that we were obliged to throw ourselves into the sea, believing that our last moment had come. They could not send boats from the port of Dunkirk to help us because they were receiving a lively cannonade from the enemy; there were heavy seas and high winds also, so that we were in the utmost peril of all being lost. However we flung ourselves onto planks of wood, although some Scottish soldiers and a captain were drowned. I reached the shore wearing nothing but my shirt, and some of Medina's soldiers who were there came to my help. It was a pitful sight to see us enter the town, once more reduced to nakedness, while almost in front of our eyes the Dutch were cutting to pieces two hundred and seventy Spaniards arriving in the boat which had brought us to Dunkirk, and leaving no more than three alive. This deed they are now paying for, as more than four hundred Dutchmen taken prisoner since then have been beheaded. I desired to write to you concerning all these things.

From the city of Antwerp, 4 October 1589.

Portuguese Maritime Disasters 1550–1650
(*Shipwrecks from* The Historia Tragico-maritima)

The Portuguese were the pioneers of European navigation and exploration. During the century, 1550–1650, the Portuguese suffered a series of maritime disasters. A collection of narratives of these disasters was published subsequently. It was entitled Historia Tragico-maritima. *The* Historia Tragico-maritima *consisted of 18 accounts of shipwrecks between 1550–1650. It was published by Bernardo Gomes de Britto, originally in 2 volumes. Six more narratives were published in the 18th century as vol III.*

The Portuguese had reached the Canaries in the first half of 14th century. Under Prince Henry the Navigator (1394–1460), Portuguese efforts at maritime exploration gained system and direction. Their ships sailed further and further south down the west African coast. The Portuguese began trading operations. They traded in slaves, gold and ivory. Under Prince Henry's successors, Afonso V and Jao II, Portuguese explorers included Diogo Cao, who reached the Congo & Angola in 1482. In 1484 he reached 1,500 miles further south to the regions of Cape Cross. The tradition of exploration culminated in Vasco da Gama. Pero de Covilha reached India overland in 1487. Bartolomeu Dias survived rounding the Cape of Good Hope (a storm blew him round) in 1488.

In 1498 Vasco da Gama sailed into a harbour near Calicut, returning to Portugal in 1499. After this, fleets were sent out annually, discovering Brazil and Madagascar on the way. In 1505 a Portuguese viceroy, Dom Francisco de Almeida, was sent to India.

The Dutch were determined to participate in the valuable spice trade. This led to outright competition with the Portuguese. The Dutch unsuccessfully attacked the Portuguese fortress of Mozambique in 1608. Between 1635–1665 the Portuguese lost Hormuz and Cochin to the English. The Portuguese also lost Malacca, Columbo and the Malabar coast to the Dutch. From 1651, a Dutch settlement at the Cape of Good Hope put them into control of the route to India. The Portuguese Eastern empire had

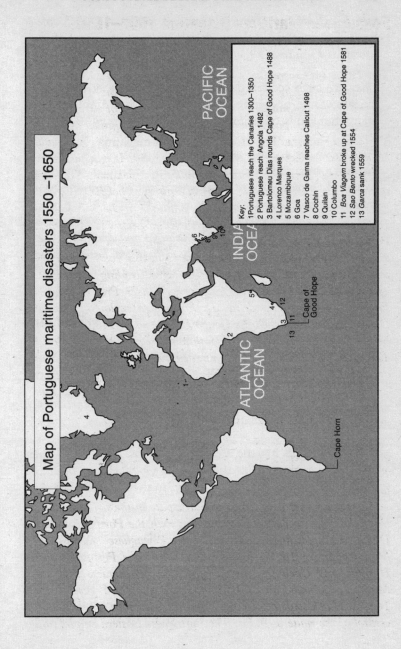

Map of Portuguese maritime disasters 1550 –1650

PACIFIC OCEAN

INDIAN OCEAN

ATLANTIC OCEAN

Cape of Good Hope

Cape Horn

Key:
1 Portuguese reach the Canaries 1300–1350
2 Portuguese reach Angola 1482
3 Bartolomeu Dias rounds Cape of Good Hope 1488
4 Lorenco Marques
5 Mozambique
6 Goa
7 Vasco de Gama reaches Calicut 1498
8 Cochin
9 Quilan
10 Columbo
11 *Boa Viagem* broke up at Cape of Good Hope 1581
12 *Sao Bento* wrecked 1554
13 *Garca* sank 1559

*been based around defensive forts and factories. The chronicler
Faria de Sousa described these possessions and outposts which were
known as Lusitania:*

They are such scattered pieces of the world that the face of
the sun would not shine upon them all if it did not travel so
many thousands of leagues in its circular journey.

*The Portuguese overseas empire depended upon the ship. Eastern
commerce was administered by the Casa da India. Portuguese
voyages took place aboard three types of vessels: caravelas, Naos
and Galleons.*

*A caravela was a small multi decked ship of c. 200 tons with a
crew of 25–150. They were of light draught and could sail close to
the wind and hug a coastline. They suffered few losses. Galleons
were larger and less seaworthy. Gomes de Britto described Naos or
carracks:*

Generally a Nao was a large merchant ship, broad in beam,
with a high poop and forecastle, lightly gunned and an
indifferent sailor; whereas a galleon was primarily a war vessel
and a lighter and handier ship.

*Ships built in India were built of teak rather than pine. French
traveller Pyrard De Laval commented:*

It is impossible for the Portuguese ships because of their
bigness, to make port at the Cape of Good Hope, while the
French and Dutch can do so easily, in their smaller vessels.

*The Portuguese ships were often overloaded. The Dutch observer
Linschoten told the story of the* As Reliquias, *which had so much
cargo placed on one side that she turned over and sank in the
harbor. Linschoten:*

God knoweth, what riches was lost in her, but nothing was
saved but some few chestes that stood above the hatches,

which the Duckers got up . . . By this it may be considered what manner the Portingales use in the lading of their ships, and that it is to bee thought, that as many ships as are cast away, whereof there hath bin heard no newes or tydinges, are onely lost by meanes of evill order and government.

Jao Baptista Lavanha criticized the sailors:

The sailors have no less blame in this matter, which is so important to them since they risk their lives in the ship, and they load the vessel without the necessary distribution of merchandise, piling the light stores on the bottom of the ship and the heavy stores on top, when just the reverse should be so. And to get rich in a hurry they overload the ship out of all proportion of cargo to size of ship, which consequently makes her impossible to handle, and when any of the forementioned accidents occur, she opens at the seams and goes to the bottom.

Linschoten described the Boa Viagem *which broke up at the Cape of Good Hope in 1588:*

[He] affirmed that the ship had at the least nine handfull high of water within it before it departed from Cochin, & although before their ships set sayle, they put the Master and other Officers to their othes (thereby to make them confesse) if the ship be strong and sufficient to performe the voyage, or to let them know the faults (which upon their said oathes is certefied, by a protestation made, wherunto the Officers set their handes:) yet though the ship have ever so many faultes, they will never confesse them, because they will not loose their places, and profit of the Voyage: yea, although they do assuredly knowe the ship is not able to continue the Voyage: for that covetousnes overthrowing wisdome (& pollicie), maketh them reject all feare: but when they fall into the danger, then they can speake faire, and promise many thinges.

Querena italiana *was a form of careening in which the ship was beached, laid over on one side and caulked, then laid over on the other. Estacio do Amaral, in the story of the* Santiago *(1602) and* Chagas, *angrily denounced his countrymen who, to save time and money, used the* querena. *He reminded them that the Portuguese* naos *were not making a three-day trip across the Mediterranean with a cargo of glass or mirrors, but instead:*

are crossing the ocean sea, from pole to pole, and are passing the Cape of Good Hope, not loaded with glass, but overloaded with great quantities of boxes and bundles and the heaviest drugs, and they contend with the fury of the four elements, and sail five or six thousands leagues in all kinds of weather.

He continued:

That the *querena* is so harmful for these ships is demonstrated by the multitude of ships that are lost after having received it, and these ships are not lost through disaster but through greed and scant attention and through letting the ships be given a *querena* and letting them be repaired piecemeal so that the contractors may make a saving.

The practice continued through the first part of the 17th century, and the Portuguese continued to lose ship after ship.

The Portuguese empire declined with its foundering ships.

The English seaman Sir Richard Hawkins admired Portuguese pilots and their navigation:

In this poynt of Steeridge, the Spaniards and Portingalls doe exceed all that I have seene, I meane for their care, which is chiefest in Navigation. And I wish in this, and in all their workes of Discipline and reformation, we should follow their examples . . .

In every Ship of moment, upon the halfe decke, or greater decke, they have a chayre, or seat; out of which whilst they

Navigate, the Pilot, or his Adiutants . . . never depart, day nor night, from the sight of the Compasse; and have another before them; whereby they see what they doe, and are ever witnesses of the good or bad Steeridge of all men that take the Helme.

A contemporary, Simao Ferreira Paes, described the lives of Portuguese seamen:

Sleeping ordinarily with death in their arms, and fighting against the four elements, driving their wretched bodies until they lose their precious lives, and wrapped in rags and tatters, and thrown to the fishes for their miserable graves, they scorn all these misfortunes and endure all these dangers . . . They sail the most distant seas, suffer the most unhealthy climates, face misery so vile that it is impossible to conceive of it.

The most flagrant case of desertion in the Historia Tragico-maritima *is revealed in the account of the* Aguia *and* Garca *(1559). Near the Cape the* Aguia *was leaking so badly that Captain Francisco Barreto of the* Aguia *asked the* Garca *to remain close at hand so that in case of an emergency she would be able to rescue his company. But on board the* Garca:

they made great protests and arguments for the ship to continue its course to Portugal, because that other ship was going to sink – it was clear that there was no help for her – and that was no reason for them on the *Garca* to sink with her.

Francisco Barreto and the Aguia *later came upon the* Garca *sinking. They took everyone off the* Garca. *The* Aguia *now carried 1,000 people. Barreto wrote a note, sealed it in a tube, then placed it in a small boat which he cast adrift. The note said:*

The ship *Garca* was lost a little beyond the Cabo dos Correntes, at a latitude of 25 degrees south, and she went to the bottom because she took in too much water. I, with the noblemen and the rest of the people [who loudly protested Barreto's generous action], saved everyone on her: and we are continuing our voyage to Portugal – with the same trouble. We ask for the love of God that all faithful Christians who hear about this recommend us to our Lord in their prayers, so that he will give us a good voyage and a safe passage to Portugal.

Francisco Barreto and the Aguia *turned back to Mozambique, where he found news of their action had already arrived.*

The fate of Nossa Senora do Bom Despacho *in 1630 was typical of the voyages described in* Historia Tragico-maritima *except that it was successfully completed.* The Historia tragico-maritima *related:*

The *Nossa Senhora do Bom Despacho* was bound from Goa to Lisbon on 4 March 1630, in spite of being obviously overloaded. Such an order may well have been the result of the viceroy's pique. This may have been caused by a mix-up on the outward voyage in which the *Bom Despacho* abandoned the flagship after the armada had left Mozambique. The early days of the homeward voyage passed without incident and the ship crossed the Equator on 21 March. The ship on 18 April met the first storm at 170 S, shortly afterwards five inches of water was discovered in the hold. The bowsprit broke in two on 8 May, several officers suggested without success to Captain Francisco de Melo that the ship turn back up the coast to Mozambique. On 23 May, at 310 S, another severe storm was encountered and the water in the hold rose to nine inches. It became necessary to throw some of the cargo into the sea, but this did not lessen the ship's list to the larboard. And as the water rose in the hold, the pepper burst from its containers and the pumps became clogged.

The captain immediately ordered several officers to inspect the ship's condition; their recommendation was that the ship tack to the nearest port, and the sooner the better. The captain publicly declared that their decision was wise, but since he was so close to the Cape he preferred to try to round it and turn back only if this proved impossible. On the next day, 24 May, the supplies of caulking, lead, and candles were exhausted, and further supplies had to be borrowed from a sister ship, the *Sao Goncalo*. On 12 June, at 350 S, winds of hurricane strength were met and with the pounding of the waves the water in the hold rose to twenty-one inches. On the following day the situation appeared so hopeless that tentative plans were made to beach the ship at the nearest Cape harbour. In the meanwhile cargo was continually thrown into the sea and the six pumps were kept going twenty-four hours a day. On the morning of the fourteenth those on *Nossa Senhora do Bom Despacho* awakened to find themselves alone on the angry seas, deserted by the other ships in the fleet. During the whole period the captain never left the deck. He slept on top of a packing crate "and, putting his hands to the pump like a common seaman," attempted to cheer up the passengers, but with little success. Among the women there were so many tears and sighs that they seemed to reach the heavens, and there was such great and general confusion that the men were afraid to talk to one another for fear of hearing worse news; and the news that was exchanged was such that everyone agreed he would be lucky if he managed to be buried in the sands of the beach, and this was the greatest consolation that anyone had.

On 24 June, when the ship was but ten leagues east of the Cape of Good Hope, another violent storm struck her, and Captain Melo was forced to sail his ship into a small bay. There water was taken on board and the most serious holes temporarily caulked. Five days later another tempest swept in on the *Bom Despacho* and after five days of steady gales, the officers finally prevailed on the captain to tack. As the vessel put about, three towering waves leveled the mainmast, ripped away every sail, and threatened to swamp the ship. It is at this point that the author earnestly begs God never again to permit Christians, especially Portuguese Christians, to suffer such agonies. Many of the crew and passengers were hiding below decks when the waves struck. Not a single one of those on deck remained uninjured. At dawn a large crucifix was tied to the mizzenmast and the entire company knelt before it to ask God's mercy. In the succeeding hours, the storm abated enough to give the captain time to investigate the case of the cowardly sailors who had refused to attend their duties during the previous night. Francisco de Melo raged that he would hang at least two of them to serve as an example to the rest, but both the passengers and the other officers declined to disclose the identity of the delinquents. There was not time for the captain to press his point, for the *Bom Despacho* was in a bad way and it was necessary to find another protected harbour where the ship could be patched up. During all these days of hovering disaster, protests against continuing the voyage were mounting, some of them coming from the officers of the ship, some coming from priests who were acting on behalf of the other passengers. Many advocated beaching the ship anywhere and taking chances of survival at the hands of the Dutch who had a tentative colony at the Cape or even at the hands of the Negro tribesmen of the region. Francisco de Melo met all complaints with a stern refusal.

Gaining momentary courage from the resolution of their captain, the others on board took heart. The nobility, displaying unusual generosity, shared their water supply with those whose supply had been exhausted or ruined. The women on the ship, including the ladies of quality, began to attend the sick and to separate oakum for caulking some of the available leaks in the vessel. Several officers felt so cheered that they renewed their former quarrelling: one officer felt constrained to go to the captain to get him to stop a fellow officer from practising his whistling at him. Everyone on board, however, was prepared for what seemed the inevitable and there were constant confessions, but on 10 July, after so many setbacks and delays, the ship finally rounded the Cape with no other incident except for a fire on board.

Two days later the *Nossa Senhora do Bom Despacho* was lashed by another storm and quickly shipped nineteen inches of water. A new danger arose as the shattered wood and casks in the hold effectively blocked the hatchways, thus preventing for a time cargo from being thrown overboard and the bucket brigade from helping to keep down the water level in the hold. During this storm neither the captain nor his fellow officers left the deck and the priests on board faithfully attended the sick and wounded. Most of the cinnamon was thrown to the sea and of that which remained the captain divided his private store with all the ordinary seamen as a reward for their loyal services. No further incidents of importance occurred as the ship sailed north toward Luanda, except for the mainsail's falling to the deck one day when the runners broke. Miraculously no one was injured, and the vessel arrived at Angola on 5 August.

Once *Nossa Senhora do Bom Despacho* was in port she was unloaded, given a *querena italiana*, and patched up in the customary manner. The captain personally supervised all the repairing done on his ship and satisfied himself that she could make the rest of the trip with a fair degree of safety. Exactly eight months later the *Nossa Senhora do Bom Despacho* sailed from the harbour of Luanda; running her pumps night and day, she reached Lisbon on 4 July with a sigh of thanksgiving from her personnel that they had encountered no further storms in the Atlantic, which surely would have sent her to the bottom. The port officials who visited the vessel swore that they had never seen a ship arrive in Lisbon in such a mauled and twisted condition. From the facts given in the narrative and from the scattered comments of the author, Father Nuno da Conceicao, it seems clear that it was the resolution and unswerving attention to duty of Captain Francisco de Melo that brought the ship into port. His determination not to yield to the pressures of either the crew, officers, or nobility when the ship seemed in gravest danger and his ability to maintain at the same

time the loyalty of almost everyone on board are evidence of a
heroic character that is seldom displayed in the pages of the
Historia Tragico-maritima.

*An impressive farewell speech was made by Dona Luisa de Melo
in the last moments of the* Chagas. *Addressing herself to a
perverted fortune, she made her own funeral oration:*

Ah, cruel fortune, how you deceived me in the wreck of the
ship *Santo Alberto,* only to place me in these straits; if on that
ship I had died, I would never be found thus afflicted. Oh,
feet of mine, who walked three hundred leagues through the
land of the Kaffirs, how much better for you to have been
bitten by a serpent there than to be burned here now by fire.
Oh, ungrateful sands of Cafraria, you swallowed and covered
D. Leonor de Sa, why did you deny me a grave, when I
walked on foot across you for three hundred and twenty
leagues? Oh, my sixteen blighted years, what decision will
you take for your bitter inevitable death: fire or water or the
arms of heretics? Farewell, sad life; farewell, false hopes.

   Having spoken, Dona Luisa tied herself to her mother with
a sash of St Francis, and they threw themselves into the sea.
Together they washed ashore, and together they were buried.

*Although ships sailed together, each ship wanted to reach port first.
Gaspar Afonso who sailed in the* Sao Francisco, *witnessed the
ships separating:*

All for the same reason that they desired to arrive first in
India and sell more dearly.

A young girl fell overboard from the deck of the Sao Paulo *in
1560.* The Historia Tragico-maritima:

The 14-year-old niece of Dom Diego Pereira de Vasconcelos
tumbled from the ship into the sea and was more than half a
league behind the Sao Paulo by the time the news of the

accident reached the captain. He immediately ordered the master to man a life-boat and the pilot to put the ship about. Both individuals protested that it was useless to take such an action, since the girl was already too far in the wake of the ship; they further maintained that it was a waste of time which would only serve to endanger the lives of everyone else on board. The pilot arrogantly told the helmsman to hold his course, but at this the captain drew his sword and swore that he would decapitate the first man disputing his decision. No one was disposed to argue with the captain's steel and a launch was finally lowered over the side. The girl was now out of sight, but after two hours of rowing in that direction, they found her unconscious on top of the water, in the last moments of life: they brought her back, and when they reached the ship she was dead, her face as serene as though she were alive; she had been in the water, alive and dead, for more than an hour without ever going to the bottom.

In the overcrowded ships sickness and death were common, especially becalmed off the fever-ridden coast of Africa. Manuel Godinho Cardoso decribed his voyage to Goa in 1614:

Ordinarily on this voyage, there are many sicknesses, swellings of the legs and gums, and so many deaths that the men of the route say that each year it is made – in addition to the great suffering from hunger and thirst – more than one hundred persons die.

Portuguese sailors were devoted to St Elmo. They preferred to believe his flames were supernatural rather than natural. If the priests on board tried to persuade them that they came from natural causes, the sailors threatened them with violence. If the blue flames appeared high two or more times high on the mast, it was a sign of good fortune; if it appeared but once and low on the mast then it was a certain augury of destruction.

The last desperate act was often throwing the cargo overboard:

In the moment of desperation, all confusion and doubts were briefly resolved in the single cry of "Cargo to the sea!"

As the danger afterwards increased there was thrown into the sea all the cargo from the gunners' quarterdeck and from the spice lockers. The sea was covered with infinite riches, thrown there by the very hands of owners who now hated and despised these treasures as much as formerly they loved and esteemed them.

A period of confusion often followed the wreck or grounding. An eyewitness aboard Nossa Senhore de Belem *wrote that, in the three hours before the ship was run aground:*

The majority of the people on board were determined to ground the ship out of fear that she would sink under them . . . I did not consent to this, and cutting through all their opinions and confusions, I ordered an anchor to be dropped. All the while some of them did not stop saying that we all were going to drown without fail, that there was no help for us unless we ran the ship aground . . . Others said that the rope was sure to break and the ship would be swept against the coast.

The chronicler Diogo Do Couto described the confusion aboard the Sao Thome *in 1589:*

The wind was whistling on every side, and it seemed to be saying to them, "Death, Death" . . . Within the ship there were only heard sighings, sobs, screams, shouts, weeping, and cries for mercy. Between the decks it seemed as though the spirits of the damned had been turned loose with the noise of all the things that were floating in the water and banging against each other, and they rolled from one side of the ship to another in such a way that to those who descended beneath decks the scene seemed like the last judgment.

As the ship broke up:

By now the sea was curdled with crates, spars, barrels, and every diversity of things which appear at the untimely hour of shipwreck; and as they were floating in the water all mixed up with the people who were swimming to land, it was a fearful thing to see, and it is a pitiable thing to tell of the carnage that the fury of the sea caused among them. All of them suffered a different torment: in one direction there were some persons who, being able to swim no more, struggled in the sea giving great and painful gasps from the quantity of water they had swallowed; there were others whose strength was even more exhausted and they commended themselves to the will of God, letting themselves with the last cry, go silently to the bottom; there were other swimmers who were killed by the crates and boxes which pressed against them and stunned them so that the waves could finish them up by sledging them against the rocks; others were pierced in various parts of the body by the spikes in the spars or pieces of ship on which they tried to push their way to shore; and everywhere the water was stained as red as the blood itself which ran from the wounds of those Portuguese whose days thus came to an end.

Faced by imminent death, people were more aware of their spiritual than their physical needs. Manuel Rangel was aboard the Conceicao *(1555):*

The wailing and shrieking that the people made caused so much fear that it seemed as though we were going down immediately, and all of us with our crucifixes in our hands or seizing the reredo begged God to forgive us for our sins and errors and we confessed to those apostles who were on the ship. The press was such that none of us gave room to his neighbour, and thus everyone embraced his neighbour with tears and affection.

The Sao Bento *was wrecked on the south-east coast of Africa in*

1554. The survivors managed to get ashore. Manuel Mesquita Perestrelo described the aftermath:

As soon as dawn began to appear, we turned in the direction of the beach to look for some clothing to cover our nakedness. The beach we found completely covered with dead bodies, with such ugly and deformed expressions that the painful manner of their death was very clear. Some were stretched out on the rocks and others beneath them, and for many of them there were only arms or legs or heads; some had their faces covered with sand or boxes or one of a hundred other things. And the space occupied by the infinity of lost cargo was not a small one, because as far as one could cast his eyes from one end of that beach to another, it was full of odoriferous drugs and an unimaginable diversity of possessions and precious things, many of them lying alongside of their owner, to whom they could be of no assistance in his present state, and indeed though they were dearly treasured by him during his lifetime, they were with their weight the cause of his death. Truly had our misfortune arranged everything there in the most confusing order possible, and we had only to remember that scene in order never again to consider poverty such a hardship that we would desert our God, our neighbours, village, country, brothers, friends, wives, and children to escape it. Nor would we trade our quiet pleasure for the luxuries that were scattered there, those luxuries which, as long as we are alive, make us suffer tempests, fire, wars, and all the other toils and dangers that cost us so dearly.

Out of 322 survivors, only 20 Portuguese and a few slaves reached Mozambique.

Manuel Godinho Carsoso described abandoning ship from the Santiago *in 1585, after it had been driven on to the Baixos da Judia shoals. The sea dashed the ship onto a coral reef. Carsoso:*

By this time the tide was rising rapidly, and five rafts that had been made came up to the launch in which those who were trying to save themselves had just embarked with great difficulty, defending their boat – since there was no help for it – with swords against all those who tried to get in it. Some women who had been on the ship clung to the sides of the boat, but they were wounded by those in it just as the men were who tried the same thing. This day's spectacle was the saddest and most heart-rending that could be seen. The reef was full of people who had been refused entrance by both the launch and the rafts; the tide was coming in and there was no longer footing for them; those that could not swim began to drown. And those who could swim postponed their death but for a short time, because they too were destined to drown. A great number of men swam in the water, some after the rafts, others after the boat, and they all drowned, as well as two women who tried to reach the rafts on which many others were. A boy of fifteen swam nearly half a league and reached the launch which was now some distance from where the rest were struggling in the water. They put a sword in front of his face, at which he showed no fear, but rather grabbed it as though it were a rope; he did not let go until they took him in the boat, although at the expense of a severely cut hand. Those who were traveling in the boat looked back at the ruins and the broken quarter-decks of the ship and saw that there still were many people on them, and all of them had red tasselled bonnets on their heads and they were wearing jackets like those of reapers cut out of scarlet cloth as well as some coloured silks that they had found on the ship; it would have been a beautiful sight at a happier time. The rafts were also something to see, because they looked like pinnaces with their green, crimson, and other coloured damask sails.

Wrecked off New England in 1635

In 1635 Anthony Thacher had recently arrived in New England. On 12 August he and his family set sail from Ipswich for Marblehead. Thacher:

But the Lord suddenly turned our cheerfulness into mourning and sad lamentation. Thus on Friday the fourteenth of August 1635 in the evening about ten of the clock our sails being old and torn, we, having a fine fresh gale of wind, were split. Our sailors, because it was something dark, would not put on new sails presently but determined to cast their sheet anchor and so to ride at anchor until the next morning and then to put [them] on. But before daylight it pleased God to send so mighty a storm as the like was never felt in New England since the English came there nor in the memory of any of the Indeans. It was [so] furious that our anchor came home, whereupon our mariners let slip more cable, yea, even to the utmost end thereof and so made it fast only about the bit, whence it slipped away end for end. Then our sailors knew not what to do but were driven as pleased the storm and waves. My cousin and we, perceiving our danger, solemnly recommended ourselves to God, the Lord both of earth and seas, expecting with every wave to be swallowed up and drenched in the deeps. And as my cousin, his wife and children and maid servant, my wife and my tender babes sat comforting and cheering on the other in the Lord against ghastly death, which every moment stares us in the face and sat triumphingly on each other's forehead, we were by the violence of the waves and fury of the winds by the Lord's permission lifted up upon a rock between two high rocks yet all was but one rock but ragged, with the stroke whereof the water came into the pinnace. So as we were presently up to the middle in water as wet, the waters came furiously and violently over us and against us but by reason of the rock's proportion could not lift us off but beat her all to pieces. Now look with me upon our distresses and consider of my misery, who beheld the ship broken, the water in her and violently overwhelming us, my goods and provision swimming in the seas, my friends almost drowned and mine own poor children so untimely (if I may so term it without offence) before mine eyes half drowned and ready to be swallowed up and dashed to pieces against the rocks by the merciless waves and myself ready to accompany them.

But I must go on to an end of this woeful relation. In the same room with us sat he that went master of the pinnace, not knowing what to do. Our foremast was cut down, our mainmast broken in three pieces, the forepart of our pinnace beaten away, our goods swimming about the seas, my children bewailing me as not pitying themselves, and myself bemoaning them, poor souls whom I had occasioned to such an end in their tender years whenas they could scarce be sensible of death. And so likewise my cousin, his wife and his children and both of us bewailing each other in Our Lord and only Saviour Jesus Christ, in whom only we had comfort and cheerfulness, insomuch that from the greatest to the least of us there was not one screech or outcry made, but all as silent sheep were contentedly resolved to die together lovingly as since our acquaintance we had lived together friendly.

Now as I was sitting in the cabinroom door, lo, one of the sailors by a wave being washed out of the pinnace was gotten in again, and coming into the cabinroom over my back, cried out, "oh, we are all cast away. Lord, have mercy on us. I have been washed overboard into the sea and am gotten in again." His speeches made me look forth, and looking toward the sea and seeing how we were, I turned myself toward my cousin and the rest and these words, "Oh, cousin, it hath pleased God here to cast us between two rocks, and the shore not far off from us, for I saw the top of trees when I looked forth." Whereupon the said master of the pinnace, looking up at the scuttle hole of the half deck went out of it, but I never saw him afterward. Then he that had been in the sea went out again by me and leaped overboard toward the rock, whom afterward also I could never see.

Now none were left in the bark that I knew or saw, but my cousin and his wife and children, myself and mine and his maidservant. I put [on] my great coat, a waistcoat of cotton but had neither sleeves nor skirts, a thin pair of breeches, a pair of boots without stockings. My coat I put off me and laid it under my poor babe's feet to raise it out of the water (a poor supporter), but my cousin thought I would have fled from him and said unto me, "Oh, cousin, leave us not. Let us die together," and reached forth his hand unto me. Then I, letting go my son Peter's hand, took him by the hand and said to him, "I purpose it not whither shall I go. I am willing and ready here to die with you. And my poor children, God be merciful to us," adding these words, "The Lord is able to help and to deliver us." He replied, saying, "True, cousin, but what His pleasure is, we know not; I fear we have been too unthankful for former mercies. But He hath promised to deliver us from sin and condemnation, through the all-sufficient satisfaction of Jesus Christ. This, therefore, we may challenge of him." To which I, replying, said, "That is all the deliverance I now desire and expect," which words I had no sooner spoken but by a mighty wave I was with a piece of the bark washed out upon part of the rock, where the wave left me almost drowned. But recovering my feet, [I] saw above me on the rock my daughter Mary, to whom I was no sooner gotten but my cousin Avary and his eldest son came to us, being all four of us washed out with one and the same wave. We went all into a small hole on the top of the rock, whence we called to those in the pinnace to come unto us. Supposing we had been in more safety than they were in, my wife, seeing us there, was crept into the scuttle of the half deck to come unto us, but presently another wave dashing the pinnace all to pieces carried away my wife in the scuttle as she was with the greater part of the half deck [carried] to the shore, where she was safely cast, but her legs were something bruised, and much timber of the vessel being there also cast, she was some time before she could get away, washed with the waves. All the rest that were in the bark were drowned in the merciless seas.

We four by that wave were clean swept away from off the rock also into the sea, the Lord in one instant of time disposing of the souls of us to his good pleasure and will. His wonderful mercy to me was thus. Standing on the rock as before you heard with my eldest daughter, my cousin, and his eldest son, [I was] looking upon and talking unto them in the bark whenas we were by that cruel wave washed off the rock as before you heard. God in his mercy caused me to fall by the stroke of the wave flat on my face, for my face was toward the sea insomuch that I was sliding down the rock into the sea. The Lord directed my toes into a joint in the rock's side as also the tops of some of my fingers with my right hand by means whereof, the waves leaving me, I remained so, having only my head above the water. On my left hand I espied a board or plank of the pinnace, and as I was reaching out my left hand to lay hold on it, by another wave coming on the top of the rock I was washed away from the rock and by the violence of the waves was driven hither and thither in the sea a great while and had many dashes against the rocks. At length past hope of life and wearied both in body and spirit I even gave out to nature, and being ready to receive in the waters of death I lifted up both my heart and hands to the God of heaven (for, note, I had my senses remaining and perfect with me all the time I was under and in the water), who at that instant lifted my head clean above the top of waters that so I might breathe without hindrance by the waters. I stood bolt upright as if I stood upon my feet but I felt no bottom nor had any footing for to stand upon but the waters. While I was thus above the waters I saw a piece of the mast as I supposed about three foot long which I laboured to catch into my arms, but suddenly I was overwhelmed with water and driven to and fro again and at last I felt the ground with my right foot. Immediately I was violently thrown grovelling on my face. When presently I recovered my feet was in the water up to my breast and through God's great mercy had my face to the shore and not to the sea. I made haste to get out but was thrown down on my hands with the waves and so with safety crept forth to the dry shore, where, blessing God, I turned about to look for my children and friends but saw neither them nor any part of the pinnace where I left them as I supposed, but I saw my wife about a butt-length from me, getting herself forth from amongst the timber of the broken bark, but before I could get unto her she was gotten to the shore. When we were come each to other we went up into the land and sat us down under a cedar tree, which the winds had thrown down, where we sat about an hour, even dead with cold, for I was glad to put off my breeches, they being rent all to pieces in the rocks.

But now the storm was broken up and the wind was calm, but the sea remained rough and fearful to us. My legs was much bruised and so was my heart, and other hurt had I none, neither had I taken in much water. But my heart would not suffer me to sit still any longer, but I would go to see if any more was gotten to the land in safety, especially hoping to have met with some of mine own poor children, but I could find none, neither dead nor yet living. You condole with me my further miseries, who now began to consider of my losses. Now [I] called to my remembrance the time and manner how and when I last saw and left my children and friends. One was severed from me sitting on the rock at my feet, the other three in the pinnace, my little babe (ah, poor Peter) sitting in his sister Edith's arms, who to the utmost of her power sheltered him out of the waters, my poor William standing close unto her, all three of them looking ruefully on me on the rock, their very countenance calling unto me to help them, whom I could not go unto, neither could they come unto me, neither could the merciless waves afford me space or time to use any means at all, either to help them or myself.

Oh I yet see their cheeks, poor, silent lambs, pleading pity and help at my hands. Then on the other side to consider the loss of my dear friends with the spoil and loss of all our goods and provisions, myself cast upon an unknown land in a wilderness, I know not where, and how to get there we did not know. Then it came into my mind how I had occasioned the death of my children, who had occasioned them out of their native land, who might have left them there, yea and might have sent some of them back again and cost me nothing. These and many such thoughts do press down my heavy heart very much, but I leave this till I see your face, before which time I fear I shall never attain comfort. Now having no friend to whom I can freely impart myself; Mr Cotten is now my chiefest friend to whom I have free welcome and access, as also Mr Mavericke, Mr Warde, Mr Ward, Mr Hocker, Mr Weles, Mr Warhad, and Mr Parker also, Mr Noyes, who use me friendly. This is God's goodness to me, as also to set the eyes of all the country on me, especially of the magistrates who much favour and comfort me.

But I let this pass and will proceed on in the relation of God's goodness unto me. While I was in that desolate island on which I was cast, I and my wife were almost naked, both of us, and wet and cold even unto death. When going down to the shore as before I said I found cast on the shore a snapsack in which I had a steel and a flint and a powder horn. Going further I found a drowned goat. Then I found a hat and my son Will's coat, both which I put on. My wife found one of her own petticoats which she put on. I found also two cheeses and some butter driven ashore. Thus the Lord sent us some clothes to put on and food to sustain our new lives which he had given lately unto us, and means also to make fire, for in my horn I had some gunpowder, which to my own and other men's admiration was dry. So, taking a piece of my wife's neckcloth, which I dried in the sun, I struck fire and so dried and warmed our wet bodies, and then skinned the goat, and having found a small brass pot we boiled some of it. Our drink was brackish water. Bread we had none. There – we remained until the Monday following, where about three o'clock in the afternoon in a boat that came that way, we went off that desolate island, which I named after my own name, "Thacher's Woe," and the rock I named "Avary his Fall," to the end their fall and loss and mine own might be had in perpetual remembrance. In the island lieth buried the body of my cousin's eldest daughter, whom I found dead on the shore. On the Tuesday following in the afternoon we arrived at Marblehed, where I am now remaining in health and good respect though very poor, and thus you have heard such relation as never before happened in New England, and as much bewailed as it was strange. What I shall do or what course I shall take I know not. The Lord in his mercy direct me that I may so lead the new life which he hath given me as may be most to his own glory.

Praise God and pray to God for me.

The Wreck of HMS *Proserpine*
31 January–22 February 1799

This account of the wreck of HMS Proserpine *in 1799 was compiled by W. O. S. Gilly from Admiralty records:*

On Monday 28 January 1799, His Majesty's frigate *Proserpine*, 28 guns, commanded by Captain James Wallis, sailed from Yarmouth to Cuxhaven. She had on board the Hon. Thomas Grenville who was the bearer of important despatches for the Court of Berlin. On Wednesday, the 30th the ship was off Heligoland, and there took in a pilot for the Elbe. The day being fine, with a fair wind from N.N.E., the *Proserpine*'s course was steered for the Red Buoy, where she anchored for the night. It was then perceived that the two other buoys at the entrance of the river had been removed: a consultation was therefore held with the pilots, in the presence of Mr Grenville as to the practicability of proceeding up the river in the absence of the buoys. The Heligoland pilot, and the two belonging to the ship, were unanimous in declaring that there was not slightest difficulty or danger in ascending the river; they professed the most perfect knowledge passage, and assured Captain Wallis they had no fear of carrying the vessel to Cuxhaven, provided only he would proceed between half ebb and half flood tide; for in that case they should be able to see the sands and to recognise their marks.

The next morning (31st), the *Proserpine* was got under weigh, and proceeded up the river, having the *Prince of Wales* packet, which had accompanied her from Yarmouth, standing on ahead.

At four o'clock in the afternoon, when they within four miles of Cuxhaven, the weather became very thick, and some snow fell, so that Captain Wallis was obliged to anchor.

At nine o'clock, p.m., the wind changed to east by south, blowing a violent gale, accompanied by a heavy fall of snow, which made it impossible to see beyond a few feet from the ship; and what was still worse, the tide and the wind brought large masses of ice against the ship, that with all hands upon deck, it was with the greatest difficulty they prevented the cables being cut, and were able to preserve their station till daylight.

By eight o'clock next morning, the flood tide had carried up most of the ice, and left a passage clear below the ship, while all above it was blocked up. The *Prince of Wales* packet had gone on shore during the night; and, warned by her fate, Captain Wallis determined to retreat out of the Elbe. Mr Grenville was very anxious to be put on shore as speedily as possible, his mission being of much importance; but the river was so completely blocked up above them, that there seemed no possibility of effecting a landing at Cuxhaven: Captain Wallis therefore got his ship under weigh, and stood out intending to land Mr Grenville on the nearest part of the coast of Jutland, if it were practicable.

The pilots were congratulating the captain on the frigate's getting safely out of the river, and clear of the sands, and the people had been allowed to go to breakfast on the supposition that all danger was past when the vessel struck upon Scharhorn Sand, with Newark Island bearing south by east, at half-past nine o'clock, a.m.

As it was blowing a very strong gale of wind, the *Proserpine* struck with great force, though she carried no other canvas than her foretopmast stay-sail. Upon sounding, there was found to be only ten feet of water under the fore part of her keel.

The boats were immediately lowered to carry out an anchor, but the ice was returning upon them so fast that this was found impossible, and the boats were hoisted on board again. All hands were then employed to shore the ship up, and make her heel towards the bank, to prevent her falling into the stream which would have been certain destruction. Happily this object was effected; for as the tide ebbed she lay towards the bank.

The next tide, however, brought down such huge masses of ice that the shores were carried away – the copper was torn from the starboard quarter, and the rudder cut in two, the lower part lying on the ice, under the counter.

Notwithstanding all these disasters, Captain Wallis still hoped to get the ship off at high water and to effect this, they proceeded to lighten her by throwing most of her guns and part of her stores overboard, all of which were borne up on the ice. One party was employed in hoisting out the provisions, another in starting the casks of wine and spirits; and such were the good discipline and right feeling of the men, that not one instance of intoxication occurred.

At ten o'clock on Friday night, they abandoned all hope of saving the vessel; it was then high water, yet the heavy gale from the south-east so kept back the tide, that upon sounding they found three feet less water than there had been in the morning, when the ship first struck.

The situation of the crew was dreadful. When the tide ebbed, they expected every moment that the ship would be driven to pieces by the ice. The cold was intense, and the darkness such that it was almost impossible to distinguish one another upon deck; and the snow, falling very thick, was driven against their faces by the wind, and froze upon them as it fell.

There was no possibility of keeping up warmth and circulation in their bodies, for the frozen snow and ice made the deck so slippery they could scarcely stand, much less walk about quickly, and all they could do was, to try to screen themselves as much as possible from the pitiless blast. Thus the night was spent in anxious fears for the future, and dread of immediate destruction. But morning came at last, though with little comfort to the sufferers, for the wind had increased, the ice was up to the cabin windows, the stern-post was found to be broken in two, and the ship otherwise seriously damaged.

In this state they could not long remain. Mr Grenville and some of the officers proposed to Captain Wallis the crew should make an attempt to get over the ice to Newark Island, as the only means of preserving their lives.

At first, Captain Wallis was inclined to reject the proposal; he saw all the danger attending such an attempt and it appeared to him, that they could scarcely expect to succeed in crossing the ice through a dense fog and heavy snow-storm, without any knowledge of the way, without a guide, and exhausted as they were by mental and bodily suffering, and benumbed with cold.

On the other hand, he confessed that the plan presented a hope of safety, and that it was their only hope. The ship's company were unanimous in wishing to adopt it, and there-fore Captain Wallis finally consented.

The people then set heartily to work to consider the diffi-culties of the undertaking, and the best means of meeting them. It was determined that they should be divided into four companies, each headed by an officer; that the strongest of the men should carry planks, to be laid down in the most dangerous places by way of assistance to the less able and active of the party; and that others should hold a long line of extended rope, to be instantly available in case of any one falling between the blocks of ice.

When all these measures were decided upon, and every man had provided himself with what was most essential for his safety and sustenance, began their perilous journey at half-past one o'clock p.m. By three o'clock, every one had left the ship except Captain Wallis, and he then followed the party, accompanied by Lieutenant Ridley, of the Marines.

To describe the dangers and difficulties which the crew of

the *Proserpine* had to encounter is almost impossible. The
snow was still falling heavily, driving against their faces, and
adhering to hair and eyebrows, where in a few minutes it
became solid pieces of ice. Sometimes they clambered over
huge blocks of ice, and at other times were obliged to plunge
through snow and water reaching to their middle.

As the wind blew from the direction in which they were
proceeding, the large flakes of snow were driven into their
eyes, and prevented them from seeing many yards in
advance. This caused them to deviate from their proper
course, and travel in a direction which, if continued, would
have carried them off the shoal and field of ice into the sea,
or at least have taken them so far from any place of shelter,
as to have left them to perish in the ice and snow during the
night.

This dreadful calamity was, however, prevented by one of
the party having in his possession a pocket compass.
Fortunately, bearings had been taken previous to their
leaving the wreck. The course they were pursuing was
examined, and to their surprise it was discovered that they
had been deviating from the direct line which they ought to
have pursued. This, however, enabled the party to correct the
march, and after a toilsome journey of six miles they at length
reached Newark.

In the course of their hazardous journey, a striking instance
was afforded of the inscrutable ways of Providence. Two
females were on board the *Proserpine* when she was stranded
– one a healthy woman, accustomed to the hardships of
maritime life: the other, exactly the reverse, weak and
delicate, had never been twelve hours on board a ship until
the evening previous to the frigate's sailing from Yarmouth.
Her husband had been lately impressed, and she had come
on board for the purpose of taking farewell. Owing to a
sudden change of the weather, and the urgency of the mission
for which the *Proserpine* had been despatched, she had been
unable to quit the ship. The poor creature was upon the eve
of her confinement and naturally being but ill . . . she was

delivered of a dead child. The reader can well imagine the sufferings endured by this helpless woman, with but one of her own sex to tend her, in a vessel tossed about in the stormy seas of the Northern Ocean.

But this was little compared with what she had yet to undergo. Before many hours the frigate stranded: the night was passed in torture of mind and body, and then was she compelled, with others, to quit the ship, and travel through masses of snow and ice, and to combat with the bitter north wind, hail and sleet.

It may well be supposed that her strength, already weakened by the sufferings she had undergone, was totally unprepared to bear up against a trial which the strongest of the crew might have shrunk but it turned out otherwise. The robust, healthy woman, with her feeble companion, left the wreck together, the former bearing in her arms an infant of nine months old. No doubt many a ready arm was stretched forth to assist them in their journey. But man could have done but little against the piercing winter's blast with which they had to contend. Before they had proceeded half the distance, the child was frozen in its mother's arms and ere long the mother herself sank on the snow into a state of stupor, and died. Not so the invalid; sustained by help from above, she still pursued her way, and ere long gained with others the hospitable shore. The inhabitants of the village received the strangers with great kindness, and did everything in their power to alleviate their sufferings. The ship's company were distributed among them for the night, but the poverty of the place afforded them little more than shelter.

The next morning a general muster was made and it was ascertained that, of the whole company, twelve seamen, a woman, and her child, only were missing; these had either been frozen to death or had died from the effects of cold, and the loss was small when compared with the hardships they had suffered. Several men had their legs and fingers frozen, but through proper medical treatment they all recovered.

The storm lasted without intermission till the night of the

fifth, and during that time the crew of the *Proserpine* were suffering much from the want of necessary food, clothing, &c. Provisions were so they were all put upon short allowance; and their scanty store being nearly exhausted, it was absolutely necessary that part of them should proceed to Cuxhaven.

They learnt that at low water it was possible to get to Cuxhaven on foot; and some of the islanders offered their services as guides, and when the tide served, it was settled that the first lieutenant and half the officers and men should start with the guides on the morning of the sixth.

Mr Grenville being very anxious to proceed on his mission to Berlin, determined to accompany the party with the secretary to the embassy, and some of the servants; and they accordingly all set off at eight o'clock in the morning, the severity of the weather having somewhat abated.

Great as had been the difficulties they had encountered in their passage from the *Proserpine* to Newark Island, the dangers of their present expedition over sand and ice, were nearly as formidable.

At one part of their journey they found themselves on the banks of a river. The guides had assured them that it was only a very narrow stream, and would most probably be frozen over: it proved, however, to be a river of considerable width; the ice was broken and floating upon it in large masses; the tide, too, was rising, and altogether the passage presented a formidable appearance. There was little time for deliberation, so the word was given to push forward, and the next moment they were up to their waists in the water, struggling against the tide and the large flakes of ice, which swept against them with such force that they had great difficulty in keeping their footing.

But through the mercy of Providence they all reached the opposite bank in safety, and by evening they arrived at Cuxhaven, without the loss of a single man. Many of them were more or less frost-bitten, but by rubbing the parts affected with snow, circulation was restored.

We must now return to Captain Wallis and the officers and men who had remained with him at Newark, in hopes of being able to save some of the stores from the frigate.

On Friday, the eighth, Mr Anthony, the master, volunteered with a party to endeavour to ascertain the state of the vessel, and if possible to bring away some bread, of which they were in much need.

They had great difficulty in reaching the ship, which they found lying on her beam ends, with seven feet and a half of water in her hold, having her quarter-deck separated six feet from her gangway, and apparently only kept together by the vast quantity of ice which surrounded her.

From this report, it was deemed unadvisable to make any more expeditions to the ship; but on the tenth, the clearness of the day induced Anthony, in company with the surgeon, a midshipman, the boatswain, and two seamen, to go off a second time.

Those who remained at Newark anxiously expected the return of the party, but they came not. Evening advanced, the tide was flowing, and at last it was too late for them to cross the sands and ice until the next ebb. The watchers were obliged to content themselves with the hope that Mr Anthony and his party had found it safe and practicable to remain on board the frigate till morning. But during the night a violent storm arose, which increased the anxiety of Captain Wallis for the safety of his people; and this anxiety became deep distress when in the morning he gazed wistfully towards the wreck, and saw nothing but the foaming waters and moving fields of ice. Not a vestige of the frigate was visible. We cannot better describe Captain Wallis' feelings on this occasion than by quoting his own words, when he communicated the intelligence to Vice-Admiral Archibald Dickson. Captain Wallis:

They got on board, but fortunately neglected, until too late in the tide, to return, which left them no alternative but that of remaining on board till next day. About ten o'clock at night the wind came on at S.S.E., and blew most violent storm; the tide, though at the neap, rose to an uncommon height, the ice got in motion, the velocity of which swept the wreck to destruction (for in the morning not a vestige of her was to be seen), and with it, I am miserably afraid, – went the above unfortunate officers and men. And if so, their loss will be a great one to the service, as, in their different departments, they a great acquisition to it.

The only hope I have is that Providence, which has so bountifully assisted us in our recent dangers and difficulties, may be extended towards them, so as to preserve their lives, by means of boat or otherwise; but I am very sorry to say my hopes are founded on the most distant degree of human probability. This melancholy accident happening so unexpectedly, added to my other misfortunes, has given so severe a shock to my health and spirits, as to prevent me hitherto undertaking the journey to Cuxhaven, where the survivors of the ship's now are, except a few who are here with me, with whom I shall set out as soon as able.

Gilly's account continued:

It is now necessary that we should follow the proceedings of Mr Anthony and his party.

They reached the wreck at ten o'clock on Sunday morning; but, being busily occupied in collecting what stores they could, they neglected to watch the tide, and whilst they were thus employed, the time passed over, and the waves rolling between them and their temporary home at Newark. They were obliged to wait till the next day's ebb. During the night, as we have stated, the wind changed to the S.S.E.: it blew a violent gale, and the tide rose to such an unusual height, that it floated the ship, and the ice that had stuck to her, without the men on board being aware of it. The next morning, to their horror and dismay, the vessel drifting out to the ocean. We can scarcely imagine a situation more terrible than that in which these unfortunate men were placed. They were in all six persons, four officers and two seamen, and these few hands had to manage a frigate of twenty-eight guns, which was actually going to pieces, and it was impossible to conjecture how long she might swim. She was merely buoyed up on the sea the fields of ice that surrounded her; and if the ice were to break away, in all probability she would not hold together for an hour.

Mr Anthony and his companions did not, however, give way to despair, nor lose time in useless repining. They set to work immediately to avoid the danger as far as circumstances would permit. Their first care was to drop the lead between two of the masses of ice, and they found that the ship was floating in eleven fathoms. They then fired several guns, to give warning of their situation. By turns they worked at the pumps; and, in order to lighten the vessel, threw all the remaining guns except four, overboard – a labour of no small magnitude for six men to perform.

Their next object was to get up the tackles for hoisting out the boat, in case of their getting into clear water, or being obliged to quit the wreck.

There was one advantage in all this hard labour, to which most of them were unaccustomed-it prevented their suffering so much as they otherwise must have done from the extreme cold; and, in one respect, they were better off than their comrades at Newark, for they had plenty of provisions on board. So passed the first day on the wreck.

The next morning, Tuesday, the twelfth, at about eleven o'clock, land was descried on their lee, on which they fired several guns, and hoisted the colours on the main-rigging, union downwards, as a signal of distress. An hour afterwards the ship struck on a rock off the island of Baltrum, about a mile and a half distant from the shore.

Mr Anthony and his companions then tried to launch the cutter, but they were obliged to give up attempt, as the sea was not sufficiently clear of ice, they therefore remained on board another night.

The next morning, however, they hoisted out the boat and pulled towards the shore; but they had not gone more than half way, when they were surrounded by fields of ice, so that they were obliged to get upon the ice, and drag the boat with them.

About noon they had reached to within a cable's length of the shore, and here they were compelled to leave the boat: they were all completely exhausted, and found it impossible to drag her further. They themselves had to leap from one piece of ice to another, often falling into the water and it was at the imminent risk of their lives that they at last gained the beach.

They were tolerably well received by the inhabitants, who took them to their houses, and allowed them to seek that repose which they so much needed.

The next day, the islanders, unable to resist the temptation of plunder, took to their boats, and made off to the ship, which they ransacked, and carried off all the arms, stores, and provisions of every kind. In vain Mr Anthony protested against this base conduct: it was as much as he could do to persuade them to spare some part of the provisions for himself and his friends.

The party were obliged to remain at Baltrum amongst their rapacious hosts until Saturday, the sixteenth, when they deemed that the ice was sufficiently cleared away to allow of their sailing for Cuxhaven; they accordingly secured the cutter, and took their departure. As there was not the remotest chance of getting the *Proserpine* afloat again, they abandoned her to the island plunderers. They reached Cuxhaven about the twenty-second, and there they found Lieutenant Wright and those who had accompanied him from Newark.

On the following day, Captain Wallis arrived with the rest of the ship's company, the sick and wounded. We can imagine the joy and gratitude with which Captain Wallis received the announcement of the safe arrival of Mr Anthony and his friends, whom he had deplored as lost.

Thus were the crew of the *Proserpine*, with the exception of fourteen persons, brought once more together after three weeks' endurance of innumerable hardships, and having been exposed to many perils. Never was the Almighty hand of Providence more visibly displayed than in the protection afforded to these gallant fellows; and never did men more to help themselves than they did. We cannot but admire the calm courage they evinced throughout that long and dismal night when almost certain destruction awaited them; as well as their obedience and cheerful alacrity through their toilsome march from the wreck to Newark, and again from Newark to Cuxhaven. Nor must we forget the fortitude displayed by Mr Anthony and his companions when they were a second time wrecked in the *Proserpine*.

Through the history of their dangers and sufferings from cold and hunger, and the other evils attending a shipwreck on such an inhospitable shore and in such a climate, there is no mention of one single instance of murmuring, discontent, or disobedience of orders.

When the Elbe was again navigable and free from ice, the crew embarked in different packets and sailed for England, where they all arrived without further disasters.

HMS *Banterer*
29 October 1808

HMS Banterer, *commanded by Captain Alexander Shippard, was sailing to Quebec on the St Lawrence river. Captain Shippard:*

Being as far as the Island of Bie in pursuance of orders, though rather an intricate navigation, with foul winds the greater part of the time, where the charge of the ship devolved upon myself, and the only chart I could procure of the navigation in question being on a very small scale, I felt relieved from much anxiety by receiving a branch pilot on board on the 28th October last, on which night at 8 p.m. we passed between that island and the south shore, with the wind north by west and very fine weather; at nine, the wind coming more round to the westward, we tacked for the north shore, in order, as the pilot said, not only to be ready to avail himself of the prevailing northerly winds in the morning, but because the current was there more in our favour. At midnight we tacked to the southward, and at 2 a.m. again laid her head to the northward; and at 4 a.m., the pilot having expressed a wish to go about, the helm was accordingly put down, and on rising tacks and sheet, it was discovered that the ship was aground. As we had then a light breeze at west, the sails were all laid aback, the land being in sight from the starboard-beam, apparently at some distance; I immediately ordered the master to sound round the ship, and, finding that the shoal lay on the starboard quarter and astern, ordered the sails to be furled, the boats hoisted out, and stream anchor and cable to be got into the launch, and the boats to tow her out two cables' length south-west from the ship, where we found the deepest water; but by this time the wind had suddenly increased to such a degree that the boats could row ahead, and latterly having lost our ground, we were obliged to let the anchor go in fifteen fathoms, about a cable's length W.S.W. from the ship on which, having got the end of the cable on board we hove occasionally as the flood made, and in the meantime got our spare topmasts over the side, with the intention of making a raft to carry out a bower anchor should it moderate; but the intense cold and the still increasing gale rendered it impossible.

About half-past 11 a.m. the stream cable being then taut ahead, the wind W.S.W., with a very heavy sea, the ship canted suddenly with her head to the southward, where we had deep water; immediately set our courses, jib and driver, and for some time had the most sanguine hopes of getting her off but were unfortunately disappointed, as the ebb made we were obliged again to sails.

As the ship was then striking very hard, with a heavy sea breaking over her in a body, we cut away the topmasts, not only to ease her, but to prevent their falling upon deck; we also endeavoured to shore up the ship, but the motion was so violent that four and six parts of a five-inch hawser were repeatedly snapped, with which we were lashing the topmasts as shores, through the maindeck ports. At about 8 p.m., fearing the inevitable loss of the ship, as the water was then gaining on the pumps, I availed myself of the first favourable moment to land the sick, and a party of marines and boys with some provisions, this could only be effected at a certain time of tide, even with the wind off shore, and employed those on board in getting upon deck what bread and other provisions could be come at.

Though the water was still gaining on the pumps as the flood made, the wind coming more round to the northward, we again set our foresail, but without the desired effect. As the stream anchor had, however, come home, the wind was too doubtful to attempt to lighten the ship.

On the morning of the thirtieth, it being moderate, with the wind off shore, we hove our guns, shot, and everything that could lighten the ship, over board, reserving two on the forecastle for signals. As the flood made, we again set what sail we could, and hove on the stream cable, though, with all hands at the pumps, we found the water increase in the hold as it flowed alongside; and it was the prevailing opinion that the ship would have foundered if got off. Being now convinced, from concurring circumstances, as well as the repeated representations of the carpenter, that the ship could not swim, the water having flowed above the orlop deck, and sand coming up with the pumps, we desisted from further attempts to get her off the shoal, and continued getting such stores and provisions as we could upon deck.

Towards the afternoon, the wind again increasing from the W.S.W., and the water being on the lower deck, I judged it proper to send some provisions, with such men as could be best spared, on shore, that, in the event of the ship going to pieces, which was expected, the boats might be the better able to save those remaining on board; and on the morning of the thirty-first, conceiving every further effort for the preservation of the ship unavailing, it then blowing strong, with every appearance of increasing, I felt myself called on, by humanity as well as duty to my country, to use every effort in saving the lives of the people entrusted to my care, and accordingly directed the boats to land as many of them as possible, keeping the senior lieutenant and a few others on board with me.

The whole of this day there was little prospect of saving those who remained with the wreck, as the surf was so great that the boats could not return to us; several guns were fired, to point to those on shore our hopeless situation, and stimulate them to use every possible effort to come to our relief: but they could not effect it, notwithstanding every exertion on their part, which we were most anxiously observing. As the only means which then occurred to me of saving the people on board, I directed a raft to be made with the spars left on the booms, which was accomplished, with much difficulty, in about six hours; the sea then breaking over the ship with great violence, and freezing as it fell with such severity, that even the alternative adopted presented little prospect of saving any one left on the wreck. During this state of awful suspense, we had every reason to think that the ship was completely bilged and were apprehensive, from the steepness of the bank, that she would fall with her decks to the lee, as the ebb made, in which case all on board must have inevitably perished.

About half-past 11 p.m. the barge came off; and as the lives of the people were now the primary consideration, I sent as many of them on shore by her as possible, as well as by the launch, when she was able to come off; and at 2 a.m., on the 1st November, having previously succeeded in sending every other person on shore, I left the ship with regret, in the jolly-boat, and landed, with some difficulty, through the surf. About 8 a.m. the same morning, I attempted to go off in the barge to save as much provisions and stores as possible, but found it impracticable, as the boat was nearly swamped. All this and the succeeding day, the gale continuing, we could not launch the boats, and were employed carrying such provisions and stores as were saved to some empty houses which were discovered about six miles to the eastward of where we landed. Finding that with all our exertions we had only been able to save three days' bread, the officers and crew were put upon half allowances, with the melancholy prospect of starving in the woods.

On Thursday 3 November, the weather moderating, we launched the boats before daylight, and despatched the jolly-boat, with the purser, to a village called Trois Pistoles, about forty-five miles distant, on the opposite side of the river, that he might find his way to Quebec, to procure us assistance and relief, there being no possibility of communicating with any inhabited quarter from where we were but by water.

During our stay near the wreck, we had repeated gales of wind, both to the eastward and westward; and so violent, and with so much sea, that the mizen mast was thrown overboard, all the upper deck beams broken, and the ship's bottom beaten out.

We embraced every intervening opportunity of going off to save stores by scuttling the decks, which were covered with ice, the ship on her broadside, and the water flowing over the quarter-deck. On these occasions we were generally away ten or twelve hours, exposed to the wet and cold, without nourishment; from which, and fatigue, I had to lament seeing the people every day become more sickly, and many of them frost-bitten from the severity of the weather. By the inde-fatigable exertions of the officers and crew we succeeded in saving all our spare sails, cables, and stores, to a considerable amount; though the cables were frozen so hard, that we were obliged to cut and saw them as junk.

On the 7th, I again sent a boat with the second-lieutenant, to Trois Pistoles, in the hope of procuring, if possible, some temporary supplies; but the wind increasing to a violent gale from the eastward, with a heavy fall of snow, they got frozen up on the oppposite shore, and did not return till the twelfth, having then only procured three hundredweight of flour, a few potatoes, and some beef – two men having deserted from the boat.

At this period, I had a respectful request made me from the people, to be allowed to go to Trois Pistoles, that they might shift for themselves whilst the weather would admit of it, dreading the consequences of remaining longer where we were; but our boats would not have carried above one-third, and I conceived the public service would have suffered from allowing them to separate. We had, also, several desertions in consequence, I believe, of hunger, and the melancholy prospect before them; two of the deserters were brought back, and one returned delirious, after five days' absence, with his feet in a state of gangrene, having had only one small cake to eat during that time. Those still missing must have perished in the woods, from the accounts of the men who were brought back.

On Sunday 20 November, we were relieved from the most painful state of anxiety by the arrival of a small schooner, with a fortnight's provisions, from Quebec, and information that a transport had been procured, and was equipping for us, which nothing but the ice setting in would prevent coming down; and on the twenty-fourth I had the satisfaction of receiving a letter by the government schooner, announcing a further supply of provisions, with some blankets for the people: it, however, then blew so hard, with a heavy fall of snow, that she was obliged to take shelter under Bie. On the twenty-fifth the schooner returned, when we embarked, and were carried to the opposite side of the river, where the transport was expected – the pilot conceiving it unsafe to bring the ship nearer to us at that season of the year.

In justice to the officers and crew, it now becomes my duty, and a very pleasing part thereof, to bear testimony to the particular perseverance with which they bore the cold, hunger, and fatigue, whilst endeavouring to save the ship, and when that idea was given up, in saving the stores with the dire prospect before them of being cut off from all supplies had the winter set in, the ice rendering all communication impracticable during that season of the year.

The Surgeon of HMS Banterer *reported:*

a considerable number of the crew were affected with inflammation of the extremities, which in nearly twenty cases produced partial mortification, and one extensive gangrene on both feet, attended with delirium and other dangerous symptoms.

Captain Shippard died, as a rear-admiral, in 1841.

The Loss of HMS *St George* and HMS *Defence*
23 December 1811

HMS St George *was the flagship of Rear-Admiral Reynolds. In November 1811 she was escorting a convoy from the Baltic. On 15 December the wind increased to a hurricane and water poured in through the hawse holes. While her crew were still attempting to veer away the cable a large merchant ship collided with her, severing her cables. The ship was driven onto a sand bank. When the weather improved, other ships from her squadron assisted her to Gottenburg where she was jury-rigged.*

On 17 December she sailed with a convoy, together with HMS Defence *and HMS* Cressy. *On 23 December she met another north westerly gale in which she lost her jury-rigged rudder. She struck her lower yards and topmasts. On 24 December HMS* St George *ran aground and began to drift towards the shore. W. O. S. Gilly compiled this account from Admiralty records:*

Upon examining the well, the carpenter reported ten feet water in the hold; and this rose so rapidly that in the space of half an hour it reached lower deck, driving the people to the main Admiral Reynolds and the captain used every effort to encourage the men to remain steady to duty, as the only chance of preserving their lives. At ten o'clock, the sea swept the main deck, so all hands were obliged to seek refuge on the poop. All the boats, except the yawl, had either been stove or washed overboard. As an instance of the obedience and discipline of the crew of the *St George*, three or four men came forward, and asked permission to attempt to reach the shore in the yawl: this request was at first granted, but as they were about to lower her into the sea, it was considered impossible that the boat could live, and the men were directed to return to their posts. Without a murmur, they instantly obeyed; and as if Providence had rewarded this implicit obedience reliance upon their officers, two of these men were of the few that were saved.

It is impossible to describe the suffering of the helpless crew. Their numbers, originally about 750, had been terribly thinned by the severity of the weather, and the surging of the waves which every instant burst over them. At eight o'clock in the evening of the 24th, fourteen men took the boat and attempted to pull from the wreck, but they had not gone many yards when she upset and her crew perished. The mizzen-mast still stood and orders were given for its being cut away, but as no axes could be found, the men were obliged to use their knives to cut the lanyards of the rigging; at this moment, a sea struck the mast, carrying away the poop, and the men who were upon it. As the poop was swept away from the wreck, it bore not only the living but the dead. The latter far outnumbered the former, and it became necessary for the general preservation to cast overboard the bodies of their dead comrades. But their strength, already weakened by previous suffering, was unequal to the performance of this painful duty; and while thus employed, a sea swept over the poop, scattering the men upon the foaming billows. Five regained it, but were again washed off, and again succeeded in reaching their former position. Of these, two died, and the other three were washed on shore.

In the fourth row lay the admiral and his friend Captain Guion; whilst the groans of the dying, mingling with the roar of the tempest, unnerved the hearts of those who had hitherto shown an undaunted front to the perils surrounding them.

There still remained about 200 men, who were employed in constructing a raft, as the last chance of saving their lives. After considerable labour, this was effected, by lashing together a topsail yard, and a cross-jack yard, the only spars that remained.

Upon this, ten men left the wreck, but the timbers being improperly secured, they broke adrift and the first sea that came washed five men off; the others gained the shore, one of whom died.

According to all accounts, even the few who survived would have perished, had it not been for the humane conduct of the Danes who came to their assistance; these, at the risk of their own lives succeeded in rescuing from the raft the seven exhausted sufferers who survived, out of the crew of 750 men.

HMS Cressy *turned downwind and avoided the danger. W. O. S.* Gilly:

The master of the *Defence* reported to Captain Atkins that the *St George* had gone on shore and that the *Cressy* had veered and was standing to the southward at the same time pointing out great danger the ship was in, and recommending that he should follow the example of the *Cressy*. The captain inquired whether the admiral had made the signal to part company; upon being answered in the negative, he replied, "I will never desert my admiral in the hour of danger and distress."

About six o'clock a.m., the hands were turned up to wear ship, but before this could be accomplished she struck, the sea made a breach over her, and washed several men overboard.

The captain gave orders to fire minute guns, and cut away the masts. Five or six guns only had been fired, before they broke adrift, so that it was impossible to fire any more; but providentially these had been heard by the look-out men on shore, to whose assistance may be attributed the preservation of the few lives that were saved.

The waves swept over the vessel, forcing numbers of the crew down the hatchways, the guns and other heavy articles had broken loose, killing some, breaking the arms and legs of others, whose agonizing cries served only to add to the horrors of a scene scarcely within the power of description.

The captain at this time stood on the poop, holding on only by a howitzer that was lashed before the mizzen-mast, the officers and crew clinging to other parts of the wreck. The boats were all stove, except the pinnace, in which about twenty men had collected, when a sea, breaking over the wreck, washed her overboard, capsized her, and all perished.

Another sea struck the *Defence* with such excessive violence as to lift a spare anchor from its berth, throw it up on end, killing in its fall upon the forecastle about thirty men. The booms were washed away, and with them nearly one hundred men who were clinging to the different spars.

One of her crew described his escape:

I got on one side of the booms that were floating among the rest of the wreck. At that time every man except two, John Platt and Ralph Teasel, two of the men who were saved, were washed off. Myself and several more were at the same swept off the mizen-top. I then made the best of my way from one spar to another, until I got on one side of the booms. At this time about forty men regained their position upon the booms, when another sea washed all off except four. I got on the booms a second time, and spoke to John Brown and told him I thought we were approaching shore. There were then about twenty men on them but when we reached the shore there were only six left.

Two Danes on the beach came to our assistance; my foot got jammed in amongst the small spars, and my comrades, seeing that I was unable to get off the raft, were coming to my help, when the Danes made signs to them to be quiet. One Dane made three attempts before he succeeded in reaching the raft, and the third time he was nearly exhausted: he managed to get hold of my foot, and wrenched it out, and carried me on shore. I was then taken up to a shed to wait for some carts which were coming for us, most of us being unable to walk. In about ten minutes a number of gentlemen arrived on horseback, and some carts came down upon the beach. We were then placed in them, and driven to a small village called Shelton. On the road the man who drove the cart spoke to a woman, and asked her if she had any liquor. She replied by drawing a bottle from her pocket, and made each of us take a dram, which I believe was in a great measure the saving of our lives.

We soon arrived at the houses in the village where we were stripped and put to bed, and treated by inhabitants with the greatest hospitality and kindness. When I awoke, I found another seaman had been placed in the same bed with me; he had come on shore some time after myself upon a piece of wreck. He said, just as he reached the shore the poop and forecastle were capsized, and not a man to be seen, except a few upon pieces of wreck. In the evening a gentleman who spoke English came to our bedside, and told us that an officer had been brought up to the house. He also told us that there was another ship on shore to the southward of us, which appeared to be a three-decker, lying with her stern on shore. We knew directly it could be none other than the *St George*.

He inquired if we were able to get up, and go and look at the body of the officer, and see if we knew of him. We answered, Yes, and, with the assistance of the people, went into the barn, and recognised our captain. We then returned to bed again, being too exhausted to stand. The gentleman told us that medical assistance could not be procured that night, but that we should have every nourishment the house could afford. He then took his leave, promising that he would return in the morning when we might be better able to speak to him.

He accordingly came in the morning, and inquired what force our ship was. We told him a 74-gun ship, with a company of 600 men. Upon our inquiring if any more of our shipmates had reached the shore, he answered, No; and we returned most hearty thanks to the Almighty for our deliverance.

On Sunday, the 29th, we put our captain into a coffin, and buried him in Shelton Churchyard, with two seamen alongside of him.

It was some time, through the bitterness of the cold and the bruises we had received, before we were able to walk about. As soon as we had gained sufficient strength, we went down to the beach, where we saw, scattered for about two miles along the beach, the wreck of the *Defence*, but not a corpse was to be seen. We supposed they had drifted away to the southward and westward, a strong current setting that way. This opinion was in a great measure confirmed by seeing our officer's things sold, and other articles belonging to the ship six miles to the southward of where we were cast away, when we went to join the few who were saved from the *St George*. On the 13th January our captain was taken up again, and carried to Rinkum Church, and placed in a vault with the honours of war.

Only six men from the *Defence* were saved, out of a crew of 600. Two days afterwards when the gale had abated, a Danish boat, with two of the English sailors, went on board the *St George* to bring away the corpses of the admiral and others, but they found the decks had been entirely swept away. Nothing could exceed the hospitality and kindness with which the Danes treated the few who were thrown upon their shore. Nor was the Danish government backward in generosity. The dead were buried with military honours, and the survivors were sent to England without exchange.

Major General Tellequist expressed the commiseration felt by the Danish government, for the lamentable catastrophe that befell the St. George *and the* Defence.

Randus, 21 January, 1812

Sir – Though the grievous misfortune which has happened his great Britannic Majesty's ships of war on the Danish coast perhaps already may be known to your Excellency; nevertheless, whereas the opposite case may be possible, I will not omit hereby to make you acquainted with the sorrowful accident, assuring you that I am very compassionating.

The 24th of last month, in the night, the English ships of the line, *St George* and *Defence*, are splitted upon the western coast of Jutland, and the violent waves made it impossible to bring the wretched crews any assistance. From both ships are saved but thirteen persons, who are cast on shore by the sea with goods of wreck. Some of them are sick, and at present under care. A part of the dead bodies are driven to land, and interred with as much ceremony as the circumstances would permit.

All possible pains have been taken to find out the bodies of the officers, in order to show them military honours, by the obsequies upon the churchyard.

Two bodies of officers were found, and buried with military honours. Among these was the body of Captain Atkins, commanding the *Defence*, which is deposited in a church till I receive the further ordaining from my most gracious sovereign.

I complain much that the body of Admiral Reynolds has not yet been found, for all the pains which are taken on this purpose.

Agreeably to the charitable sensibility of the Danish nation, the inhabitants have been very grieved to see the English warriors in such a distress, without being able to assist them; and I am very sorry, Sir, that I cannot give your Excellency of this accident an account less sorrowful

With great esteem I remain, Sir,

&c. &c. &c.

Tellequist

The body of Rear-Admiral Reynolds was found a few days after

the date of Major General Tellequist's letter. It was buried with military honours near that of Atkins, in Rinkum Church.

The surviving officers and men of the St George were tried by a court-martial at Sheerness, and acquitted of all blame with reference to the loss of that vessel.

The Wreck of HMS *Penelope*
31 April 1815

On 31 March 1815, HMS Penelope, *a troopship, Commander James Galloway, sailed from Spithead for Canada. Off the Banks of Newfoundland, she encountered ice, fog and strong SE winds. On 25 April she was surrounded by ice but finally entered the Gulf of St Lawrence. On 30 April, she was using a lead to take sound-ings when she ran aground. Commander Galloway:*

I cannot describe my feelings, at that moment; for having, for a long been almost deprived of my eyesight by night, and also afflicted with rheumatic pains and other complaints, I was unable to judge correctly of the extent of our danger.

They lowered their boats and anchored in five and a half fathoms. The anchor held but did not move the vessel. They heaved the guns overboard to lighten the vessel. The wind increased. It was a cold north east wind carrying sleet and snow. In the morning they cut away the masts but it was apparent that the ship would break up. They tried to save some provisions but they were already damaged by salt water.

W. O. S. Gilly compiled this account from Admiralty records:

The masts were about this time cut away, in order to ease the ship as much as possible; they fell towards the shore about a cable's length from the beach. The master was sent in a cutter to try to fasten a rope to the shore, but the surf ran so high that the boat was stove, and the crew with difficulty gained the beach.

In this condition, with very little prospect of saving the lives of the crew, the captain, anxious for the preservation of the public dispatches, entrusted them to the purser, who, with Captain Murray (aide-de-camp to Lieut.-General Sir George Murray) in charge of the military dispatches, embarked in the life-boat, to which a small line was attached. They had, however, no better success than the other boat, for as soon as they reached the surf, the boat capsized, and the two officers swam to the shore with the dispatches tied round their necks.

Another cutter was then sent off in hopes that she would be more successful, but she filled almost immediately; and they were obliged to abandon the rope which was fastened to her.

By this time it was impossible to stand upon the deck, the sea made a fair breach over the ship, and the water having rushed into the cabin, the few bags of bread that had been stowed there for protection were destroyed.

The captain, being unable from ill health to make any great exertion to save his life, was lowered into the pinnace, into which were already crowded as many men as she could hold, and they took another rope on board, to make a last attempt to form a cominunication with the shore. The boat had scarcely left the side of the ship before a sea struck and upset her. The captain, supported by two men, made his way through the surf with great difficulty and got on shore, followed by the rest of the boat's crew, who, some by swimming, and others by help of oars and spars, saved themselves from destruction. The gig was now the only boat left on board; she was lowered from the stern, and the first and second lieutenants, with eighteen men, jumped into her. They were all fortunate enough to reach the shore, and some of the men gallantly return to the vessel, and succeeded in landing about twenty others. Again the gig repaired to the wreck, and took off some more of the crew, but this time she was unfortunately upset in the surf, though no lives were lost.

When the men left on the wreck saw themselves thus deprived of the last chance of escape, though they raised the most piteous cries for assistance, although they knew that their comrades had no means of affording it. These were in all probability the men who had betaken themselves to their hammocks a short time before, and had refused to assist in providing for their own safety; they had disobeyed orders, and despised discipline, and now we find them imploring others for that deliverance which they had neglected to provide for themselves. Most of them had been drinking the spirits, and were so stupified that they were incapable of taking advantage of the floating spars and planks to which they might have clung, and so gained the land.

By drunkenness the bed of the ocean has been rendered a foul and gloomy charnel-house, where the bones of thousands of our fellow-men await the summons of the Archangel's trumpet, when "the sea shall give up her dead". The reckless seamen, though unprepared for another world, hurry themselves into the presence of their Judge, to meet the drunkard's doom.

Unfortunate as was the situation of the helpless creatures on the wreck of the *Penelope*, it was only a few degrees more wretched than that of the officers and men on the shore. They had been cast at the base of a steep mountain, bruised and benumbed by the cold; their clothes were actually freezing on their backs, and they were without provisions of any kind. Their first care was to search for wood and kindle fires, which they at last succeeded in doing, and then they dried their clothes – but before they could derive any benefit from the fire, the intensity of cold had caused many of them extreme suffering; they were frost-bitten in the hands and feet, and several lost their toes. Some of the people were employed in constructing a tent with branches of trees and blankets, others were searching for provisions and securing such articles as were washed on shore from the ship. In the evening they found about sixty pieces of pork, – and with this and some melted snow they satisfied the cravings of hunger and thirst. Later in the evening several casks of wine, which had been stowed in the ward-room were washed on shore;

but these, which might have proved a blessing to all, were seized by a party of the men, who broke open the casks and drank to such an excess that they fell asleep, and were found almost frozen to death. During the whole of the day the unhappy men upon the wreck had never ceased supplicating their more fortunate comrades to go to their assistance, but this was impossible: no human effort could save them. As night drew on, their cries were redoubled, and were still heard far above the howling and roaring of the tempest when darkness had hidden the ill-fated vessel from view. About twelve o'clock three fearful crashes were followed by a still more fearful sound – the last agonized shriek of many perishing creatures.

At daylight, the remains of the *Penelope* were again visible, but in three separate pieces; all that were left on board had perished, save one man, who was washed on shore nearly lifeless.

The sufferings of these poor wretches must have been awful in the extreme, for their agonies of mind appear to have surpassed those of the body, and to have prolonged their lives by preventing them falling into the torpor which precedes death from cold. So severe was the frost, that the wreck had the appearance of huge masses of ice; and on shore nothing but the very large fires that were kept burning could have preserved the existence of the rest of the crew.

Upon the ship breaking up, the spirits floated on shore, when there ensued such a scene of tumult and insubordination as, happily for the honour of the service, seldom occurs in the British navy. The men broke open the casks, and before the officers were aware of it, scarcely a man was to be seen sober. This brought with it its own punishment; many had drunk to such a degree that they fell lifeless in the snow. The officers then caused the (barrels) of the rum to be stove, excepting a certain quantity placed under their own care; but when discipline is once broken, it is not easily restored. The next day, forty-eight men deserted, after plundering several of their shipmates, and breaking open every trunk that was washed up. These paid the penalty of their crimes, for many of them were found dead in the woods by the Canadians.

One of the surviving officers described:

With the remaining part of the crew the boats were hauled up, which we began to repair the best way we could. Sails were made from a lower and topmast studding-sail, which was fortunately washed ashore; a cask of flour was also found, a part of which was made into dough, and preparations were made to proceed to Quebec.

On the third day a Canadian boat was passing when the captain ordered her to be detained to proceed to that port. With the assistance of the cooking utensils found in the Canadian boat, all the pork that could be found was cooked and served out to the different boats, which was a very short allowance for two days.

On the sixth day of our misery, the weather moderated, the boats were launched, and all hands embarked; sixty-eight persons in all, including two women. The wind was favourable, but light; with rowing and sailing, we got to Great Fox River that night, at which place we were hospitably entertained with potatoes and salt at a Canadian hut. Next morning we sailed for Gaspar Bay, and reached Douglas Town in the evening.

The captain and officers were accommodated at Mr Johnston's, and the crew lodged at the different huts around the place. After three days' rest, we walked nine miles over the ice to where the transports lay; leaving the sick at Douglas Town. The captain hoisted his pendant on board the *Ann* transport, and put a lieutenant in each of the others and an equal number of men. When the ice broke up, which was seven days after we got on board, we dropped down to Douglas Town, and embarked the sick, one of whom died, and two deserted. The next morning we sailed for Quebec, where we arrived on the 28th, many of us not having a change of clothes of any description.

Captain Galloway reported:

I feel it my duty, to state to you the infamous conduct of the whole of the crew, with a very few exceptions. From the time that the ship struck, their behaviour was not in the character of British seamen in general; they had neither principle nor humanity; some, in consequence, have suffered severely, and several died from drunkenness.

The Wreck of the *Medusa*
July 2 1816

In 1816 the French frigate, Medusa, *was taking out the governor of Senegal and his suite to St. Louis on the coast of west Africa. The* Medusa *was carrying 400 men, women, and children, including 160 crew, and Colonel Julien-Désiré Schmaltz, Commander in Chief and new Governor of Senegal. The captain, de Chaumereys, owed his appointment to political favour rather than experience.*

Schmaltz was impatient to reach St Louis by the most direct route. This route took them dangerously close to the shoreline. There were navigational problems along the entire length of the African coast, including the notorious Arguin bank. Despite the danger, Governor Schmaltz insisted that they take the most direct route.

On 2 July, although they were taking soundings, the ship ran aground on the Arguin bank. According to witnesses, a strange transformation came over the faces of de Chaumereys and the navigator, "a silent fever . . . a great anxiety."

Seconds later, the navigator was subjected to a volley of abuse, and very nearly assaulted. The captain was speechless.

The crew began throwing things overboard. It was high spring tide, and each high tide was going to be lower than the last. De Chaumereys stopped the lightening of the ship. The ship settled on the sandbank. De Chaumereys decided to abandon ship. He held a conference to to discuss what to do about the lack of lifeboats.

Governor Schmaltz suggested building a raft to carry the soldiers and crew to shore. The more "important" of the passengers would take the lifeboats. Strung together, the lifeboats would tow the raft to safety. The raft was made of the masts and cross-beams of the boat. It was crudely constructed, roughly 65 feet by 23 feet (or 20m × 7m). It had no means of navigation and no oars. When the men were loaded onto it, some 150 of them, they sank down in the sea to their waists. It was hopelessly overcrowded; each man only had a square three feet (1 m) on a side to stand in. Without even enough room to lie down in, they stood in the water, and their legs shriveled up like prunes. W. O. S. Gilly compiled this account from contemporary documents:

A total relaxation of discipline, and absence of all order, precaution, and presence of mind, and a contemptible disregard of everything and of everybody but self, in the hour of common danger, filled up the full measure of horrors poured out upon the guilty crew of the *Medusa*. She struck on a sand-bank under circumstances which admitted of the hope of saving all on board. The shore was at no great distance, and the weather was not so boisterous as to threaten the speedy destruction of the ship, when the accident first happened.

There were six boats of different dimensions available to take off a portion of the passengers and crew: there was time and there was opportunity for the construction of a raft to receive the remainder. But the scene of confusion began among the officers and men at the crisis, when an ordinary exercise of forethought and composure would have been the preservation of all. Every man was to shift for himself, and every man did shift for himself, in that selfish or bewildered manner which increased the general disaster. The captain was not among the last, but among the first to scramble into a boat; and the boats pushed off from the sides of the frigate, before they had taken in as many as each was capable of holding. Reproaches, recrimination, and scuffling took the place of order and of the word of command, both in the ship and in the boats, when tranquillity and order were indispensable for the common safety.

When the raft had received the remaining 150 in number, for whom the boats had no room, or would make no room, it was found when it was too late to correct the evil that the raft had been put together with so little care. It was so ill provided with necessaries, that the planking was insecure; there was not space enough for protection from the waves; and charts, instruments, spars, sails, and stores were all deficient. A few casks of wine and some biscuits, enough for a single meal only, were all the provision made for their sustenance. The rush and scramble from the wreck had been accomplished with so little attention to discipline, that the raft had not a single naval officer to take charge of her. At first the boats took the raft in tow, but in a short time though the sea was calm and the coast was known to be within 15 leagues, the boats cast off the tow-lines: and in not one of the 6 was there a sufficient sense of duty, or of humanity left, to induce the crew to remain by the floating planks – the forlorn hope of 150 of their comrades and fellow-countrymen! Nay, it is related by the narrators of the wreck of the *Medusa*, that the atrocious cry resounded from one boat to another "Nous les abandonnons!" "We leave them to their fate," – until one by one all the tow-lines were cast off. During the long interval of 17 days the raft struggled with the waves. A small pocket compass was the only guide of the unhappy men, who lost even this in one of the quarrels which ensued every hour for a better place on the raft or a morsel of biscuit. On the first night 12 men were jammed between the timbers and died under the agonies of crushed and mangled limbs. On the second night more were drowned, and some were smothered by pressure towards the centre of the raft. Common suffering, instead of softening, hardened the hearts of the survivors against each other. Some of them drank wine till they were in a frenzy of intoxication, and attempted to cut the ropes which kept the raft together. A general fight ensued, many were killed, and many were cast into the sea during the struggle; and thus perished from 60 to 65. On the third day, portions of the bodies of the dead were devoured by some of the survivors. On the fourth night another quarrel and another fight, with more bloodshed, broke out. On the fifth morning, 30 only out of the 150 were alive. Two of these were flung to the waves for stealing wine: a boy died, and 27 remained, not to comfort and to assist each other, but to hold a council of destruction, to determine who should be victims for the preservation of the rest. At this hideous court twelve were pronounced too weak to outlive much more suffering, and that they might not needlessly consume any part of the remaining stock of provisions, such as it was (flying-fish mixed with human flesh), these twelve helpless wretches were deliberately thrown into the sea. The 15, who thus provided for their own safety by the sacrifice of their weaker comrades, were rescued on the 17th day after the wreck by a brig, sent out in quest of the wreck of the *Medusa* by the 6 boats which reached the shore in safety; and which might have been the means of saving all on the raft, had not the crews been totally lost to every sentiment of generosity and humanity, when they cast off the tow-lines.

A writer in the Quarterly Review *of October, 1817 wrote:*

It is impossible not to be struck with the extraordinary difference of conduct in the officers and crew of the *Medusa* and the *Alceste*, wrecked nearly about the same time. In the one case all the people were kept together in a perfect discipline and subordination, and brought safely home from the opposite side of the globe; in the other, every one seems to have been left to shift for himself and the greater part perished in the horrible way we have seen.

The similarities between the Medusa *and the* Alceste *invite comparison. Both ships were frigates, both were carrying diplomatic*

*passengers. Both ships ran aground in 1816–17. The subsequent
fates of their crews and passengers were a contrast which was represented by the painter Gericault. He completed the painting in 1819.
It is now entitled* Le Radeau De La Medusa *(The Raft of the
Medusa), but was originally titled* Scene de naufrage *(Scene of
shipwreck). It hangs in Salle 77 of the Denon wing of the Louvre
Museum. The painter's sources were published accounts and
personal interrogations of two of the survivors named Correard and
Savigny.*

The Wreck of HMS *Alceste*

This account of the wreck of HMS Alceste *in 1817 was compiled
from Admiralty records by W. O. S. Gilly:*

At the close of 1815, the Court of Directors of the East India
Company having represented to the British Government the
impediments thrown in the way of our trade with China, by
the impositions practised by the local authorities at Canton,
it was determined to send an embassy to the court of Peking.

Lord Amherst was selected to undertake the mission and
Mr Henry Ellis was appointed secretary to the embassy.

The *Alceste*, a frigate of 46 guns, under the command of
Captain, afterwards Sir Murray Maxwell, was fitted up for
the reception of the ambassador and his suite.

On 9 February 1816, the expedition sailed from Spithead,
and arrived in the China seas about the middle of July
following. It is not in our province to give any account of the
proceedings of the embassy, which have already been so ably
described, and are well known.

His excellency, having accomplished the object of his
mission, took his departure from China on 9 January 1817,
arrived at Manilla on 3 February, and finally sailed from
thence to the *Alceste*, on the 9th of the same month.

Captain Maxwell directed the ship's course to be steered

towards the Straits of Gaspar, in preference to those of Banca, as affording, at that period of the monsoon, the most convenient and speedy egress from the China seas; and though this pass is not so often taken as that of Banca, the Gaspar Straits appeared by the plans and surveys laid down in the Admiralty charts, as well as in those of the East India Company, to be not only wider, but to have a much greater depth of water, and to offer fewer difficulties to navigation.

Early on the morning of 18 February, they made the Island of Gaspar, and in a short time, Pulo Leat, or Middle Island, was descried from the masthead. The weather was remarkably fine and clear – a mild breeze blowing from the north-west, and the surface of the water gently agitated by the current, which perpetually sets through the Straits, either to the south-east or south-west, according to the monsoon.

The sea, which is usually so clear in these climates, had been greatly discoloured that morning by a quantity of fish-spawn, a circumstance of not unfrequent occurrence in those seas; and the navigation being thus rendered more dangerous, unusual precautions were taken for ensuring the safety of the ship. A man was stationed at the foretop mast head and and others at the fore-yardarms. Captain Maxwell, with the master and other officers, was upon deck. An eye-witness wrote:

> steering under all these guarded circumstances, the soundings corresponding so exactly with the charts, and following the express line prescribed by all concurring directions, to clear every danger, and it was the last danger of this sort between us and England, when the ship, about half-past seven in the morning, with a horrid crash on a reef of sunken rocks, and remained immoveable.

Captain Maxwell himself recalled:

What my feelings were at this momentary transition from a state of perfect security to all the horrors of a shipwreck, I will not venture to depict but I must acknowledge, it required whatever mental energy I possessed to control them, and to enable me with coolness and firmness the necessary orders preparatory to abandoning the ship – which a very short period of hard working at all the pumps showed the impracticability of saving.

Gilly's account continued:

The carpenter very soon reported the water above the tanks in the main hold, and in a few minutes more, over the orlop deck.

The quarter boats had been instantly lowered to sound and reported deep water all round the reef, ten fathoms immediately under the stern, and seventeen about a quarter of a cable further off, so that it was but too evident that the preservation of the crew depended solely upon the vessel's remaining fast where she was.

The first care of Captain Maxwell was for the safety of Lord Amherst and his suite; the boats were quickly hoisted out, and before half-past eight, he had the melancholy satisfaction of seeing the ambassador and all his attendants safely embarked in them.

For the better protection of the embassy, an officer was sent to the barge, with a guard of marines, to conduct them to Pulo Leat, between three and four miles distant, and from which it was hoped that plenty of water and abundance of tropical fruits might be procured.

Meanwhile the officers and men exerted themselves most indefatigably to save some of the provisions – a task by no means easy of accomplishment, as the holds and everything in them were submerged in water. Towards the afternoon, the boats returned from the shore, and the men reported that they had great difficulty in landing his excellency, from the mangrove trees growing out to a considerable distance in the water; and it was not until they had pulled three or four miles from the place where they had first attempted to land that they were enabled to reach terra firma. They also stated that neither food nor water could be discovered on the island. Unpromising as appearances were, there was no alternative but to seek shelter on the inhospitable shore. Accordingly, every preparation was made and by 8 p.m., the people were all landed, excepting one division, who remained on board the wreck, with the captain, first-lieutenant and some other officers.

About midnight, the wind had greatly increased and the ship became so uneasy from her heeling to windward, that fears were entertained for the safety of those on board. To prevent her falling further over, the topmasts were cut away, and as the wind became more moderate towards the ship remained stationary, and all apprehensions were removed. The boats did not return to the wreck till between six and seven o'clock in the morning, and they brought no better tidings as to the capabilities of the island to furnish food and other necessaries for the subsistence of so many human beings.

A raft had been constructed during the previous day which the small quantity of provisions they had been able to collect, together with some of the baggage of the embassy, and clothes and bedding of the officers and men, had been transported to the shore.

In the course of the forenoon, Captain Maxwell thought it right to confer with Lord Amherst as to his further movements; he accordingly quitted the wreck and went on shore. He left the vessel in charge of Mr Hick, the first-lieutenant, with orders that every effort should be made to get at the provisions and the water, and that a boat should remain, by the wreck for the safety of the men in case of emergency. Captain Maxwell reached the shore about half-past 11 a.m., and we may imagine the bitterness of his distress on finding the ambassador, surrounded by his suite, and the officers and men of the *Alceste*, in the midst of a pestilential salt-water marsh.

One of the officers, named McLeod, described the scene:

The spot in which our party were situated was sufficiently romantic, but seemed, at the same time, the abode of ruin and havoc. Few of its inhabitants (and among the rest the ambassador) had now more than a shirt or a pair of trousers on. The wreck of books, or, as it was not unaptly termed, "a literary manure", was spread about in all directions; whilst parliamentary robes, court dresses, and mandarin habits, intermixed with check shirts and tarry jackets, were hung around in wild confusion on every tree.

W. O. S. Gilly:

The situation in which Captain Maxwell was placed was, indeed, a most trying one, and such he felt it to be, for, from the lowest seaman to the ambassador himself; every one looked to him for relief and direction in his perilous position. Captain Maxwell was fully competent to meet the emergency; and, said he, "I had the consolation left me, to feel with confidence that all would follow my advice, and abide by my decision, whatever it might be."

His first care was for the safety of Lord Amherst and in a short conference with his excellency Mr Ellis, the second commissioner, it was arranged that the embassy should proceed to Batavia in the barge and cutter, with a guard of marines to the boats from any attack of the pirates. Mr Ellis promised that if they arrived safely at Batavia, he would himself return, in the first vessel that put off, to the assistance of those who remained on the island.

A small quantity of provisions, and nine gallons of water, was all that could be spared from their very scanty store; but at sunset every heart was exhilarated by hope and sympathetic courage, on seeing the ambassador strip, and wade off to the boats with as much cheerfulness as if he had stepped into them under a salute. At seven o'clock the barge, under the charge of Lieutenant Hoppner, and the cutter, commanded by Mr Mayne, the master, containing in all 47 persons took their departure for Batavia, accompanied by the anxious thoughts and good wishes of their fellow-sufferers, who were left to encounter new dangers.

Captain Maxwell's first order was to direct a party to dig in search of water. The men had begun to suffer greatly from thirst, as for the last two days they had had scarcely a pint of water each – one small cask only having been saved from the ship. The next step was to remove their encampment to higher ground, where they could breathe a purer air, and be in greater safety in case of attack.

In a short time the island presented a scene of bustle and activity strangely at variance with the solitude it had exhibited two days before; and the once silent woods resounded with the voices of men and the strokes of the axe and the hammer. One party was employed in cutting a path to the summit of the hill, another in removing thither their small stock of provisions. A few men were on board the wreck, endeavouring to save every article that might prove of general use.

About midnight, the men who had been employed for so many hours on a most fatiguing and harassing duty, and exposed to the vertical rays of a burning sun began to suffer most painfully from increased thirst. And it was at that moment when they were bereft of hope that they experienced one of the many merciful interpositions of Providence by which the Almighty displays His tender care for His creatures: a plentiful shower of rain fell, which the people caught by spreading out their table-cloths and clothes; and then, by wringing them, a degree of moisture was imparted to their parched lips, and their hearts were revived, and prepared to hear the joyful news, which was communicated by the diggers soon after midnight, that they had found water in the well, and a small bottle of this most dearly prized treasure was handed to the captain. So great was the excitement of the people on receiving the announcement, that it became necessary to plant sentries, in order to prevent their rushing to the well and impeding the work of the diggers.

On the morning of the 20th, the captain called all hands together, and pointed out to them the critical nature of their position, and the absolute necessity of their uniting as one man to overcome the difficulties by which they were surrounded. He reminded them that they were still amenable to the regulations of naval discipline, and assured them that discipline would be enforced with even greater rigour, if necessary, than on board ship; and that in serving out the provisions the strictest impartiality should be observed, and all should share alike until the arrival of assistance from Lord Amherst.

During the day, the well afforded a pint of water to each man; the water is said to have tasted like milk and water, and when a little rum was added to it, the men persuaded themselves that it tasted like milk punch, and it became a favourite with them.

The people were employed during the 20th much in the same manner as on the previous day but very few things could be obtained from the ship, every article of value being under water.

On Friday, the 21st, the party stationed on board the wreck observed a number of proahs [native craft made from reeds] full of Malays, apparently well armed, coming towards them. Being without a single weapon of defence they could only jump into their boats without loss of time, and push for the land. The pirates followed closely in pursuit, but retreated when they saw two boats put out from the shore to the assistance of their comrades. The Malays then returned to the ship and took possession of her. In an instant all was activity and excitement in the little camp.

McLeod wrote:

Under all the depressing circumstances attending shipwreck, of hunger, thirst and fatigue, and menaced by a ruthless foe, it was glorious to see the British spirit staunch and unsubdued. The order was given for every man to arm

himself in the best manner he could, and it was obeyed with
the utmost promptitude and alacrity. Rude pike staves were
formed by cutting down young trees; small swords, dirks,
knives, even large spike nails sharpened, were firmly fixed to
the ends of these poles, and those who could find nothing
better hardened the end of the wood in the fire, and
bringing it to a sharp point formed a tolerable weapon.
There were, perhaps a dozen cutlasses; the marines had
about thirty muskets and bayonets; but we could muster no
more than seventy-five ball cartridges among the whole
party.

We had fortunately preserved some loose powder from the
upper deck guns after the ship had struck (for the magazines
were under water in five minutes,) and the marines, by
hammering their buttons round, and by rolling up pieces of
broken bottles in cartridges, did their best to supply
themselves with a sort of shot that would have some effect at
close quarters, and strict orders were given not to throw away
a single discharge until sure of their aim.

Mr Cheffy, the carpenter, and his crew, under the direction of the captain, were busied in forming a sort of abattis by
felling trees, and enclosing in a shape the ground we
occupied; and by interleaving loose branches with the stakes
driven in among these, a breastwork was constructed, which
afforded us some cover, and must naturally impede the
progress of any enemy unsupplied with artillery.

Gilly's account continued:

The Malays had taken possession of some rocks, at no great
distance from where the crew of the *Alceste* were encamped,
and here they deposited the plunder they had taken from the
wreck. It now became necessary for Captain Maxwell to
prepare against an attack. With a very small stock of
provisions, which, even if husbanded with the greatest care,
could last only a few days, he had to contend with a handful
of men, many of them unarmed against a host of savages,

perhaps the most merciless and inhuman that are to be found in any part of the world.

In the evening a general muster was called and a rude and motley group presented itself to the eye of the commander. But rough as was the exterior he well knew that there was that within which would bid defiance to danger and outrage so long as life should last.

McLeod's account continued:

Even the boys had managed to make fast table-forks on the end of sticks for their defence. One of them, who had been severely bruised by the falling of the masts, and was slung in his hammock between two trees, had been observed carefully fixing with two sticks and a rope yarn, the blade of an old razor. On being asked what he meant to do he replied, "You know I cannot stand, but if any of these fellows come within reach of my hammock I'll mark them."

Gilly:

The officers and men were divided into companies and every precaution adopted to secure the garrison from being taken by surprise. The boats were hauled closer up to the landing-place, and put under the charge of an officer and guard.

On Saturday morning, the 22nd, every effort was made to induce the Malays to come to an amicable conference but without success. Mr Hay, the second lieutenant, was, therefore, ordered to proceed to the ship, with the barge, cutter, and gig (armed in the best manner possible under the circumstances), and to gain possession of her by fair means or by force. No sooner did the pirates see the boats put out towards the wreck, than they left the vessel though not before they had set fire to her, thus performing an act which was of great service to the crew of the *Alceste*; for by burning her upperworks everything buoyant could float up from below and be more easily laid hold of. The ship continued to burn during the night, and the flames as they darted from her side, shed a ruddy glare upon the wild scenery around, and, breaking through the shade of the thick and lofty trees, rested upon a landscape worthy of the pencil of Salvator Rosa.

Upon the summit of a hill, and under the spreading branches of the majestic trees, was a rude encampment, formed by the erection of a few wig-wams; whilst here and there, collected together in groups and reclining in different attitudes, were parties of men armed with pikes or cutlasses, in their ragged, unwashed, and unshorn appearance resembling rather a gang of banditti, than the crew of a British ship of war.

It was with the most painful feelings that both officers and men witnessed the gradual destruction of the gallant ship, which had been their home for so many months.

During the night that followed this sad scene, an incident occurred which, though it occasioned considerable alarm at the time, became a source of amusement afterwards.

A sentry, startled by the approach of a very suspicious-looking personage, who was making towards him, levelled his musket and fired. In an instant the whole camp was alive with excitement, supposing that they were attacked by the savages, when behold, the enemy turned out to be a large baboon, one of a race that abounded in the island. These creatures became very troublesome; they were most audacious thieves, and even carried away several ducks which had been saved from the wreck; till at last the poor birds were so frightened that they left their little enclosure and voluntarily sought for safety and protection amongst the people.

From the morning of Sunday the 23rd, till Wednesday the 26th, the men were busied in saving whatever they could from the hull of the *Alceste*, and they were fortunate enough to obtain several casks of flours, a few cases of wine, and a cask of beer, besides between fifty and sixty boarding pikes and eighteen muskets, all of which proved most acceptable.

A second well had been sunk, which supplied clearer water, and in great abundance, so that they possessed one of the chief necessaries of life in plenty.

Everything now wore a more favourable aspect. The Malays had retired behind a little island (called Palo Chalacca, or Misfortune's Isle) about two miles distant; and although they were expected to return speedily with a reinforcement, the crew of the *Alceste* were better prepared for them. The gunner had been actively employed in forming musket cartridges; and, by melting down some pewter basins and jugs, with a small quantity of lead obtained from the wreck, balls had been cast in clay moulds, which not a little increased their confidence and feeling of security.

Under the able command of Captain Maxwell, the greatest regularity and order prevailed amongst the people. Every man appeared happy and contented with his lot; for each man, from the highest to the lowest, encouraged his neighbour by his own good conduct, whilst he in turn received encouragement from the example of those above him. The provisions were served out with the strictest impartiality.

Mr McLeod wrote:

The mode adopted by Captain Maxwell, to make things go as far as possible, was to chop up the allowance for the day into pieces, whether fowls, salt beef, pork, mixing the whole hotch-potch, boiling them together, and serving out a measure to each and openly, and without any distinction. By these means no nourishment was lost: it could be more equally divided than by any other way; and although necessarily a scanty, it was by no means an unsavoury, mess.

Early on Wednesday morning, Lieutenant Hay, who had charge of the boats, observed two pirate proahs nearing the island, as if to reconnoitre; he immediately made a dash at them, with the barge, cutter, and gig. The barge closed with the Malays first, and a desperate conflict ensued. There was only one musket in the boat, which Mr Hay used to some purpose, for he killed two of the savages with his own hand. In the meantime, the other two boats had come up to the assistance of their comrades. One more pirate was shot dead, and another knocked down with the butt-end of a musket yet the rest continued to fight with savage ferocity until, seeing that resistance was fruitless, they jumped into the sea and drowned themselves, choosing to perish rather than yield. During the engagement an officer who was on the beach observed a canoe, which had been cut away from one of the proahs, drifting not many yards from the spot where he stood; and as he thought the prize worth securing, he entered the water and swam towards it. He had nearly attained his object, when those who watched him from the shore perceived an enormous shark hovering about. They were almost petrified with horror; anxious to make their friend aware of the danger, yet not daring to call out to warn him, lest a sudden perception of the perils of his situation, and of the proximity of his formidable enemy, should unnerve him, and thus deprive him of the slight chance of escape that remained. Breathless and silent then they stood and marked the movements of the shark with trembling anxiety. He seemed to be so sure of his prey, that he was in no haste to seize it, but swam leisurely about, crossing and recrossing between the doomed victim and the shore, as if gloating himself, and sharpening his appetite by gazing on the antici-pated feast. The officer, too, seemed to be luxuriating in the refreshing coolness of the water, calmly approaching the canoe, happily unconscious of his danger; but the shark followed him closely: his life depended upon a swimmer's stroke, or the whim of a moment. The anxiety of the specta-tors became agony; but that moment was decisive – the swimmer struck out once more – the canoe was gained, and he was saved.

Then, and then only, did he become aware of the horrible fate that had threatened him of the merciful interposition of Providence in his behalf.

In the course of this day fourteen proahs and smaller boats were observed standing towards the island, from the Banca side, and every heart bounded with joy in the full anticipation that it was a party sent by Lord Amherst from Batavia to their relief. Their joy, however, did not last long, for they soon found that the boats had come only to gather a kind of seaweed much esteemed by Chinese epicures, who use it, as they do birds' nests, in their soup.

Consultations were held that night as to the policy of negotiating with these people, so as to induce them, by promises of reward, to convey part of the crew of the *Alceste* to Java – the four remaining boats would then be sufficient for the transport of the rest.

But the morning dawn put all such plans to flight, and revealed the true character of these people. No sooner did they perceive the wreck, than they started off to her and plundered the hull of everything they could carry away. No assistance was to be expected from these rapacious thieves; and as the time had elapsed which was required to bring succour from Batavia, measures were taken to repair the launch and to construct a raft to enable the people to leave the island before their provisions should be completely exhausted.

Matters now began to assume a more formidable aspect, for on Saturday, 1 March, the Malay was increased by the arrival of several proahs, who joined in breaking up the remains of the wreck.

At daybreak on Sunday, the 2nd, the camp was alarmed and all were called to arms by the yells of savages, who, firing their partereroes [heavy firearms on a mounting], and beating their gongs, advanced with about twenty of their heaviest vessels towards the landing-place, and anchored within a cable's length of the shore.

After a short deliberation, a boat full of men armed with creeses approached the shore, and was met by a canoe containing an officer and party with a letter from Captain Maxwell, addressed to the chief authority at Minto, stating the situation of the *Alceste*'s crew, and praying that assistance might be sent to them.

The officer placed this letter in the hands of the Malays,

repeatedly pronounced the word Minto, and showed them a dollar, to intimate that they would be well rewarded if they returned with an answer. They appeared to understand the mission, and to be willing to execute it; but, as may be supposed, the service was never performed.

Meantime the Malay forces continued to increase; no less than 50 proahs and boats of different sizes were collected, and on a moderate computation, they had 500 men on board. Their mischievous intentions were too evident; they drew closer and closer to the shore, prevented the escape of any of the ship's boats, and even had recourse to stratagem in order to gain possession of the much-desired booty.

One party declared that all the Malays except themselves were hostile, and urged that they might be allowed to go to the camp to guard the crew of the *Alceste*. This kind offer was of course refused. "We can trust to ourselves," was the reply. The plot began to thicken; the odds seemed fearfully against the heroic little band, who, badly armed and worse provisioned, had to make good their position against a multitude of foes matchless amongst savages in cunning and cruelty. But in proportion to the imminence of the danger rose the courage of our countrymen.

Mr McLeod relates that, in the evening, when Captain Maxwell had assembled, as usual, the men under arms, for the purpose of inspecting them he addressed them in these words:

My lads, you must all have observed this day, as well as myself, great increase of the enemy's force (for enemies we must now consider them), and the threatening position they have assumed. I have, on various grounds, strong reason to believe they will attack us this night. I do not wish to conceal our real state because I think there is not a man here who is afraid to face any sort of danger. We are now strongly fenced in, and our position in all respects is so good that, armed as we are, we ought to make a formidable defence even against regular troops; what then, would be thought of us, if we allowed ourselves to be surprised by a set of naked savages with their spears and their creeses?

It is true they have swivels in their boats but they cannot act here; I have not observed that they have any matchlocks or muskets; but if they do, so have we!

I do not wish to deceive you as to the means of resistance in our power. When we were first thrown together on shore we were almost defenceless. Seventy-five ball cartridges only could be mustered; we have now 600. They cannot, I believe send up more than 500 men, but, with 200 such as now stand around me, I do not fear 1,000 – nay, 1,500 of them! I have the fullest confidence that we shall beat them. The pikemen standing firm, we can give them such a volley of musketry as they will be little prepared for, and when we find they are thrown into confusion, we'll sally out among them, chase them into the water, and ten to one but we secure their vessels. Let every man, therefore, be on the alert with his arms in his hands; and should these barbarians this night attempt our hill, I trust we convince them that they are dealing with Britons!

This short but spirited appeal had its full effect upon the hearts to which it was addressed. It was answered by three wild hurrahs, which were taken up by the picquets and outposts, and resounded through the woods. The British cheer struck the savages with terror; they no doubt thought it preceded an attack and they were observed making signals with lights to some of their tribe behind the islet.

The night passed undisturbed, and daylight discovered the pirates in the same position, their force increased by ten proahs, making their number at least 600 men. The situation of Captain Maxwell and his party became hourly more critical; the provisions could not last long – something must be done – some plan must be decided on. They had but little choice; they must either make a dash at the pirates, and seize their boats, with the certainty of being all butchered should they not succeed – and the odds were fearfully against them – or they must maintain their present position, in the hope that aid might be sent from Java, in time to save them from a fate scarcely less horrible – the lingering death of famine.

Under these depressing circumstances, the spirits of the men never for a moment seemed to flag. True "hearts of oak," their courage increased with their difficulties, and the prevailing desire amongst them was to rush upon the enemy and get possession of their boats, or perish in the attempt.

But for this day, at least, they were ordered to remain passive; perhaps in coming to this decision, the wise and brave commander of the party may have remembered another captain who was "in a great strait", and who said, "Let us fall now into the hands of the Lord, for his mercies are great and let me not fall into the hand of man." The decision then, was, to wait; and the hours rolled on till afternoon, when an officer ascended one of the loftiest trees, and thence he thought he descried a sail at a great distance. The joyful news seemed too good to be true.

A signalman was sent up with a telescope to sweep the horizon. The eager and intense anxiety that pervaded the little band, until he could report his observations, may be better imagined than described. At last, he announced that the object was indeed a brig, or a ship, standing towards the island under all sail. The joy was unbounded and overpowering. Men felt as if awaking from some horrible dream; and, doubtless, many an honest heart was uplifted in thankfulness to the Almighty, for the mercy vouchsafed in delivering them from what had appeared, a few minutes before, to be certain destruction.

There remains little more to be told; the vessel proved to be the *Ternate*, which Lord Amherst had sent to their assistance. The pirates took to flight as soon as they discovered the ship, but not before they had received a volley from the *Alceste*'s people, unfortunately without effect.

It was not till Friday 7 March, that all were embarked on board the *Ternate*. They arrived safely at Batavia on the 9th, and were most kindly received by Lord Amherst, who converted his table into a general mess for the officers, as well as the embassy; comfortable quarters were also provided for the men; and in their present enjoyment they all soon forgot the hardships they had suffered.

In conclusion, we will quote the following passage from the pen of Mr McLeod:

It is a tribute due to Captain Maxwell to state (and it is a tribute that all will most cheerfully pay) that, by his judicious arrangements, we were preserved from all the horrors of anarchy and confusion. His measures inspired confidence and hope, while his personal example in the hour of danger gave courage and animation to all around him.

Stove in by a whale
20 November 1820

In 1819, Owen Chase was first mate of the whaling ship Essex. *The* Essex *was stove in by a whale. The crew abandoned ship. Owen Chase:*

The ship *Essex*, commanded by captain George Pollard junior, was fitted out at Nantucket, and sailed on the 12 August 1819, for the Pacific Ocean, on a whaling voyage. Of this ship I was first mate. She had lately undergone a thorough repair in her upper works, and was at that time, in all respects, a sound, substantial vessel: she had a crew of twenty-one men, and was victualled and provided for two years and a half. We left the coast of America with a fine breeze, and steered for the Western Islands. On the second day out, while sailing moderately on our course in the Gulf Stream, a sudden squall of wind struck the ship from the SW and knocked her completely on her beam-ends, stove one of our boats, entirely destroyed two others, and threw down the cambouse. We distinctly saw the approach of this gust, but miscalculated altogether as to the strength and violence of it. It struck the ship about three points off the weather quarter, at the moment that the man at the helm was in the act of putting her away to run before it. In an instant she was knocked down with her yards in the water; and before hardly a moment of time was allowed for reflection, she gradually came to the wind, and righted. The squall was accompanied with vivid flashes of lighting, and heavy and repeated claps of thunder. The whole ship's crew were, for a short time, thrown into the utmost consternation and confusion; but fortunately the violence of the squall was all contained in the first gust of the wind, and it soon gradually abated, and became fine weather again. We repaired our damage with little difficulty, and continued on our course, with the loss of the two boats. On 30 August we made the island of Floros, one of the western group called the Azores. We lay off and on the island for two days, during which time our boats landed and obtained a supply of vegetables and a few hogs: from this place we took the NE trade-wind, and in sixteen days made the Isle of May, one of the Cape de Verds.

As we were sailing along the shore of this island, we discovered a ship stranded on the beach, and from her appearance took her to be a whaler. Having lost two of our boats, and presuming that this vessel had probably some belonging to her that might have been saved, we determined to ascertain the name of the ship, and endeavour to supply if possible the loss of our boats from her. We accordingly stood in towards the port, or landing place. After a short time three men were discovered coming out to us in a whale boat. In a few moments they were alongside, and informed us that the wreck was the *Archimedes* of New York, captain George B. Coffin, which vessel had struck on a rock near the island about a fortnight previously; that all hands were saved by running the ship on shore, and that the captain and crew had gone home. We purchased the whale boat of these people, obtained some few more pigs, and again set sail.

Our passage thence to Cape Horn was not distinguished

for any incident worthy of note. We made the longitude of the Cape about 18 December having experienced head winds for nearly the whole distance. We anticipated a moderate time in passing this noted land, from the season of the year at which we were there, being considered the most favourable; but instead of this, we experienced heavy westerly gales, and a most tremendous sea, that detained us off the Cape five weeks, before we had got sufficiently to the westward to enable us to put away. Of the passage of this famous Cape it may be observed, that strong westerly gales and a heavy sea are its almost universal attendants: the prevalence and constancy of this wind and sea necessarily produce a rapid current, by which vessels are set to leeward; and it is not without some favourable slant of wind that they can in many cases get round at all. The difficulties and dangers of the passage are proverbial; but as far as my own observation extends, (and which the numerous reports of the whalemen corroborate), you can always rely upon a long and regular sea; and although the gales may be very strong and stubborn, as they undoubtedly are, they are not known to blow with the destructive violence that characterizes some of the tornadoes of the western Atlantic Ocean.

On 17 January 1820, we arrived at the island of St Mary's lying on the coast of Chili, in latitude 36° 59' S. longitude 73° 41' W. This island is a sort of rendezvous for whalers, from which they obtain their wood and water, and between which and the main land (a distance of about ten miles) they frequently cruise for a species of whale called the right whale. Our object in going in there was merely to get the news.

We sailed thence to the island of Massafuera, where we got some wood and fish, and thence for the cruising ground along the coast of Chili, in search of the spermaceti whale. We took there eight, which yielded us 250 barrels of oil; and the season having by this time expired, we changed our cruising ground to the coast of Peru. We obtained there 550 barrels.

After going into the small port of Decamas, and

replenishing our wood and water, on 2 October we set sail for the Gallipagos Islands. We came to anchor, and laid seven days off Hood's Island, one of the group; during which time we stopped a leak which we had discovered, and obtained 300 turtle. We then visited Charles Island, where we procured 60 more. These turtle are a most delicious food, and average in weight generally about 100 pounds, but many of them weigh upwards of 800. With these, ships usually supply themselves for a great length of time, and make a great saving of other provisions. They neither eat nor drink, nor is the least pains taken with them; they are strewed over the deck, thrown under foot, or packed away in the hold, as it suits convenience. They will live upwards of a year without food or water, but soon die in a cold climate.

We left Charles Island on 23 October, and steered off to the westward, in search of whales. In latitude 1° 0' S. longitude 118° W. on 16 November, in the afternoon, we lost a boat during our work in a shoal of whales. I was in the boat myself, with five others, and was standing in the fore part, with the harpoon in my hand, well braced, expecting every instant to catch sight of one of the shoal which we were in that I might strike; but judge of my astonishment and dismay, at finding myself suddenly thrown up in the air, my companions scattered about me, and the boat fast filling with water. A whale had come up directly under her, and with one dash of his tail, had stove her bottom in, and strewed us in every direction around her. We, however, with little difficulty, got safely on the wreck, and clung there until one of the other boats which had been engaged in the shoal, came to our assistance, and took us off. Strange to tell, not a man was injured by this accident. Thus it happens very frequently in the whaling business, that boats are stove; oars, harpoons, and lines broken; and ankles and wrists sprained; boats upset, and whole crews left for hours in the water, without any of these accidents extending to the loss of life. We are so much accustomed to the continual recurrence of such scenes as these, that we become familiarized to them, and consequently always feel that confidence and self-possession, which teaches us every expedient in danger, and inures the body, as well as the mind, to fatigue, privation, and peril, in frequent cases exceeding belief. It is this danger and hardship that makes the sailor; indeed it is the distinguishing qualification amongst us; and it is a common boast of the whaleman, that he has escaped from sudden and apparently inevitable destruction oftener than his fellow. He is accordingly valued on this account, without much reference to other qualities.

On 20 November (cruising in latitude 0° 40' S. longitude 119° 0' W.) a shoal of whales was discovered off the lee-bow. The weather at this time was extremely fine and clear, and it was about 8 o'clock in the morning, that the man at the mast-head gave the usual cry of, "there she blows". The ship was immediately put away, and we ran down in the direction for them. When we had got within half a mile of the place where they were observed, all our boats were lowered down, manned, and we started in pursuit of them. The ship, in the mean time, was brought to the wind, and the main-top-sail hove aback, to wait for us. I had the harpoon in the second boat; the captain preceded me in the first. When I arrived at the spot where we calculated they were, nothing was at first to be seen. We lay on our oars in anxious expectation of discovering them come up somewhere near us. Presently one rose, and spouted a short distance ahead of my boat; I made all speed towards it, came up with, and struck it; feeling the harpoon in him, he threw himself, in an agony, over towards the boat (which at that time was up alongside of him) and, giving a severe blow with his tail, struck the boat near the edge of the water, amidships, and stove a hole in her. I immediately took up the boat hatchet, and cut the line, to disengage the boat from the whale, which by this time was running off with great velocity.

I succeeded in getting clear of him, with the loss of the harpoon and line; and finding the water to pour fast in the boat, I hastily stuffed three or four of our jackets in the hole, ordered one man to keep constantly bailing, and the rest to pull immediately for the ship; we succeeded in keeping the boat free, and shortly gained the ship. The captain and the second mate, in the other two boats, kept up the pursuit, and soon struck another whale. They being at this time a considerable distance to leeward, I went forward, braced around the mainyard, and put the ship off in a direction for them; the boat which had been stove was immediately hoisted in, and after examining the hole, I found that I could, by nailing a piece of canvas over it, get her ready to join in a fresh pursuit, sooner than by lowering down the other remaining boat which belonged to the ship. I accordingly turned her over upon the quarter, and was in the act of nailing on the canvass, when I observed a very large spermaceti whale, as well as I could judge, about 85 feet in length; he broke water about 20 rods off our weather-bow, and was lying quietly, with his head in a direction for the ship. He spouted two or three times, and then disappeared. In less that two or three seconds he came up again, about the length of the ship off, and made directly for us, at the rate of about three knots. The ship was then going with about the same velocity. His appearance and attitude gave us at first no alarm; but while I stood watching his movements, and observing him but a ship's length off, coming down for us with great celerity, I involuntarily ordered the boy at the helm to put it hard up; intending to sheer off and avoid him. The words were scarcely out of my mouth, before he came down upon us with full speed, and struck the ship with his head, just forward of the fore-chains; he gave us such an appalling and tremendous jar, as nearly threw us all on our faces. The ship brought up as suddenly and violently as if she had struck a rock, and trembled for a few seconds like a leaf. We looked at each other with perfect amazement, deprived almost of the power of speech.

Many minutes elapsed before we were able to realize the dreadful accident; during which time he passed under the ship, grazing her keel as he went along, came up alongside of her to leeward, and lay on the top of the water (apparently stunned with the violence of the blow), for the space of a minute; he then suddenly started off, in a direction to leeward. After a few moments' reflection, and recovering, in some measure, from the sudden consternation that had seized us, I of course concluded that he had stove a hole in the ship, and that it would be necessary to set the pumps going. Accordingly they were rigged, but had not been in operation more than one minute, before I perceived the head of the ship to be gradually settling down in the water; I then ordered the signal to be set for the other boats, which, scarcely had I despatched, before I again discovered the whale, apparently in convulsions, on the top of the water, about 100 rods to leeward. He was enveloped in the foam of the sea, that his continual and violent thrashing about in the water had created around him, and I could distinctly see him smite his jaws together, as if distracted with rage and fury. He remained a short time in this situation, and then started off with great velocity, across the bows of the ship, to windward.

By this time the ship had settled down a considerable distance in the water, and I gave her up as lost. I however, ordered the pumps to be kept constantly going, and endeavoured to collect my thoughts for the occasion. I turned to the boats, two of which we then had with the ship, with an intention of clearing them away, and getting all things ready to embark in them, if there should be no other resource left; and while my attention was thus engaged for a moment, I was aroused with the cry of a man at the hatchway, "here he is – he is making for us again." I turned around, and saw him about 100 rods directly ahead of us, coming down apparently with twice his ordinary speed, and to me at that moment, it appeared with tenfold fury and vengeance in his aspect. The surf flew in all directions about him, and his course towards us was marked by a white foam of a rod in width, which he made with the continual violent thrashing of his tail; his head was about half out of water, and in that way he came upon, and again struck the ship. I was in hopes when I descried him making for us, that by a dexterous movement of putting the ship away immediately, I should be able to cross the line of his approach, before he could get up to us, and thus avoid, what I knew, if he should strike us again, would prove our inevitable destruction. I bawled out to the helmsman, "hard up!" but she had not fallen off more than a point, before we took the second shock. I should judge the speed of the ship to have been at this time about three knots, and that of the whale about six. He struck her to windward, directly under the cathead, and completely stove in her bows. He passed under the ship again, went off to leeward, and we saw no more of him.

Our situation at this juncture can be more readily imagined than described. The shock to our feelings was such, as I am sure none can have an adequate conception of, that were not there: the misfortune befell us at a moment when we least dreamt of any accident; and from the pleasing anticipations we had formed, of realizing the certain profits of our labour, we were dejected by a sudden, most mysterious, and overwhelming calamity. Not a moment, however, was to be lost in endeavouring to provide for the extremity to which it was now certain we were reduced. We were more than 1,000 miles from the nearest land, and with nothing but a light open boat, as the resource of safety for myself and companions. I ordered the men to cease pumping, and every one to provide for himself; seizing a hatchet at the same time, I cut away the lashings of the spare boat, which lay bottom up, across two spars directly over the quarter deck, and cried out to those near me, to take her as she came down. They did so accordingly, and bore her on their shoulders as far as the waist of the ship. The steward had in the mean time gone down into the cabin twice, and saved two quadrants, two practical navigators, and the captain's trunk and mine; all which were hastily thrown into the boat, as she lay on the deck, with the two compasses which I snatched from the binnacle. He attempted to descend again; but the water by this time had rushed in, and he returned without being able to effect his purpose. By the time we had got the boat to the waist, the ship had filled with water, and was going down on her beam-ends: we shoved our boat as quickly as possible from the plant-shear into the water, all hands jumping in her at the same time, and launched off clear of the ship. We were scarcely two boats' lengths distant from her, when she fell over to windward, and settled down in the water.

Amazement and despair now wholly took possession of us. We contemplated the frightful situation the ship lay in, and thought with horror upon the sudden and dreadful calamity that had overtaken us. We looked upon each other, as if to gather some consolatory sensation from an interchange of sentiments, but every countenance was marked with the paleness of despair. Not a word was spoken for several minutes by any of us; all appeared to be bound in a spell of stupid consternation; and from the time we were first attacked by the whale, to the period of the fall of the ship, and of our leaving her in the boat, more than ten minutes could not certainly have elapsed! God only knows in what way, or by what means, we were enabled to accomplish in that short time what we did; the cutting away and transporting the boat from where she was deposited would of itself, in ordinary circumstances, have consumed as much time as that, if the whole ship's crew had been employed in it. My companions had not saved a single article but what they had on their backs; but to me it was a source of infinite satisfaction, if any such could be gathered from the horrors of our gloomy situation, that we had been fortunate enough to have preserved our compasses, navigators, and quadrants.

After the first shock of my feelings was over, I enthusiastically contemplated them as the probable instruments of our salvation; without them all would have been dark and hopeless. Gracious God! what a picture of distress and suffering now presented itself to my imagination. The crew of the ship were saved, consisting of twenty human souls. All that remained to conduct these twenty beings through the stormy terrors of the ocean, perhaps many thousand miles, were three open light boats. The prospect of obtaining any provisions or water from the ship, to subsist upon during the time, was at least now doubtful. How many long and watchful nights, thought I, are to be passed?

How many tedious days of partial starvation are to be endured, before the least relief or mitigation of our sufferings can be reasonably anticipated. We lay at this time in our boat, about two ships' lengths off from the wreck, in perfect silence, calmly contemplating her situation, and absorbed in our own melancholy reflections, when the other boats were discovered rowing up to us. They had but shortly before discovered that some accident had befallen us, but of the nature of which they were entirely ignorant. The sudden and mysterious disappearance of the ship was first discovered by the boat-steerer in the captain's boat, and with a horror-struck countenance and voice, he suddenly exclaimed, "Oh, my God! where is the ship?" Their operations upon this were instantly suspended, and a general cry of horror and despair burst from the lips of every man, as their looks were directed for her, in vain, over every part of the ocean. They immediately made all haste towards us.

The captain's boat was the first that reached us. He stopped about a boat's length off, but had no power to utter a single syllable: he was so completely overpowered with the spectacle before him, that he sat down in his boat, pale and speechless. I could scarcely recognise his countenance, he appeared to be so much altered, awed, and overcome, with the oppression of his feelings, and the dreadful reality that lay before him. He was in a short time however enabled to address the inquiry to me, "My God, Mr Chase, what is the matter?"

I answered, "We have been stove by a whale." I then briefly told him the story. After a few moments' reflection he observed, that we must cut away her masts, and endeavour to get something out of her to eat. Our thoughts were now all accordingly bent on endeavours to save from the wreck whatever we might possibly want, and for this purpose we rowed up and got on to her. Search was made for every means of gaining access to her hold; and for this purpose the lanyards were cut loose, and with our hatchets we commenced to cut away the masts, that she might right up again, and enable us to scuttle her decks. In doing which we were occupied about three quarters of an hour owing to our having no axes, nor indeed any other instruments, but the small hatchets belonging to the boats.

After her masts were gone she came up about two-thirds of the way upon an even keel. While we were employed about the masts the captain took his quadrant, shoved off from the ship, and got an observation. We found ourselves in latitude 0° 40' S. longitude 119° W. We now commenced to cut a hole through the planks, directly above two large casks of bread, which most fortunately were between decks, in the waist of the ship, and which being in the upper side, when she upset, we had strong hopes was not wet. It turned out according to our wishes, and from these casks we obtained 600 pounds of hard bread. Other parts of the deck were then scuttled, and we got without difficulty as much fresh water as we dared to take in the boats, so that each was supplied with about 65 gallons; we got also from one of the lockers a musket, a small canister of powder, a couple of files, two rasps, about two pounds of boat nails, and a few turtle.

In the afternoon the wind came on to blow a strong breeze; and having obtained every thing that occurred to us could then be got out, we began to make arrangements for our safety during the night. A boat's line was made fast to the ship, and to the other end of it one of the boats was moored, at about fifty fathoms to leeward; another boat was then attached to the first one, about eight fathoms astern; and the third boat, the like distance astern of her. Night came on just as we had finished our operations; and such a night as it was to us! so full of feverish and distracting inquietude, that we were deprived entirely of rest. The wreck was constantly before my eyes. I could not, by any effort, chase away the horrors of the preceding day from my mind: they haunted me

the live-long night. My companions – some of them were like
sick women; they had no idea of the extent of their deplorable
situation. One or two slept unconcernedly, while others
wasted the night in unavailing murmurs.

I now had full leisure to examine, with some degree of
coolness, the dreadful circumstances of our disaster. The
scenes of yesterday passed in such quick succession in my
mind that it was not until after many hours of severe reflection that I was able to discard the idea of the catastrophe as
a dream. Alas! it was one from which there was no awaking;
it was too certainly true, that but yesterday we had existed as
it were, and in one short moment had been cut off from all
the hopes and prospects of the living! I have no language to
paint out the horrors of our situation. To shed tears was
indeed altogether unavailing, and withal unmanly; yet I was
not able to deny myself the relief they served to afford me.

After several hours of idle sorrow and repining I began
to reflect upon the accident, and endeavoured to realize by
what unaccountable destiny or design (which I could not at
first determine), this sudden and most deadly attack had
been made upon us: by an animal, too, never before
suspected of premeditated violence, and proverbial for its
insensibility and inoffensiveness. Every fact seemed to
warrant me in concluding that it was anything but chance
which directed his operations; he made two several attacks
upon the ship, at a short interval between them, both of
which, according to their direction, were calculated to do
us the most injury, by being made ahead, and thereby
combining the speed of the two objects for the shock; to
effect which, the exact manoeuvres which he made were
necessary His aspect was most horrible, and such as indicated resentment and fury. He came directly from the shoal
which we had just before entered, and in which we had
struck three of his companions, as if fired with revenge for
their sufferings. But to this it may be observed, that the
mode of fighting which they always adopt is either with
repeated strokes of their tails, or snapping of their jaws

together; and that a case, precisely similar to this one, has never been heard of amongst the oldest and most experienced whalers.

To this I would answer, that the structure and strength of the whale's head is admirably designed for this mode of attack; the most prominent part of which is almost as hard and as tough as iron; indeed, I can compare it to nothing else but the inside of a horse's hoof, upon which a lance or harpoon would not make the slightest impression. The eyes and ears are removed nearly one-third the length of the whole fish, from the front part of the head, and are not in the least degree endangered in this mode of attack. At all events, the whole circumstances taken together, all happening before my own eyes, and producing, at the time, impressions in my mind of decided, calculating mischief, on the part of the whale, (many of which impressions I cannot now recall) induce me to be satisfied that I am correct in my opinion. It is certainly, in all its bearings, a hitherto unheard of circumstance, and constitutes, perhaps, the most extraordinary one in the annals of the fishery.

21 November

The morning dawned upon our wretched company. The weather was fine, but the wind blew a strong breeze from the SE. and the sea was very rugged. Watches had been kept up during the night, in our respective boats, to see that none of the spars or other articles (which continued to float out of the wreck) should be thrown by the surf against, and injure the boats. At sunrise, we began to think of doing something; what, we did not know: we cast loose our boats, and visited the wreck, to see if anything more of consequence could be preserved, but everything looked cheerless and desolate, and we made a long and vain search for any useful article; nothing could be found but a few turtle; of these we had enough already; or at least, as many as could be safely stowed in the boats, and we wandered around in every part of the ship in a sort of vacant idleness for the greater part of the morning.

We were presently aroused to a perfect sense of our destitute and forlorn condition, by thoughts of the means which we had for our subsistence, the necessity of not wasting our time, and of endeavouring to seek some relief wherever God might direct us. Our thoughts, indeed, hung about the ship, wrecked and sunken as she was, and we could scarcely discard from our minds the idea of her continuing protection. Some great efforts in our situation were necessary, and a great deal of calculation important, as it concerned the means by which our existence was to be supported during, perhaps, a very long period, and a provision for our eventual deliverance. Accordingly, by agreement, all set to work in stripping off the light sails of the ship, for sails to our boats; and the day was consumed in making them up and fitting them. We furnished ourselves with masts and other light spars that were necessary, from the wreck. Each boat was rigged with two masts, to carry a flying-jib and two sprit-sails; the sprit-sails were made so that two reefs could be taken in them, in case of heavy blows.

We continued to watch the wreck for any serviceable articles that might float from her, and kept one man during the day, on the stump of her foremast, on the look out for vessels. Our work was very much impeded by the increase of the wind and sea, and the surf breaking almost continually into the boats, gave us many fears that we should not be able to prevent our provisions from getting wet; and above all served to increase the constant apprehensions that we had, of the insufficiency of the boats themselves, during the rough weather that we should necessarily experience. In order to provide as much as possible against this, and withal to strengthen the slight materials of which the boats were constructed, we procured from the wreck some light cedar boards (intended to repair boats in cases of accidents) with which we built up additional sides, about six inches above the gunwale; these, we afterwards found, were of infinite service for the purpose for which they were intended; in truth, I am satisfied we could never have been preserved without them;

the boats must otherwise have taken in so much water that all the efforts of twenty such weak, starving men as we afterwards came to be, would not have sufficed to keep her free; but what appeared most immediately to concern us, and to command all our anxieties, was the security of our provisions from the salt water. We disposed of them under a covering of wood, that whale-boats have at either end of them, wrapping it up in several thicknesses of canvass.

I got an observation today, by which I found we were in latitude 0° 6' S. longitude 119°30' W. having been driven by the winds a distance of forty-nine miles the last twenty-four hours; by this it would appear that there must have been a strong current, setting us to the NW. during the whole time. We were not able to finish our sails in one day; and many little things preparatory to taking a final leave of the ship were necessary to be attended to, but evening came and put an end to our labours. We made the same arrangements for mooring the boats in safety, and consigned ourselves to the horrors of another tempestuous night. The wind continued to blow hard, keeping up a heavy sea, and veering around from SE. to E. and E.S.E.

As the gloom of night approached, and obliged us to desist from that employment, which cheated us out of some of the realities of our situation, we all of us again became mute and desponding: a considerable degree of alacrity had been manifested by many the preceding day, as their attention had been wholly engaged in scrutinizing the wreck, and in constructing the sails and spars for the boats; but when they ceased to be occupied, they passed to a sudden fit of melancholy, and the miseries of their situation came upon them with such force, as to produce spells of extreme debility, approaching almost to fainting. Our provisions were scarcely touched – the appetite was entirely gone; but as we had a great abundance of water, we indulged in frequent and copious draughts, which our parched mouths seemed continually to need. None asked for bread.

Our continued state of anxiety during the night, excluded

all hopes of sleep; still (although the solemn fact had been before me for nearly two days) my mind manifested the utmost repugnance to be reconciled to it; I laid down in the bottom of the boat, and resigned myself to reflection; my silent prayers were offered up to the God of mercy, for that protection which we stood so much in need of. Sometimes, indeed, a light hope would dawn, but then, to feel such an utter dependence on and consignment to chance alone for aid and rescue, would chase it again from my mind. The wreck – the mysterious and mortal attack of the animal – the sudden prostration and sinking of the vessel – our escape from her, and our then forlorn and almost hapless destiny, all passed in quick and perplexing review in my imagination; wearied with the exertion of the body and mind, I caught, near morning, an hour's respite from my troubles, in sleep.

22 November

The wind remained the same, and the weather continued remarkably fine. At sunrise, we again hauled our boats up, and continued our search for articles that might float out. About 7 o'clock, the deck of the wreck began to give way, and every appearance indicated her speedy dissolution; the oil had bilged in the hold, and kept the surface of the sea all around us completely covered with it; the bulk-heads were all washed down, and she worked in every part of her joints and seams, with the violent and continual breaking of the surf over her. Seeing, at last, that little or nothing further could be done by remaining with the wreck, and as it was all important that while our provisions lasted, we should make the best possible use of time, I rowed up to the captain's boat, and asked him what he intended to do. I informed him that the ship's decks had bursted up, and that in all probability she would soon go to pieces; that no further purpose could be answered, by remaining longer with her, since nothing more could be obtained from her; and that it was my opinion, no time should be lost in making the best of our way towards the nearest land. The captain observed, that he would go once more to the wreck, and survey her, and after waiting until 12 o'clock for the purpose of getting an observation, would immediately after determine. In the mean time, before noon all our sails were completed, and the boats otherwise got in readiness for our departure.

Our observation now proved us to be in latitude 0° 13' N. longitude 120° 00' W. as near as we could determine it, having crossed the equator during the night, and drifted nineteen miles. The wind had veered considerably to the eastward, during the last twenty-four hours. Our nautical calculations having been completed, the captain, after visiting the wreck, called a council, consisting of himself and the first and second mates, who all repaired to his boat, to interchange opinions, and devise the best means for our security and preservation. There were, in all of us, twenty men; six of whom were blacks, and we had three boats.

We examined our navigators, to ascertain the nearest land, and found it was the Marquesas Islands. The Society Islands were next; these islands we were entirely ignorant of; if inhabited, we presumed they were by savages, from whom we had as much to fear, as from the elements, or even death itself. We had no charts from which our calculations might be aided, and were consequently obliged to govern ourselves by the navigators alone; it was also the captain's opinion, that this was the season of the hurricanes which prevail in the vicinity of the Sandwich Islands, and that consequently it would be unsafe to steer for them.

The issue of our deliberations was, that, taking all things into consideration, it would be most advisable to shape our course by the wind, to the southward, as far as 25° or 25° S. latitude, fall in with the variable winds, and then, endeavour to get eastward to the coast of Chili or Peru. Accordingly, preparations were made for our immediate departure; the boat which it was my fortune, or rather misfortune to have, was the worst of the three; she was old and patched up, having been stove a number of times, during the cruise.

At best, a whale-boat is an extremely frail thing; the most

so of any other kind of boat; they are what is called clinker built, and constructed of the lightest materials, for the purpose of being rowed with the greatest possible celerity, according to the necessities of the business for which they are intended. Of all species of vessels, they are the weakest, and most fragile, and possess but one advantage over any other—that of lightness and buoyancy, that enables them to keep above the dash of the sea, with more facility than heavier ones. This qualification is, however, preferable to that of any other, and, situated as we then were, I would not have exchanged her, old and crazy as she was, for even a ship's launch. I am quite confident, that to this quality of our boats we most especially owed our preservation, through the many days and nights of heavy weather, that we afterwards encountered. In consideration of my having the weakest boat, six men were allotted to it; while those of the captain and second mate, took seven each, and at half past 12 we left the wreck, steering our course, with nearly all sail set, S.SE. At four o'clock in the afternoon we lost sight of her entirely. Many were the lingering and sorrowful looks we cast behind us.

It has appeared to me often since to have been, in the abstract, an extreme weakness and folly, on our parts, to have looked upon our shattered and sunken vessel with such an excessive fondness and regret; but it seemed as if in abandoning her we had parted with all hope, and were bending our course away from her, rather by some dictate of despair. We agreed to keep together, in our boats, as nearly as possible to afford assistance in cases of accident, and to render our reflections less melancholy by each other's presence. I found it on this occasion true, that misery does indeed love company; unaided, and unencouraged by each other, there were with us many whose weak minds, I am confident, would have sunk under the dismal retrospections of the past catastrophe, and who did not possess either sense or firmness enough to contemplate our approaching destiny, without the cheering of some more determined countenance than their own. The wind was strong all day; sea ran very high, our boat taking in water from her leaks continually, so that we were obliged to keep one man constantly bailing. During the night the weather became extremely rugged, and the sea every now and then broke over us.

By agreement, we were divided into two watches; one of which was to be constantly awake, and doing the labours of the boat, such as bailing; setting, taking in, and trimming the sails. We kept our course very well together during this night, and had many opportunities of conversation with the men in the other boats, wherein the means and prospects of our deliverance were variously considered; it appeared from the opinions of all, that we had most to hope for in the meeting with some vessel, and most probably some whale ship, the great majority of whom, in those seas, we imagined were cruising about the latitude we were then steering for; but this was only a hope, the realization of which did not in any degree depend on our own exertions, but on chance alone. It was not, therefore, considered prudent, by going out of our course, with the prospect of meeting them, to lose sight, for one moment, of the strong probabilities which, under Divine Providence, there were of our reaching land by the route we bad prescribed to ourselves; as that depended, most especially, on a reasonable calculation, and on our own labours we conceived that our provision and water, on a small allowance, would last us 60 days; that with the trade-wind, on the course we were then lying, we should be able to average the distance of a degree a day, which, in 26 days, would enable us to attain the region of the variable winds, and then, in 30 more, at the very utmost, should there be any favour in the elements, we might reach the coast.

With these considerations we commenced our voyage; the total failure of all which, and the subsequent dismal distress and suffering, by which we were overtaken, will be shown in the sequel. Our allowance of provision at first consisted of bread; one biscuit, weighing about one pound three ounces, and half a pint of water a day, for each man. This small quantity (less than one third which is required by an ordinary person), small as it was, we however took without murmuring, and, on many an occasion afterwards, blest God that even this pittance was allowed to us in our misery. The darkness of another night overtook us; and after having for the first time partook of our allowance of bread and water, we laid our weary bodies down in the boat, and endeavoured to get some repose.

Nature became at last worn out with the watchings and anxieties of the two preceding nights, and sleep came insensibly upon us. No dreams could break the strong fastenings of forgetfulness in which the mind was then locked up; but for my own part, my thoughts so haunted me that this luxury was yet a stranger to my eyes; every recollection was still fresh before me, and I enjoyed but a few short and unsatisfactory slumbers, caught in the intervals between my hopes and my fears. The dark ocean and swelling waters were nothing; the fears of being swallowed up by some dreadful tempest, or dashed upon hidden rocks, with all the other ordinary subjects of fearful contemplation, seemed scarcely entitled to a moment's thought; the dismal-looking wreck, and the horrid aspect and revenge of the whale, wholly engrossed my reflections, until day again made its appearance.

23 November

In my chest, which I was fortunate enough to preserve, I had several small articles, which we found of great service to us; among the rest, some eight or ten sheets of writing paper, a lead pencil, a suit of clothes, three small fish hooks, a jack-knife, a whetstone, and a cake of soap. I commenced to keep a sort of journal with the little paper and pencil which I had; and the knife, besides other useful purposes, served us as a razor. It was with much difficulty, however, that I could keep any sort of record, owing to the incessant rocking and unsteadiness of the boat, and the continual dashing of the spray of the sea over us. The boat contained, in addition to the articles enumerated, a lantern, tinder-box, and two or three candles, which belonged to her, and with which they are kept always supplied, while engaged in taking whale. In addition to all which, the captain had saved a musket, two pistols, and a canister, containing about two pounds of gunpowder; the latter he distributed in equal proportions between the three boats, and gave the second mate and myself each a pistol.

When morning came we found ourselves quite near together, and the wind had considerably increased since the day before; we were consequently obliged to reef our sails; and although we did not apprehend any very great danger from the then violence of the wind, yet it grew to be very uncomfortable in the boats, from the repeated dashing of the waves, that kept our bodies constantly wet with the salt spray. We, however, stood along our course until twelve o'clock, when we got an observation, as well as we were able to obtain one, while the water flew all over us, and the sea kept the boat extremely unsteady. We found ourselves this day in latitude 0° 58' S. having repassed the equator. We abandoned the idea altogether of keeping any correct longitudinal reckoning, having no glass, nor log-line. The wind moderated in the course of the afternoon a little, but at night came on to blow again almost a gale. We began now to tremble for our little barque; she was so ill calculated, in point of strength, to withstand the racking of the sea, while it required the constant labours of one man to keep her free of water. We were surrounded in the afternoon with porpoises that kept playing about us in great numbers, and continued to follow us during the night.

24 November

The wind had not abated any since the preceding day, and the sea had risen to be very large, and increased, if possible, the extreme uncomfortableness of our situation. What added more than anything else to our misfortunes, was, that all our efforts for the preservation of our provisions proved, in a great measure, ineffectual; a heavy sea broke suddenly into the boat, and, before we could snatch it up, damaged some part of it; by timely attention, however, and great caution, we managed to make it eatable, and to preserve the rest from a similar casualty. This was a subject of extreme anxiety to us; the expectation, poor enough of itself indeed, upon which our final rescue was founded, must change at once to utter hopelessness, deprived of our provisions, the only means of continuing us in the exercise, not only of our manual powers, but in those of reason itself; hence, above all other things, this was the object of our utmost solicitude and pains.

We ascertained, the next day, that some of the provisions in the captain's boat had shared a similar fate during the night; both which accidents served to arouse us to a still stronger sense of our slender reliance upon the human means at our command, and to show us our utter dependence on that divine aid which we so much the more stood in need of.

25 November

No change of wind had yet taken place, and we experienced the last night the same wet and disagreeable weather of the preceding one. About eight o'clock in the morning we discovered that the water began to come fast in our boat, and in a few minutes the quantity increased to such a degree as to alarm us considerably for our safety; we commenced immediately a strict search in every part of her to discover the leak, and, after tearing up the ceiling or floor of the boat near the bows, we found it proceeded from one of the streaks or outside boards having bursted off there; no time was to be lost in devising some means to repair it. The great difficulty consisted in its being in the bottom of the boat, and about six inches from the surface of the water; it was necessary, therefore, to have access to the outside, to enable us to fasten it on again: the leak being to leeward, we hove about, and lay to on the other tack, which brought it then nearly out of water; the captain, who was at the time ahead of us, seeing us manoeuvring to get the boat about, shortened sail, and presently tacked, and ran down to us. I informed him of our situation, and he came immediately alongside to our assistance. After directing all the men in the boat to get on one side, the other, by that means, heeled out of the water a considerable distance, and, with a little difficulty, we then managed to drive in a few nails, and secured it, much beyond our expectations.

Fears of no ordinary kind were excited by this seemingly small accident. When it is recollected to what a slight vessel we had committed ourselves; our means of safety alone consisting in her capacity of endurance for many weeks, in all probability, yet to come, it will not be considered strange that this little accident should not only have damped our spirits considerably, but have thrown a great gloominess over the natural prospects of our deliverance. On this occasion, too, were we enabled to rescue ourselves from inevitable destruction by the possession of a few nails, without which (had it not been our fortune to save some from the wreck) we would, in all human calculation, have been lost: we were still liable to a recurrence of the same accident, perhaps to a still worse one, as, in the heavy and repeated racking of the swell, the progress of our voyage would serve but to increase the incapacity and weakness of our boat, and the starting of a single nail in her bottom would most assuredly prove our certain destruction. We wanted not this additional reflection, to add to the miseries of our situation.

26 November
Our sufferings, heaven knows, were now sufficiently increased, and we looked forward, not without an extreme dread, and anxiety, to the gloomy and disheartening prospect before us. We experienced a little abatement of wind and rough weather today, and took the opportunity of drying the bread that had been wet the day previously; to our great joy and satisfaction also, the wind hauled out to E.NE. and enabled us to hold a much more favourable course; with these exceptions, no circumstance of any considerable interest occurred in the course of this day.

27 November was alike undistinguished for any incident

worthy of note; except that the wind again veered back to E. and destroyed the fine prospect we had entertained, of making a good run for several days to come.

28 November

The wind hauled still further to the southward, and obliged us to fall off our course to S. and commenced to blow with such violence, as to put us again under short sail; the night set in extremely dark, and tempestuous, and we began to entertain fears that we should be separated. We however, with great pains, managed to keep about a ship's length apart, so that the white sails of our boats could be distinctly discernable. The captain's boat was but a short distance astern of mine, and that of the second mate a few rods to leeward of his.

At about 11 o'clock at night, having laid down to sleep, in the bottom of the boat, I was suddenly awakened by one of my companions, who cried out, that the captain was in distress, and was calling on us for assistance. I immediately aroused myself, and listened a moment, to hear if any thing further should be said, when the captain's loud voice arrested my attention. He was calling to the second mate, whose boat was nearer to him than mine. I made all haste to put about, ran down to him, and inquired what was the matter; he replied, "I have been attacked by an unknown fish, and he has stove my boat."

It appeared that some large fish had accompanied the boat for a short distance, and had suddenly made an unprovoked attack upon her, as nearly as they could determine, with his jaws; the extreme darkness of the night prevented them from distinguishing what kind of animal it was, but they judged it to be about twelve feet in length, and one of the killer-fish species. After having struck the boat once, he continued to play about her, on every side, as if manifesting a disposition to renew the attack, and did a second time strike the bows of the boat, and split her stem. They had no other instrument of offence, but the sprit-pole (a long slender piece of wood, by which the peak of the sail is extended) with which, after repeated attempts to destroy the boat, they succeeded in beating him off.

I arrived just as he had discontinued his operations, and disappeared. He had made a considerable breach in the bows of the boat, through which the water had began to pour fast; and the captain, imagining matters to be considerably worse than they were, immediately took measures to remove his provisions into the second mate's boat and mine in order to lighten his own, and by that means, and constant bailing, to keep her above water until daylight should enable him to discover the extent of the damage, and to repair it.

The night was spissy darkness itself; the sky was completely overcast, and it seemed to us as if fate was wholly relentless, in pursuing us with such a cruel complication of disasters. We were not without our fears that the fish might renew his attack, some time during the night, upon one of the other boats, and unexpectedly destroy us; but they proved entirely groundless, as he was never afterwards seen. When daylight came, the wind again favoured us a little, and we all lay to, to repair the broken boat; which was effected by nailing on thin strips of boards in the inside; and, having replaced the provisions, we proceeded again on our course.

Our allowance of water, which in the commencement, merely served to administer to the positive demands of nature, became now to be insufficient; and we began to experience violent thirst, from the consumption of the provisions that had been wet with the salt water, and dried in the sun; of these we were obliged to eat first, to prevent their spoiling; and we could not, nay, we did not dare, to make any encroachments on our stock of water. Our determination was, to suffer as long as human patience and endurance would hold out, having only in view, the relief that would be afforded us, when the quantity of wet provisions should be exhausted. Our extreme sufferings here first commenced.

The privation of water is justly ranked among the most dreadful of the miseries of our life; the violence of raving thirst has no parallel in the catalogue of human calamities. It was our hard lot, to have felt this in its extremest force, when necessity subsequently compelled us to seek resource from one of the offices of nature. We were not, at first, aware of the consequences of eating this bread; and it was not until the fatal effects of it had shown themselves to a degree of oppression, that we could divine the cause of our extreme thirst. But, alas! there was no relief. Ignorant, or instructed of the fact, it was alike immaterial; it composed a part of our subsistence, and reason imposed upon us the necessity of its immediate consumption, as otherwise it would have been lost to us entirely.

29 November

Our boats appeared to be growing daily more frail and insufficient; the continual flowing of the water into them, seemed increased, without our being able to assign it to any thing else, than a general weakness, arising from causes that must in a short time, without some remedy or relief, produce their total failure. We did not neglect, however, to patch up and mend them, according to our means, whenever we could discover a broken or weak part. We this day found ourselves surrounded by a shoal of dolphins; some, or one of which, we tried in vain a long time to take. We made a small line from some rigging that was in the boat, fastened on one of the fish-hooks, and tied to it a small piece of white rag; they took not the least notice of it, but continued playing around us, nearly all day, mocking both our miseries and our efforts.

30 November

This was a remarkably fine day; the weather not exceeded by any that we had experienced since we left the wreck. At one o'clock, I proposed to our boat's crew to kill one of the turtle; two of which we had in our possession. I need not say, that the proposition was hailed with the utmost enthusiasm; hunger had set its ravenous gnawings upon our stomachs, and we waited with impatience to suck the warm flowing blood of the animal. A small fire was kindled in the shell of the turtle, and after dividing the blood (of which there was about a gill) among those of us who felt disposed to drink it, we cooked the remainder, entrails and all, and enjoyed from it an unspeakably fine repast. The stomachs of two or three revolted at the sight of the blood, and refused to partake of it; not even the outrageous thirst that was upon them could induce them to taste it; for myself, I took it like a medicine, to relieve the extreme dryness of my palate, and stopped not to inquire whether it was anything else than a liquid. After this, I may say exquisite banquet, our bodies were considerably recruited, and I felt my spirits now much higher than they had been at any time before. By observation, this day we found ourselves in latitude 7°53' S. our distance from the wreck, as nearly as we could calculate, was then about 480 miles.

1 December

From the 1st to the 3rd of December, exclusive, there was nothing transpired of any moment. Our boats as yet kept admirably well together, and the weather was distinguished for its mildness and salubrity. We gathered consolation too from a favourable slant which the wind took to NE. and our situation was not at that moment, we thought, so comfortless as we had been led at first to consider it; but, in our extravagant felicitations upon the blessing of the wind and weather, we forgot our leaks, our weak boats, our own debility, our immense distance from land, the smallness of our stock of provisions; all which, when brought to mind, with the force which they deserved, were too well calculated to dishearten us, and cause us to sigh for the hardships of our lot. Up to 3 December, the raging thirst of our mouths had not been but in a small degree alleviated; had it not been for the pains which that gave us, we should have tasted, during this spell of fine weather, a species of enjoyment, derived from a momentary forgetfulness of our actual situation.

3 December

With great joy we hailed the last crumb of our damaged bread, and commenced this day to take our allowance of healthy provisions. The salutary and agreeable effects of this change were felt at first in so slight a degreee, as to give us no great cause of comfort or satisfaction; but gradually, as we partook of our small allowance of water, the moisture began to collect in our mouths, and the parching fever of the palate imperceptibly left it. An accident here happened to us which gave us a great momentary spell of uneasiness. The night was dark, and the sky was completely overcast, so that we could scarcely discern each other's boats, when at about ten o'clock, that of the second mate was suddenly missing. I felt for a moment considerable alarm at her unexpected disappearance; but after a little reflection I immediately hove to, struck a light as expeditiously as possible, and hoisted it at the mast-head, in a lantern. Our eyes were now directed over every part of the ocean, in search of her, when, to our great joy, we discerned an answering light, about a quarter of a mile to leeward of us; we ran down to it, and it proved to be the lost boat.

Strange as the extraordinary interest which we felt in each other's company may appear, and much as our repugnance to separation may seem to imply of weakness, it was the subject of our continual hopes and fears. It is truly remarked, that misfortune more than anything else serves to endear us to our companions. So strongly was this sentiment engrafted upon our feelings, and so closely were the destinies of all of us involuntarily linked together, that, had one of the boats been wrecked, and wholly lost, with all her provisions and water, we should have felt ourselves constrained, by every tie of humanity, to have taken the surviving sufferers into the other boats, and shared our bread and water with them, while a crumb of one or a drop of the other remained. Hard, indeed, would the case have been for all, and much as I have since reflected on the subject, I have not been able to realize, had it so happened, that a sense of our necessities would have allowed us to give so magnanimous and devoted a character to our feelings. I can only speak of the impressions which I recollect I had at the time.

Subsequently, however, as our situation became more straitened and desperate, our conversation on this subject took a different turn; and it appeared to be an universal sentiment, that such a course of conduct was calculated to weaken the chances of a final deliverance for some, and might be the only means of consigning every soul of us to a horrid death of starvation. There is no question but that an immediate separation, therefore, was the most politic measure that could be adopted, and that every boat should take its own separate chance: while we remained together, should any accident happen, of the nature alluded to, no other course could be adopted, than that of taking the survivors into the other boats, and giving up voluntarily, what we were satisfied could alone prolong our hopes, and multiply the chances of our safety, or unconcernedly witness their struggles in death, perhaps beat them from our boats, with weapons, back into the ocean.

The expectation of reaching the land was founded upon a reasonable calculation of the distance, the means, and the subsistence; all which were scanty enough, God knows, and ill adapted to the probable exigences of the voyage. Any addition to our own demands, in this respect, would not only injure, but actually destroy the whole system which we bad laid down, and reduce us to a slight hope, derived either from the speedy death of some of our crew, or the falling in with some vessel. With all this, however, there was a desperate instinct that bound us together; we could not reason on the subject with any degree of satisfaction to our minds, yet we continued to cling to each other with a strong and involuntary impulse. This, indeed, was a matter of no small difficulty, and it constituted, more than any thing else, a source of continual watching and inquietude. We would but turn our eyes away for a few moments, during some dark nights, and presently, one of the boats would be missing.

There was no other remedy than to heave to immediately and set a light, by which the missing boat might be directed to us. These proceedings necessarily interfered very much with our speed, and consequently lessened our hopes; but we preferred to submit to it, while the consequences were not so immediately felt, rather than part with the consolation which each other's presence afforded.

Nothing of importance took place on 4 December; and on the 5th, at night, owing to the extreme darkness, and a strong wind, I again separated from the other boats. Finding they were not to be seen in any direction, I loaded my pistol and fired it twice; soon after the second discharge they made their appearance a short distance to windward, and we joined company, and again kept on our course, in which we continued without any remarkable occurrence, through 6 and 7 of December. The wind during this period blew very strong, and much more unfavourably. Our boats continued to leak, and to take in a good deal of water over the gunwales.

8 December

In the afternoon of this day the wind set in E.SE. and began to blow much harder than we had yet experienced it; by 12 o'clock at night it had increased to a perfect gale, with heavy showers of rain, and we now began, from these dreadful indications, to prepare ourselves for destruction. We continued to take in sail by degrees, as the tempest gradually increased, until at last we were obliged to take down our masts. At this juncture we gave up entirely to the mercy of the waves. The sea and rain had wet us to the skin, and we sat down, silently, and with sullen resignation, awaiting our fate. We made an effort to catch some fresh water by spreading one of the sails, but after having spent a long time, and obtained but a small quantity in a bucket, it proved to be quite as salt as that from the ocean: this we attributed to its having passed through the sail which had been so often wet by the sea, and upon which, after drying so frequently in the sun, concretions of salt had been formed. It was a dreadful night – cut off from any imaginary relief – nothing remained but to await the approaching issue with firmness and resignation.

The appearance of the heavens was dark and dreary, and the blackness that was spread over the face of the waters dismal beyond description. The heavy squalls, that followed each other in quick succession, were preceded by sharp flashes of lightning, that appeared to wrap our little barge in flames. The sea rose to a fearful height, and every wave that came looked as if it must be the last that would be necessary for our destruction. To an overruling Providence alone must be attributed our salvation from the horrors of that terrible night. It can be accounted for in no other way: that a speck of substance, like that which we were, before the driving terrors of the tempest, could have been conducted safely through it. At 12 o'clock it began to abate a little in intervals of two or three minutes, during which we would venture to raise up our heads and look to windward. Our boat was completely unmanageable; without sails, mast, or rudder, and had been driven, in the course of the afternoon and night, we knew not whither, nor how far. When the gale had in some measure subsided we made efforts to get a little sail upon her, and put her head towards the course we had been steering. My companions had not slept any during the whole night, and were dispirited and broken down to such a degree as to appear to want some more powerful stimulus than the fears of death to enable them to do their duty. By great exertions, however, towards morning we again set a double-reefed mainsail and jib upon her, and began to make tolerable progress on the voyage. An unaccountable good fortune had kept the boats together during all the troubles of the night: and the sun rose and showed the disconsolate faces of our companions once more to each other.

9 December

By 12 o'clock this day we were enabled to set all sail as usual; but there continued to be a very heavy sea running, which opened the seams of the boats, and increased the leaks to an alarming degree. There was, however, no remedy for this but continual bailing, which had now become to be an extremely irksome and laborious task. By observation we found ourselves in latitude 17° 40' S. At 11 o'clock at night, the captain's boat was unexpectedly found to be missing. After the last accident of this kind we had agreed, if the same should again occur, that, in order to save our time, the other boats should not heave to, as usual, but continue on their course until morning, and thereby save the great detention that must arise from such repeated delays. We, however, concluded on this occasion to make a small effort, which, if it did not immediately prove the means of restoring the lost boat, we would discontinue, and again make sail. Accordingly we hove to for an hour, during which time I fired my pistol twice, and obtaining no tidings of the boat, we stood on our course. When daylight appeared she was to leeward of us, about two miles; upon observing her we immediately ran down, and again joined company.

10 December

I have omitted to notice the gradual advances which hunger and thirst, for the last six days, had made upon us. As the time had lengthened since our departure from the wreck, and the allowance of provision, making the demands of the appetite daily more and more importunate, they had created in us an almost uncontrollable temptation to violate our resolution, and satisfy, for once, the hard yearnings of nature from our stock; but a little reflection served to convince us of the imprudence and unmanliness of the measure, and it was abandoned with a sort of melancholy effort of satisfaction. I had taken into custody, by common consent, all the provisions and water belonging to the boat, and was determined that no encroachments should be made upon it with my consent; nay, I felt myself bound, by every consideration of duty, by every dictate of sense, of prudence, and discretion, without which, in my situation, all other exertions would have been folly itself, to protect them, at the hazard of my life. For this purpose I locked up in my chest the whole quantity, and never, for a single moment, closed my eyes without placing some part of my person in contact with the chest; and having loaded my pistol, kept it constantly about me. I should not certainly have put any threats in execution as long as the most distant hopes of reconciliation existed; and was determined, in case the least refractory disposition should be manifested (a thing which I contemplated not unlikely to happen, with a set of starving wretches like ourselves), that I would immediately divide our subsistence into equal proportions, and give each man's share into his own keeping. Then, should any attempt be made upon mine, which I intended to mete out to myself, according to exigences, I was resolved to make the consequences of it fatal.

There was, however, the most upright and obedient behaviour in this respect manifested by every man in the boat, and I never had the least opportunity of proving what my conduct would have been on such an occasion. While standing on our course this day we came across a small shoal of flying fish: four of which, in their efforts to avoid us, flew against the mainsail, and dropped into the boat; one, having fell near me, I eagerly snatched up and devoured; the other three were immediately taken by the rest, and eaten alive. For the first time I, on this occasion, felt a disposition to laugh, upon witnessing the ludicrous and almost desperate efforts of my five companions, who each sought to get a fish. They were very small of the kind, and constituted but an extremely delicate mouthful, scales, wings, and all for hungry stomachs like ours.

From the eleventh to the thirteenth of December inclusive, our progress was very slow, owing to light winds and calms; and nothing transpired of any moment, except that on the eleventh we killed the only remaining turtle, and enjoyed another luxuriant repast, that invigorated our bodies, and gave a fresh flow to our spirits. The weather was extremely hot, and we were exposed to the full force of a meridian sun, without any covering to shield us from its burning influence, or the least breath of air to cool its parching rays. On the thirteenth day of December we were blessed with a change of wind to the northward, that brought us a most welcome and unlooked for relief.

We now, for the first time, actually felt what might be deemed a reasonable hope of our deliverance; and with hearts bounding with satisfaction, and bosoms swelling with joy, we made all sail to the eastward. We imagined we had run out of the trade-winds, and had got into the variables, and should, in all probability, reach the land many days sooner than we expected. But, alas! our anticipations were but a dream, from which we shortly experienced a cruel awaking. The wind gradually died away, and at night was succeeded by a perfect calm, more oppressive and disheartening to us, from the bright prospects which bad attended us during the day. The gloomy reflections that this hard fortune had given birth to, were succeeded by others, of a no less cruel and discouraging nature, when we found the calm continue during the fourteenth, fifteenth, and sixteenth of December inclusive. The extreme oppression of the weather, the sudden and unexpected prostration of our hopes, and the consequent dejection of our spirits, set us again to thinking, and filled our souls with fearful and melancholy forebodings.

In this state of affairs, seeing no alternative left us but to employ to the best advantage all human expedients in our power, I proposed, on the fourteenth, to reduce our allowance of provisions one half. No objections were made to this arrangement: all submitted, or seemed to do so, with an admirable fortitude and forbearance. The proportion which our stock of water bore to our bread was not large; and while the weather continued so oppressive, we did not think it advisable to diminish our scanty pittance; indeed, it would have been scarcely possible to have done so, with any regard to our necessities, as our thirst had become now incessantly more intolerable than hunger, and the quantity then allowed was barely sufficient to keep the mouth in a state of moisture, for about one-third of the time. "Patience and long-suffering" was the constant language of our lips: and a determination, strong as the resolves of the soul could make it, to cling to existence as long as hope and breath remained to us. In vain was every expedient tried to relieve the raging fever of the throat by drinking salt water, and holding small quantities of it in the mouth, until, by that means, the thirst was increased to such a degree, as even to drive us to despairing, and vain relief from our own urine.

Our sufferings during these calm days almost exceeded human belief. The hot rays of the sun beat down upon us to such a degree, as to oblige us to hang over the gunwale of the boat, into the sea, to cool our weak and fainting bodies. This expedient afforded us, however, a grateful relief, and was productive of a discovery of infinite importance to us. No sooner had one of us got on the outside of the gunwale than he immediately observed the bottom of the boat to be covered with a species of small clam, which, upon being tasted, proved a most delicious and agreeable food. This was no sooner announced to us, than we commenced to tear them off and eat them, for a few minutes, like a set of gluttons; and, after having satisfied the immediate craving of the stomach, we gathered large quantities and laid them up in the boat; but hunger came upon us again in less than half an hour afterwards, within which time they had all disappeared. Upon attempting to get in again, we found ourselves so weak as to require each other's assistance; indeed, had it not been for three of our crew, who could not swim, and who did not, therefore, get overboard, I know not by what means we should have been able to have resumed our situations in the boat.

On the fifteenth our boat continued to take in water so fast from her leaks, and the weather proving so moderate, we concluded to search out the bad places, and endeavour to mend them as well as we should be able. After a considerable search, and, removing the ceiling near the bows, we found the principal opening was occasioned by the starting of a plank or streak in the bottom of the boat, next to the keel. To remedy this, it was now absolutely necessary to have access to the bottom. The means of doing which did not immediately occur to our minds. After a moment's reflection, however, one of the crew, Benjamin Lawrence, offered to tie a rope around his body, take a boat's hatchet in his hand, and thus go under the water, and hold the hatchet against a nail, to be driven through from the inside, for the purpose of clenching it. This was, accordingly, all effected, with some little trouble, and answered the purpose much beyond our expectations. Our latitude was this day 21° 42' South.

The oppression of the weather still continuing through the sixteenth, bore upon our health and spirits with an amazing force and severity. The most disagreeable excitements were produced by it, which, added to the disconsolate endurance of the calm, called loudly for some mitigating expedient – some sort of relief to our prolonged sufferings. By our observations to day we found, in addition to our other calamities, that we had been urged back from our progress, by the heave of the sea, a distance of ten miles; and were still without any prospect of wind. In this distressing posture of our affairs, the captain proposed that we should commence rowing, which, being seconded by all, we immediately concluded to take a double allowance of provision and water for the day, and row, during the cool of the nights, until we should get a breeze from some quarter or other. Accordingly, when night came, we commenced our laborious operations: we made but a very sorry progress. Hunger and thirst, and long inactivity, had so weakened us, that in three hours every man gave out, and we abandoned the further prosecution of the plan. With the sunrise the next morning, on the seventeenth, a light breeze sprung up from the SE. and, although directly ahead, it was welcomed with almost frenzied feelings of gratitude and joy.

18 December

The wind had increased this day considerably, and by 12 o'clock blew a gale; veering from SE. to E.SE. Again we were compelled to take in all sail, and lie to for the principal part of the day. At night, however, it died away, and the next day, the nineteenth, proved very moderate and pleasant weather, and we again commenced to make a little progress.

20 December

This was a day of great happiness and joy. After having experienced one of the most distressing nights in the whole catalogue of our sufferings, we awoke to a morning of comparative luxury and pleasure. About 7 o'clock, while we were sitting dispirited, silent, and dejected, in our boats, one of our companions suddenly and loudly called out, "there is land!"

We were all aroused in an instant, as if electrified, and casting our eyes to leeward, there indeed, was the blessed vision before us, "as plain and palpable" as could be wished for. A new and extraordinary impulse now took possession of us. We shook off the lethargy of our senses, and seemed to take another, and a fresh existence. One or two of my companions, whose lagging spirits, and worn out frames had begun to inspire them with an utter indifference to their fate, now immediately brightened up, and manifested a surprising alacrity and earnestness to gain, without delay, the much wished for shore.

It appeared at first a low, white, beach, and lay like a basking paradise before our longing eyes. It was discovered nearly at the same time by the other boats, and a general burst of joy and congratulation now passed between us. It is not within the scope of human calculation, by a mere listener to the story, to divine what the feelings of our hearts were on this occasion. Alternate expectation, fear, gratitude, surprise, and exultation, each swayed our minds, and quickened our exertions. We ran down for it, and at 11 a.m. we were within a quarter of a mile of the shore. It was an island, to all appearance, as nearly as we could determine it, about six miles long, and three broad; with a very high, rugged shore, and surrounded by rocks; the sides of the mountains were bare, but on the tops it looked fresh and green with vegetation.

Upon examining our navigators, we found it was Ducie's Island, lying in latitude 24° 40' S. longitude 124° 40' W. A short moment sufficed for reflection, and we made immediate arrangements to land. None of us knew whether the island was inhabited or not, nor what it afforded, if any thing; if inhabited, it was uncertain whether by beasts or savages; and a momentary suspense was created, by the dangers which might possibly arise by proceeding without due preparation and care. Hunger and thirst, however, soon determined us, and having taken the musket and pistols, I, with three others, effected a landing upon some sunken rocks, and waded thence to the shore. Upon arriving at the beach, it was necessary to take a little breath, and we laid down for a few minutes to rest our weak bodies, before we could proceed. Let the reader judge, if he can, what must have been our feelings now! Bereft of all comfortable hopes of life, for the space of 30 days of terrible suffering; our bodies wasted to mere skeletons, by hunger and thirst, and death itself staring us in the face; to be suddenly and unexpectedly conducted to a rich banquet of food and drink, which subsequently we enjoyed for a few days, to our full satisfaction; and he will have but a faint idea of the happiness that here fell to our lot. We now, after a few minutes, separated, and went different directions in search of water; the want of which bad been our principal privation, and called for immediate relief.

They managed to catch some fish, crabs and birds which they ate. The next day they found a spring of fresh water. They decided to set sail for Easter Island which bore E.S.E in latitude 27° 9' S, 109° 35' W. Three of the crew decided to remain on Ducie's Island.

27 December

I went, before we set sail this morning, and procured for each boat a flat stone, and two armsful of wood, with which to make a fire in our boats, should it become afterwards necessary in the further prosecution of our voyage; as we calculated we might catch a fish, or a bird, and in that case be provided with the means of cooking it; otherwise, from the intense beat of weather, we knew they could not be preserved from spoiling. At ten 10 a.m. the tide having risen far enough to allow our boats to float over the rocks, we made all sail, and steered around the island, for the purpose of making a little further observation, which would not detain us any time, and might be productive of some unexpected good fortune. Before we started we missed our three companions, and found they had not come down, either to assist us to get off, nor to take any kind of leave of us. I walked up the beach towards their rude dwelling, and informed them that we were then about to set sail, and should probably never see them more. They seemed to be very much affected, and one of them shed tears. They wished us to write to their relations, should Providence safely direct us again to our homes, and said but little else. They had every confidence in being able to procure a subsistence there as long as they remained: and, finding them ill at heart about taking any leave of us, I hastily bid them "good-bye", hoped they would do well, and came away. They followed me with their eyes until I was out of sight, and I never saw more of them.

On the NW. side of the island we perceived a fine white beach, in which we imagined we might land, and in a short time ascertain if any further useful discoveries could be effected, or any addition made to our stock of provisions; and having set ashore five or six of the men for this purpose, the rest of us shoved off the boats and commenced fishing. We saw a number of sharks, but all efforts to take them proved ineffectual; and we got but a few small fish, about the size of a mackerel, which we divided amongst us. In this business we were occupied for the remainder of the day, until 6 o'clock in

the afternoon, when the men, having returned to the shore
from their search in the mountains, brought a few birds, and
we again set sail and steered directly for Easter Island.
During that night, after we had got quite clear of the land, we
had a fine strong breeze from the NW.; we kept our fires
going, and cooked our fish and birds, and felt our situation as
comfortable as could be expected. We continued on our
course, consuming our provisions and water as sparingly as
possible, without any material incident, until the thirtieth,
when the wind hauled out E.SE. directly ahead, and so
continued until the thirty-first, when it again came to the
northward, and we resumed our course.

On the third of January we experienced heavy squalls from
the W.SW. accompanied with dreadful thunder and lightning, that threw a gloomy and cheerless aspect over the
ocean, and incited a recurrence of some of those heavy and
desponding moments that we had before experienced. We
commenced from Ducie's Island to keep a regular reckoning, by which, on the fourth of January, we found we had
got to the southward of Easter Island, and the wind
prevailing E.NE. we should not be able to get on to the
eastward, so as to reach it. Our birds and fish were all now
consumed, and we had begun again upon our short
allowance of bread. It was necessary, in this state of things,
to change our determination of going to Easter Island, and
shape our course in some other direction, where the wind
would allow of our going. We had but little hesitation in
concluding, therefore, to steer for the island of Juan
Fernandez, which lay about E.SE. from us, distant 2,500
miles. We bent our course accordingly towards it, having
for the two succeeding days very light winds, and suffering
excessively from the intense beat of the sun. The seventh
brought us a change of wind to the northward, and at twelve
o'clock we found ourselves in latitude 30° 18' S. longitude
117° 29' W. We continued to make what progress we could
to the eastward.

10 January

Matthew P. Joy, the second mate, had suffered from debility, and the privations we had experienced, much beyond any of the rest of us, and was on the eighth removed to the captain's boat, under the impression that he would be more comfortable there, and more attention and pains be bestowed in nursing and endeavouring to comfort him. This day being calm, he manifested a desire to be taken back again; but at 4 o'clock in the afternoon, after having been, according to his wishes, placed in his own boat, he died very suddenly after his removal. On the eleventh, at 6 o'clock in the morning, we sewed him up in his clothes, tied a large stone to feet, and, having brought all the boats to, consigned him in a solemn manner to the ocean. This man did not die of absolute starvation, although his end was no doubt very much hastened by his sufferings. He had a weak and sickly constitution, and complained of being unwell the whole voyage. It was an incident, however, which threw a gloom over our feelings for many days. In consequence of his death, one man from the captain's boat was placed in that from which he died, to supply his place, and we stood away again on our course.

On 12 January we had the wind from the NW. which commenced in the morning, and came on to blow before night a perfect gale. We were obliged to take in all sail and run before the wind. Flashes of lightning were quick and vivid, and the rain came down in cataracts. As however the gale blew us fairly on our course, and our speed being great during the day, we derived, I may say, even pleasure from the uncomfortableness and fury of the storm. We were apprehensive that in the darkness of this night we should be separated, and made arrangements, each boat to keep an E.SE course all night. About eleven o'clock my boat being ahead a short distance of the others, I turned my head back, as I was in the habit doing every minute, and neither of the others were to be seen. It was blowing and raining at this time as if the heavens were separating, and I knew not hardly at the moment what to do. I hove my boat to the wind, and lay drifting about an hour, expecting every moment that they would come up with me, but not seeing anything of them, I put away again, and stood on the course agreed upon, with strong hopes that daylight would enable me to discover them again.

When the morning dawned, in vain did we look over every part of the ocean for our companions; they were gone! and we saw no more of them afterwards. It was folly to repine at the circumstances; it could neither be remedied, nor could sorrow secure their return; but it was impossible to prevent ourselves feeling all the poignancy and bitterness that characterizes the separation of men who have long suffered in each other's company, and whose interests and feelings fate had so closely linked together. By our observation, we separated in lat. 32° 165. long. 112° 20 W. 14 For many days after this accident, our progress was attended with dull and melancholy reflections. We had lost the cheering of each other's faces, that, which strange as it is, we so much required in both our mental and bodily distresses.

The 14 January proved another very squally and rainy day. We had now been nineteen days from the island, and had only made a distance of about 900 miles: necessity began to whisper us, that a still further reduction of our allowance must take place, or we must abandon altogether the hopes of reaching the land, and rely wholly on the chance of being taken up by a vessel. But how to reduce the daily quantity of food, with any regard to life itself, was a question of the utmost consequence. Upon our first leaving the wreck, the demands of the stomach had been circumscribed to the smallest possible compass; and subsequently before reaching the island, a diminution had taken place of nearly one-half; and it was now, from a reasonable calculation, become necessary even to curtail that at least one-half; which must, in a short time, reduce us to mere skeletons again. We had a full allowance of water, but it only served to contribute to our debility; our bodies deriving but the scanty support which an ounce and a half of bread for each man afforded. It required a great effort to bring matters to this dreadful alternative, either to feed our bodies and our hopes a little longer, or in the agonies of hunger to seize upon and devour our provisions, and coolly await the approach of death.

We were as yet, just able to move about in our boats, and slowly perform the necessary labours appertaining to her; but we were fast wasting away with the relaxing effects of the water, and we daily almost perished under the torrid rays of a meridian sun; to escape which, we would lie down in the bottom of the boat, cover ourselves over with the sails, and abandon her to the mercy of the waves. Upon attempting to rise again, the blood would rush into the head, an intoxicating blindness come over us, almost to occasion our suddenly falling down again. A slight interest was still kept up in our minds by the distant hopes of yet meeting with the other boats, but it was never realized.

An accident occurred at night, which gave me a great cause of uneasiness, and led me to an unpleasant rumination upon the probable consequences of a repetition of it. I had laid down in the boat without taking the usual precaution of securing the lid of the provision-chest, as I was accustomed to do, when one of the white men awoke me, and informed me that one of the blacks had taken some bread from it. I felt at the moment the highest indignation and resentment at such conduct in any of our crew and immediately took my pistol in my hand, and charged him that if he had taken any, to give it up without the least hesitation, or I should instantly shoot him! – He became at once very much alarmed and, trembling, confessed the fact, pleading the hard necessity that urged him to it: he appeared to be very penitent for his crime, and earnestly swore that he would never be guilty of it again. I could not find it in my soul to extend towards him the least severity on this account, however much, according to the strict imposition which we felt upon ourselves it might demand it. This was the first infraction; and the security of our lives, our hopes of redemption from our sufferings, loudly called for a prompt and signal punishment; but every humane feeling of nature plead in his behalf, and he was permitted to escape, with the solemn injunction, that a repetition of the same offence would cost him his life.

I had almost determined upon this occurrence to divide our provisions, and give to each man his share of the whole stock; and should have done so in the height of my resentment, had it not been for the reflection that some might, by imprudence, be tempted to go beyond the daily allowance, or consume it all at once, and bring on a premature weakness or starvation: this would of course disable them for the duties of the boat, and reduce our chances of safety and deliverance.

On 15 January, at night, a very large shark was observed swimming about us in a most ravenous manner, making attempts every now and then upon different parts of the boat, as if he would devour the very wood with hunger; he came several times and snapped at the steering oar, and even the stern-post. We tried in vain to stab him with a lance, but were so weak as not to be able to make any impression upon his hard skin; he was so much larger than an ordinary one, and manifested such a fearless malignity, as to make us afraid of him; and our utmost efforts, which were at first directed to kill him for prey, became in the end self-defence. Baffled however in all his hungry attempts upon us, he shortly made off.

On 16 January, we were surrounded with porpoises in great numbers, that followed us nearly an hour, and which also defied all manoeuvres to catch them. The 17th and 18th proved to be calm; and the distresses of a cheerless prospect and a burning hot sun, were again visited upon our devoted heads.

We began to think that Divine Providence had abandoned us at last; and it was but an unavailing effort to endeavour to prolong a now tedious existence. Horrible were the feelings that took possession of us! – The contemplation of a death of agony and torment, refined by the most dreadful and distressing reflections, absolutely prostrated both body and soul. There was not a hope now remaining to us but that which was derived from a sense of the mercies of our Creator.

The night of the 18th was a despairing era in our sufferings; our minds were wrought up to the highest pitch of dread and apprehension for our fate, and all in them was dark, gloomy, and confused. About 8 o'clock, the terrible noise of whale-spouts near us sounded in our ears: we could distinctly hear the furious thrashing of their tails in the water, and our weak minds pictured out their appalling and hideous aspects. One of my companions, the black man, took an immediate fright, and solicited me to take out the oars, and endeavour to get away from them. I consented to his using any means for that purpose; but alas! it was wholly out of our power to raise a single arm in our own defence. Two or three of the whales came down near us, and went swiftly off across our stern, blowing and spouting at a terrible rate; they, however, after an hour or two disappeared, and we saw no more of them.

The next day, 19 January, we had extremely boisterous weather, with rain, heavy thunder and lightning, which reduced us again to the necessity of taking in all sail and lying to. The wind blew from every point of the compass within the twenty-four hours, and at last towards the next morning settled at E.NE. a strong breeze.

20 January

The black man, Richard Peterson, manifested today symptoms of a speedy dissolution; he had been lying between the seats in the boat, utterly dispirited and broken down, without being able to do the least duty, or hardly to place his hand to his head for the last three days, and had this morning made up his mind to die rather than endure further misery: he refused his allowance; said he was sensible of his approaching end, and was perfectly ready to die: in a few minutes he became speechless, the breath appeared to be leaving his body without producing the least pain, and at four o'clock he was gone. I had two days previously, conversations with him on the subject of religion, on which he reasoned very sensibly, and with much composure; and begged me to let his wife know his fate, if ever I reached home in safety.

The next morning we committed him to the sea, in latitude 35° 07' S. longitude 105° 46' W. The wind prevailed to the eastward until 24 January, when it again fell calm. We were now in a most wretched and sinking state of debility, hardly able to crawl around the boat, and possessing but strength enough to convey our scanty morsel to our mouths. When I perceived this morning that it was calm, my fortitude almost forsook me. I thought to suffer another scorching day, like the last we had experienced, would close before night the scene of our miseries; and I felt many a despairing moment that day, that had well nigh proved fatal.

It required an effort to look calmly forward, and contemplate what was yet in store for us, beyond what I felt I was capable of making; and what it was that buoyed me above all the terrors which surrounded us, God alone knows. Our ounce and a half of bread, which was to serve us all day, was in some cases greedily devoured, as if life was to continue but another moment; and at other times, it was hoarded up and eaten crumb by crumb, at regular intervals during the day, as if it was to last us for ever.

To add to our calamities, biles began to break out upon us, and our imaginations shortly became as diseased as our bodies. I laid down at night to catch a few moments of oblivious sleep, and immediately my starving fancy was at work. I dreamt of being placed near a splendid and rich repast, where there was every thing that the most dainty appetite could desire; and of contemplating the moment in which we were to commence to eat with enraptured feelings of delight; and just as I was about to partake of it, I suddenly awoke to the cold realities of my miserable situation. Nothing could have oppressed me so much. It set such a longing frenzy for victuals in my mind, that I felt as if I could have wished the dream to continue for ever, that I never might have awoke from it. I cast a sort of vacant stare about the boat, until my eyes rested upon a bit of tough cow-hide, which was fastened to one of the oars; I eagerly seized and commenced to chew it, but there was no substance in it, and it only served to fatigue my weak jaws, and add to my bodily pains.

My fellow sufferers murmured very much the whole time, and continued to press me continually with questions upon the probability of our reaching land again. I kept constantly rallying my spirits to enable me to afford them comfort. I encouraged them to bear up against all evils, and if we must perish, to die in our own cause, and not weakly distrust the providence of the Almighty, by giving ourselves up to despair. I reasoned with them, and told them that we would not die sooner by keeping up our hopes; that the dreadful sacrifices and privations we endured were to preserve us from death, and were not to be put in competition with the price which we set upon our lives, and their value to our families: it was, besides, unmanly to repine at what neither admitted of alleviation nor cure; and withal, that it was our solemn duty to recognise in our calamities an overruling divinity, by whose mercy we might be suddenly snatched from peril, and to rely upon him alone, "Who tempers the wind to the shorn lamb."

The three following days, the 25th, 26th, and 27th, were not distinguished by any particular circumstances. The wind still prevailed to the eastward, and by its obduracy, almost tore the very hopes of our hearts away: it was impossible to silence the rebellious repinings of our nature, at witnessing such a succession of hard fortune against us. It was our cruel lot not to have had one bright anticipation realized – not one wish of our thirsting souls gratified. We had, at the end of these three days, been urged to the southward as far as latitude 36° into a chilly region, where rains and squalls prevailed; and we now calculated to tack and stand back to the northward: after much labour, we got our boat about; and so great was the fatigue attending this small exertion of our bodies, that we all gave up for a moment and abandoned her to her own course. – Not one of us had now strength sufficient to steer, or indeed to make one single effort towards getting the sails properly trimmed, to enable us to make any headway. After an hour or two of relaxation, during which the horrors of our situation came upon us with a despairing force and effect, we made a sudden effort and got our sails into such disposition, as that the boat would steer herself; and we then threw ourselves down awaiting the issue of time to bring us relief, or to take us from the scene of our troubles. We could now do nothing more; strength and spirits were totally gone; and what indeed could have been the narrow hopes, that in our situation, then bound us to life?

28 January

Our spirits this morning were hardly sufficient to allow of our enjoying a change of the wind, which took place to the westward. It had nearly become indifferent to us from what quarter it blew: nothing but the slight chance of meeting with a vessel remained to us now: it was this narrow comfort alone, that prevented me from lying down at once to die. But fourteen days' stinted allowance of provisions remained, and it was absolutely necessary to increase the quantity to enable us to live five days longer: we therefore partook of it, as pinching necessity demanded, and gave ourselves wholly up to the guidance and disposal of our Creator.

The 29th and 30th of January, the wind continued west, and we made considerable progress until the 31st, when it again came ahead, and prostrated all our hopes. On 1 February, it changed again to the westward, and on the 2nd and 3rd blew to the eastward; and we had it light and variable until 8 February.

Our sufferings were now drawing to a close; a terrible death appeared shortly to await us; hunger became violent and outrageous, and we prepared for a speedy release from our troubles; our speech and reason were both considerably impaired, and we were reduced to be at this time, certainly the most helpless and wretched of the whole human race. Isaac Cole, one of our crew, had the day before this, in a fit of despair, thrown himself down in the boat, and was determined there calmly to wait for death. It was obvious that he had no chance; all was dark he said in his mind, not a single ray of hope was left for him to dwell upon; and it was folly and madness to be struggling against what appeared so palpably to be our fixed and settled destiny. I remonstrated with him as effectually as the weakness both of my body and understanding would allow of; and what I said appeared for a moment to have a considerable effect: he made a powerful and sudden effort, half rose up, crawled forward and hoisted the jib, and firmly and loudly cried that he would not give up; that he would live as long as the rest of us – but alas! this effort was but the hectic fever of the moment, and he shortly again relapsed into a state of melancholy and despair.

This day his reason was attacked, and he became about 9 o'clock in the morning a most miserable spectacle of madness: he spoke incoherently about every thing, calling loudly for a napkin and water, and then lying stupidly and senselessly down in the boat again, would close his hollow eyes, as if in death. About 10 o'clock, we suddenly perceived that he became speechless; we got him as well as we were able upon a board, placed on one of the seats of the boat, and covering him up with some old clothes, left him to his fate. He lay in the greatest pain and apparent misery, groaning piteously until 4 o'clock, when he died, in the most horrid and frightful convulsions I ever witnessed.

We kept his corpse all night, and in the morning my two companions began as of course to make preparations to dispose of it in the sea; when, after reflecting on the subject all night, I addressed them on the painful subject of keeping the body for food!! Our provisions could not possibly last us beyond three days, within which time, it was not in any degree probable that we should find relief from our present sufferings, and that hunger would at last drive us to the necessity of casting lots. It was without any objection agreed to, and we set to work as fast as we were able to prepare it so as to prevent its spoiling.

We separated his limbs from his body, and cut all the flesh from the bones; after which, we opened the body, took out the heart, and then closed it again – sewed it up as decently as we could, and committed it to the sea. We now first commenced to satisfy the immediate craving of nature from the heart, which we eagerly devoured, and then eat sparingly of a few pieces of the flesh; after which, we hung up the remainder, cut in thin strips about the boat, to dry in the sun: we made a fire and roasted some of it, to serve us during the next day. In this manner did we dispose of our fellow-sufferer; the painful recollection of which, brings to mind at this moment, some of the most disagreeable and revolting ideas that it is capable of conceiving.

We knew not then, to whose lot it would fall next, either to die or be shot, and eaten like the poor wretch we had just dispatched. Humanity must shudder at the dreadful recital. I have no language to paint the anguish of our souls in this dreadful dilemma. The next morning, 10 February, we found that the flesh had become tainted, and had turned of a greenish colour, upon which we concluded to make a fire and cook it at once, to prevent its becoming so putrid as not to be eaten at all: we accordingly did so, and by that means preserved it for six or seven days longer; our bread during the time, remained untouched; as that would not be liable to spoil, we placed it carefully aside for the last moments of our trial.

About three o'clock this afternoon a strong breeze set in from the NW. and we made very good progress, considering that we were compelled to steer the boat by management of the sails alone: this wind continued until the thirteenth, when it changed again ahead. We contrived to keep soul and body together by sparingly partaking of our flesh, cut up in small pieces and eaten with salt-water. By the fourteenth, our bodies became so far recruited, as to enable us to make a few attempts at guiding our boat again with the oar; by each taking his turn, we managed to effect it, and to make a tolerable good course. On the fifteenth, our flesh was all consumed, and we were driven to the last morsel of bread, consisting of two cakes; our limbs had for the last two days swelled very much, and now began to pain us most excessively.

We were still, as near as we could judge, 300 miles from the land, and but three days of our allowance on hand. The hope of a continuation of the wind, which came out at west this morning, was the only comfort and solace that remained to us: so strong had our desires at last reached in this respect, that a high fever had set in, in our veins, and a longing that nothing but its continuation could satisfy. Matters were now with us at their height; all hope was cast upon the breeze; and we tremblingly and fearfully awaited its progress, and the dreadful development of our destiny. On the sixteenth, at night, full of the horrible reflections of our situation, and panting with weakness, I laid down to sleep, almost indifferent whether I should ever see the light again. I had not lain long, before I dreamt I saw a ship at some distance off from us, and strained every nerve to get to her, but could not. I awoke almost overpowered with the frenzy I had caught in my slumbers, and stung with the cruelties of a diseased and disappointed imagination.

On the seventeenth, in the afternoon, a heavy cloud appeared to be settling down in an E. by N. direction from us, which in my view, indicated the vicinity of some land, which I took for the island of Massafuera. I concluded it could be no other; and immediately upon this reflection, the life blood began to flow again briskly in my veins. I told my companions that I was well convinced it was land, and if so, in all probability we would reach it before two days more. My words appeared to comfort them much; and by repeated assurances of the favourable appearance of things, their Spirits acquired even a degree of elasticity that was truly astonishing. The dark features of our distress began now to diminish a little, and the countenance, even amid the gloomy bodings of our hard lot, to assume a much fresher hue. We directed our course for the cloud, and our progress that night was extremely good.

The next morning, before daylight, Thomas Nicholson, a boy about seventeen years of age, one of my two companions who had thus far survived with me, after having bailed the boat, laid down, drew a piece of canvas over him, and cried out, that he then wished to die immediately. I saw that he had given up, and I attempted to speak a few words of comfort and encouragement to him, and endeavoured to persuade him that it was a great weakness and even wickedness to abandon a reliance upon the Almighty, while the least hope, and a breath of life remained; but he felt unwilling to listen to any of the consolatory suggestions which I made to him; and, notwithstanding the extreme probability which I stated there was of our gaining the land before the end of two days more, he insisted upon lying down and giving himself up to despair. A fixed look of settled and forsaken despondency came over his face: he lay for some time silent, sullen, and sorrowful – and I felt at once satisfied, that the coldness of death was fast gathering upon him: there was a sudden and unaccountable earnestness in his manner, that alarmed me, and made me fear that I myself might unexpectedly be overtaken by a like weakness, or dizziness of nature, that would bereave me at once of both reason and life; but Providence willed it otherwise.

At about seven o'clock this morning, while I was lying asleep, my companion who was steering, suddenly and loudly called out, "There's a sail!" I know not what was the first movement I made upon hearing such an unexpected cry: the earliest of my recollections are, that immediately I stood up, gazing in a state of abstraction and ecstasy upon the blessed vision of a vessel about seven miles off from us; she was standing in the same direction with us, and the only sensation I felt at the moment was, that of a violent and unaccountable impulse to fly directly towards her. I do not believe it is possible to form a just conception of the pure, strong feelings, and the unmingled emotions of joy and gratitude, that took possession of my mind on this occasion: the boy, too, took a sudden and animated start from his despondency, and stood up to witness the probable instrument of his salvation.

Our only fear was now, that she would not discover us, or that we might not be able to intercept her course: we, however, put our boat immediately, as well as we were able, in a direction to cut her off; and found, to our great joy, that we sailed faster than she did. Upon observing us, she shortened sail, and allowed us to come up to her. The captain hailed us, and asked who we were. I told him we were from a wreck, and he cried out immediately for us to come alongside the ship. I made an effort to assist myself along to the side, for the purpose of getting up, but strength failed me altogether, and I found it impossible to move a step further without help.

We must have formed at that moment, in the eyes of the captain and his crew, a most deplorable and affecting picture of suffering and misery. Our cadaverous countenances, sunken eyes, and bones just starting through the skin, with the ragged remnants of clothes stuck about our sun-burnt bodies, must have produced an appearance to him affecting and revolting in the highest degree. The sailors commenced to remove us from our boat, and we were taken to the cabin, and comfortably provided for in every respect. In a few minutes we were permitted to taste of a little thin food, made from tapioca, and in a few days, with prudent management, we were considerably recruited. This vessel proved to be the brig *Indian*, captain William Crozier, of London; to whom we are indebted for every polite, friendly, and attentive disposition towards us, that can possibly characterize a man of humanity and feeling. We were taken up in latitude 33° 45' S longitude 81° 03' W. At twelve o'clock this day we saw the island of Massafuera, and on 25 February, we arrived at Valparaiso in utter distress and poverty. Our wants were promptly relieved there.

The captain and the survivors of his boat's crew were taken up by the American whale-ship, the *Dauphin*, Captain Zimri Coffin, of Nantucket, and arrived at Valparaiso on the 17th of March following: he was taken up in latitude 37° S. off the island of St Mary. The third boat got separated from him on 28 January, and has not been heard of since. The names of all the survivors, are as follows: Captain George Pollard, junr.

Charles Ramsdale, Owen Chase, Benjamin Lawrence and Thomas Nicholson, all of Nantucket. There died in the captain's boat, the following: Brazilla Ray of Nantucket, Owen Coffin of the same place, who was shot, and Samuel Reed, a black.

The captain relates, that after being separated, as herein before stated, they continued to make what progress they could towards the island of Juan Fernandez, as was agreed upon; but contrary winds and the extreme debility of the crew prevailed against their united exertions. He was with us equally surprised and concerned at the separation that took place between us; but continued on his course, almost confident of meeting with us again. On the 14th, the whole stock of provisions belonging to the second mate's boat, was entirely exhausted, and on the 25th, the black man, Lawson Thomas, died, and was eaten by his surviving companions. On the 21st, the captain and his crew were in the like dreadful situation with respect to their provisions; and on the 23rd, another coloured man, Charles Shorter, died out of the same boat, and his body was shared for food between the crews of both boats.

On the 27th, another, Isaac Shepherd (a black man), died in the third boat; and on the 28th, another black, named Samuel Reed, died out of the captain's boat. The bodies of these men constituted their only food while it lasted; and on the 29th, owing to the darkness of the night and want of sufficient power to manage their boats, those of the captain and second mate separated in latitude 35° S longitude 100° W. On 1 February, having consumed the last morsel, the captain and the three other men that remained with him were reduced to the necessity of casting lots. It fell upon Owen Coffin to die, who with great fortitude and resignation submitted to his fate. They drew lots to see who should shoot him: he placed himself firmly to receive death, and was immediately shot by Charles Ramsdale, whose hard fortune it was to become his executioner. On the 11th Brazilla Ray died; and on these two bodies the captain and Charles

Rarnsdale, the only two that were then left, subsisted until the morning of the 23rd, when they fell in with the ship *Dauphin*, as before stated, and were snatched from impending destruction. Every assistance and attentive humanity, was bestowed upon them by Capt. Coffin to whom Capt. Pollard acknowledged every grateful obligation. Upon making known the fact, that three of our companions had been left at Ducie's Island, to the captain of the U.S. frigate *Constellation* which lay at Valparaiso when we arrived, he said he should immediately take measures to have them taken off.

On the 11 June following I arrived at Nantucket in the whale-ship the *Eagle*, Capt. William H. Coffin. My family had received the most distressing account of our shipwreck, and had given me up for lost. My unexpected appearance was welcomed with the most grateful obligations and acknowledgements to a beneficent Creator, who had guided me through darkness, trouble, and death, once more to the bosom of my country and friends.

Owen Chase's Narrative of the most Extaordinary and Distressing Shipwreck of the Whale ship Essex *was published in New York in October 1821. In 1841 or 1842, Herman Melville, the author of* Moby Dick, *met Owen Chase's son William Henry on his first voyage on a whaling ship, the* Acushnet. *William Henry Chase lent Melville his copy of the* Narrative. *Melville's own copy of the* Narrative *is heavily annotated.*

The *Royal Charter* Storm
25–6 October 1859

During a two-day storm in October 1859, 133 ships were sunk and 90 badly damaged. At Penrhyn harbour, Bangor, on the coast of North Wales a witness described:

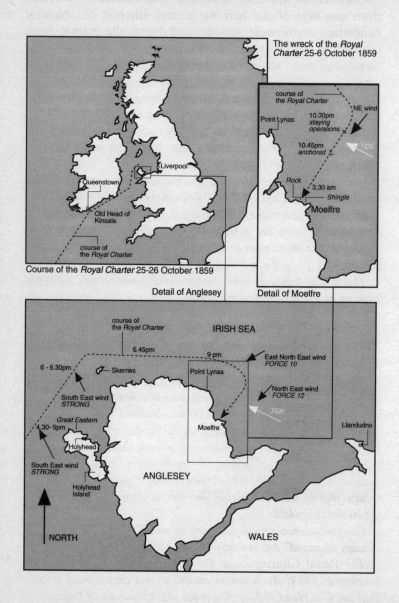

The wreck of the *Royal Charter* 25-6 October 1859

course of the *Royal Charter*

Point Lynas

NE wind

10.30pm staying operations

10.45pm anchored

TIDE

Rock

3.30 am

Shingle

Moelfre

Detail of Moelfre

Liverpool

Queenstown

Old Head of Kinsale

course of the *Royal Charter*

Course of the *Royal Charter* 25-26 October 1859

Detail of Anglesey

course of the *Royal Charter*

IRISH SEA

6.45pm

9 pm

East North East wind *FORCE 10*

6 - 6.30pm

Skerries

Point Lynas

North East wind *FORCE 12*

South East wind *STRONG*

TIDE

Great Eastern

4.30- 5pm

Moelfre

Llandudno

Holyhead

South East wind *STRONG*

Holyhead Island

ANGLESEY

WALES

NORTH

. . . the effect was truly appalling. The vessels were driven from one side of the harbour to the other in the greatest confusion; some were run into, and actually ridden over; others scuttled or dismasted, with their sides or their sterns ripped open and their boats smashed.

Admiral Fitzroy, of the Meteorological Office, described the storm as "complete horizontal cyclone."

Eight hundred lives were lost. The previous year, 1858, the total number of lives lost at sea had been 340. It was a transitional period in the construction of ships. Ships were changing from wood to steel. During this transitional period some ships were made from iron, including the Great Eastern. *In the storm of October 1859, most of the ships lost were small sailing vessels, but one of them was a large iron ship, the auxiliary steam clipper* Royal Charter. *Nearly 450 men, women and children lost their lives in the* Royal Charter.

The Royal Charter *was an iron-built sailing ship, equipped with an auxiliary steam engine. Her engines were for use when the wind was calm or contrary. She was 2,719 tons and 320 feet long. She had three tall clipper masts and a single steam funnel. Her engine was only capable of 200 horse power. She was intended to sail to Australia and back.*

At that time there was a gold rush in Australia. Gold had been discovered at Ballarat, near Melbourne, in 1851. The news, and £50,000 worth of gold, had reached Great Britain in 1852. Between 1852–7 226,000 people landed in Australia. The Royal Charter *reached Australia in 60 days, breaking the existing record for all types of vessels except steamships. She became a famous ship which never lacked passengers. On her return trip in 1859, she was carrying a small cargo and over £320,000 of gold bullion.*

Contemporaries agreed that her captain, Thomas Taylor, was a "rough diamond" but a "very smart man".

The Royal Charter *sailed for Liverpool, from Melbourne, on 26 August 1859. At daybreak on 24 October they sighted land, it was the Old Head of Kinsale on the southern coast of Ireland.*

The Royal Charter *hove to off Queenstown. She was 58 days out of Melbourne. After three hours she sailed for Liverpool. At dawn on Tuesday, 25 October she was off the coast of Caernarvonshire, Wales. She passed the* Great Eastern *which was in Holyhead harbour. A* Times *special correspondent was aboard the* Great Eastern. *He noted the changing weather:*

The wind gradually freshened during the afternoon, though not very much, till over the mountain came a thin black haze, which rose into the air with ominous rapidity and overspread the sky. The sea and wind kept rising as the glass fell, and before eight it blew a heavy gale from the eastward, with fierce squalls and storms of rain. As night wore on, the wind increased and came in fearful gusts, tearing away among the spars and rigging with a hoarse sustained roar that was awful to listen to, especially when one bore in mind that the glass was still falling, and that what we saw was only the commencement of the gale.

The Royal Charter *signalled for a pilot off Point Lynas on Anglesey, before entering Liverpool Bay. By 8 p.m. a gale had blown up. The pilot was unable to board. Thomas Grundy, a first class passenger described:*

When the gale became so strong, opposite the Skerries, the ladies and passengers became exceedingly nervous.

Rowland Hughes was at sea in a small fishing smack. He described the wind:

It chapped round to the north-east between 10 and 11 o'clock that night, and then it began to blow a complete hurricane.

Soon after midnight Rowland Hughes landed at Moelfre.

Hughes observed:

The sea upon that beach was such as I have never seen in my life before.

After the wind changed from SE to ENE, the Royal Charter *was making sternway towards the shore. Captain Taylor ordered his crew to prepare to anchor but a squall hit her. They tried to set some sail to take them out to sea. John Sheppard was in command of a Liverpool pilot boat not far away. He described:*

At 11 p.m., the gale was more violent than before; it was dreadful, we could not hear each other speak at a distance of eight feet on deck.

At 11 p.m. the Royal Charter *anchored, letting go her port anchor until 75 fathoms of anchor chain lay on the bottom. This relieved some of the strain on the port anchor. The engine was still going. She let go her starboard anchor. Despite the anchor and the engine, the* Royal Charter *was dragging herself and her anchors towards the shore.*

    At about 1.30 a.m. her port anchor cable parted near the hawse hole. The starboard anchor still held. The masts, rigging and funnel were acting as sails and needed to be cut away. This would probably foul the screw which was keeping the strain on the cable from becoming too great.

    But at about 2.30 a.m. the starboard anchor cable parted. Thomas Grundy was below in the passenger saloon:

It was crowded with ladies and gentlemen in the utmost state of terror. Families all clinging to each other; children were crying out piteously, whilst parents were endeavouring to soothe them with cheering hopes.

Captain Taylor came below and said:

Now, ladies, you need not be at all afraid. We are on a sandy beach and embedded in the sand. We are not ten paces from the shore, and the tide will leave us dry, and in ten minutes you will all be safe.

The Royal Charter *had struck the shore bows on. Another passenger, Mr Gapper, expressed: "the fact is she was driven ashore like a log of wood". She had then swung broadside on to the surf, listing to seaward. The crew finally managed to cut away the mainmast. The foremast fell perhaps an hour later, followed by the mizzen mast. They were firing signal guns and flares and rockets as distress signals. They had struck the shore below the village of Moelfre. There was no hope of getting ashore in the boats. William Barton, a rigger who was aboard, said:*

It was as dark as pitch, we could not see our hands before us. We were in total ignorance as to what sort of coast it was. And the sea was so rough that no boat could have lasted five minutes in it. Instead we set up a tar barrel, ready to set fire to, to send ashore to light the coast and let us know what kind of place it was. But the ship thumped so heavily, and danger was so imminent, that the idea was not carried out.

Dawn broke at about 6 a.m. They saw that they were barely 25 yards from land. The nearest land was a rocky shelf. Waves were breaking over the wreck. A seaman, Joseph Rodgers, volunteered to try to swim to shore with a line. Later, he described:

The sea between the ship and the rock was very heavy. I partly swam and partly was washed ashore. I was three times washed back to the ship.

Local fishermen on shore, linked hands to pull Rodgers and his line onto the rock. They pulled a hawser ashore, fastened it and rigged a bosun's chair. Safety was in sight but the rising tide lifted the wreck up and the next breaker flung her down hard upon the rocky bottom to seaward. William Foster, the ship's carpenter was one of the crew waiting to try to get ashore using the bosun's chair. A female passenger had the opportunity to try but, at the court of inquiry, Foster said:

The female refused to go, and then I went along the hawser and was thus saved; about three of the crew came ashore in the same way after me.

Conditions were considered to be too bad for the female passengers to wait on the deck. At the court of inquiry, Foster also stated that the hurricane broke up the ship by beating her on the rocks:

Nothing could withstand the beating she got there. She was a very strong ship. I would be glad to go out in her if she had had the luck to get home safe. She was perfectly tight during the voyage.

Samuel Grenfell, a passenger, described:

The sea was breaking over the ship in an awful manner, carrying everything before it; no one could keep his feet, and most of them were washed overboard.

Thomas Grundy was on deck when the enormous wave completed the damage begun by the pounding of the iron hull on the rocks:

A great sea came against the broadside, and divided the ship in two, just at the engine house, as one would smash a pipe stem, and the sea washed quite through her. People were carried down by the debris and as many must have been killed as drowned.

James Russell was a passenger who was accompanied by his family. They were clinging to the rail. Russell:

We found we were on the stern part of the vessel, separated from the fore part by a yawning chasm, into which every moment human beings were dropping, or being driven by the waves.

James Dean, another passenger, agreed:

She broke like the snapping of a tobacco stump. The people on board stood petrified at the catastrophe, seemingly unable to make the slightest struggle for their lives, whilst the terror was increased by the awful scenes as unfortunate creatures fell and were crushed to atoms between the chasm separating the two sides of the ship.

One of them was Walter Hughes, an apprentice. He said later; "I felt as if I was being killed"; his last memory of the shipwreck was of "three little children, standing on deck, holding each other's hands, screaming." Hughes was hammered by the sea until his hands and face were bloody but was cast onto the rocks after a few minutes. John Judge, a passenger, was washed out of the ship from below decks: "I saw hundreds of people closed up in the jaws of death around me." Judge caught hold of a spar, held on and was washed ashore. James Dean observed people being crushed by heavy floating bits of wreckage:

They were crushed to death, the bodies dreadfully mutilated against the rocks by the great weight of these materials. Mangled corpses, arms, legs, even heads were discernible on the crest of many a retreating wave.

Most of the people in the sea were clothed. Their waterlogged clothes made it extremely difficult for them to stand up if they were thrown onto the rocks. Those who were "nearly naked" had a better chance of survival. Villagers on the rocks helped. James Dean was thrown a rope which he was able to grasp:

By it, I was finally drawn out of danger without experiencing any injuries or bruises other than of a very trifling description.

Owen Williams, a quartermaster, got ashore using the bosun's chair. Edward Wilson, an able seaman, watched his shipmates struggling in the water:

It was dreadful, dreadful. There were mangled bodies floating about in the water; men women and children standing on the deck and shrieking for assistance; others on their knees and praying; others being washed overboard. There were a large number of passengers huddled on the deck to the end; the shrieks of the poor creatures as they met their death was absolutely appalling.

Thomas Grundy went into the water on the lee side, as he struggled up towards the surface, he felt a blow on his head: "My head had to open a passage, for the water here was thickly strewn with timber." One of the ship's yards was to seaward of him and another man. Grundy: "but, strange to say, it was carried over me, and we were both pitched on shore for a moment together".

   Both were dragged back by the retreating surf, but some villagers hauled him out. Henry Carew Taylor, a first-class passenger, observed:

masses of people in the water on the lee side of the ship, clustered as thickly as grapes . . . the struggle was so desparate I had not the slightest hope of being saved.

He held on to a spar which was thrown high onto the rocks where he was grasped by two villagers "just as another wave was going to nip me back".

Captain Taylor, Thomas Cormick, a steward and James M'Cappin, a passenger, got into a boat which had torn loose from its davits. The boat was shattered on the rocks. M'Cappin and Cormick were grabbed by rescuers. M'Cappin observed the last few to die, they were clustered around a single spar in the water: "A wave dashed them with terrible violence against the side of the ship; there were masses of timber heaped above them."

There were only 40 survivors: 22 passengers and 18 crew. It was never known exactly how many people were on board because the ship's papers were lost. It was estimated that between 472 and 498 people were on board. By 8 a.m. the Royal Charter *had disappeared from sight. The hurricane continued. Nearby, at Llandudno, the* Caernarvon *and* Daily Herald *reported:*

At 9.45 a.m., a part of the railway, with a large proportion of the roadway of the New Pier erected this year, was carried away by a heavy wave; and shortly after this, about 10 o'clock, one grand wave swept over the pier from one end to the other, which for a second or two was completely concealed from view, and struck the timber with such violence as to cause a report like distant thunder, and to shake the earth under my feet at a distance of nearly a quarter of a mile. In another moment, piles, 30 feet long, sprang with great violence into the air, and the sea had made a complete breach through about one-third of the pier. At about high tide another wave swept over the inshore portion, and carried away about one-third more, with equal, if not greater force. The whole of the beach is covered with wreckage and the Esplanade with hundreds of tons of shingle and large pieces of rock. There is a vessel at this moment lying at anchor about four miles from shore, without masts or rigging with two men and a boy on board, and we have no life-boat or any craft fit to go out to them.

At Moelfre villagers were searching for valuables. They helped the survivors, putting them in their own beds and giving them their spare clothes. A visitor from Liverpool, Mr J. H. Gregory wrote:

it is to be hoped that a competent staff of either coastguard or military will be immediately despatched to the scene of the disaster, to protect as much as possible so valuable a cargo,

which so far as the passengers' gold is concerned, is very
much scattered about. I saw men picking sovereigns out of
the holes of the rocks, as they would shellfish.

Mr J. H. Gregory continued:

In the midst of fragments of massive ironwork, with fearful
evidence of violence and death all around, there was found
perfect and unbroken on the rocks a small photograph, the
portrait of a lady and gentleman, both young and evidently of
superior position. The Collector of Customs at Beaumaris,
who, today, is the principal person in authority at the wreck,
carries the photograph in his hand, and compares it with the
lineaments of the dead washed up but as yet without having
succeeded in establishing the identity of either of the origi-
nals.

*Local detachments of coastguard and Marines were sent to enforce
martial law.*

*Charles Dickens was among many who visited Moelfre,
although he came several months later. By the time he arrived
divers had raised most of the gold bullion from the wreck. By 1859
divers used compressed air and diving suits with rigid helmets. In
"The Uncommercial Traveller" Dickens described the wreck:*

A reader, haply turning this page by the fireside at Home,
and hearing the night wind rumble in the chimney, that slight
obstruction was the uppermost fragment of the wreck of the
Royal Charter, Australian trader and passenger ship,
Homeward bound, that struck here on the terrible morning
of the twenty-sixth of this October, broke into three parts,
went down with her treasure of at least five hundred human
lives, and has never stirred since!

From which point, or from which, she drove ashore stern
foremost; on which side, or on which, she passed the little
Island in the bay for ages henceforth to be aground certain
yards outside her; these are rendered bootless questions by

the darkess of that night and the darkness of death. Here she went down.

Even as I stood on the beach with the words "Here she went down!" in my ears, a diver in his grotesque dress, dipped heavily over the side of the boat alongside the lighter, and dropped to the bottom. On the shore by the water's edge, was a rough tent, made of fragments of wreck, where other divers and workmen sheltered themselves, and where they had kept Christmas-day with rum and roast beef, to the destruction of their frail chimney. Cast up among the stones and boulders of the beach, were great spars of the lost vessel, and masses of iron twisted by the fury of the sea into the strangest forms. The timber was already bleached and iron rusted, and even these objects did no violence to the prevailing air the whole scene wore, of having been exactly the same for years and years.

Yet, only two short months had gone, since a man, living on the nearest hill-top overlooking the sea, being blown out of bed at about daybreak by the wind that had begun to strip his roof off, and getting upon a ladder with his nearest neighbour to construct some temporary device for keeping his house over his head, saw from the ladder's elevation as he looked down by chance towards the shore, some dark troubled object close in with the land. And he and the other, descending to the beach, and finding the sea mercilessly beating over a great broken ship, had clambered up the stony ways, like staircases without stairs, on which the wild village hangs in little clusters, as fruit hangs on boughs, and had given the alarm. And so, over the hill-slopes, and past the waterfall, and down the gullies where the land drains off into the ocean, the scattered quarrymen and fishermen inhabiting that part of Wales had come running to the dismal sight – their clergyman among them. And as they stood in the leaden morning, stricken with pity, leaning hard against the wind, their breath and vision often failing as the sleet and spray rushed at them from the ever forming and dissolving mountains of sea, and as the wool which was a part of the vessel's cargo blew in with the salt foam and remained upon the land when the foam melted, they saw the ship's life-boat put off from one of the heaps of wreck; and first, there were three men in her, and in a moment she capsized, and there were but two; and again, she was struck by a vast mass of water, and there was but one; and again, she was thrown bottom upward, and that one, with his arm struck through the broken planks and waving as if for the help that could never reach him, went down into the deep.

It was the clergyman himself from whom I heard this, while I stood on the shore, looking in his kind wholesome face as it turned to the spot where the boat had been. The divers were down then, and busy. They were "lifting" today the gold found yesterday – some five-and-twenty thousand pounds. Of three hundred and fifty thousand pounds' worth of gold, three hundred thousand pounds worth, in round numbers, was at that time recovered. The great bulk of the remainder was surely and steadily coming up. Some loss of sovereigns there would be, of course; indeed, at first sovereigns had drifted in with the sand, and been scattered far and wide over the beach, like sea-shells; but most other golden treasure would be found. As it was brought up, it went aboard the Tug-steamer, where good account was taken of it. So tremendous had the force of the sea been when it broke the ship, that it had beaten one great ingot of gold, deep into a strong and heavy piece of her solid iron-work: in which, also, several loose sovereigns that the ingot had swept in before it, had been found, as firmly embedded as though the iron had been liquid when they were forced there. It had been remarked of such bodies come ashore, too, as had been seen by scientific men, that they had been stunned to death, and not suffocated. Observation, both of the internal change that had been wrought in them, and of their external expression, showed death to have been thus merciful and easy. The report was brought, while I was holding such discourse on the beach, that no more bodies had come ashore since last night. It began to be very doubtful whether many more would be thrown up, until the north-east winds of the early spring set in. Moreover, a great number of the passengers, and particularly the second-class women-passengers, were known to have been in the middle of the ship when she parted, and thus the collapsing wreck would have fallen upon them after yawning open, and would keep them down. A diver made known, even then, that he had come upon the body of a man, and had sought to release it from a great superincumbent weight; but that, finding he could not do so without mutilating the remains, he had left it where it was.

The Wreck of the *Serica*
13 March 1868

Thomas Cubbin was master and owner of the Serica, *a 560 ton merchant sailing ship. The* Serica *sailed from Liverpool for Aden on 8 December 1867. Cubbin had his wife and two sons aboard. His eldest son was eleven years old, the younger was only eighteen months old. He described them as "ocean born". They reached the tropic of Capricorn 38 days out. The ship's crew of 14 included two boys, Radcliffe and Clarke. They met storms off the Cape of Good Hope. During February they had difficulty making progress eastwards. By 10 March 1868 they were in strong gales which continued. Thomas Cubbin:*

12 March
At 2 a.m. there was no improvement in the weather; yet the barometers were still steady. I decided to run no further, shortened sail, wore ship, and hove-to on the port-tack under lower maintopsail. Daylight, wind increasing to a heavy gale, yet the barometers gave no indication of a coming storm. But I determined to prepare; had royal yards and all possible top hamper sent down; had the sails doubly made fast to the spars; extra lashings on the spare spars and boats; double relieving tackles on the rudder head; covered and battened

cabin skylights and windows, barricaded front of the poop, and made all about the ship as secure as we possibly could.

During that day I felt sure there was a hurricane passing over Mauritius, and often said so; but thought we were on the southern edge of it, and would escape its destructive rotary force, by having only a steady gale. The barometers were steady throughout the day, at 29.80; which strengthened my opinion; but we did not relax our labours in making our ship ready for the worst that might come. Towards evening, it was blowing a very heavy gale; our good ship was lying-to splendidly; the gale continued during the night, increasing in violence.

13 March

At day-break, a fearful gust came down upon us; all hands were called to shorten sail. The lower maintopsail was the only sail set. We waited, as we thought, for a lull, and started to clew up, but it was blown to pieces. We got up tarpaulins and hammocks in the mizzen rigging to keep ship's head to wind. The storm was now down upon us in all its fury. I went to see the barometers, they were still steady; but shortly afterwards began to fall rapidly; the two men were lashed at the wheel. I myself, for the first time in my life, was lashed on the poop to prevent me being washed overboard. By noon, the storm was past all description, being almost as dark as midnight, with a spectral light. The barometer had fallen to 29.00. We had only a small place in the after companion to communicate with the cabin. My wife was there, wishing to speak to me; she asked what I thought of the weather, and our prospect of getting through it. I said, "There was still hope, but at the same time the ship might founder any moment, and that her hope and trust should be in God. Go down with the children and pray, and prepare for the worst." She replied, "If our case is so hopeless, you come down with us." I said, "No; if I do that the ship would soon be given up and left to herself. I must remain at my post until the last."

Past noon, if possible it blew harder, barometers still

falling. I ordered a part of the lee bulwarks to be rammed out, to allow the weight of water to escape off the decks. Our ship was still tight, for I ordered the pumps to be often tried, and found very little water in her. The scene was fearful to look upon. At 4 p.m. my wife was at the companion; she wished to know what the weather was like. I told her I was unable to describe it, she said, "What does it look like?" (forgive the answer) I said, "It looks like the mouth of hell," and told her to attend to her prayers. Those were strong expressions to make use of; but at the very time my wife came up, I was contemplating the scene, and I thought it was a good representation of that place of everlasting torments. The sea looked like great avalanches coming out of the clouds; around was like a boiling cauldron, and sometimes the ship looked as if in a deep vortex. It was not the first or second hurricane the writer had experienced in the vicinity of Mauritius, but all other storms dwindle into insignificance compared to this awful one.

If I had been a short time in this sad reverie, I was suddenly roused by some very heavy seas striking the ship, one of them damaged the rudder. The barometer had fallen to 28.60. I had been expecting all day to see the masts go over the side; but still everything held on well aloft. Night was again approaching, the barometers still falling. Another heavy sea had struck the rudder, and bent the iron tiller. I signalled the officers to get the fore-topmast cut away. They went about it, but not in the proper manner, by cutting the rigging, without separating aloft. Signalled again that such would not do; told them, if they so cut, it would most likely fall inboard, and be the loss of the ship; told the mate they must separate the upper from the lower topsail yards, natch the mast above the cap, to save the foremast head, and then cut the rigging. He soon returned to say that no man would lay aloft. At that time the iron tiller carried away short off by the rudder head. I then ordered the foremast to be cut away, feeling sure that if the ship fell off into the trough of the sea, she must soon founder. The wind was veering to eastward at the time.

The foremast was cut away; the main and mizzen soon followed. By this time it was getting dark. We cut and got the wreck away from the ship as quickly as possible, and then got to the pumps, often up to our necks at them, yet kept them going. The storm continued all night, with very little abatement, the ship (if I might call her that name then) laid well along.

14 March

At daylight, the wind had veered to the N.E. The scene, our ship a miserable derelict, the sea breaching heavily over her, our best boat was smashed to pieces by the falling of the mainmast, our next best had her stem knocked out by the sea, and her gunwales badly broken in the lashings, the smallest, a double end boat, was split open at both ends, through the sea striking and crushing her in the lashing. The rudders and tillers, etc., of both boats, were washed away. At noon, the wind was north and moderating, and a heavy cross sea on. We kept the pumps going, allowing the men to get something to eat, only two at one time. I ordered the mate to give the crew grog as often as he thought it would do them good. We got the wreck that was about the decks overboard, except such as might be useful in constructing a raft was securely lashed. The crew wanted to sound, and find out what water was in her. I would not allow it. I ordered them plenty of the best fare in the ship, and that they must work away. The only place my poor wife and children could find to keep themselves dry, was sitting holding on in our bed. During the afternoon I was below for a few minutes, standing with my head resting on the bed. The cook had come down for stores. After he had got all he required, I overheard him say to the young steward, "Now I must have some bottles of grog." The young man said, "I dare not give it, the Captain would not allow it." "What," he replied, "there is no Captain now; we are all equal." At these words, I confronted him, and asked who had sent him for the grog? He said, "the crew. I said, "I do not believe you; but if it even is so that they have sent you, go back and tell them that the ship is still under command, and that I am, and will be Master as long as she floats; and if you ever dare to put your foot in this place again, without my permission, I will punish you, even though we should all go into eternity an hour after."

Our only way into the cabin was by the aft companion, the front of the poop being barricaded to resist the sea striking it. The cabin leaked very much, and took the two boys baling out to prevent the water getting down the store room hatch. By the evening the crew were very much exhausted and complaining. I arranged that during the night we would set watches, one watch resting and relieving every two hours.

15 March
At 2 a.m., I fancied the ship was settling down, and determined on more active measures. Had all hands on deck again at the pumps. Afterwards, taking two with myself, we began getting everything of any weight overboard. We threw over the anchors from the forecastle; part of the cables that was in the fore-hold we let run overboard, and everything heavy, until we got at the coals. Then we divided, one half pumping, the other throwing cargo overboard. I was working the forehold, when, during the forenoon, the cry rang through the ship, "Sail ho!" I went on deck, and there was a vessel steering right down upon us; all hands were rejoiced at the sight, and dropped the pumps. I sent them back, saying they must pump away, for if even the vessel did come to our assistance, they might think there was too much sea on to put out a boat, and, would only lay by us until it went down. I enquired what the time was, and found it was half an hour to noon. Then taking the bearing of the vessel, said he must see us when he takes his meridian altitude at noon, for we bore due north from him, right in the sun blade.

We got our ensign, union down, elevated on a ladder, and another signal to a pole, one lashed to the stump the main and mizzen masts. The wind at that time had veered W.S.W., and was moderating. The vessel came on under easy sail, until we got glimpses of her hull, when she trimmed sail, and hauled off to the eastward for a few miles, and then made off again. We all made sure they saw us. If they did, may God forgive them for their cruel conduct. This was an awful blow to my poor wife; she had got the children and herself ready to leave our ill-fated ship. My only hope now was to keep her afloat. We all went to work again, throwing cargo overboard and keeping the pumps going.

I overheard the cook inciting the men at the pumps to break into the cabin and help themselves to the drinkables. I called him to account for his insubordinate talk, and was on the point of chastising him for it, and with difficulty I restrained myself from so doing, ordered him to the pumps, and told him if he used such talk again, or left the pumps till he was relieved, his body should suffer for it. This cook was about the most idle, insolent, and mutinous character I ever knew. He professed being an infidel, and not caring for death. If he did show neglect, after this caution, he took care not to let me find him away from his post.

Towards evening, the crew were complaining of the work, and said they could not keep at it. I said, "What do you mean? You are not working for me; everyone is working for his life; and I am working as hard as any of you." The crew no doubt were fatigued; I was very much so myself; yet I think the cook's evil counsels had a very bad effect; he was indeed a bad man. My wife by this time had informed me, that he somehow got into the cabin during the height of the storm, and was then asking the young steward to give him some grog, which she overheard, and spoke to him about. He said he might as well have some, it would be his last, for we might all go to the bottom any minute. She said, he should not have it. I think it was well for us all that my wife was there, else I believe he would have helped himself, and during my absence working in other parts of the ship, others of the crew might have done the same, and perhaps all been lost.

My chief mate and some of the crew worked well. The mate up to this time was all I could have wished him to be.

During the afternoon, the carpenter was overhauling the starboard pump. He was stupidly driving the lower box down with the iron break in my absence. I once saw him do so before, but stopped it, and made him get a handspike, and told him never to use the break for that purpose again. Yet he had done so on that occasion with fatal effect, knocking a hole in the chamber of the pump.

As soon as I knew of this to us sad accident, I got a derrick rigged, and hove the pump up, secured the hole with white lead, canvas and sheet lead over. When we lowered again, we could not get the pump tail into the well after trying all possible means. A good deal of water got down through the pump hole during the operation, darkness came on us, and we had to secure it for the night to keep out water; intending by the morning light to have it up again, and cut the end off, where it would not enter the well.

Through this sad disaster, we were able to work only one pump during the night.

16 March

Long before daylight, I had all hands out again, leaving one watch at the pumps; commenced with the rest getting up stores and provisions by the after companion, to clear away to get at the cargo. Threw all overboard as we got it up. Before daylight, we were working out the cargo from the after-hold. I was working in the hold, in the after-run. There was very little cargo right aft, and the water was making a great noise there. My gang wanted very much to work under the break of the store room deck, to find out what depth of water was there, but I would not allow it. The crew were murmuring, and slipping away when a chance offered. My wife and son were assisting at the cargo with them, and reported. When some went away, I went and got them back again.

At 8 a.m. fear began to take possession of their hearts, that the ship would suddenly sink, and take all down with her. I expostulated with them, and said the ship was our only chance of saving our lives, and that it would require good boats to live in the sea that was on then; besides, the weather looked wild, and our boats that were left were shattered and broken in the storm. I got them to work again, and while down had a little water passed up into the cabin. In a very short time they broke again, and their cry was, "She will founder and take all hands with her." I strove to cheer them, saying, "We had over two months water on board, and plenty of provisions; let us only keep the ship afloat, and we will be all right." But it was all to no purpose, for by this time fear had taken full possession of them. Finding that the hold was clear of gas, the last thing I did before I came up out of it, was to go round with a light and examine the ship's upper works, and in the way of the channels, expecting to find her very much strained and opened; but it was not so, she was tight in all her upper works, to my great astonishment. I then felt sure that the damage must be in her bottom, through falling on the wreck of her spars, during the storm, before we got clear of it.

Up to this time my wife had confidence in my opinion, that the ship might be kept afloat, and was urging on the crew to get the cargo overboard, and also helping herself; but during my absence below examining the ship, the chief mate having fallen into the same fears as the crew, distressed her by telling her that the ship might founder any minute with all on board, and advised her to prevail on me to abandon the ship.

When I got on deck again, all on board were clamouring to leave her; but I would not yield, and ordered them to get the hose of the deck pump down the forward ventilator, and work that until we got the starboard main pump cut and placed. It was to no purpose, they refused to do so. I told them there was very little hope of our lives being saved by the boats; that the nearest land, the islands of Mauritius and Bourbon, were at least 250 miles off; bearing north. But still they were determined to abandon the ship, by taking to the boats. I then ordered the carpenter to repair the boat on the fore deck house that had her stern knocked out, and otherwise damaged, telling the crew at the same time that there would be very little chance of saving our lives by the boats; and ordered and showed them how to construct a raft that would answer as a floating breakwater to hang the boats to. I then told them above all things they must get some water from below; not one would go in the hold for it.

I took two or three men with myself to get the small boat off the skids on to the poop to repair her, which I did in a very rude manner, for it would have taken a long time to do her properly. I told my wife to get the children and herself ready to go in the boat. When finished, we got her in the davits, put a small breaker with some water in her, two bags of bread, and three or four cheeses. I then got my poor wife and children in her, I kissed them, thinking it might be the last time. They wished me to be in the boat with them. I said no, I must be the last to abandon the ship. We lowered, and got the boat safely afloat, the chief mate and Hall, A.B., being in her to attend the tackles.

It was intended that the mate should come up out of the boat again, that she should hang astern, and Hall attend her. From what they afterwards said, she would not hang astern, and they cut her adrift, and kept her with the oars.

After the small boat was afloat, I went to get the raft completed. At this time our infidel cook was as much afraid of his life as any other on board. He went to the pumps, and said he would pump until he dropped; beforetime he had to be driven to them. About noon, the raft was completed, and got it successfully launched; a good rope was attached to it, which I ordered should be kept on the top ready at any time to cut; it was passed astern with one man on it.

The carpenter by that time had finished the other boat, and we got her safely launched. I told them again that it was most necessary that they should get some water from below, but none of them would go down for it.

I then told them, there was plenty of preserved provisions and stores in the cabin and store-room; that they might go down and help themselves to everything except wines or spirits. Two men were minding the boat, and the rest went down and got what they pleased. I reminded them again that they should get up water. They began to disagree about which ought to go. Some of them commenced crying, saying, "the ship would go down before they got away from her." This was indeed a trying scene. I ordered them into their boats. Andrew Stout got down and found a lot of cutlasses and bottles of grog, which he very properly threw overboard. The rest of them soon followed him into the boat. Radcliffe and Clarke, were crying bitterly, and said my wife had promised them that they should be with her to the last; I said, "So you shall, but for the present, get into the boat." When they were all in, they said they would not go without me. I told them to go to the raft, naming two or three that should come back to me with the boat, and leave all the rest of them on the raft, intending when the boat came back, to get some water up. Again they said they would not go without me; when I told them, if they would not obey my orders, I would have nothing more to do with them. They then went, and I passed their raft-rope, and made it fast right aft on the ship.

As soon as they got to the raft, and some upon it, they began shouting and screaming for me to let them go. I said, "I would not; when it is requisite, you can cut the raft-rope;" they replied, "No, it is foul under the raft, and the ship will go down, and take us with her." They screamed again, and I let them go. I called them in the boat to come to the ship, but they would not. Except my dog, I was then alone on board the doomed ship. I went down and looked at the barometers, although this was the third day from the storm, the reading was only 28.95, and the weather looked squally. I got up as high as I could and looked around, hoping there might be some friendly sail in sight; but alas, there was no such succour near.

I was then utterly hopeless, and knew not what further to do, I did not think the boats could live many hours. I knelt down and prayed Almighty God to guide and assist me, and surely He heard my prayers; for I rose up refreshed, and felt again a ray of hope; and the first time for many days I felt anhungered. I went forward and found a kettle of hot coffee that had been prepared for the crew, who in the hurry had left without using it. I got a mug of it, and waded aft again, got some bread, and made a hearty meal, it being the first food I had eaten for some time. My wife by that time was very anxious I should leave the sinking ship, she and the children had been calling a long time, to which I fear I paid very little attention. I then told them, I would soon be with them; went down into the cabin, and picked up a few things the sailors had left strewed about, a few bottles of port wine, two or three tins of sardines, two or three tins of preserved meats, and one jar of jelly. I sent these afloat in a case for them to pick up. The boat looked so deep, that I dare not send anything heavy. She was indeed a very poor boat to stand any bad weather. The other boat was double as capable for it, and much larger. I looked at her low gunwales, and only sent a few light things that might be useful; a chronometer and a box with the ship papers, a compass, nautical almanac, and sextant. All these things we might have left behind, for all the good we had of them.

I went round to take a last look through our doomed ship, and see that the pigs, sheep, and every living thing was let loose. The water in the ship made her race ahead, the boat and the raft being out of sight of the small boat astern. I had then been about two hours alone on board the ship, and the time must have been about 3 p.m., when remembering my wife's promise to the two boys, Radcliffe and Clarke, took a bearing of the raft and other boat, and left the ship. The dog was ready to leap into the boat with me, and very sorry I was to have to beat him back. I got in and we pulled for the raft.

I thought then as we were leaving the ill-fated ship, and think so still, that had we all used our utmost exertions, we might have kept our ship afloat until we were picked up, or rigged jury masts and temporary rudder, and got to Mauritius.

We got up to the raft. The other boat was hanging to it; I

called to the boys that they must jump on our oars. We could go no nearer, fearing our boat might be stoved. We got them in. We threw over a bag of bread, so that the other boat might pick it up; and we threw them about half the cheeses. Andrew Stout asked me if I would have another hand. I counted, and found that would make nine persons to each boat. I told him if he came he must jump like the others. He did so. We left the second mate and eight men with the raft and other boat. He had previously been informed of our position, distance and bearing. I said, "I must now go back to see the last of the ship." The compass we soon threw overboard finding it was useless.

At this point they separated from the raft and the other boat which held the second mate and eight men. Thomas Cubbin's boat went back under the lee of the wreck. The next day the wreck sank.

They sailed toward Isle Bourbon which was closer than Mauritius and reached driftwood and landbirds off shore but the wind was against them. They had to turn and run before the wind to Madagascar. By 22 March they were suffering from thirst. On 24 March they were attacked by a shark. Thomas Cubbin:

24 March

About 3 a.m. the mate was steering. I was laid on a thwart, resting my head. I felt something striking the boat very hard. I inquired what it was. The mate said it was a great shark. I said, "Make him shift, or he will stove the boat's bottom; and look out that he does not break your steer oar."

The mate said, "How can I do it?" Hall at the same time said, "It is no use, he will never leave until he gets some of us to eat." I said, "I will give him a broad hint that I have no wish that he should make a meal out of me." His way of action, was dropping astern about thirty yards, then coming full speed, striking the boat under the stern, and rushing up alongside with his great jaws above the boat's gunwale. I got the loose thwart and placed myself in a position to astonish him. The mate let me know when he was coming, and as he came alongside, I made the timber ring on his big head; and he took the hint, so far as not to strike the boat any more. It was then my turn to steer. I had scarcely got hold of the oar, when I felt Mr Shark at the point of it, and I gave him so severe a poke, that, with this second hint, he declined our further acquaintance, and we were not the least grieved at losing such company.

On 26 March they sighted land. By the time they reached the surf, it was dark. Thomas Cubbin:

Soon after noon, we got a light breeze of wind, but still we pulled all we could, striving to get to land before dark, for I warned that there would be a heavy surf on the coast, although I had never been there; for this coast of the Island being exposed to the south-east trade wind, must certainly have a surf we pulled hard with what strength there was in us. At sunset, it was the mate's turn steering, I was at the oars. He called to me, saying, it was time I came to steer her in. I went, but I told them I was sorry to have to say we were yet much over a mile from the surf. I scanned the coast. Along it there was one unbroken line of surf; I took a bearing of the place where the surf broke nearest the shore, and steered for that spot. We got in close to the surf when it was getting dark. I told them it would be better for us to keep out for the night, and have daylight to run it, when they all cried out that they could not live until the morning, my poor wife also saying that neither the child or her could live to see the morning light. When I found remonstrance had no effect, I said, "Stop the oars, and let us make our arrangements." I reminded the mate that he had always promised, if he were saved himself; he would save the child James. I knew he was a splendid swimmer. The two children were passed forward to where he was at the oar, the eldest sitting and holding the little fellow on his knees.

I appealed to them to act like men at the last – to try and save my children, and help each other, saying, at the same time, I would look after my wife. I put a swimming belt on her, the only one we had, and that she had brought herself and I placed her on the thwart next to myself. These arrangements made, I told them to give way on the oars; our dear little boy cried bitterly. The elder said, "Hush, Jimmy, darling; plenty of water in a few minutes," and commenced singing the evening hymn. As soon as we got on the back of the surf my wife said, "Turn back." I replied, "Too late, Mary, give way men, life or death." The first breaker we came to, I saw, would be fatal to our boat, and called out, "We are gone." I could have leaped and cleared the boat, but there were others that I cared for more than myself. The boat turned upon us, and we were a short time under her. I confess I was unable to assist my wife in that position. I was first from under and got out at the stern, I was swimming after her, and from that position could see all. The boy Clarke came from under next, and immediately my wife, on the opposite side. I called to them to get hold of her keel; while I spoke, the boy Radcliffe came out beside Clarke. I could see my wife could not hold long; she had lost hold with one hand. I called to the boys that each should get hold of her hands across the boat. They answered me and did so. Stout was holding on at fore part.

Immediately afterwards I had hold, and was just at my wife's side, reaching to take hold of her, when the boat turned over again. We were then all four thrown together, my wife and the boys keeping fast hold of each other, I told them to hold fast, and was behind them swimming, and pushing them in before me. Not more than one minute from this, the boat either turned again, or fell off the sea upon me, giving me a fearful blow, which dislocated some of my ribs. Very shortly after my feet touched ground, between the seas. I then shifted my position, got before them, dragging them in as the sea came, and holding against the drawback.

Soon after Stout was rushing in past; I caught hold of him by the waistband of his trousers. He shouted, and screamed to let him go, or he would be drowned. I said, "No! you pull away, my wife and the two boys are drowning," but still he screamed. A very heavy sea passed over us; it loosened my hold on them, and while mending my grip on them I lost his waistband, grasped again, and caught his shirt, he all the time screaming, made a wrench, and left part of his shirt in my hand, and was rushing in through the surf. I thought when he got to the beach, he would turn back to assist us.

We were all the time getting nearer in, with hard struggling, for the drawback was very strong. I knew my wife was in the group I was dragging, but I did not know whether she and Radcliffe were living or dead, both having lost their footing; while looking after the retreating form of Stout, pass up the beach and out of sight, I saw a large man walking along the beach line past us. There was still a little light in the Western sky, that enabled me to see that he was perfectly naked. I thought it was a native, and called out, "Who is that walking along the beach there?" I got the answer, "It is me, sir." I was astonished, for I recognised the voice to be the mate's. "What you," I said, "walking past and looking at my wife and these boys perishing, if not dead already, come down and help me." At that call he came down, but by the time he got to us, we were near the beach. He helped to carry my wife clear of the water, the boys crawled up with us. As soon as we laid her down, not knowing whether living or dead, I thought the first time about my children. Asked him where they were, thinking he had got them ashore. "They are lost, I suppose," he said. "What," I said, "is that all you know about them?" and rushed out into the surf again near to the boat, which was tumbling about, but could see nothing clinging to her. I returned with a sad heart, and accused him of having deserted my poor children. "At the last, oh! miserable cowards all." He said, "Be thankful, sir, you have got your wife." I said, "I know I have got her, either dead or alive, but I have no need to thank you for that; you were passing by looking at me struggling with the three, and would not come down to help until you saw they were through the surf; and not then, until I called you to help in bringing them." While speaking, I was examining if my wife was alive, and found her still breathing. He said, my children were not the only ones, that Thomas Hall was also lost.

We carried my wife further up the beach, where the shore-bank projected and afforded a little shelter, and laid her down on the sand. I opened her dress, and tended as well as I could, and she soon showed signs of life. Stout had made his way to this place, and was lying not far off. I accused him of his miserable, cowardly conduct, in making off from us in the surf leaving a piece of his shirt in my hand, whilst I was struggling to save the three, and not even turning round to see if we got through. He said, "At such a time as that, it was every man for himself." "You mean, contemptible heap of humanity!" I replied, "You are not worthy to be called a man."

We scraped some holes in the sand, as deep as we could, to find water. We then knelt down and prayed, thanking God that He had permitted us to land, and acknowledging His chastening hand in those He had taken away from us. We afterwards examined the holes we had made in the sand, but found no appearance of water. The mate went down the beach to try what he could find that might wash up from the boat; he found the blanket and ensign which we had used for sails. I took the blanket to cover my wife; the ensign he took to wrap round himself for he was perfectly nude of everything except shoes. He went again, and found our Bible and the pint bottle that yet had a little wine in it; when he returned, my wife was rallying to consciousness. I must do him the justice to state, that he gave me the bottle with a spoonful of wine in it for her, which I put into her mouth. If the night before was a miserable one, I cannot explain how wretched this night was. We wished for the morning light, yet did not know what to expect when it came.

They managed to squeeze some water out of the trees which appear to have been a kind of cactus known as a traveller's tree. They made contact with some natives who gave them water and a little boiled rice.

On 27 March, they received help from two natives of Mauritius, a Mr Liger and a Mr Raphel. Mr Raphel spoke English. On 3 April Cubbin was shown the remains of his eldest son. They were reunited with the members of the crew who had been in the other boat. On 4 April they buried the remains of their son and began a journey by canoe and by foot to the capital, Tamatave. There was a British consulate in Tamatave. They arrived in Tamatave on 16 April. The rest of the crew arrived on 28 April. On 30 April they took passage in a vessel carrying bullocks to Mauritius. It was an old vessel. It spent three days rolling in the harbour of Tamatave. Thomas Cubbin:

Sunday 3 May

At an early hour, the captain came on board, and said he would sail. Miserable as it was to us lying there, we should very much have liked him to put it off until the next day, remembering how unfortunate our last Sunday sailing had been; but we had no voice in the matter, being merely passengers. So, away we went past the reefs and surf, and glad we were when we got clear of our enemy's awful noise. The wind was a brisk breeze from the south, and the weather cloudy. The bullocks seemed to stand it well, for stand they must; if any of them attempted to lie down, the men on watch beat them until they got up again. During the day they were served with some water and hay.

4 May

Strong breeze from the southward, and cloudy weather. Bullocks are better sailors than I thought they would have been. There was nothing of importance occurred except splitting some of the sails, and carrying away the gear, which did not require much force of wind to effect it.

5 May

We had a strong breeze from the Southward, and cloudy weather. The bullocks were standing well, but there was two deaths among them, the carcasses were cast into the sea.

There was no attempt made to clean, and the reader may imagine how foul an atmosphere we had to breathe.

6 May

We had a brisk breeze from S.W., and gloomy weather. I did not at all like the appearance of the weather. The barometer, like nearly everything else on board, was French, and I could not read it, but could see, by the position of the mercury, that it was rather low; but still there was the thought, it is the month of May. The fall in the barometer may be for rain.

7 May

Commenced a moderate breeze from S, S.W., and gloomy. I did not like the appearance of the weather, although it was the month of May. I spoke to the captain, explaining as well as I could my opinion of things in general, and pointed to the barometer. He admitted it was very low, but said, "Hurricane no month May." During the evening, the wind decreased to a very moderate breeze, but the appearance of the weather was worse, and the barometer still falling. I spoke again to the captain, and advised that we should run northward, and try to avoid the coming storm. He said, "If it were the stormy season, he would do so, but month of May no hurricane." We retired, but not to sleep, I was going about most of the night. The barometer still falling.

8 May

At 1 a.m. I went up on the poop. It was the chief mate's watch. He and my late chief were having a long talk, their bodies being placed in a very comfortable position. The wind at the time was a very moderate breeze from the westward; but the weather looked very bad. I asked the mate of the ship where the captain was. He replied that he was in bed. I asked if he knew how low the barometer was. He said, it was no lower than the evening before. I said, be the barometer how it would, the weather looked very bad, and it was full time that he was on deck, attending to his duty.

He took no notice of my expressions, but quietly resumed the conversation.

I suppose, thinking it was the month of May, and being in the vicinity of where he was born, thought he knew more about the weather I did. I went below; my wife enquired how I thought the weather looked. I said that it looked very bad, and it would, before long, burst upon us; and related the manner in which I was insulted by the mate of the ship. She asked me if I would call the captain; I said I would not. He had no right to be asleep at such a time, and if let alone, he might wake to find his masts alongside. She said, "I will call him," and had him out quick.

I pointed to him the barometer, and the appearance of the weather, and made him understand that I thought it was full time for him to prepare his ship for the worst. He said he would shorten sail, but hurricane no month May. He went on deck, and commenced taking in the small sails, for the old ship had all possible sail set. Our brave captain was none too soon in reducing his canvas, for, by the time he had got in the small sails, the wind commenced to pipe, and he still reduced. At daybreak, the wind was rapidly increasing. As soon as we had daylight, although the crew did not understand English, I easily made them understand the danger of the great openings in the deck. While the captain was commanding on the poop, I took the liberty of giving orders on the main deck, in laying spars and planks across the openings, and sails to cover over at hand.

At 9 a.m. the main topsail was taken in, the old ship was then running under the lower fore topsail. I had often to go in and see my wife; indeed, I told her there was very little hope, and we both wished we had gone with our children in the surf. We prayed together, supposing it would be the last time; after which, I went on deck to see that the men were standing by the rails, ready to cover up the openings. The lightning flashed, and thunder roared, the fore topsail burst into shreds. I called out to the men to cover up, they attended to my order, assisted myself and told them that if the ship broached to before these openings were secured, and shipped one sea, we would all be lost. The covering up was death to all the bullocks below.

I told my wife there was again a little hope. So much thunder and lightning denoted the storm to be of the cyclone character, and would not last long. At this time the steward came for the Limas, saying the captain wanted to destroy them; we did not share in their superstition, and were not prepared to give them up; but he said the sailors will do no more until they are killed. Then I said, "Take them." I went to see what they did with the Limas. The second mate took them, swung each three times round his head, then dashed them with all his strength on the deck, and threw them into the sea. The ship soon after broached to on the starboard tack, which was the proper tack for our position; but she shipped a large quantity of water. The ship was laying very badly along. The captain and crew seemed to have lost all presence of mind, and left the poor old ship to her fate. I and my late chief mate went on the poop, and for the time being took charge, and whole of the crew willingly obeying my orders; braced the yards, got relieving tackles on the rudder-head, and a storm sail in the mizzen rigging, to keep ship's head to wind, means that they evidently had never before seen adopted.

It was a very severe cyclone, and the old ship laboured and strained heavily. The captain and his officers were often slipping down into the cabin, and were drinking deep; the effect of which was soon apparent upon them; I suppose their idea was to die gloriously drunk. My wife found an opportunity of speaking to the steward, telling him not to let them have any more, or the ship would be lost. He acted on this advice, and told them all the strong drink was broken and lost. We got the ship trimmed about noon, when I urged the captain to have the deckload of bullocks thrown overboard, many of them at that time being almost dead, with broken limbs, and lying in heaps, gored by falling upon each other, and altogether in an awful state. He agreed, and part of the crew were told off for that duty, the remainder working the pumps, for there was a great deal of water in the ship.

It was a fearful afternoon, blowing very hard, vivid flashes of lightning, peals of thunder, and a deluge of rain, but in this phenomena was our hope, that it would not last so long as the dreaded hurricane. Before sunset, the atmosphere began to break, and it was apparent that the heaviest of the storm was past. The old ship was in a most deplorable state, the hurricane or spar deck had given way, and all fallen in. The groans of bullocks below, that were dying of suffocation, and otherwise, the filth, the stench, the spars flying about, expecting every moment that the whole of her spars would go over the side. She had eased herself of some of the small spars. The old ship looked an awful wreck. Before dark, half the deck load of bullocks was thrown overboard, and it was impossible to get at any more, through the spar deck that had fallen having blocked them up. The bullocks below did not groan very long, their noise ended soon after dark. But the awful effluvias that arose were unbearable in the cabin, where all was in a heterogeneous mass.

From the setting of the sun, the weather gradually moderated, and very glad we were to find it so, for the old ship would not have stood much more; as it was, she laboured and strained heavily all night, and was making a great deal of water. Both pumps were constantly going, and still I think the water was gaining. To breathe in the cabin doorway was a difficulty, and every moment the foul odours were increasing. At midnight, the wind was north, and all the while moderating. At daybreak, the wind was N.E. As soon as possible I got my wife up on the poop, the only place where it was possible to get a little sweet air. After a little consultation, it was decided to let the old ship run; our course being to the S.W.; but it was requisite to find sails to run with, the old fore topmast staysail, that had been in the mizen rigging was taken down to bend, in place of one that had been blown to pieces. The foresail had been saved by furling it in time. These two sails were set, and the old ship put before the wind. Orders were then given to loose and set the lower main topsail, but when they went aloft for that purpose, found the main topmast badly sprung in the doublings; secured it with a chain, what seamen call a Spanish cap, and afterwards set the sail.

9 May

Some time after daylight, the weather cleared off a little, and we were thankful to the Almighty when the sun once more shone out upon us. The old ship by daylight did look a miserable wreck. Of the bullocks that remained on deck, some were dead and some dying, with the wreck of the spar deck lying upon them, and only some fourteen or sixteen of the whole cargo were saved alive. There was still a great deal of water in the ship, and both pumps were constantly going. We had good hopes again, if she could only be cleared of the water that was in her. At the best, our living on board the bullocker was very coarse; but during the storm the cookhouse and apparatus were smashed, and strewn amongst the debris on deck, so that cooking operations were entirely suspended; but they got some temporary arrangement, and by noon-day we had some breakfast prepared for us. We took ours on deck, for the stench was unbearable below; indeed, we had to remain all our time on the poop, until we arrived at Mauritius.

At noon, the old ship was bounding on her way with all possible sail set; and, by observation, we were eighty miles distant from that island. During the afternoon, the crew were employed at the pumps, and getting the dead bullocks overboard. From the time the hatches were opened, it is impossible to describe the awful stench. The crew of the bullocker no doubt are inured to filth and stench, but it was even too much for them, for several had to part with their breakfast much quicker than they liked. When darkness set in, the hatches were covered up, which was a little relief, but still it was unbearable in the cabin. During the evening the ship was pumped dry, which was a great relief to our minds.

At 11 p.m. we sighted the light on the island. The pumps were regularly attended during the night. Midnight, the wind decreased to a light breeze from the eastward.

10 May
Daylight, we sighted the land, which gladdened our hearts; for the old ship was very much disabled, and she had only two miserable small and old boats. With the daylight, the extreme stench was again opened to us by uncovering the hatches to get more of the dead carcasses overboard. A little before noon the hatches were covered up again, and about noon we anchored in the roads outside Port Louis. Soon after we had anchored, a pilot came alongside. I suppose he thought the old ship smelled too strong to be taken into port, for he would not come on board. However, the state of the ship was reported to him in a modified form. We also reported ourselves being on board, and wished to get out of the filth and stench as soon as possible. He promised to make the report, and immediately left. Soon afterwards, we had a heavy fall of rain; which lasted about one hour. The old awning we had spread, saved us very little from its force, yet it was more pleasant to get wet than endure the foul odours below.

About 2 p.m. the health visit came alongside. The doctor made a very short visit, no doubt feeling that the foul atmosphere on board the old ship was neither wholesome nor agreeable. When leaving, he made my wife and me the offer of a passage on shore with him, which we very gladly and thankfully accepted. While we were passing on shore, the harbour master had sent a small tug to convey us. They took all that was left of my late crew. On landing, Mr Morgan, the harbour master, and other officials, gave us a very kindly welcome to their port, and sympathized with us in our bereavement and distress. While speaking to them, the owner of the *Caprice* and the bullocks came up, asking me if I did not think the bullocks might have been saved. Saying, he thought the captain had too soon sealed their fate, and I suppose thinking, at the same time, that the bullocks had as much, if not more right than us to live. Considering they were his property, and the ship his own, I replied, that the only fault I could find with the captain was, that he spared the bullocks' lives too long, thereby very greatly endangering our own lives. He then very quickly made his exit.

Mr Morgan recommended us to put up at the sailors' home; where he said we would get apartments, and fare better than at any hotel in the place. He sent a person as our guide to that institution, where we arrived about 4 p.m. The superintendent, a British subject, and old shipmaster, received us very coolly, and long hesitated to accommodate us; but said we had better try some of the hotels. We told him we were perfect strangers, and who it was that did recommend us. But still he hesitated, saying, he had no apartments for us; but, after a long consideration, he sent us to look at a sleeping apartment. It was anything but grand, nor had it any appearance of respectability; yet on the whole it was more comfortable than any we had occupied for some time.

On 13 May a Board of Enquiry was held regarding the loss of the Serica. *It concluded that her abandonment was necessary and that nobody should be blamed. Thomas Cubbin, his wife and the two ship's boys sailed back to England on board the* Canopus, *an iron ship. They arrived at Plymouth on 8 September 1868.*

The Sinking of the *Titanic*
14 April 1912

The passenger steamship, Titanic, *left Queenstown on 11 April 1912. She was bound for New York on her maiden voyage. At 11.40 p.m. on 14 April she struck an iceberg which punctured 5 watertight compartments. By 2.20 a.m. she had sunk. She was carrying 1,316 passengers and 885 crew. The* Titanic *was owned by the White Star Line. The British and the Americans both held*

Courts of Inquiry into the disaster. The Wreck Commissioner, Lord Mersey, presided over the British Court of Inquiry. The other assessors were mainly experienced naval officers. Many of the following accounts are taken from the report of the Inquiry which was based on the testimonies of survivors:

At 9 a.m., 1.42 p.m. and 1.45 p.m. on 14 April, the *Titanic* received wireless messages warning of ice. At 7.30 p.m. she picked up a fourth message from the SS *Californian* to the SS *Antillian*. It reported "three large bergs to southward of us".

The wireless operator, Harold Bride, did not remember to which officer he delivered this message. The report continued:

At 9.40 p.m. the *Titanic* received another warning from a steamer called the *Mesaba*. It included an "Ice report in lat. 42° N to 41° 25' N, long. 49° to long. 50° 30' W. Saw much heavy pack ice and great number large icebergs. Also field ice. Weather 'good clear'." The report of the Inquiry concluded that this warning never reached any of the *Titanic*'s officers. At the time, the wireless operator was very busy with transmitting and receiving messages to and from the passengers.

The Titanic *made its entire passage at high speed. At the time of the collision, the report concluded it was making an average speed of 22 knots. The report described the collision with the iceberg:*

Mr Lightoller turned over the ship to Mr Murdoch, the first officer, at 10 o'clock, telling him that the ship was within the region where ice had been reported. He also told him of the message he had sent to the crow's nest, and of his conversation with the Master, and of the latter's orders.

The ship appears to have run on, on the same course, until, at a little before 11.40, one of the look-outs in the crow's-nest struck three blows on the gong, which was the accepted warning for something ahead, following this immediately afterwards by a telephone message to the bridge "Iceberg right ahead". Almost simultaneously with the three-gong signal Mr Murdoch, the officer of the watch, gave the order "hard-a-starboard", and immediately telegraphed down to the engine-room, "Stop. Full speed astern." The helm was already "hard over," and the ship's head had fallen off about two points to port, when she collided with an iceberg well forward on her starboard side.

Mr Murdoch at the same time pulled the lever over which closed the watertight doors in the engine and boiler rooms.

These watertight doors dropped vertically, by gravity, and were controlled by an electro magnetic switch. The report continued:

The Master "rushed out" on to the bridge and asked Mr Murdoch what the ship had struck.

Mr Murdoch replied: "An iceberg, Sir. I hard-a-starboarded and reversed the engines, and I was going to hard-a-port round it but she was too close. I could not do any more. I have closed the watertight doors."

Robert Hichens, Quartermaster, described:

All went along very well until 20 minutes to 12, when three gongs came from the lookout, and immediately afterwards a report on the telephone, "Iceberg right ahead." The Chief Officer (First Officer Murdoch) rushed from the wing to the bridge. He rushed to the engines. I heard the telegraph bell ring, also give the order "Hard-a-starboard". The sixth officer repeated the order, "The helm is hard-a-starboard, sir." But during the time, she was crushing the ice, or we could hear the grinding noise along the ship's bottom. I heard the telegraph ring. The skipper came rushing out of his room – Captain Smith – and asked, "What is that?" Mr Murdoch said, "An iceberg."

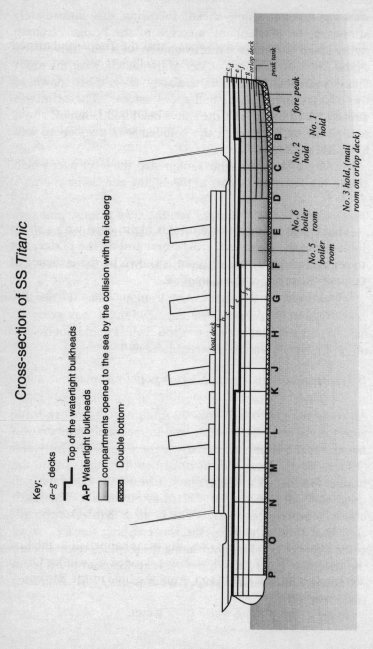

Cross-section of SS *Titanic*

Key:

a–g decks

⌐ Top of the watertight bulkheads

A-P Watertight bulkheads

▨ compartments opened to the sea by the collision with the iceberg

▨ Double bottom

boat deck

a
b
c
d
e
f
g

peak tank

fore peak

No. 1 hold

No. 2 hold

No. 3 hold, (mail room on orlop deck)

No. 6 boiler room

No. 5 boiler room

orlop deck

A B C D E F G H J K L M N O P

The report continued:

From the evidence given it appears that the *Titanic* had turned about two points to port before the collision occurred. From various experiments subsequently made with the SS *Olympic*, a sister ship to the *Titanic*, it was found that travelling at the same rate as the *Titanic*, about 37 seconds would be required for the ship to change her course to this extent after the helm had been put hard-a-starboard. In this time the ship would travel about 460 yards, and allowing for the few seconds that would be necessary for the order to be given, it may be assumed that 500 yards was about the distance at which the iceberg was sighted either from the bridge or crow's-nest.

That it was quite possible on this night, even with a sharp look-out at the stemhead, crow's-nest and on the bridge, not to see an iceberg at this distance is shown by the evidence of Captain Rostron, of the *Carpathia*.

The injuries to the ship . . . were of such a kind that she foundered in two hours and forty minutes.

The report described the damage to the Titanic*:*

The collision with the iceberg, which took place at 11.40 p.m., caused damage to the bottom of the starboard side of the. vessel at about 10 feet above the level of the keel, but there was no damage above this height. There was damage in: – The fore peak, No. 1 hold, No. 2 hold, No. 3 hold, No. 6 boiler room, No. 5 boiler room.

The damage extended over a length of about 300 ft.

As the ship was moving at over 20 knots, she would have passed through 800 ft. in less than 10 seconds, so that the damage was done in about this time.

At first it is desirable to consider what happened in the first 10 minutes. The forepeak was not flooded above the Orlop deck – i.e., the peak tank top, from the hole in the bottom of the peak tank.

In No. 1 hold there was 7 ft. of water.

In No. 2 hold five minutes after the collision water was seen rushing in at the bottom of the firemen's passage on the starboard side, so that the ship's side was damaged abaft of bulkhead B sufficiently to open the side of the firemen's passage, which was 34 ft. from the outer skin of the ship, thereby flooding both the hold and the passage.

In No. 3 hold the mail room was filled soon after the collision. The floor of the mail room is 24 ft. above the keel.

Norman Chambers, a first class passenger, described:

... I looked at the starboard end of our passageway, where there was the companion leading to the quarters of the mail clerks and farther on to the baggage room, and I believe, the mail sorting room, and at the top of these stairs I found a couple of mail clerks wet to their knees, who had just come up from below, bringing their registered mail bags. As the door in the bulkhead in the next deck was open, I was able to look directly into the trunk room which was then filled with water, and within 18 inches or 2 feet of the deck above. We were standing there joking about our baggage being completely soaked and about the correspondence which was seen floating about on the top of the water. While we were standing there three of the ship's officers descended the first companion and looked into the baggage room, coming back up immediately, saying that we were not making any more water. This was not an announcement, but merely a remark passed from one to the other. Then my wife and myself returned in the direction of our stateroom, a matter of a few yards only, and as we were going down our own alleyway to the stateroom door our room steward came by and told us that we could go on back to bed again, that there was no danger.

The report continued:

In No. 6 boiler room, when the collision took place, water at once poured in at about 2 feet above the stokehold plates, on the starboard side, at the after end of the boiler room. Some of the firemen immediately went through the watertight door opening to No. 5 boiler room because the water was flooding the place. The watertight doors in the engine-rooms were shut from the bridge almost immediately after the collision. Ten minutes later it was found that there was water to the height of 8 feet above the double bottom in No.6 boiler room.

No. 5 boiler room was damaged at the ship's side in the starboard forward bunker at a distance of 2 feet above the stokehold plates, at 2 feet from the watertight bulkhead between Nos. 5 and 6 boiler rooms. Water poured in at that place as it would from an ordinary fire hose. At the time of the collision this bunker had no coal in it. The bunker door was closed when water was seen to be entering the ship.

In No. 4 boiler room there was no indication of any damage at the early stages of the sinking.

It will thus be seen that all the six compartments forward of No. 4 boiler room were open to the sea by damage which existed at about 10 feet above the keel. At 10 minutes after the collision the water seems to have risen to about 14 feet above the keel in all these compartments except No. 5 boiler room. After the first ten minutes, the water rose steadily in all these six compartments. The fore peak above the peak tank was not filled until an hour after the collision when the vessel's bow was submerged to above C deck. The water then flowed in from the top through the deck scuttle forward of the collision bulkhead. It was by this scuttle that access was obtained to all the decks below C down to the peak tank top on the orlop deck.

At 12 o'clock water was coming up in No. 1 hatch. It was getting into the firemen's quarters and driving the firemen out. It was rushing round No. 1 hatch on G deck and coming mostly from the starboard side, so that in 20 minutes the water had risen above G deck in No. 1 hold.

In No. 2 hold about 40 minutes after the collision the water was coming in to the seamen's quarters on F deck through a burst fore and aft wooden bulkhead of a third-class cabin opposite the seamen's wash place. Thus, the water had risen in No. 2 hold to about 3 ft. above F deck in 40 minutes.

In No. 3 hold the mail room was afloat about 20 minutes after the collision. The bottom of the mail room which is on the Orlop deck, is 24 feet above the keel.

The watertight doors on F deck at the fore and after ends of No. 3 compartment were not closed then.

The mail room was filling and water was within 2 ft. of G deck, rising fast, when the order was given to clear the boats.

There was then no water on F deck.

There is a stairway on the port side on G deck which leads down to the first-class baggage room on the Orlop deck immediately below. There was water in this baggage room 25 minutes after the collision. Half an hour after the collision water was up to G deck in the mail room.

Thus the water had risen in this compartment to within 2 ft. of G deck in 20 minutes, and above G deck in 25 to 30 minutes.

No. 6 boiler room was abandoned by the men almost immediately after the collision. Ten minutes later the water had risen to 8 ft. above the top of the double bottom, and probably reached the top of the bulkhead at the after end of the compartment, at the level of F deck, in about one hour after the collision.

In No. 5 boiler room there was no water above the stoke-hold plates, until a rush of water came through the pass between the boilers from the forward end, and drove the leading stoker out.

It has already been shown in the description of what happened in the first ten minutes, that water was coming into No. 5 boiler room in the forward starboard bunker at 2 ft. above the plates in a stream about the size of a deck hose. The door in this bunker had been dropped probably when water was first discovered, which was a few minutes after the collision. This would cause the water to be retained in the bunker until it rose high enough to burst the door which was weaker than the bunker bulkhead. This happened about an hour after the collision.

No. 4 boiler room. – One hour and 40 minutes after collision water was coming in forward, in No. 4 boiler room, from underneath the floor in the forward part, in small quantities. The men remained in that stokehold till ordered on deck.

Nos. 3, 2 and 1 boiler rooms. – When the men left No. 4 some of them went through Nos. 3, 2 and 1 boiler rooms into the reciprocating engine room, and from there on deck. There was no water in the boiler rooms abaft No. 4 one hour 40 minutes after the collision (1.20 a.m.), and there was then none in the reciprocating and turbine engine rooms.

Electrical engine room and tunnels. – There was no damage to these compartments.

From the foregoing it follows that there was no damage abaft No. 4 boiler room.

All the watertight doors aft of the main engine room were opened after the collision.

Half an hour after the collision the watertight doors from the engine room to the stokehold were opened as far forward as they could be to No. 4 boiler room.

The later stages of the sinking cannot be stated with any precision, owing to a confusion of the times which was natural under the circumstances.

The forecastle deck was not under water at 1.35 a.m. Distress signals were fired until two hours after the collision (1.45 a.m.). At this time the fore deck was under water. The forecastle head was not then submerged though it was getting close down to the water, about half an hour before she disappeared (1.50 a.m.).

Third Officer Herbert Pitman described the firing of the distress signals:

I should say about a dozen rockets were fired. They were fired from the rail. They make a report while leaving the rail, and also an explosion in the air, and they throw stars, of course, in the air.

The Titanic *was equipped with twenty lifeboats, including four Engelhardt collapsible boats. The 14 regular lifeboats could each carry 65 persons. The four Engelhardt collapsible boats could each carry 47 persons. The two cutters, or emergency boats, could each carry 40 persons. Consequently, if each lifeboat was full, there was room for 1,178 persons. Under the maritime regulations of the time: the number of lifeboats carried was based upon the tonnage of the ship not upon the number of people aboard. There had been no compulsory boat drills.*

Colonel Archibald Gracie, an American first-class passenger, recounted the experience of Mrs J. J. Brown of Denver, Colorado, which she had told him:

Instead of retiring to slumber, Mrs Brown was absorbed in reading and gave little thought to the crash at her window overhead which threw her to the floor. Picking herself up, she proceeded to see what the steamer had struck; but thinking nothing serious had occurred, though realizing that the engines had stopped immediately after the crash and the boat was at a standstill, she picked up her book and began reading again. Finally she saw her curtains moving while she was reading, but no one was visible. She again looked out and saw a man whose face was blanched, his eyes protruding, wearing the look of a haunted creature. He was gasping for breath and in an undertone gasped, "Get your life-preserver." He was one of the buyers for Gimbel Bros, of Paris and New York.

She got down her life-preserver, snatched up her furs and hurriedly mounted the stairs to A Deck, where she found passengers putting on life-belts like hers. Mrs Bucknell approached and whispered, "Didn't I tell you something was going to happen?" She found the lifeboats lowered from the falls and made flush with the deck. Madame de Villiers appeared from below in a nightdress and evening slippers, with no stockings. She wore a long woollen motorcoat. Touching Mrs Brown's arm, in a terrified voice she said she was going below for her money and valuables. After much persuasion Mrs Brown prevailed upon her not to do so, but to get into the boat. She hesitated and became very much excited, but was finally prevailed upon to enter the lifeboat. Mrs Brown was walking away, eager to see what was being done elsewhere. Suddenly she saw a shadow and a few seconds later someone seized her, saying: "You are going, too," and she was dropped fully four feet into the lowering lifeboat. There was but one man in charge of the boat. As it was lowered by jerks by an officer above, she discovered that a great gush of water was spouting through the porthole from D Deck, and the lifeboat was in grave danger of being submerged. She immediately grasped an oar and held the lifeboat away from the ship.

When the sea was reached, smooth as glass, she looked up and saw the benign, resigned countenance, the venerable white hair and the Chesterfieldian bearing of the beloved Captain Smith with whom she had crossed twice before, and only three months previous on the *Olympic*. He peered down upon those in the boat, like a solicitous father, and directed them to row to the light in the distance – all boats keeping together.

Because of the fewness of men in the boat she found it necessary for someone to bend to the oars. She placed her oar in an oarlock and asked a young woman nearby to hold one while she placed the other on the further side. To Mrs. Brown's surprise, the young lady immediately began to row like a galley slave, every stroke counting. Together they managed to pull away from the steamer.

By this time E and C Decks were completely submerged. Those ladies who had husbands, sons or fathers on the doomed steamer buried their heads on the shoulders of those near them and moaned and groaned. Mrs Brown's eyes were glued on the fast-disappearing ship. Suddenly there was a rift in the water, the sea opened up and the surface foamed like giant arms and spread around the ship and the vessel disappeared from sight, and not a sound was heard.

Mrs Charlotte Collyer was a third-class passenger, who was rescued on lifeboat No. 14:

A little further on we saw a floating door that must have been torn loose when the ship went down. Lying upon it, face downward, was a small Japanese. He had lashed himself with a rope to his frail raft, using the broken hinges to make the knots secure. As far as we could see, he was dead. The sea washed over him every time the door bobbed up and down, and he was frozen stiff. He did not answer when he was hailed, and the officer hesitated about trying to save him.

"What's the use?" said Mr Lowe. "He's dead, likely, and if he isn't there's others better worth saving than a Jap!"

He had actually turned our boat around, but he changed his mind and went back. The Japanese was hauled on board, and one of the women rubbed his chest, while others chafed his hands and feet. In less time than it takes to tell, he opened his eyes. He spoke to us in his own tongue; then, seeing that we did not understand, he struggled to his feet, stretched his arms above his head, stamped his feet and in five minutes or so had almost recovered his strength. One of the sailors near to him was so tired that he could hardly pull his oar. The Japanese bustled over, pushed him from his seat, took his oar and worked like a hero until we were finally picked up. I saw Mr Lowe watching him in open-mouthed surprise.

"By Jove!" muttered the officer, "I'm ashamed of what I said about the little blighter. I'd save the likes o' him six times over if I got the chance."

The report continued:

When the last boat, lowered from davits (D), left the ship, A deck was under water, and water came up the stairway under the Boat deck almost immediately afterwards. After this the other port collapsible (B), which had been stowed on the officers' house, was uncovered, the lashings cut adrift, and she was swung round over the edge of the coamings of the deckhouse on to the Boat deck.

Elizabeth Shutes, a first-class passenger, described:

Our lifeboat, with 36 in it, began lowering to the sea. This was done amid the greatest confusion. Rough seamen all giving different orders. No officer aboard. As only one side of the ropes worked, the lifeboat at one time was in such a position that it seemed we must capsize in mid-air. At last the ropes worked together, and we drew nearer and nearer the black, oily water. The first touch of our lifeboat on that black sea came to me as a last good bye to life, and so we put off – a tiny boat on a great sea – rowed away from what had been a safe home for five days. The first wish on the part of all was to stay near the *Titanic*. We all felt so much safer near the ship. Surely such a vessel could not sink. I thought the danger must be exaggerated, and we could all be taken aboard again. But surely the outline of that great, good ship was growing less. The bow of the boat was getting black. Light after light was disappearing . . .

Lawrence Beesley was a second class passenger in lifeboat No. 13:

. . . And all the time we got closer to the sea and the exhaust roared nearer and nearer – until finally we floated with the ropes still holding us from above, the exhaust washing us away and the force of the tide driving us back against the side. The resultant of these three forces was that we were carried parallel to the ship, directly under the place where boat 15 would drop from her davits into the sea. Looking up we saw her already coming down rapidly from B deck; she must have filled almost immediately after ours. We shouted up, "Stop lowering 14" [He did not know the correct number of the boat at the time] and the crew and passengers in the boat

above, hearing us shout and seeing our position immediately
below them, shouted the same to the sailors on the boat deck;
but apparently they did not hear, for she dropped down foot
by foot – twenty feet, fifteen, ten – and a stoker and I in the
bows reached up and touched her bottom swinging above our
heads, trying to push away our boat from under her. It
seemed now as if nothing could prevent her dropping on us,
but at this moment another stoker sprang with his knife to the
ropes that still held us and I heard him shout, "One! Two!"
as he cut them through. The next moment we had swung
away from underneath 15, and were clear of her as she
dropped into the water in the space we had just before
occupied.

Fifth Officer Harold Lowe described:

Numbers 12, 14, and 16 were down about the same time. I
told Mr Moody that three boats had gone away and that an
officer ought to go with them. He said: 'You go.' There was
difficulty in lowering when I got near the water. I dropped
her about five feet because I was not going to take the chance
of being dropped down upon by somebody. While I was on
the Boat Deck, two men tried to jump into the boat. I chased
them out. We filled boats 14 and 16 with women and
children. Lightoller was there part of the time. They were all
women and children, barring one passenger, and he sneaked
in dressed like a woman. He had a shawl over his head. As I
was being lowered, I expected every moment that my boat
would be doubled up under my feet. I had overcrowded her,
but I knew that I had to take a certain amount of risk. I
thought if one additional body was to fall into that boat – that
slight additional weight might part the hooks, or carry away
something. So as we were coming down past the open decks,
I saw a lot of people all along the ship's rails. They were
glaring more or less like wild beasts, ready to spring. That is
why I yelled out to "look out" and let go, bang! . . . right
along the ship's side. There was a space I should say of about

three feet between the side of the boat and the ship's side, and as I went down I fired these shots without any intention of hurting anybody and with the positive knowledge that I did not hurt anybody. I fired, I think three times.

George Rowe, a crewman, described:

All the time my boat was being lowered the rubbing strake kept on catching on the rivets down the ship's side, and it was as much as we could do to keep her off. When the boat was in the water the well deck was submerged. It took us a good five minutes to lower the boat on account of this rubbing going down.

Hugh Woolner, a first-class passenger, described:

. . . the electric lights along the ceiling of A Deck were beginning to turn red, just a glow, a red sort of glow. So I said to Steffanson: "This is getting rather a tight corner. I do not like being inside these closed windows. Let us go out through the door at the end." And as we went out through the door the sea came in onto the deck at our feet. Then we hopped up onto the gunwale, preparing to jump out into the sea, because if we had waited a minute longer we should have been boxed in against the ceiling. And as we looked out we saw this collapsible, the last boat on the port side, being lowered right in front of our faces. It was full up to the bow, and I said to Steffanson: "There is nobody in the bows. Let us make a jump for it. You go first." And he jumped out and tumbled in head over heels into the bow, and I jumped too, and hit the gunwale with my chest, which had on this life preserver, of course, and I sort of bounced off the gunwale and caught the gunwale with my fingers, and slipped off backwards. As my legs dropped down I felt that they were in the sea. Then I hooked my right heel over the gunwale, and by this time Steffanson was standing up, and he caught hold of me and lifted me in. Then we looked over into the sea and saw a man swimming in the sea just beneath us, and pulled him in. By that time we were bumping against the side of the ship. She was going down pretty fast by the bow. We were exactly opposite the end of the glass windows on the A Deck.

The report continued:

Very shortly afterwards the vessel, according to Mr Lightoller's account, seemed to take a dive, and he just walked into the water. When he came to the surface all the funnels were above the water.

Second Officer Lightoller himself described:

Just then the ship took a slight but definite plunge – probably a bulkhead went – and the sea came rolling along up in a wave, over the steel-fronted bridge, along the deck below us, washing the people back in a dreadful huddled mass. Those that didn't disappear under the water right away instinctively started to clamber up that part of the deck still out of water, and work their way towards the stern, which was rising steadily out of the water as the bow went down. It was a sight that doesn't bear dwelling on – to stand there, above the wheelhouse, and on our quarters, watching the frantic struggles to climb up the sloping deck, utterly unable to even hold out a helping hand.

George Crowe, a dining room steward, described:

After getting clear of the ship the lights were still burning very bright, but as we got away she seemed to go lower and lower, and she almost stood up perpendicular . . .

Edward Buley, Able Seaman, described:

She went down as far as the afterfunnel, and then there was a little roar, as though the engines had rushed forward, and she snapped in two, and the bow part went down and the afterpart came up . . . She uprighted herself for about five minutes, and then tipped over and disappeared.

The passengers Colonel Archibald Gracie and James Clinch Smith attempted to help launching the collapsible, Engelhardt boats. Colonel Gracie described:

I was now working with the crew at the davits on the starboard side forward, adjusting them ready for lowering the Engelhardt boat from the roof of the officers' house to the Boat Deck below. Some one of the crew on the roof, where it was, sang out, "Has any passenger a knife?" I took mine out of my pocket and tossed it to him, saying, "Here is a small penknife, if that will do any good." It appeared to me then that there was more trouble than there ought to have been in removing the canvas cover and cutting the boat loose, and that some means should have been available for doing this without any delay. Meantime, four or five long oars were placed aslant against the walls of the officers' house to break the fall of the boat, which was pushed from the roof and slipped with a crash down on the Boat Deck, smashing several of the oars. Clinch Smith and I scurried out of the way and stood leaning with our backs against the rail, watching this procedure and feeling anxious lest the boat might have been stove in, or otherwise injured so as to cause her to leak in the water. The account of the junior Marconi operator, Harold S. Bride, supplements mine. "I saw a collapsible boat," he said, "near a funnel, and went over to it. Twelve men were trying to boost it down to the Boat Deck. They were having an awful time. It was the last boat left. I looked at it longingly a few minutes, then I gave a hand and over she went."

About this time I recall that an officer on the roof of the house called down to the crew at this quarter, "Are there any seamen down there among you?" "Aye, aye, sir," was the response, and quite a number left the Boat Deck to assist in what I supposed to have been the cutting loose of the other Engelhardt boat up there on the roof. Again I heard an inquiry for another knife. I thought I recognized the voice of the second officer working up there with the crew. Lightoller has told me, and has written me as well, that "boat A on the starboard side did not leave the ship," while "B was thrown down to the Boat Deck," and was the one on which he and I eventually climbed. The crew had thrown the Engelhardt boat to the deck, but I did not understand why they were so long about launching it, unless they were waiting to cut the other one loose and launch them both at the same time. Two young men of the crew, nice looking, dressed in white, one tall and the other smaller, were coolly debating as to whether the compartments would hold the ship afloat. They were standing with their backs to the rail looking on at the rest of the crew, and I recall asking one of them why he did not assist.

At this time there were other passengers around, but Clinch Smith was the only one associated with me here to the last. It was about this time, fifteen minutes after the launching of the last lifeboat on the port side, that I heard a noise that spread consternation among us all. This was no less than the water striking the bridge and gurgling up the hatchway forward. It seemed momentarily as if it would reach the Boat Deck. It appeared as if it would take the crew a long time to turn the Engelhardt boat right side up and lift it over the rail, and there were so many ready to board her that she would have been swamped. Probably taking these points into consideration, Clinch Smith made the proposition that we should leave and go toward the stern, still on the starboard side, so he started and I followed immediately after him. We had taken but a few steps in the direction indicated when there arose before us from the decks below, a mass of humanity several lines deep, covering the Boat Deck, facing us, and completely blocking our passage toward the stern.

There were women in the crowd, as well as men, and they

seemed to be steerage passengers who had just come up from the decks below.

Olaus Abelseth was a third-class passenger:

I was standing there, and I asked my brother-in-law if he could swim and he said no. I asked my cousin if he could swim and he said no. So we could see the water coming up, the bow of the ship was going down, and there was kind of an explosion. We could hear the popping and cracking, and the deck raised up and got so steep that the people could not stand on their feet on the deck. So they fell down and slid on the deck into the water right on the ship.

Gracie continued:

Instantly, when they saw us and the water on the deck chasing us from behind, they turned in the opposite direction towards the stern. This brought them at that point plumb against the iron fence and railing which divide the first and second cabin passengers. Even among these people there was no hysterical cry, or evidence of panic, but oh, the agony of it! Clinch Smith and I instantly saw that we could make no progress ahead, and with the water following us behind over the deck, we were in a desperate place. I can never forget the exact point on the ship where he and I were located, viz., at the opening of the angle made by the walls of the officers' house and only a short distance abaft the *Titanic*'s forward "expansion joint". Clinch Smith was immediately on my left, nearer the apex of the angle, and our backs were turned toward the ship's rail and the sea.

Looking up toward the roof of the officers' house, I saw a man to the right of me and above lying on his stomach on the roof, with his legs dangling over. Clinch Smith jumped to reach this roof, and I promptly followed. The efforts of both of us failed. I was loaded down with heavy long-skirted overcoat and Norfolk coat beneath, with clumsy life-preserver over all, which made my jump fall short. As I came down, the water struck my right side. I crouched down into it preparatory to jumping with it, and rose as if on the crest of a wave on the seashore. This expedient brought the attainment of the object I had in view. I was able to reach the roof and the iron railing that is along the edge of it, and pulled myself over on top of the officers' house on my stomach near the base of the second funnel. The feat which I instinctively accomplished was the simple one, familiar to all bathers in the surf at the seashore. I had no time to advise Clinch Smith to adopt it. To my utter dismay, a hasty glance to my left and right showed that he had not followed my example, and that the wave, if I may call it such, which had mounted me to the roof, had completely covered him, as well as all people on both sides of me, including the man I had first seen athwart the roof.

With this second wind under water there came to me a new lease of life and strength, until finally I noticed by the increase of light that I was drawing near to the surface. Though it was not daylight, the clear star-lit night made a noticeable difference in the degree of light immediately below the surface of the water. As I was rising, I came in contact with ascending wreckage, but the only thing I struck of material size was a small plank, which I tucked under my right arm. This circumstance brought with it the reflection that it was advisable for me to secure what best I could to keep me afloat on the surface until succour arrived. When my head at last rose above the water, I detected a piece of wreckage like a wooden crate, and I eagerly seized it as a nucleus of the projected raft to be constructed from what flotsam and jetsam I might collect. Looking about me, I could see no *Titanic* in sight. She had entirely disappeared beneath the calm surface of the ocean and without a sign of any wave. That the sea had swallowed her up with all her precious belongings was indicated by the slight sound of a gulp behind me as the water closed over her. The length of time that I was under water can be estimated by the fact that

I sank with her, and when I came up there was no ship in sight. The accounts of others as to the length of time it took the *Titanic* to sink afford the best measure of the interval I was below the surface.

What impressed me at the time that my eyes beheld the horrible scene was a thin light-grey smoky vapour that hung like a pall a few feet above the broad expanse of sea that was covered with a mass of tangled wreckage. That it was a tangible vapour, and not a product of imagination, I feel well assured. It may have been caused by smoke or steam rising to the surface around the area where the ship had sunk. At any rate it produced a supernatural effect, and the pictures I had seen by Dante and the description I had read in my Virgil of the infernal regions, of Charon, and the River Lethe, were then uppermost in my thoughts. Add to this, within the area described, which was as far as my eyes could reach, there arose to the sky the most horrible sounds ever heard by mortal man except by those of us who survived this terrible tragedy. The agonizing cries of death from over a thousand throats, the wails and groans of the suffering, the shrieks of the terror-stricken and the awful gaspings for breath of those in the last throes of drowning, none of us will ever forget to our dying day. "Help! Help! Boat ahoy! Boat ahoy!" and "My God! My God!" were the heart-rending cries and shrieks of men, which floated to us over the surface of the dark waters continuously for the next hour, but as time went on, growing weaker and weaker until they died out entirely.

The report described what Gracie missed while he was underwater:

Her stern was gradually rising out of the water, and the propellers were clear of the water. The ship did not break in two: and she did eventually attain the perpendicular, when the second funnel from aft about reached the water. There were no lights burning then, though they kept alight practically until the last.

Before reaching the perpendicular when at an angle of 50

or 60 degrees, there was a rumbling sound which may be attributed to the boilers leaving their beds and crashing down on to or through the bulkheads. She became more perpendicular and finally absolutely perpendicular, when she went slowly down.

After sinking as far as the after part of the Boat deck she went down more quickly. The ship disappeared at 2.20 a.m.

The report made the observation that the flooding of the forward boiler room doomed her:

I am advised that the *Titanic* as constructed could not have remained afloat long with such damage as she received. Her bulkheads were spaced to enable her to remain afloat with any two compartments in communication with the sea. She had a sufficient margin of safety with any two of the compartments flooded which were actually damaged.

In fact any three of the four forward compartments could have been flooded by the damage received without sinking the ship to the top of her bulkheads.

Even if the four forward compartments had been flooded, the water would not have got into any of the compartments abaft of them, though it would have been above the top of some of the forward bulkheads. But the ship, even with these four compartments flooded, would have remained afloat. But she could not remain afloat with the four forward compartments and the forward boiler room (No. 6) also flooded.

The flooding of these five compartments alone would have sunk the ship sufficiently deeply to have caused the water to rise above the bulkhead at the after end of the forward boiler room (No. 6) and to flow over into the next boiler room (No. 5), and to fill it up until in turn its after bulkhead would be overwhelmed and the water would thereby flow over and fill No. 4 boiler room, and so on in succession to the other boiler rooms till the ship would ultimately fill and sink.

The report continued:

As soon as the dangerous condition of the ship was realised, messages were sent by the Master's orders to all steamers within reach. At 12.15 a.m. the distress signal C.Q.D. was sent. This was heard by several steamships and by Cape Race. By 12.25, Mr Boxall, the fourth officer, had worked out the correct position of the *Titanic*, and then another message was sent: *Come at once, we have struck a berg.* This was heard by the Cunard steamer *Carpathia*, which was at this time bound from New York to Liverpool and 58 miles away. The *Carpathia* answered, saying that she was coming to the assistance of the *Titanic*. This was reported to Captain Smith on the Boat deck. At 12.26 a message was sent out, "Sinking; cannot hear for noise of steam." Many other messages were also sent, but as they were only heard by steamers which were too far away to render help it is not necessary to refer to them. At 1.45 a message was heard by the *Carpathia*, "Engine room full up to boilers." The last message sent out was "C.Q.," which was faintly heard by the steamer *Virginian*. This message was sent at 2.17. It thus appears that the Marconi apparatus was at work until within a few minutes of the foundering of the *Titanic*.

The report continued:

At 12.35 the message from the *Carpathia* was received announcing that she was making for the *Titanic*. This probably became known and may have tended to make the passengers still more unwilling to leave the ship, and the lights of a ship (the *Californian*) which were seen by many people may have encouraged the passengers to hope that assistance was at hand. These explanations are perhaps sufficient to account for so many of the lifeboats leaving without a full boat load; but I think, nevertheless, that if the boats had been kept a little longer before being lowered, or if the after gangway doors had been opened, more passengers might have been induced to enter the boats. And if women could not be induced to enter the boats, the boats ought then to have been filled up with men. It is difficult to account for so many of the lifeboats being sent from the sinking ship, in a smooth sea, far from full. These boats left behind them many hundreds of lives to perish. I do not, however, desire these observations to be read as casting any reflection on the officers of the ship or on the crew who were working on the Boat deck. They all worked admirably, but I think that if there had been better organization the results would have been more satisfactory.

Charles Hendricksen, a fireman, was in No. 1 lifeboat:

When the ship sank we picked up nobody. The passengers would not listen to our going back. Of the twelve in the boat, seven were of the crew. Symons, who was in charge, said nothing and we all kept our mouths shut. None of the crew objected to going back. It was a woman who objected, Lady Duff Gordon, who said we would be swamped. People screaming for help could be heard by everyone in our boat. I suggested going back. Heard no one else do so. Mr Duff Gordon upheld his wife.

After we got on the *Carpathia* Gordon sent for them all and said he would make them a present. I was surprised to receive five pounds from him the day after docking in New York.

Another fireman, R. W. Pusey, recounted:

After the ship went down we heard cries for a quarter of an hour, or twenty minutes. Did not go back in the direction the *Titanic* had sunk. I heard one of the men say: "We have lost our kit," and then someone said: "Never mind, we will give you enough to get a new kit." I was surprised that no one suggested going back. I was surprised that I did not do so, but we were all half dazed. It does occur to me now that we might have gone back and rescued some of the strugglers. I heard Lady Duff Gordon say to Miss Francatelli: "You have lost your beautiful nightdress," and I said: "Never mind, you have saved your lives; but we have lost our kit;" and then Sir Cosmo offered to provide us with new ones.

Mr A. Clement Edwards, MP, Counsel for the Dock Workers' Union, brought a charge against Sir Cosmo Duff Gordon at the British inquiry:

Here was a boat only a short distance from the ship, so near that the cries of those struggling in the water could be heard. Symons had been told to stand by the ship, and that imposed upon him a specific duty. It was shown in Hendricksen's evidence that there was to the fullest knowledge of those in the boat a large number of people in the water, and that someone suggested that they should return and try to rescue them. Then it was proved that one of the ladies, who was shown to be Lady Duff Gordon, had said that the boat might be swamped if they went back, and Sir Cosmo Duff Gordon had admitted that this also represented his mental attitude at the time. He (Mr Edwards) was going to say, and to say quite fearlessly, that a state of mind which could, while within the hearing of the screams of drowning people, think of so material a matter as the giving of money to replace kits was a state of mind which must have contemplated the fact that there was a possibility of rescuing some of these people, and the danger which might arise if this were attempted.

He was not going to say that there was a blunt, crude bargain, or a deal done with these men: "If you will not go back I will give you five pounds;" but he was going to suggest as a right and true inference that the money was mentioned at that time under these circumstances to give such a sense of ascendancy or supremacy to Sir Cosmo Duff Gordon in the boat that the view to which he gave expression that they should not go back would weigh more with the men than if he had given it as a piece of good advice. There were twenty-eight places on that boat and no one-on board had a right to save his own life by avoiding any possible risk involved in filling the vacant places. To say the least of it, it was most reprehensible that there should have been any offer of money calculated to influence the minds of the men or to seduce them from their duty.

The British inquiry decided:

I heard much evidence as to the conduct of the boats after the *Titanic* sank and when there must have been many struggling people in the water, and I regret to say that in my opinion some, at all events, of the boats failed to attempt to save lives when they might have done so, and might have done so successfully. This was particularly the case with boat No. 1. It may reasonably have been thought that the risk of making the attempt was too great; but it seems to me that if the attempt had been made by some of these boats it might have been the means of saving a few more lives. Subject to these few adverse comments, I have nothing but praise for both passengers and crew. All the witnesses speak well of their behaviour. It is to be remembered that the night was dark, the noise of the escaping steam was terrifying, the peril, though perhaps not generally recognized, was imminent and great, and many passengers who were unable to speak or to understand English, were being collected together and hurried into the boats.

Mr Edwards also charged Mr Bruce Ismay, Managing Director of the White Star Line, with failing to do his duty to the passengers when he himself abandoned ship:

Coming to Mr Ismay's conduct, Mr Edwards said it was clear that that gentleman had taken upon himself to assist in getting women and children into the boats. He had also admitted that when he left the *Titanic* he knew she was doomed, that there were hundreds of people in the ship, that he didn't know whether or not there were any women or children left, and that he did not even go to the other side of the Boat Deck to see whether there were any women and children waiting to go. Counsel submitted that a gentleman occupying the position of managing director of the company owning the *Titanic*, and who had taken upon himself the duty of assisting at the boats, had certain special and further duties beyond an ordinary passenger's duties, and that he had no more right to save his life at the expense of any single person on board that ship than the captain would have had. He [Mr Edwards] said emphatically that Mr Ismay did not discharge his duty at that particular moment by taking a careless glance around the starboard side of the Boat Deck. He was one of the few persons who at the time had been placed in a position of positive knowledge that the vessel was doomed, and it was his clear duty, under the circumstances, to see that someone made a search for passengers in other places than in the immediate vicinity of the Boat Deck.

Lord Mersey: Moral duty to you mean?

Mr Edwards: I agree; but I say that a managing director going on board a liner, commercially responsible for it and taking upon himself certain functions, had a special moral obligation and duty more than is possessed by one passenger to another passenger.

Lord Mersey: But how is a moral duty relative to this inquiry? It might be argued that there was a moral duty for every man on board that every woman should take precedence, and I might have to inquire whether every passenger carried out his moral duty.

The British inquiry decided:

As to the attack on Mr Bruce Ismay, it resolved itself into the suggestion that, occupying the position of Managing Director of the Steamship Company, some moral duty was imposed upon him to wait on board until the vessel foundered. I do not agree. Mr Ismay, after rendering assistance to many passengers, found "C" collapsible, the last boat on the starboard side, actually being lowered. No other people were there at the time. There was room for him and he jumped in. Had he not jumped in he would merely have added one more life, namely, his own, to the number of those lost.

The British inquiry described the other attempts to make distress signals:

Meanwhile Mr Boxall was sending up distress signals from the deck. These signals (rockets) were sent off at intervals from a socket by No. 1 emergency boat on the Boat deck. They were the ordinary distress signals, exploding in the air and throwing off white stars. The firing of these Signals began about the time that No. 7 boat was lowered (12.45 a.m.), and it continued until Mr Boxall left the ship at about 1.45.

Mr Boxall was also using a Morse light from the bridge in the direction of a ship whose lights he saw about half a point on the port bow of the *Titanic* at a distance, as he thought, of about five or six miles. He got no answer. In all, Mr Boxall fired about eight rockets. There appears to be no doubt that the vessel whose lights he saw was the *Californian*. The evidence from the *Californian* speaks of eight rockets having been seen between 12.30 and 1.40. The *Californian* heard none of the *Titanic*'s messages; she had only one Marconi operator on board and he was asleep.

The British inquiry described the assistance rendered by the SS Carpathia:

On 15 April the SS *Carpathia*, 13,600 tons gross, of the Cunard Line, Mr Arthur Henry Rostron, Master, was on her passage to Liverpool from New York. She carried some 740 passengers and 325 crew.

On receipt of the *Titanic*'s first distress message the Captain immediately ordered the ship to be turned round and driven at her highest speed (17½ knots) in the direction of the *Titanic*. He also informed the *Titanic* by wireless that he was coming to her assistance, and he subsequently received various messages from her. At about 2.40 a.m. he saw a green flare which, as the evidence shows, was being sent up by Mr Boxall in No. 2 boat. From this time until 4 a.m. Captain Rostron was altering his course continually in order to avoid icebergs. He fired rockets in answer to the signals he saw from Boxall's boat. At 4 o'clock he considered he was practically up to the position given and he stopped his ship at 4.05. He sighted the first boat (No. 2) and picked her up at 4.10. There was then a large number of icebergs round him, and it was just daylight. Eventually he picked up in all 13 lifeboats, two emergency boats and two collapsible boats, all of which were taken on board the *Carpathia*, the other boats being abandoned as damaged or useless. From these boats he took on board 712 persons, one of whom died shortly afterwards. The boats were scattered over an area of four to five miles, and it was 8 a.m. before they had all been picked up. He saw very little wreckage when he got near to the scene of the disaster, only a few deck chairs, cork lifebelts, etc., and only one body. The position was then 41° 46' N., 50° 14' W.

The Carpathia *subsequently returned to New York with the passengers and crew she had rescued.*

The British inquiry expressed:

The Court desires to record its great admiration of Captain Rostron's conduct. He did the very best that could be done.

Captain Arthur Rostron of the SS Carpathia, *in his testimony to the US inquiry, described:*

We picked up the first boat, which was in charge of an officer who I saw was not under full control of his boat. He sang out that he had only one seaman in the boat – so I had to manoeuvre the ship to get as close to the boat as possible, as

I knew well it could be difficult to do the pulling. By the time we had the first boat's people it was breaking day, and then I could see the remaining boats all around within an area of about four miles. I also saw icebergs all around me. There were about twenty icebergs that would be anywhere from about 150 to 200 feet high, and numerous smaller bergs; also numerous ones we call "growlers" anywhere from 10 to 12 feet high and 10 to 15 feet long, above the water.

The ship Mr Boxall had seen between 12.30 and 1.40 was almost certainly the SS Californian. *The British inquiry examined the evidence concerning the SS* Californian. *The* Californian *had stopped earlier in the evening because it was surrounded by ice. It only had one radio operator who had gone off duty and was asleep. He did not come back on duty until shortly before 6am. Once he did, Captain Lord of the* Californian *reacted immediately. The report described:*

At about 6 a.m. Captain Lord heard from the *Virginian* that "the *Titanic* had struck a berg, passengers in boats, ship sinking"; and he at once started through the field ice at full speed for the position given. that Captain Lord stated that about 7.30 a.m. he passed the *Mount Temple*, stopped, and that she was in the vicinity of the position given him as where the *Titanic* had collided (lat. 41° 46' N.; long. 50° 14' W.). He saw no wreckage there, but did later on near the *Carpathia*, which ship he closed soon afterwards. and he stated that the position where he subsequently left this wreckage was 41° 33' N.; 50° 1' W. It is said in the evidence of Mr Stewart that the position of the *Californian* was verified by stellar observations at 7.30 p.m. on the Sunday evening, and that he verified the Captain's position given when the ship stopped (42° 5' N.; 50° 7' W.) as accurate on the next day. The position in which the wreckage was said to have been seen on the Monday morning was verified by sights taken on that morning.

With regard to the Californian, *the report concluded:*

There are contradictions and inconsistencies in the story as told by the different witnesses. But the truth of the matter is plain. The *Titanic* collided with the berg at 11.40. The vessel seen by the *Californian* stopped at this time. The rockets sent up from the *Titanic* were distress signals. The *Californian* saw distress signals. The number sent up by the *Titanic* was about eight. The *Californian* saw eight. The time over which the rockets from the *Titanic* were sent up was from about 12.45 to 1.45 o'clock. It was about this time that the *Californian* saw the rockets. At 2.40 Mr Stone called to the Master that the ship from which he had seen the rockets had disappeared.

At 2.20 a.m. the *Titanic* had foundered. It was suggested that the rockets seen by the *Californian* were from some other ship not the *Titanic*. But no other ship to fit this theory has ever been heard of.

These circumstances convince me that the ship seen by the *Californian* was the *Titanic*, and if so, according to Captain Lord, the two vessels were about five miles apart at the time of the disaster. The evidence from the *Titanic* corroborates this estimate, but I am advised that the distance was probably greater, though not more than eight to ten miles. The ice by which the *Californian* was surrounded was loose ice extending for a distance of not more than two or three miles in the direction of the *Titanic*. The night was clear and the sea was smooth. When she first saw the rockets the *Californian* could have pushed through the ice to the open water without any serious risk and so have come to the assistance of the *Titanic*. Had she done so she might have saved many if not all of the lives that were lost.

The Report of the British inquiry concluded:

The Court, having carefully inquired into the circumstances of the above mentioned shipping casualty, finds . . . that the loss of the said ship was due to collision with an iceberg, brought about by the excessive speed at which the ship was being navigated.

The Report made a number of recommendations, including some suggestions for improved watertight sub-divisions. Most significantly it recommended that:

The provision of life boat and raft accommodation on board such ships should be based on the number of persons intended to be carried in the ship and not upon tonnage.

It also recommended that in all such ships there should be an installation of wireless telegraphy, and that such installation should be worked with a sufficient number of trained operators to secure a continuous service by night and day. In this connection regard should be had to the resolutions of the International Conference on Wireless Telegraphy recently held under the presidency of Sir H. Babington Smith. That where practicable a silent chamber for "receiving" messages should form part of the installation.

Another ship of the same class as Titanic *was being built. Because of the loss of* Titanic, *there were many changes made. The new ship was renamed, from* Gigantic *to* Britannic. *Her bulkheads were made higher and stronger. Unlike her two sisters (*Olympic *and* Titanic*), which could have any two adjoining watertight compartments flooded and still survive: the new ship could survive with any six compartments flooded (one more than the number of compartments breached on the* Titanic*). Furthermore, she had special lifeboat davits, which could launch up to six boats over either side of the ship, regardless of listing. As a result of these modifications, the* Britannic *was larger than the* Titanic, *at 48,000 tons.*

The Last of the Windjammers
1920

In 1920 "Frank" Haakon Chevalier was a student at Stamford University. Chevalier was 17. He had recently begun to read the seafaring novels of Joseph Conrad. He and a friend decided to spend their summer vacation working on board a steamship bound for the orient. They went to San Francisco to try to find a ship. The only ship looking for crew was the Rosamund. *She was a 1,000 ton four-masted sailing schooner. She was carrying a cargo of lumber from Seattle to Cape Town, South Africa. Her crew was only 10 men including the captain and the mate. He and his friend, Donald Snedden, signed on as cabin boys (unskilled hands). Chevalier described the* Rosamund:

We watched her with mounting excitement as we came closer. Her hull was built of wood and was painted black, with a white trim. Piled way above the bulwarks and lashed down by chains was an incredible load of lumber extending from the fo'c'sle to the poop deck, causing her to ride, I thought, dangerously low. Seen from the side, the jib-boom stuck forward smartly from the bow, braced by the stays above and the martingale below; the name *Rosamund* was painted in conventional white letters on a black panel against the white trim of the fo'c'sle bulwark just forward of the sidelights on either side. There was nothing fancy about her – no figurehead, no carving. She was, in fact, plain: a working ship.

One of the other crew members was an Australian sailor called George. George was in his forties. Chevalier:

George obviously loved to talk, and he bore the brunt of the conversation, rattling on at a great rate in a colourful lingo sprinkled with obscenities and marked by a strong Australian accent.

"What was your last ship?" was one of his first questions,

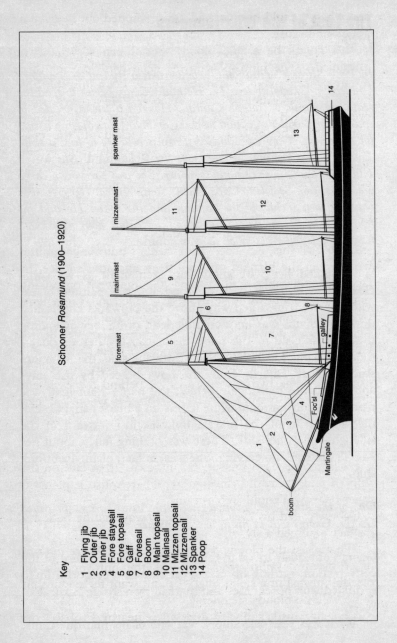

Schooner *Rosamund* (1900–1920)

Key

1 Flying jib
2 Outer jib
3 Inner jib
4 Fore staysail
5 Fore topsail
6 Gaff
7 Foresail
8 Boom
9 Main topsail
10 Mainsail
11 Mizzen topsail
12 Mizzensail
13 Spanker
14 Poop

and when we told him we had never shipped out he gave us a look of disgust.

"It's gonna be a fine bloody trip, I can see that," he grumbled. "The bleedin' ship 'as been lyin' 'ere for three months rottin' away, waitin' for a crew. It's a jinx ship. No honest bleedin' sailor will come near 'er." He screwed up his eyes and looked at us searchingly. "You know what 'appened, don't you? The bleedin' tub was wrecked off the coast somewhere outside Los Angeles. Started down from Seattle. Lost 'er 'ole bloody deckload. She was towed to San Pedro and put in the bloody dry-dock for repairs and then brought 'ere. She's been 'ere at anchor ever since and that was way back last bleedin' fall. And now they can't even get together a crew of real bleedin' sailors to sail 'er."

During all this, Feliciano Rosero, alert but noncommittal, wrapped in the blanket of some deep ancestral silence, his face indecipherable, said nothing. George went on talking, reminiscing about other ships he had sailed in – big square-riggers with crews of thirty or forty salts, "*real* bloody ships" – coming back now and again to the *Rosamund* only to belittle her and her skipper, to say nothing of her crew.

. . . "A hell of a bloody crew this is goin' to be!" he exploded. "The two of you, still wet behind the ears, and then the other two we've seen, neither of whom 'as ever seen the business end of a bleedin' 'alyard . . . bloody steamboat sailors!' he huffed, "Probably can't even tie a bloody knot!"

I was getting pretty upset. "If things are that bad on this ship," I said, "why did you sign on? There must be plenty of other boats you could ship out on."

George rolled his eyes in a peculiar way that he had, and his face assumed a sly look.

"That's just the bloody trouble!" he said. "There *ain't* no other bleedin' sailin' ships. This is the only one in the bleedin' port. I'm a sailin' man. I don't want to 'ave nothin' to do with no bloody steamer."

A hoarse whistle sounded somewhere nearby. Probably our

launch – anxious to take off. I glanced at Don, who looked up as the whistle blared.

"Maybe we could just have a look at the fo'c'sle,' he said, 'and then I guess we'll have to be off."

"Sure thing," said George, leading the way across the foot-high step.

The fo'c'sle was a snug low-ceilinged triangular area, about eight feet wide at the entrance and narrowing to a point at the bow end, the deck sloping up, with four upper and four lower bunks built against the ship's side. An inner bulkhead with a sliding door separated it from the central space in the fo'c'sle, the 'tween decks, where the anchor chain cables passed via the capstan shaft from the hawsehole down into the hold. On the starboard side was a small oilet, a tiny cubicle with a toilet bowl emptying into a hole in the ship's side, but of course with no flush. A recess in the after part of the fo'c'sle next to the galley had a built-in mess table and benches, hardly big enough for six, which evidently served as mess-room.

I was completely at a loss. "Wh– where are the other bunks?" I finally said.

"What other bunks?"

"Well, the bunks for the rest of the crew."

"The rest of the crew!" George laughed uproariously. I noticed that his teeth were in bad condition, several of them missing. He ran the back of his hand across his face. "Eight is all the bloody crew she's supposed to 'ave," he said, giving me a wise look. "And I've got a damn good 'unch the bleedin' skipper is plannin' to sail without a full crew."

Noticing my crestfallen look, he quickly added, "Well, there's one thing you won't have to worry about: you won't be wakin' up some mornin' and findin' a bloody rat scamperin' across your face. All the rats left the ship the night before she was towed out 'ere in the bloody 'arbour."

The deck was loaded with additional lumber. This was stacked directly on top of the cargo in the hold. The *Rosamund* had no engine and no radio. It had a diesel engine. This was supposed to be used for winching up cargo and driving the pumps. Because of the deck load it was inoperable.

The crew was divided into two watches. At sea for the first time, Chevalier described:

There was first of all the wind, a strong, aggressive wind which swept down over us from the northeast, filling our sails, straining masts and stays and halyards, driving the ship forward in a plunging course amid a crash of waves and a spray of foam. The wind itself, of course, was no novelty. What was new was its overriding presence, and the fact that from now on wind was going to be the governing factor of our lives.

But what was even more estranging was being plunged into a new world of incessant and compelling motion that shook one's whole being – the swaying and tossing, the need at every moment to compensate, by posture and muscle, the careening and yawing, the rise and fall, the seesaws, the rolling and the treacherous jolts that threatened to throw one off balance. After the first day or two on board, while still at anchor in the harbour, the rocking had been so gentle as to become quickly unnoticeable. But now the ship seemed to have sprung alive, was like a creature that had long been shackled and was suddenly released. It danced and pranced and tossed, as if intoxicated by the wind and the waves, seeming to rejoice in its recovered freedom. Walking, and even just standing, on the heaving, slanting deck or deckload, and at the same time bracing oneself against the fitful, ever-varying pressure of the wind, was a feat of equilibrium requiring constant alertness.

But besides wind and motion, there was also sound. The roar of the wind as it swept over us, humming and whistling through the rigging, filling the sails to a quivering tautness, the restless stir of the sea, waves pounding against the ship's hull and leaping up in occasional salt-stinging sprays that blew in our faces, combined to produce a many-voiced and infinitely varied song, a song that one not only heard, but whose polyphony penetrated one's skin and vibrated in one's being.

At the same time that we were running back and forth in execution of the rapid succession of orders and getting the ship under full sail, I became aware of another sensation. The up and down motion of the ship, as she plunged and lurched at the will of wind and sea, was beginning to affect me rather peculiarly. At each rise something inside my head seemed to want to keep on going up even after the peak was reached, and at each fall I felt an odd sinking in my stomach. The sensation at first was not disagreeable, and was even at moments exhilarating.

After the four big sails had been hoisted and set, we had immediately been put to work spreading the rest of the canvas – first the fore staysail, then the flying jib, the outer jib and the inner jib, and finally the three topsails, on the fore, main and mizzen masts. I was glad I was not sent aloft to undo the gaskets of any of the furled topsails, for those eighty-or-so feet up to the wildly swaying trestle-trees seemed to me at the time an impossibly dangerous climb. I did not in fact feel too steady on my pins even here on deck, and I marvelled at the agility of George and Feliz, who climbed up the riggings like monkeys and went about their work up there as though it were an everyday lark, shaking out the stiff topsails which had been lashed to the topmasts for months, getting them on the lee side of the peak halyards, fastening the clew to the sheet and bringing the tack to the weather side. We on deck then had only to heave away on the corresponding lines to bring head, clew and tack successively into position to give the big triangular topsails their full spread.

It was only when we had made fast on its belaying pin the last bight of the mizzen topsail tack that the *Rosamund* was at last under sail – eleven sails in all, swelling to the steady northeast wind that struck us on our port quarter. The strain and movement, the buffeting and roar of the wind and the tumult of the sea combined to create a sense of tremendous agitation and momentum. I had the feeling that we were moving at breakneck speed. How fast were we actually going? I later learned that under the best of circumstances the ship was capable at most of between seven and eight knots. It was the wind, probably, and all the sound and stir, which gave the illusion that we were moving much faster. Looking back at the receding shore, the features of which were gradually becoming blurred by mist and distance, I felt a curious kind of excitement, as though this was an important turning-point in my life, and I had just now suddenly realized it. There was no turning back. I had committed myself to this ship: I was bound to it for the months to come, whatever happened.

His first job was to grease the masts from a bosun's chair suspended from the masthead. But he had not yet gained his "sea legs". He vomited and dropped a can of grease on the sail.

There was a second mate aboard. He was addressed as "bos'n". He was a Finn named Lauri Sippola. Chevalier described their daily schedule:

Four hours on and four hours off; with the schedule alternating in the dogwatches, became an established rhythm, to which our minds and our bodies became accustomed. We each took our two-hour turn at the wheel, so that each of us was helmsman four hours a day, which meant that by the end of our globe-circling voyage each of us would have steered the ship some five thousand nautical miles. Although the working day was long, the work itself, in good weather on ordinary days, was not excessive.

The worst chore was manning the pump. For half an hour or more in all the daylight watches two of us had to pump water out of the hold. We had to climb down into the well left in the deck-load for this purpose to the pump that stood on the deck just aft of the mizzen mast. It had two large flywheels with a handle on each one wide enough to hold with two hands. It took a lot of elbow-grease to keep it turning, and by the time the half hour was up we were pretty tired, and it was hot down there besides. The rotating wheels drove two plungers working up and down in the suction pipes on shafts connected to a crank, bringing the bilge water out of the hull bottom in alternating streams that gushed out from the nozzles onto the deck at our feet and spilled down to the scuppers in the leeside bulwarks through the ventilation space left under the deckload, big slushes of water splashing up against our feet with the swaying of the deck. Sippola would stand by and, depending on his mood, would either encourage us or make sarcastic remarks about what weaklings we were and periodically plunge a rod at the end of a rope to the bottom of the hold to measure the amount of water.

When we first began to man the pump, some four or five days out, the water in the hold was up to an alarming five feet or so. That was a hell of a lot of water, and the ship was already heavily loaded. We speculated among the crew about the danger of the ship's becoming waterlogged and foundering, remembering that she had been wrecked on the leg down from Seattle. She was twenty years old, after all, having been built in 1900, and George had explained to us that a carvel-built ship, like the *Rosamund*, on which the boards of the skin were laid edge to edge, was more subject to leakage than the earlier clinker-built ships, the planking of which was edge-lapped, as on the old Viking ships. A kind of primitive fear incited us to pump away with a vengeance, until after days and days of pumping we brought the level down to two feet or less. What riled us, though, was the fact that there was a perfectly good and brand-new diesel engine that had been installed abaft the galley just for the purpose of pumping out the hold (as well as to serve as a winch for the hoisting of a sail) and a tunnel had been left under the deckload leading from it to the pump for a belt to connect up with it. It was another example of the skipper's tightness. We had to pay for it with our sweat, and we did a good deal of grumbling about it.

Apart from this no great demands were made on our energies in the everyday routine. The oil lamps for the sidelights and for the fo'c'sle had to be regularly filled (Sippola took care of the binnacle lights and the cook kept the poop deck-house lamps filled). The poop deck had to be kept spick and span. Its Oregon pine deck had to be regularly washed down with buckets-full of seawater, and periodically treated with boiled linseed oil. There were brasses to be polished, and shackles and chains to be kept greased, and iron parts – clevises, cleats, chocks, the anchors and anchor chains, and the capstan from which the rust had to be chipped off with a chisel and which then had to be coated with red lead and one or two coats of paint.

I was sent up again to grease down the mizzen mast once I had completely found my sea legs. This time there was no getting out of it. It was ticklish being suspended up there on a slim bos'n's chair, seventy feet or so above the deck, from a slender line passed over one of the trestletrees and being let down two or three feet at a time by the second mate, who each time secured the line to a belaying pin on the mizzen mast pinrail. I had not realized until now that the surface of the masts was entirely covered from gaff to boom with great splinters, like the back of a hedgehog, from the friction of the hoops. The big tin of hot grease hung from one side of the bos'n's chair, and I daubed the stinking stuff onto the mast with a rag, which progressively got full of splinters, as did my hands. The swinging of the mast made it harder and harder to hang on as I got lower. My hands were sticky with grease, and as I was not supposed to touch either the sail or even the bolt rope on its luff the only possible hold was by the hoops. But these kept slapping unpredictably against the mast, and several times I got my fingers caught between a hoop and the mast, with excruciating results. Once I lost my hold and was swung some twenty feet or more away from the mast to leeward, and when the ship righted herself I was brought back full speed to windward. I just barely managed to twist myself round and wildly grab the main topping lift that came

within my reach, in time to keep my head and back from
smashing against the mast. When at last I got down to the
deckload, sweating, smeared with grease, bruised and with
my hands covered with splinters, I felt that I had had a real
work-out and I thanked my stars that I had managed to get
out of it at least that first day when I had been so seasick.

Most of our work, however, was with the sails. The
skipper, who kept pretty much to the poop deck, was
constantly looking up at the sails and giving orders to bring
in or let out this or that sheet, to raise or lower one or another
sail a little. Or else one of the booms was up too high, so that
the topping lift had to be let out a little. Unless it was the
other way around. Every time there was some slight change
of wind, something would have to be done about the sails.
The topsails were always giving trouble: the tack was too
slack or too taut or someone had forgotten to make it fast, or
the sheet needed pulling in . . . The skipper would pop up in
the companion unexpectedly at all hours of the day or night
and find fault with something that had been done while he
was below deck. We were forever hauling away at purchases,
tacks and sheets, coiling and recoiling ropes, and our palms
grew hard with calluses while our backs became strong and
our muscles sinewy.

The twelve hours a day that we were not working were of
course not wholly spent in eating and sleeping. After the sun
was down, though, there was not much else to do. Don and
I had brought a chess set and a board and also a set of
checker men. Neither Joe nor Feliz could play chess, but we
sometimes played checkers. Greg had a deck of cards and
liked to play solitaire. George would only play poker, but as
he invariably won, and insisted on playing for money, Greg
got discouraged and seldom took him on. I would often read
in the fo'c'sle in the evening, either at the mess table or in my
bunk by the light of the kerosene lamp that hung on the galley
bulkhead above the table and was kept burning all night.

We had a greater range of activity in the daytime. We had
the freedom of the ship in our off-hours, as long as we did not

interfere with the watch on duty, though we usually confined our activities to the fo'c'sle and the forward part of the ship. We had to do all our personal chores, of course, during our off-hours – wash, shave, keep our bunks and everything clean and tidy, sweep or mop the fo'c'sle deck, do our laundry (with seawater), mend or darn our clothes if necessary.

They passed Pitcairn Island south of the Tropics, heading for Cape Horn. A steamer crossed their bows. This made the sailors furious because as a sailing ship they had right of way. Chevalier described a dangerous incident:

The next day the weather had changed for the worse. The wind was coming from the north and, though steady, it was blowing with a kind of wicked intensity. The skipper spent much of his time on deck.

"It's about time we got our hard-weather sails up," I heard him say to the first mate, who had by now recovered some of his old bounce. "As soon as this gale lets up we'd better get started on it. Meanwhile, let's take in all the tops'ls."

We took in the fore- and mizzen-topsails and the three jibs. The wind continued to blow and the waves became huge. I had never seen them so high. A terrific downpour swept upon us that lasted all night, and by morning the wind suddenly veered and became so violent that the ship was nearly on her beam ends, and the course had to be quickly altered to southwest by south. All hands were called on deck.

"We've got to reef down the sails!" the captain ordered. "A double reef. Bring down the fores'l quickly! I'll take the wheel."

We all scampered to the port foresail rigging just by our fo'c'sle, wearing our oilskins, sou'westers and boots for the first time. The foremast was the only mast with a gaff sail which had its halyards made fast to the built-in bulwark pinrail. The mainmast and the mizzen, because of the deckload, had jury pinrails raised to waist-height above the deckload.

The mate was in charge of the operation, while the second mate stood by to give a hand. Normally a sail was lowered by slowly letting out the halyards, after the purchases, peak and throat alternately, with one or two bights of rope round the belaying pin, slipping the rope-end through gently until the strain relaxed sufficiently for the hands to be able to lower the sail the rest of the way.

The wind was blowing with increasing fury, and the ship was labouring heavily, with waves breaking over the gunwales and spraying us. After the purchases had been let out, the mate began working on the peak halyard, trying to unbend the top bight. The night's driving rain had soaked, swelled and hardened the rope too tight to be budged by hand.

"Get me a marlin spike," the mate barked, amid an explosion of curses.

Feliz brought a marlin spike, and with it the mate finally succeeded in unwedging the first bight that locked all the others. He was sweating and cursing and dripping from the waves that had splashed over him, as we all were. The halyard to be released lay in a large coil on the deck, and in his struggle with the bight, the mate, violating an elementary rule of seamanship, had put both feet in the middle of the coil.

"Now you boys grab the halyard," he yelled to us crew members, "and put all your weight to it!" As I was the tallest, I jumped up on the bulwark and grabbed the rope as high up as I could reach both hands. Feliz, the next tallest, grabbed it just below my grasp, then Don, then George, then Greg, and Joe last.

From where I was I couldn't see what was going on. The halyard we were holding was soaked, and the water trickled down my hands and arms all the way to my armpits and down my bare sides. The mate was presumably unbending one or more bights preparatory to letting the halyard slip inch by inch until the very considerable initial strain was reduced.

There we were, the six of us, holding on to the dripping halyard for dear life, twelve hands, one above the other, mine at the top. I figured that between us we weighed about half a ton. The ship was tossing, the waves were pounding us and the wind was making a deafening roar. The violence of the elements was such that my mind was a complete blank.

Suddenly something gave way. What had happened? I felt myself abruptly wrenched and swept upward, and the whole ship sank beneath me, spread out from stem to stern in bird's eye view. It all happened in a matter of seconds. Inexplicably I continued to hang on to the rope as I was being lifted up at a dizzying speed, and Feliz's hands were just below mine. For a split second the question as to what would happen when my hands reached the block below the trestletrees through which the halyard passed must have flashed through my mind. Flesh and bones mangled to a pulp – and the rest of me? . . .

By a sheer miracle something jammed, and the halyard, with a jerk, was immobilized just as my upper hand reached to within a few inches of the block. I was some ninety feet above the deck, dangling by my two hands from a wet piece of rope swaying violently in the storm. How did I manage to hang on? I looked down and saw that all five of my shipmates were also hanging there by their hands, one below the other, a chain of bodies swathed in sou'westers and oilskins precariously suspended between life and death.

"Get down quick!" I yelled, frantic by now.

It had all happened so fast that I had not had time to realize the danger I was in, but now it suddenly occurred to me that the halyard, shaken as it was by the wild movements of the ship, might at any moment continue racing madly through the block. With the haunting fear that every second might be our last, Joe, and then Greg, and then George, and then Don, Feliz and finally I, one after another, somehow managed to wind our legs round the halyard and shinny down. Once back on deck we all stared at one another, glassy-eyed. No one could say a word. Joe was crying like a baby. It had been a close shave and we were badly shaken.

But here on deck another shock awaited us. The mate, as he had tried to let the halyard slip slowly round the belaying pin, had fumbled and the halyard had suddenly got away from him. Standing as he did in the middle of the coil, when the halyard had broken loose it had picked him right up in its loops, whirled him in the air and thrown him on his back, after he had knocked over the galley chimney, clear across to the galley skylight. Sippola, before all this happened, had relieved the skipper at the wheel, and the skipper was now on the galley trying to move the mate, who was screaming with pain, his body all twisted.

The storm was now upon us with a vengeance and the ship, with too much sail on her, was yawing wildly and becoming difficult to manage. I saw now what had miraculously saved our lives: when it had broken loose with the runaway peak halyard (though still held by the throat halyard), the gaff had been blown as it dropped by the terrific pressure of the wind right against the starboard rigging, where its peak had got caught and where it was still jammed. Some merciful providence had calculated to within three or four inches just how far up that rope should be allowed to go.

With the ship becoming unruly, all the sails needing tending to, the mate in a critical condition, having perhaps suffered a broken back, and all the crew unnerved by the harrowing experience it had just been through, we were facing our gravest emergency.

In this predicament the skipper proved to be remarkably cool-headed. Feliz had already run up on the fo'c'sle head and onto the deck of the galley deckhouse. The skipper ordered George to go and relieve the bos'n and have him come forward, and then he and Feliz gently eased the mate off the skylight and on to the galley deck. The mate was obviously suffering excruciating pain. The skipper told Feliz and Don to stand by with the mate, left Joe and Greg standing by the foremast rigging, and then had me hurry aft with him. From a supply locker next to the officers' cabins he pulled out a stretcher, which I carried forward to the galley. Meanwhile he had ordered the bos'n to take care of the foresail gaff with Don, Greg, Joe and me. He and Feliz got the mate on the stretcher and, with some help from us in getting him down from the galley deck and up on the deckload, and then down from the deckload aft, carried him to his cabin.

Sippola proved to be an efficient demon in an emergency. He looked at the foresail and sized up the situation, cursed the mate for his poor seamanship and then ordered Don, Greg, Joe and myself to stand by the peak halyard while he climbed the starboard rigging to extricate the gaff which had its peak caught between the stays. He signaled us to haul up on the halyard a little, managed, after some straining, to pry the gaff free, and then had us haul the gaff up enough to give its crotch a good hold on the mast.

We were sailing before the wind, way out of our course, with the sheets pulled in to give as little resistance as possible to the raging wind. The waves were battering the hull with a force which I thought would shatter it and the high-tossed spray stung our faces. Feliz came forward and joined us after leaving the skipper to do what he could to make the mate temporarily comfortable. It was the bos'n's turn now to see what he could do with the fore throat halyard on the starboard pinrail. The purchase had already been let out.

Instead of trying to let out the halyard with the terrific strain that the wind was putting on it, he took a block-and-tackle with double blocks, caught the hook of the lower block to a shackle on the bulwark rail and tied the strap of the upper block securely to the halyard. This gave us a rope-end with a strain only one-fourth of the strain on the halyard itself, which could easily be managed by hand. The halyard, with the strain taken off it, came off the belaying pin fairly easily. The tackle line was then let up as far as it would go, the halyard was again made fast to the belaying pin, and the strap of the upper block was brought down close to the bulwark rail and the slack of its line taken in, the process being repeated until the five of us could handle the halyard itself. This device, which works on the same principle as the built-in purchase, is known to all sailors. We had often used it before, both to hoist and to lower a sail when the strain was too great, or when we were shorthanded, and it was surprising that the mate had not thought of it when he had to lower the first sail.

We used the block and tackle on both the throat and the peak halyards, and all went smoothly – or as smoothly as it could go under the existing weather conditions.

The skipper appeared on deck again and came forward, nodded a glum approval of what had been done, and ordered us next to lower the spanker, which gave us no trouble. We wound a few loops of gasket round it as a temporary measure to keep it from billowing, and were next sent to lower the mizzen. We used the block-and-tackle again and the sail came down in slow stages, throat and peak alternately, slapping and struggling fearfully as it was lowered, until it finally collapsed, panting like an exhausted animal.

"Now let's get the double reef into the foresail," shouted the skipper, without giving us a minute's breathing-spell.

We were all a little groggy after what we had already been through, but there was no letting up before we had got the ship in her weather trim. We went forward and lined up along the fore boom. Sippola brought the reef points and we proceeded to roll up the sail to the second reef band, worked the points through the reef cringles and around the foot of the sail and tied them. Then back to the halyards we went and hauled away, and finally brought the sail up taut with the purchases. With the double reef the sail had about two-thirds of its full spread.

We next lowered the mainsail, reefed it and hoisted it again, and finally put reefs in the mizzen and hoisted it. We had now reduced our canvas spread to four sails – the fore staysail and the three reefed-down gaff sails – and with that she should reasonably be able to ride out the storm. Both wind and waves had increased in intensity, and once again I was beginning to feel a little sick in my stomach. We were hemmed in by cloud and mist. There was no horizon, and visibility had shrunk to a radius of less than a mile. The sea was a boiling cauldron of foam and spray.

It was now way past noon. We were on our last legs, and we were starving. But we couldn't help worrying about the mate. For the second time he was taking bad punishment, and this time it really looked bad. The skipper had gone below to see to him and had come up on deck again. But he was not communicative, and we were left to wonder how the mate was faring.

The storm raged with unabated violence for three days. We were able to partly correct our course to between south by east and southeast by south, but the drift of the seas was pushing us in a southwesterly direction. No bearings were taken during those days, for a thick pall hung over us day and night, and a dead reckoning could not be very accurate because of the drift and the uncertainty of the currents. Life aboard, after the sunny tropics, had suddenly become grim. It was cold and damp. Through the deafening roar of the wind, came lugubrious piercing howls and whistles and moans as it swept through the rigging, and the pounding of the seas was incessant, each assault sending shuddering movements through the ship. Whenever we were on deck we needed our boots, oilskins and sou'westers. Keeping our footing on the bounding deckload with its steep slant against the fitful pressure of the wind and the waves that would occasionally crash over the edge had become a feat that required unrelaxing attention. The steel cable stretched at waist-height between the riggings could hardly be depended on if we should happen to be caught off balance. Joe was completely demoralized and wailed shamelessly. It got to be terribly embarrassing. He could not be depended upon for anything, except to stand at the wheel. George was no great help. Every time he had a chance he bawled him out mercilessly, and whenever poor Joe started weeping, which was more and more frequently, George threatened to kill him.

"You better get hold of yourself, you bloody wop!" he

would snarl. "One of these bleedin' nights you're goin' to find yourself overboard!"

What chance would a man have if he should go overboard in weather like this? This was a question we discussed in the fo'c'sle. George, and especially Sippola, had a whole collection of sombre stories about men lost at sea.

Chevalier described how they came close to disaster rounding Cape Horn:

The storm that we had been through had opened the ship's seams, as the skipper put it, and we had taken in a lot of water. For several days we were made to man the bilge pump at least an hour every watch except the dogwatch, so that the pump was kept going five hours a day or more. This was reduced when the water in the hold was brought down to a level of two to three feet, but pumping remained an almost daily chore all the way to Cape Town.

Our holiday of relatively fair wind and weather ended abruptly by the time we got to within a thousand miles of the Horn. The skipper was keeping a close eye on the barometer, and one mid-morning it fell alarmingly. He at once ordered the jibs and topsails to be taken in, and then we pulled down the spanker and put double reefs in the three big sails. We were on the port tack. The albatross, a dozen or so of them, which had been making wide circles about the ship, now suddenly spread their wings wide, scudded before the wind at breakneck speed and disappeared. The barometric pressure had been dropping steadily during all this, and we were just putting the last reef points on the mizzen when the hurricane hit us. Hunraken, the Carib Indians' god of stormy weather, from whom the word hurricane is derived, was on a rampage.

It came so suddenly that George and Feliz, who had finished before the rest of us and were standing away from the boom, were knocked over and sent rolling. Feliz was saved by the mizzen mast as he was carried down the slanting deckload, and George managed to grab hold of a deckload chain long enough for some of us to bring him up against the boom. The other three of us, who were still busy with the reefs, had the wind knocked out of us when we were banged against the boom, and I was blown right over the boom and into the folds of the sail on the lee side, where I was in the safest possible position for the fireworks that followed.

The first blast laid the ship on her beam ends, so that her masts were nearly parallel with the surface of the sea. As she was righting herself the heavens opened up and the sky was filled with a blinding, many-branched tree of lightning immediately followed by a crash of thunder so powerful that it seemed to split the whole world asunder; I was sure my eardrums had burst and were bleeding.

The wind continued to increase in velocity and in volume, blowing spray that felt like shot when it hit my skin and that blinded me when I tried to look in its direction. The scream and booming of the raging blast grew so loud that it drowned out all other sound. With my eyes shielded by the boom and the screen of the sail, I could now see the almost continuous flashes of lightning, but the sound of the cataclysmic claps of thunder itself was suffocated by the overpowering din made by the wind, which seemed to penetrate to my bones and tear my nerves to shreds. I found it hard to breathe. Suddenly I had the impression that the ship was being lifted clear out of the water, and then almost immediately was brutally slapped down again. She next proceeded to go through the strangest antics I had ever witnessed, having no apparent relation either to wind or wave, leaping and quivering and churning in a mad, hysterical way while the water all around us rose in fantastic whirls of spume and spray and the air at moments seemed to want to suck us up. To my stupefaction I saw Greg's wool cap, which he had recently bought in the captain's locker, lifted right off his head, fly upwards and vanish.

Don was at the wheel, the skipper must be somewhere up there on the poop if he had not been blown overboard, and the bos'n had disappeared.

I kept wondering about the mate and how he must be faring. The fearful beating that the ship was taking must be making it very uncomfortable for him with his bad back. We had not seen him now for some two weeks.

I didn't know – I guess no one of us knew – what was happening to the ship. We could see only a few hundred yards, and when the lightning flashed it seemed to set everything afire. The violence of the wind and the sea was so great that no one could venture to move about the deck while it lasted. There was nothing to do but to ride it out and I only hoped that Don was still at the wheel and that he was able to keep the ship, despite her erratic movements, with her tail to the wind.

In my cocoon of sail I was relatively snug and I tried, by gesture and by yelling against the wind across the few feet that separated me from them, to persuade the other four to climb over the boom and join me. But they seemed to be only intent on holding on where they were. Joe was almost hysterical. He was shaking and seemed barely able to hang on to the foot rope. His face was completely distorted and flooded with tears, and I was afraid that George might at any moment give him a shove that would send him overboard. Now that there seemed to be no immediate danger of my being washed overboard, my other fear was that the lightning would hit us and a further fear was that the ship would go to pieces under the terrific battering she was taking. Remarkably enough, the two sails that I could see – the mainsail and the foresail – seemed to be holding.

After a time which seemed endless, the noise of the wind became somewhat less deafening, and once again I could hear the crash of thunder breaking through its thick wall. I noticed that the lag between the bursts of lightning and the thunder seemed to increase. I had only just begun to take some small comfort from this when, to my utter amazement, the wind suddenly veered round 180 degrees and hit us with a terrific whack from the other side. The mainsail was ripped from head to foot. I looked about in alarm. The ship with its antic movements slowly turned round, the foresail – our only remaining sail, unless the fore staysail was still intact – slapping helplessly. The skipper must be up there giving Don the course. We continued to turn round till the wind again came from our port quarter. Fortunately we were close-hauled, so that the swinging of the booms from starboard to port and back again was not too violent. We were now probably heading northwards.

It was several hours before the storm had abated sufficiently to make it possible for us to move without holding on for dear life to some fixed solid object. We had been, the skipper later told us, in the very eye of the hurricane, and at its height the wind that had swept us must have reached considerably more than 100 miles per hour, with its coil of wind whirling at up to 250 miles per hour round its centre – the "eye" where, several thousand feet up, Greg's wool cap was perhaps still being held.

The waves that it left behind were now mountain-high, and this added to our difficulty in getting about. Our mainsail was ruined, and on the poop deck, we saw, the port lifeboat had snapped the gripes that held it and been knocked off its chocks, and one of its davits had been bent out of shape. The skipper and bos'n had both taken shelter in the companion during the worst part of the hurricane and Don, braced against the wheel, had managed to stick to his post, with directions and encouragement from the skipper.

As soon as we could, we got the ripped mainsail down and hoisted the reefed-down mizzen. The skipper, as usual, wailed over the magnitude of the loss – though the price he mentioned this time was $1,600, and not $1,400, which he had given as the cost of the mizzen I had ruined. The fore staysail had come through undamaged. It was on this occasion, I seem to remember, that he came out with a theory of his to the effect that the Germans and the "Bushelviks" were responsible for bad weather or absence of weather.

After a time the wind veered round to northeast, and we were able to resume a southeast course. Almost too exhausted to be hungry, we were served what should have been lunch late in the afternoon.

As we approached the Horn the wind became increasingly erratic. We sometimes had to tack several times a day and we must have changed our course during the days that followed the hurricane to almost every point of the compass. We were forever climbing up the riggings to shift the topsail tack from port to starboard and back again.

After the hurricane I took the first opportunity to look up what Thorn's *Navigation* had to say about storms. I had to make my way through a maze of technical language in my effort to extract a few basic notions as to the factors affecting weather and causing wind. It was all immensely complicated. Essentially, variations in weather are caused by differences in temperature, which in turn affect atmospheric pressure. Cold air from the two poles, which is at high pressure, flows toward the Equator where the sun's rays are most powerful and where the pressure is low. This creates winds, but these are complicated by the rotation of the earth and by the great masses of land and water on the earth's surface. Moisture is a further factor. Over oceans moisture collects quickly and warmth slowly, whereas over the land the air collects less moisture but is more quickly warmed by the heat of the sun, since this is reflected from land but absorbed by water. Warm air can hold more moisture than cold air, so that if air is cooled to the point that it can no longer hold its moisture, this has to condense in some form such as clouds or rain.

This was all fascinating. I went on to read about anticyclones, which are areas of high pressure, and cyclones, which are areas of low pressure, and which result from the contact of warm tropical air and polar air, in which the winds tend to blow toward the centre of the low-pressure area and are deflected by the earth's rotation in a clockwise or anticlockwise direction depending on whether they occur in the southern or the northern hemisphere.

A cyclone is formed by the movement of great masses of

air. When a mass of warm tropical air meets a mass of cold polar air they mix and form a cyclone. The whole system then moves along a definite track which is in the opposite direction to the prevailing wind.

A hurricane, I learned, is a violent type of cyclone, formed by winds sweeping round in a coil of decreasing circles. It is shaped like a gigantic disk, some thousands of feet thick, with a diameter of about 500 miles. The "eye" that the skipper had told me about is a calm area in the centre. An object caught up in a hurricane, like Greg's cap, is whirled round and round till it reaches this "eye" and is held there till the storm subsides. A hurricane moves like a top, travelling across the sea at a speed of ten to fifteen miles per hour or more with its whirling mass of winds which, as the skipper had also said, may reach a speed of up to 250 miles per hour.

The skipper refused to be drawn out on the subject of the hurricanes or typhoons he himself had been through, but he told me several tales showing the destructive force of these storms, the most terrifying of which was his account of the hurricane in the Bay of Bengal in October 1737, when waves forty feet high destroyed thousands of ships and killed over a quarter of a million people.

The day after the hurricane had left us we had lashed the port lifeboat back on its chocks, had tidied up the decks and gone back to extra duty on the bilge pump. We now enjoyed a succession of days of strong, though shifting winds. The days grew shorter, the sun – a heatless winter sun – made only brief and irregular appearances, and every day it got colder.

And then one day – it was 22 September – far over to our port, we sighted land. Yes, it was Cape Horn, the skipper assured us. We gazed and gazed at that fabled point of land which, as we saw it, blurred by mist to a thin slice of darker grey with a broken outline, could have been an island or promontory anywhere in the world, but which in the minds of thousands of sailors had been for centuries a challenging and often dreaded goal which, once reached, remained in

their memories as an outstanding milepost in a life dedicated
to hardship and adventure.

*They had been at sea for 81 days and sailed 8,000 miles at an
average of 112 miles per day. Their average speed was 4.5 knots.
They were close to the sixtieth parallel and it was very cold. The
captain told Chevalier that he and his friend had been put on the
payroll as ordinary seamen.*

The next day the wind shifted southward again, and we had
to change our course back to southeast. The mate came up
on deck at noon for the shooting of the sun. His beard had
grown into a thick grey mat around his face, but his cheeks
were rosy and his guileless blue eyes were bright. He looked
kind of thick around the middle, and I guessed the skipper
had provided him with a brace of some sort. He walked
awkwardly and kept putting one hand against the small of his
back.

The skipper's face looked sombre again as he made his
calculations. The mate wrinkled up his face in turn.

"It's gettin' dangerous," he said, and then the two walked
out of earshot.

I gathered that we were getting dangerously far south, close
to the Antarctic Circle. When I looked at my atlas I saw that
we were within the limit of drift ice. It had been getting
steadily colder. The next morning when I came on deck, sure
enough, there, far ahead of us, but ominous-looking, was
what looked like a huge iceberg. I pointed it out to George as
he was coming forward at the end of his watch.

"*One* bleedin' iceberg!" he practically screamed. "Look
there! And there! And there!" He pointed to a series of
points, to starboard, to port, and aft.

I looked, and was startled to confirm that we were in fact
more or less surrounded by icebergs. As the morning wore
on, however, these apparently disappeared. What looked like
a bank of mist covered the horizon.

"That's the trouble, Frank," the skipper explained to me

later when I was at the wheel. "They're still there, but you can't see them. They chill the air around them below dew-point and become surrounded by *fog*."

The problem was how to get out of the trap we were in. The limit of drift ice extends as far north as 52° in the area where we were, and further east, between 0° and 10° east, it reaches up to 48° south. Our only way of escape was north-ward, but from where we were, north of Elephant Island, it would take us several days to get clear of the drift ice even if we could steer a northeast, or northeast by north course, and the wind was contrary. And now the fog was closing in on us, and the thermometer was way below zero.

We tacked and turned our bow northwest – the only direction in which we had not sighted icebergs – with the wind on our starboard. But the fog did not clear and speed, which theoretically was our salvation, was also dangerous. We had to take in sail. But climbing the riggings and handling tackle was quite a different matter in this freezing weather from what it had been before. The thermometer registered twenty below zero. The first time I grabbed hold of a steel stay when I was sent aloft to make a topsail fast my hand stuck to the stay, and I could get it loose only by an excruciating effort, which practi-cally tore my skin off. I learned, when climbing the riggings in freezing weather, to hold on to the wood battens only, and not to the steel stays. The backs of our hands were already covered with chilblains, and we could not use mittens for work up aloft.

We took in jibs and topsails, and then the spanker, and put double reefs in the gaff sails, and even so we were going too fast. The fog was now all around us and we could hardly see further than fifty fathoms.

We now had to submit to what seemed to me the supreme indignity, which was to get up on the fo'c'sle head and, hour after hour, and all through the night, blow our foghorn. The foghorn was a primitive contraption which had to be cranked by hand. Blowing a foghorn in the situation we were in was of course a requirement according to the rules of navigation. But the chance of encountering a ship in these parts was so remote as to be negligible. The only floating objects likely to hear our warning were the icebergs themselves, and the idea that we might be giving these warning before we crashed into them struck me as a bad joke.

Sippola, despite his sardonic turn of mind, was as glum as the skipper and the mate.

"Those icebergs are sons of bitches," he said. "Floating death, we call dem. If ve hit von of dem ve vill be smashed into a tousand pieces."

Icebergs can be huge, 250 feet high and of vast expanse, and only one-ninth of their mass shows above the water. They can travel hundreds of miles from their place of origin in the polar icefields.

Joe was in a complete funk and refused to leave his bunk. Sippola threatened him with loss of his pay, but this had no effect. "Throw him overboard," said George. Even the skipper, who had never yet set foot in the fo'c'sle, could not make him budge.

As night fell, and the fog persisted, we lowered the mizzen sail to cut down our speed still further. All night we kept the lugubrious foghorn going. The night was pitch-black, and we had of course no kind of searchlight. Two of us, cranking the foghorn alternately, were on the lookout on the fo'c'sle head while the third man on the watch was at the helm. If suddenly we were to see a vast pale shape loom up ahead of us we were supposed to give an immediate signal with repeated strokes on the pipe that we used to sound the bells, so that the helmsman could at once put the wheel over. But by that time it would of course already be too late. It was rather terrifying to find ourselves so defenceless against so great and so present a menace.

We were never so glad to greet the dawn and to find ourselves still afloat and intact. The fog slowly lifted in the course of the morning and we were able to give the foghorn a rest. By noon a wan sun was outlined against the high mist.

We saw no icebergs, but the visibility was poor, and by mid-afternoon we sighted an enormous ice plateau ahead of us emerging from the mist. We promptly changed our course, almost due west this time. In the middle of the night watch we again turned round and set our course at southeast by south. We kept the foghorn going all night, and the uncertainty, the suspense, were even more nerve-racking than the night before.

The morning rose fairly clear, and now we saw five, six, seven icebergs at different points of the compass, some much nearer than we had seen before and one, to our starboard, towering dazzling white above the water with caves and cliffs of fantastic shades of blue and green, and something that looked like cascades pouring down its sides. A film of ice had formed on the stays of our riggings.

At the rate at which we were going we would be here forever, if we were lucky enough not to crash into one of those formidable blocks of ice in a thick fog or in the darkness of the night. The skipper seemed to have made up his mind, too, that something had to be done to escape, for he ordered all sails to be hoisted or let out, and we were able to head almost due north in a direction about half way between two menacing icebergs. With a good wind in our favour we managed to get beyond them, but in the late afternoon we saw a series of other vague shapes ahead of us. He decided then to reduce our sails to the minimum, and we spent another agonizing night in which none of us did much sleeping.

The next morning we were again surrounded by the jagged white masses of ice. With our raw hands we again proceeded to hoist the sails. We now had the southeast trade wind and we could head again in a northeasterly direction, and while we had good daylight and clear visibility we took the chance of going fairly close to one of the icebergs. A kind of thick vapour hung round the lower part of it and we could see an area of white in the water around it. At one point we were violently shaken by a series of vast waves in a relatively quiet sea. The mate told George this could have been caused by a whole big berg capsizing as the warm sea melted the underwater portion away. By nightfall we were still in the midst of the drift ice and we again had to bring down most of our canvas.

We kept the foghorn going all night, and even before the night was over we became aware of the fact that if the foghorn ever had any point it surely had one now, for the fog was coming over us so thick that we could not see ten feet away and had more or less to feel our way about the ship.

On 11 November 1920 they docked in Cape Town. They left on 16 December to make the return trip in ballast. They weathered a storm in the Tasman Sea:

On 24 January we cleared Tasmania and entered upon the thousand-mile stretch of stormy sea – the Tasman Sea – that separates that island from New Zealand. That afternoon the wind began to blow threateningly from the north. As soon as our watch got back on deck in the middle of the dogwatch we hauled down the square sail from the foremast and made it fast. Then we dewed up the fore and main gaff topsails, the mizzen having been made fast the day before. I was sent aloft to make the fore top fast – a beastly job, at best.

A mizzly fog was rolling over us as I went up, and all the ropes and riggings were dripping. The sail, too, was heavy as lead, and had blown itself round the outrigger and between the back stays, so that it took me more than half an hour to make the thing fast. I was consoling myself, however, that in a short time I would be snugly sleeping in my bunk. Just as I started to come down, a pelting rain assaulted me and by the time I reached the deck I was drenched. As luck would have it, my wardrobe at that time was limited to what I was then wearing. The rest of my clothes, except for some woollens, were soaking in a tub of soapy water. I was about to retire to the fo'c'sle when all hands were called on deck to reef down.

The wind was blowing so hard that as we tried to lower the

sails the canvas would press against the stays and remain stuck there until a momentary lurch of the ship to windward or a let-up in the wind allowed the gaff to drop a few feet at a time. The huge surface of canvas would bulge like a balloon, then begin to shake madly and collapse, only to swell out again with an explosive bang. Each time the skipper would rage, look up at the sky and shake his fists. "Oh, you brute!" he would shout, addressing the Almighty. On our passage across the South Atlantic we had lost a mizzen sail in this way as we were lowering it for a reef. For days thereafter we had had to listen to the skipper's despairing groans. Fourteen hundred dollars was the sum he had mentioned then, though more generally he spoke of "a thousand dollars worth of canvas". "And these," he would explain, speaking of our sails which had seen considerable service and many of which were patched, "are just as good as new – to us, anyway."

This time, however, we lost no sails. We reefed the mizzen, then the foresail and made the spanker fast. The flying jib also came down, and an hour later the cap jib. At midnight we reefed the mainsail, still assailed by the pelting downpour and occasionally rushed at close quarters by a huge sea that crashed against the ship's side and swept across the deck.

At midnight I took the wheel, and at just about that time streaks of lightning began to play across the sky. There was something indescribably weird and unreal about the scene lit up by the intermittent blinding flashes. The sea was a roaring, seething mass of phosphorescent foam rising to billows mountain-high. As the thunderclouds swept dizzily along they would sometimes rip apart momentarily and a few brights stars would shine through the rift and then almost immediately be blotted out. The ship reared and plunged and rolled and lurched violently without let-up, and still the wind increased and the mountainous seas grew higher.

The second mate sent Feliz aloft to take care of the main top-sail. It had broken loose from its gasket. After a time the rain became only intermittent, driven across our path in sheets by sweeping squalls. Suddenly the moon, of which there had been no sign throughout the night, bared its bright round face, and a magic silver glow fell upon the water. Besides being highly phosphorescent, the sea was alive with a kind of jelly-fish which glow at night like huge fireflies. From my point of vantage at the wheel on the prancing poop deck I was thus treated to a rather impressive pyrotechnical display, composed of countless glittering sprays of foam tossed skyhigh, studded with smouldering sparks, writhing, shapeless forms and bright windstreaks in the troughs of the waves, pale, lurid stars dancing beyond the silver-edged clouds, and the ghastly moon breaking through at brief moments and turning everything into gold and silver – all of which was again and again blotted out by the heaven-shattering bursts of lightning followed by claps of thunder. Amid all this our little ship laboured and tossed, a mere straw before the fury of the elements.

At two o'clock I was relieved by Oscar, and went into the fo'c'sle for an hour, according to our routine. In this regard our starboard watch was more fortunate than the port watch. The mate required his men to remain on deck throughout their watch, even in the night watches, whereas the bos'n allowed us to relieve one another for the lookout every hour and spend the rest of the time in our bunks, when there was no sail work to be done. At three o'clock I relieved Feliz for the lookout. The ship was then rolling so violently that it required considerable skill and agility to preserve one's balance while walking down the length of the deck and clear the occasional seas that swept over the bulwarks. Sometimes I would just underestimate the lurch the ship was about to make and then in order to regain my balance I would have to scamper at full speed down the slanting deck and endeavour to catch hold of a boom or a mast. Once I tripped on the fore hatch. A few seconds later I was picking myself up from the lee waterway, dripping wet.

I have already mentioned the noise made by the elements and by the ship itself in such a storm. The din is so intense and so overwhelming that after a time one becomes deafened and almost unconscious of the very phenomenon of sound. It is only when one attempts to speak, roaring at the top of one's lungs while no sound comes, or when another person right in front of you tries to say something, and you see the violent effort he is making to have himself understood and you can hear nothing of what he is saying, that you realize what a considerable number of decibels are flying around.

The wind continued with undiminished violence for three days. Then gradually both wind and sea died down, although dark, menacing clouds still hovered about. Finally we fell into a calm. The skipper sighed and groaned, as usual, and spoke harshly to God. He also mentioned the Germans and the "Bushelviks", as he was wont to do whenever the weather put on a particularly bad performance. In the course of our voyage I made a small collection of some of the skipper's favourite expressions which he used on occasions like this. They would usually be muttered under his breath, but loud enough to be overheard, or else he would address one of us in confidential tones, as though he were imparting some rare secret. "Dangerous locality." "Treacherous water." "Bad season for hurricanes." "If we catch a storm in this part of the world, look out!" "This is one of the worst places we can get into." And I have already mentioned his remark to me a few days after we had passed Cape Horn: "We are now entering upon the most desolate stretch of water on the face of this globe."

They touched at Seattle. They were ordered to San Francisco. The company that owned the Rosamund *had gone bankrupt while they were at sea. It had been her last voyage. The* Rosamund *was anchored in San Francisco bay. She remained there until she was finally laid up at Lake Union, Seattle in October 1926. Chevalier's account was published in 1970.*

Storm at Sea
1941

Nicholas Monsarrat served in corvettes during the Battle of the Atlantic (1939–45). Corvettes were small warships. They were used to escort convoys of Allied merchant ships. Monsarrat:

A corvette would roll on wet grass.

Our measure of rough weather is domestic, but reliable. Moderate sea, the lavatory seat falls down when it is tipped up; rough sea, the radio set tumbles off its bracket in the wardroom.

Some trips are good, some not. There was one, in calm weather, with an easy-going Gibraltar convoy, that was a picnic, the kind of jaunt which costs a guinea a day, with fancy-dress thrown in, in peace-time there was another, that took us far North and West that was a long nightmare. For when, seven days out, we turned round to go home, an easterly gale set in: we went five hundred miles in the teeth of it before it moderated – five hundred miles, and six days, of screaming wind and massed, tumbling water, of sleet and snow-storms, of a sort of frozen malice in the weather which refused us all progress. Nothing could keep it out: helmets, mittens, duffle-coats, sea-boot stockings – all were like so much tissue paper. "Cold?" said the signalman, as he pulled his hand away from the Morse-lamp and left a patch of skin on the handle: "Cold? I reckon this would freeze the ears of a brass monkey."

There are cumulative miseries to be endured during a really wet night on the bridge: icy water finds its way everywhere – neck, wrists, trouser-legs, boots: one stands out there like a sodden automaton, ducking behind the rail as every other wave sends spray flying over the compass-house – and then standing up to face, with eyes that feel raw and salt-caked and streaming, the wind and the rain and the treachery of the sea. Of course, heavy weather need not always make life so miserable: if corvettes are in no hurry, and can afford to ease down and lie-to with their bows just off the wind, they do very well – as far as that's concerned, they are prime sea-boats; but if they have to proceed with any determination, they put their nose smack into it every time. Twice we have had windows smashed up on the bridge by seas which curled up and broke right on top of them: surprise-packets we could have done without. We're not complaining: just remarking on the facts . . .

Cheerful dialogue on being called for the middle watch, rough weather:

"Is it raining?"

"No, sir – just washing over."

Midnight means taking it all on again: mounting the ladder with an effort, watching for the square of sky (sometimes scarcely perceptible) which will tell you what the visibility is going to be like: listening to see if it is still blowing as hard as when you were last on watch. It usually is.

Apart from the noise it produces, rolling has a maddening rhythm that is one of the minor tortures of rough weather. It never stops or misses a beat, it cannot be escaped anywhere. If you go through a doorway, it hits you hard: if you sit down, you fall over; you get hurt, knocked about continuously, and it makes for extreme and childish anger. When you drink, the liquid rises towards you and slops over: at meals, the food spills off your plate, the cutlery will not stay in place. Things roll about, and bang, and slide away crazily: and then come back and hurt you again. The wind doesn't howl, it screams at you, and tears at your clothes, and throws you against things and drives your breath down your throat again. And off watch, below, there is no peace: only noise, furniture adrift, clothes and boots sculling about on the deck, a wet and dirty chaos. Even one's cabin can be a vicious cage, full of sly tricks and booby-traps: not a refuge at all, rather a more subtle danger-spot, catching you relaxed, and unawares and too dead-tired to guard your balance. Sometimes, at the worst height of a gale, you may be hove-to in this sort of fury for days on end, and all the time you can't forget that you are no nearer shelter than you were twenty-four hours before: you are gaining nothing, simply holding your own: the normal rigours of the trip are still piled up, mountains high, in front of you.

A most unholy chaos can be caused on the upper deck when, in bad weather, things get adrift and are not immediately secured.

We once had some heavy oil drums whlch broke away aft, and were washing about with a tremendous noise, dragging all sorts of oddments – planks, fenders, heaving-lines – in their train: to get them under control again we had almost to stalk them, dodging out of the way as they crashed to leeward, gradually getting more and more ropes secured and finally smothering them. And another time, a rough, pitch-dark night, one of the boats which was swung out rolled itself right under water, smashing the griping-spar and jumping its releasing gear at one end: it hung down by the after falls, its bows in the water at one moment and then lifting and crashing against the ship's side as we rolled. It looked, and sounded, nasty.

"Have a crack at securing that," said the captain, after watching it for a couple of minutes. "But don't kill yourself. If it's no good, cut it adrift."

The right order . . . It took an hour, and the six toughest hands of the watch, but we got it inboard in the end, not much the worse for wear, and securely lashed in its chocks. I think I almost enjoyed the struggle, floundering about on the boat-deck with the seas washing over, leaning outboard at the end of a life-line to try to get the falls hooked on again. It was nearer the sea-going of the past, less official, less organized, less war-like.

Discussion on the bridge, at the height of a gale, of how we came to be drafted to corvettes.

Captain: "I was told it would be like luxury motoring."

Self: "I was told I was damned lucky to get one."

Voice of Asdic rating: "I was detailed off, sir."

When the ship crosses the storm-centre, there comes a

sudden lull, and then the wind starts to blow from the opposite direction, setting up a baffling sea. It seems to come at you from all angles, rather like the meeting of the tides in Pentland Firth at the top of Scotland: shapeless humps of water are thrown together crazily, and when the wave-tops break they are caught and blown back like a horse's mane, or a crest of white hair suddenly whipped up.

Running with a heavy following sea at night has its own hard-won loveliness. The long streaks of foam are lit eerily by the moonlight: the enormous pile-up of water which collects, and roaring, under the bow, seems suddenly to explode into broad phosphorescent smother which in a moment is left behind. Looking aft, one sees the stern cant up before a black wall of water: the water overtakes, slides underneath and past, and breaks at the bow, its attack spent. The ship yaws, the compass swings: from below comes the quartermaster's muttered curse as he braces his feet and hauls the wheel over to meet the next ponderous weight of sea.

Simile-spinning in the middle watch.

Northern lights – like giant streamers stirred by a sky-wide fan: like an amateur-operatic rendering of Don Giovanni's purgatory: like the fake flames of a pale electric fire . . .

"Bosun's mate!"

"Bosun's mate, sir."

"Get me a cup of tea and the notebook in my top drawer."

It is pleasant to notice the first patch of drying deck after a storm. It spreads. It means peace. But it covers, between decks, a chaos which until then there has been no chance to set to rights.

In the mess-decks, water is everywhere: there are benches broken, things washing about on the deck, off-watch stokers trying to sleep and cursing the sweepers at work cleaning up. The ward-room is like an abandoned battle-field: armchairs have slipped their moorings and crashed the whole length of it, packed book-cases have burst open, and in the pantry all the steward's cunning has not prevented a formidable expense of broken crockery.

There's a respite now, anyway: hot meals again instead of tea
and corned-beef sandwiches: sleep without being tipped out of
your bunk, a whole watch without once getting wet. The upper-
deck Petty Officer gets to work squaring up, the seaman-gunner
of the watch cleans the Lewis and Hotchkiss guns, the Leading
Signalman checks over his rockets and flares, the Torpedoman
greases the depth-charge releasing gear, examines all the
primers, test the electric circuits. Work comes as a relief, after
the discomfort and the cramping inactivity of the past few days.

Plymouth to Sydney in One Stage
1966

*Francis Chichester (1901–71) became the second person to fly solo
to Australia in 1929. In 1953 he changed from flying to ocean
racing in yachts. In 1960 he made a record-breaking solo crossing
of the Atlantic. His yacht was named* Gipsy Moth III. *(The
original* Gipsy Moth *was one of the famous "clipper" ships;*
Gipsy Moth II *was his previous yacht).*

*He decided to circumnavigate the world in an interesting and
attractive way. Previous attempts had followed a well-beaten path
along the "belt" of the trade winds. Chichester:*

I told myself for a long time that anyone who tried to round
the Horn in a small yacht must be crazy. Of the eight yachts
I knew to have attempted it, six had been capsized or somer-
saulted, before, during or after the passage. I hate being
frightened, but, even more, I detest being prevented by fright.
At the same time the Horn had a fearsome fascination, and it
offered one of the greatest challenges left in the world.

Chichester assessed his possible speed and progress:

To sail a yacht from Plymouth to Sydney in one stage was a
most formidable proposition: could it be done? I measured it

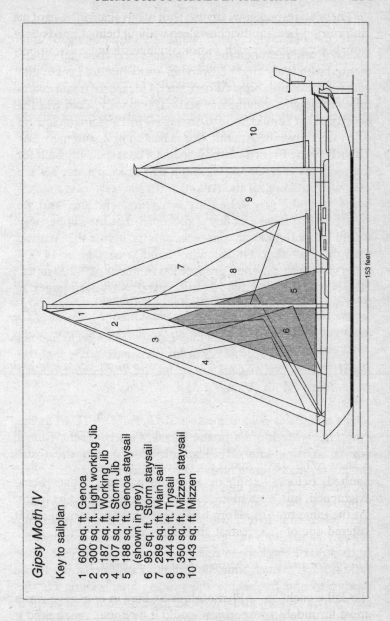

Gipsy Moth IV

Key to sailplan

1 600 sq. ft. Genoa
2 300 sq. ft. Light working Jib
3 187 sq. ft. Working Jib
4 107 sq. ft. Storm Jib
5 188 sq. ft. Genoa staysail
  (shown in grey)
6 95 sq. ft. Storm staysail
7 289 sq. ft. Main sail
8 144 sq. ft. Trysail
9 350 sq. ft. Mizzen staysail
10 143 sq. ft. Mizzen

153 feet

off somewhat hurriedly, and made it 13,750 miles. This was along the old clipper way, which the square-rigged ships followed, and reckoned the fastest route after they had experimented with every kind of diversion over a hundred years, and with ten thousand ships. (When, later, I measured it more carefully and slowly, it came out at 14,100 miles.) What was the best time that I could hope to do this in? In 1964, in the second solo race across the Atlantic, I was beaten by Lieutenant Eric Tabarly of the French Navy, who had a boat specially built for the race; his speed was 105 and a half miles per day for the east–west crossing of the Atlantic. On the west–east passage home after the race I had my son Giles with me, and we averaged 126 miles per day. I reckoned that the clipper way would be more like the west–east passage across the Atlantic than the east–west. On the other hand, a passage of 14,000 miles was a very different proposition from one of 3,200 miles. However, I reckoned that 126 miles per day was a fair target, at least one that I could aim for, and hope to hit.

On 12 August 1966 he started from London with his wife and son aboard. On 27 August he began his circumnavigation from the Royal Western Yacht Club's start line off Plymouth Hoe. His yacht, Gipsy Moth IV, *was a 53 foot, 13 ton boat.*

Sheila and Giles helped me to sail *Gipsy Moth IV* from the mooring at Mashford's to the Royal Western Yacht Club's normal starting line off Plymouth Hoe. I had the usual sinking feeling before a race. Sid Mashford in his launch took off Sheila and Giles, and after that I was alone. I ought, I suppose, to have experienced a sense of thankfulness, or at least relief, that here I was after all the years of planning, actually at sea with my great adventure before me, but the truth is that I was kept so rushed inanoeuvring the yacht that I did not have much time for feeling of any sort at all. I was tacking to and fro behind the starting line, waiting for the eleven o'clock gun; and short-tacking a 53-foot boat keeps a one-man crew fully occupied. However, I managed it without too great an effort. I had a jib and the mainsail set, and by timing the tack right, letting go the jib sheet at the right moment, and hauling it in the other side while steering with my backside against the tiller, I could avoid the grind of using a winch.

Off Madeira he lost control:

By evening I was past the eastern end of Madeira, and was sailing some miles south of Funchal. But by 21.00 that night I was in trouble. I was in the lee of the island and, although it was about 8 miles away, I was being struck by minor squalls from wind eddies whirling down from the 6,000-foot peaks. I had my first experience of *Gipsy Moth*'s being out of control, and I didn't like it. I had a desperate feeling when I couldn't move the tiller; the sails were pressed right down, and the boat was tearing through the water out of control. Gradually I got the mainsail down, followed by the mizzen. Then she was under control again, but almost immediately the wind died away to a complete calm. These whirling gusts were repeated time after time. I longed to escape from the wind shadow of the island. "No wonder," I logged, "the clippers kept outside Madeira. What a fool I have been! And I am worked out." During the intervals of being becalmed, the self-steering wind vane, released, rotated, swinging through whole circles. A clipper under these conditions would be in pretty serious trouble. With each burst of wind I gained a few miles to the south-west, and finally got clear of the island, determined if possible to keep well to windward of any other groups of islands on the voyage.

He made improvements for better handling:

In the afternoon I made various improvements for better gear-handling. Success in singlehanded sailing depends on easy gear-handling, and being able to keep the boat in control all the time. Some of the improvements I made were to fit blocks, so that the mizzen boom vangs could be led into the cockpit; blocks amid-ships for leading the after-guys of the poles back to the mast, where I fitted two camcleats to the deck on each side of the mast to take the boom guys. This arrangement enabled me to hoist a boom while all the time keeping control of it from where I stood at the mast. All the same it was quite a feat of juggling, because I had to control, at the same time, the foreguy, the aft-guy, the topping lift, the uphaul of the heel of the pole, and the downhaul of the pole heel, also the outhaul of the clew of the sail to the end of the pole and the sheet from the cockpit to the clew. (As the pole foreguy is paid out, for instance, the aft-guy needs taking in the same amount.) I have only myself to blame for the frightful number of operations involved in a gybe, for I designed the rig and layout of these poles myself. When I am working with normal efficiency, they do enable me to hoist and keep control of the two big running sails. Also, with this gear, I can drop the sails without much trouble if hit suddenly by a squall, whereas if I set a spinnaker of the same size as these two running sails (1,200 square feet) as is the usual practice in a racing boat in off-shore races, I should soon be in big trouble. Even yachts with big full crews usually get into trouble with their spinnakers.

In spite of all this fine talk about improvement, I got landed in a super-shemozzle that night. I had finished a gybe, and was looking forward to a peaceful noggin of brandy in the cabin, when along came a squall. It was not a severe one, but with more than 1,600 square feet of sail set, *Gipsy Moth* began to get out of control – that is to say, the self-steering gear could not hold her on course, and I could not take the helm as well as drop the sails. It was all very well galloping along at 9 knots, but no good if this was in the wrong direction! So I decided to drop the big genny which was poled out to starboard. I stupidly overlooked a step in my standard drill – a bad slip-up while working in a near gale-force wind. I let go the halliard and brought the luff of the sail down the topmast stay, and now had the bunt of the sail partly muzzled by my body and arms right in the stem of the boat inside the pulpit. The mistake I made was that I had left the running part of the clew outhaul cleated up at the mast, instead of bringing it forward with me to the pulpit. I had to leave the pulpit and let go the bunt of the sail, so that I could release this outhaul. The clew and foot of the sail stretched 20 feet outboard to the end of the pole, and this part of the sail filled out with wind to the shape of a banana, and began flogging madly up and down in the near-gale. Then I made a second blunder. I should have robbed a furled headsail near by of its sail tie, and used this to secure to the pulpit as much of the big genny as I had managed to smother in my arms. But the wind was freshening fast, the situation was getting serious, and I decided that the best thing to do was to dash for the mast and slack away the outhaul with a run. Before I got back to the pulpit, the sail had caught the wind, bellied out, and blown round to the leeward side of the stem. That sail is a piece of Terylene the size of a room 20 feet by 30 feet, and once it gets out of control it is a really tough proposition for a singlehander. When it was round to the leeward side of the fast-moving stem, the water caught it, and my heart sank with it as it disappeared under the stem and the ship sailed over it. My lovely sail, so essential to this project, ridden under the keel! I must slow up the ship as soon as possible, but first I had to slack away any ropes holding the sail to the windward side of the boat. The strain on all this gear from a huge bag of Terylene under water, in a speed of 8 to 9 knots, must have been terrific. I let the outhaul fly. The rope disappeared into the sea like a thin snake. I then let go the foreguy to the pole; this allowed the sheet from the cockpit to the clew of the sail to pass under the keel. Now, the sail under water was held only by the hanks fastening it to the forestay. It should be streaming freely in the water, and no more harm should happen to it.

I dropped the big genny on the leeward side, then the mainsail, and lastly the mizzen and, with the boat nearly stopped, I first housed the pole on deck, and then began hauling the sail inboard foot by foot until it would come no farther. I was puzzled by this until I realised that the sheet was still fast to the winch in the cockpit on the starboard side, and was holding the clew under the keel to the weather side of the ship. I let go of the sheet, and got the rest of the sail inboard. This may sound simple enough, but it was no fun at the time. It was dark and blowing hard, and it was all hard work. I was immensely pleased to find later that though both sail and sheet had plenty of red anti-fouling paint on them from the keel, the sail was intact. But I was depressed at losing a night's sailing. The boat was too big, no doubt of it. I felt that I had had to put out a much bigger physical effort than I thought I was normally good for. I went below and had my brandy at last, but I had no appetite at all, although I had had only a sandwich for lunch. However, I could not bear to lose the good wind, so I donned my lifeline again and hoisted the big port-side genoa once more. The yacht began moving, and I went below to try and get some sleep.

But my leg ached too much to sleep. The rolling was bad without the mainsail, so I decided to have another go. I went on deck yet again, and rehoisted the mainsail. I finished the whole operation at 14 minutes before midnight. The giant shemozzle itself had lasted over three hours. There was a time when I had thought sailing would be no good to me because it provided no physical effort and exercise! At that moment, that seemed a pretty good joke.

On 10 September he wrote in his log:

"Roughish going," and one and a half hours later my log read, "Most puzzling: I was woken by a shattering shock, and got the impression that things were jumping about in the cabin due to it. I thought of what could have caused it, the mast broken, the main boom adrift and banging the cabin, a pole come down from aloft. I dressed in full war paint-shorts, lifeline, harness and cap-and went on deck to find out the worst. I could see nothing wrong at all. I inspected everything right up to the stem. I believe *Gipsy Moth* must have sailed full tilt into a whale, and got away with it. Very fortunately there was no more water in the bilge. I suppose it could have been a dream or a nightmare."

On 17 September he celebrated his 65th birthday. He was sleeping after enjoying the occasion with champagne cocktails.

I could have done without a celebration hangover at 2 a.m., when a sharp squall of wind laid *Gipsy Moth* over on her side. I staggered out of my bunk with difficulty, as I was on the lee side of the boat and was still pretty full of brandy and bonhomie. I started looking for clothes, getting the best footholds I could at the side of the boat and on the bunk, but with a shot of panic in my vitals I realised that this was a serious emergency; there was no time for clothes. I grabbed a lifeline harness and put that on as I climbed into the cockpit. *Gipsy Moth* was pressed over on her side, with the sails dipping in the water and out of control of the self-steering gear. No wonder at that, because after I had released the self-steering gear from the tiller I could not move the tiller even with a tiller line to help. The situation was serious, because if she went over further and the sails got completely below the water, the companion being wide open, the water could easily rush in there and the boat founder. *Gipsy Moth* was carrying every square foot of sail I had been able to set. I let go the mizzen staysail (350 square feet) with a run, and hauled it into the cock-pit, which it half filled, until I could get at the mainsheet and pay off the main boom. Slowly the boat righted, and I was able to turn her downwind and engage the self-steering gear again to control her. This enabled me to get forward to drop the big 600-square-foot genoa. That left the staysail genoa and the mainsail. After the squall eased I waited a few minutes because of the heavy rain, and by 03.17 I had added the big jib and the mizzen. I was tempted to reset the mizzen staysail, but did not want to be turned out again that night for another shemozzle with the boat out of control, so left it down. As I turned in again I made a note that I must devise a better arrangement for the tiller lines.

Gipsy Moth IV *was not without its faults.*

I trimmed up the ship carefully to sail as close as possible to the south-east wind. The wind had dropped to a gentle and ideal breeze and the sea had moderated. The waves were now quite small – ripples, I felt like calling them – but I found that they made *Gipsy Moth* hobbyhorse in such a way that three waves in succession would each knock three-quarters of a knot off the speed. The first wave would cut the speed down from 5 and a half knots to 4 and three-quarters, the second to 4 knots and the third to 3 and a quarter knots. If there was a fourth or fourth and fifth they would bring the yacht up head to wind and it would stop dead. The only way of avoiding this with the self-steering gear in control was to head off the wind another 20°. This meant that I could not sail any closer to the wind than the clippers, and the plan that I had set so much store on collapsed in ruins. This hobbyhorsing was the first of *Gipsy Moth*'s nasty tricks that I was to suffer from on the voyage. It was a tiresome and trying period of the voyage. If I kept *Gipsy Moth* going fast on the wind, she slammed damnably into the seas, which worried me for the safety of her hull. Yet I had to keep going as fast as I could if I was not to fall hopelessly behind the clippers. I could make no good radio contacts, and I had trouble trying to charge the batteries. I could not get a good charge into them. At night I was troubled by cramp in my legs which would hit me after I had been asleep about two hours, and would let go only if I stood up. This meant that I never got more than about two hours' sleep at a time. It was hot, and I sweated profusely; I wondered if my body might be losing too much salt. I decided to drink half a glassful of seawater a day to put back salt.

After crossing the line on 22 September 1966:

It was now that *Gipsy Moth*'s second vicious habit began to take effect. Now and then when the wind eased I would log that I was having some lovely sailing, but alas a few minutes or hours later there was sure to be a complaint about the difficulty of keeping *Gipsy Moth* to her heading. The log is littered with entries such as, "*Gipsy Moth* keeps on edging up to the wind and slowing up then", "I feel she is too much heeled, labouring and pinned down", "The self-steering could not settle down and keep to a heading: too much weather helm", "I see she is sailing too free now; I must have another go at her, drat it!", "I could not stand the violent slamming which built up when the wind increased above 20 knots and the 40° heel is pretty excessive", "I think the vane must be slipping in some of the big bumps", "*Gipsy Moth* is sailing 65° off the true wind." (She ought to have been sailing within 50° of the true wind at the most.)

From now on, except when the wind dropped and the sea moderated, I had an almost endless struggle trying to keep *Gipsy Moth* to a heading close-hauled. I thought at the time that it was due to the self-steering gear being unable to hold the tiller, Eventually, however, I discovered the trouble. I was standing on the deck one day looking forward, when the wind increased suddenly in a puff from 20 knots to 25 knots. The boat heeled over more, and to my astonishment I saw the bows slide over the water downwind about 30°. It was like a knife spreading butter, sliding over a piece of bread. What had plagued and puzzled me became quite clear; there was a critical angle of heel for the boat. If the hull came a degree or two more upright it would start griping up to windward and slowing up. If; however, the hull heeled over a degree or two more than this critical angle, the forepart of the boat slid off to leeward, the boat lying more on its side had quite different sailing character-istics, and would romp off at great speed on a heading 300 downwind. On this heading *Gipsy Moth* went at racing speed, but of course this was unfortunate if the heading I wanted was

30° different. When I did discover this trick, it explained something else which had puzzled me. Normally, when sailing hard on the wind if you want to ease off 5 or 10°, the drill is to slack the mainsail sheet, and the heading will at once ease off a few degrees downwind. With *Gipsy Moth IV* it was necessary to do exactly the opposite; to head a few degrees away from the wind it was necessary to harden in the sails! What happened was that this changed the angle of heel, and she would romp off downwind at a great pace.

On 26 September he was alarmed by a big bang.

It was not comfortable sailing in the strong winds, Big "slams" would slow the boat right down, and then she would pinch up to windward as if the self-steering had been "forced". I thought, indeed, that this was what was happening, and I would go and give the self-steering a downwind twitch. I felt that I needed both a monkey and an elephant for supplementary crew – the monkey to tackle things when Gipsy Moth was heeled to 35° or more, and the elephant to take the helm when it got out of control in a squall.

On Monday night (26 September) I had just settled nicely in my berth, absorbed by Maigret and *La Grande Perche*, when there was a big bang astern. A big sail flap followed, and I thought that something in the self-steering gear had burst. I got on deck as fast as I could, but it was no weather to be there without a safety belt. I was relieved to find that it was only a tiller line which had broken. I robbed one of the spinnaker pole guys, and rigged that hoping that the old rope had just perished and that the new rope would hold. It was quite a long job, in a strong wind and rough sea, but I got it done and got back to my berth feeling so sleepy that I could hardly keep my eyes open. I was not allowed to sleep for long – *Gipsy Moth* was getting such a bashing that I could not stand it. I went on deck again and dropped the mainsail, and then I did manage to get a bit of rest.

I got up after a couple of hours, intending to go on deck and get the mainsail up again, but I decided to have a cup of hot chocolate first. The wind increased to 25 knots while I sipped my chocolate, so I hoisted the small staysail, and left the main down. That morning might have seen the end of the voyage as far as I was concerned, for I had a narrow escape in a nasty, though rather absurd, accident. The weather continued dirty, and *Gipsy Moth* was much thrown about. I went to the heads [lavatory] and the door was twice thrown open, and I pushed it shut. Without warning the door burst open again, smashed back downhill from behind me, and the handle struck me a crack on the forehead, sending my spectacles flying. The blow cut my head about two inches above my eye, and left me feeling nearly stunned. Amazingly, the spectacles were not damaged, and some dabbing with disinfectant seemed all that the cut needed. But my escape seemed a miracle – supposing that handle had caught me on the eye, after smashing through my glasses!

He compared his progress with that of the clipper ships; he calculated that he was 1,140 miles behind Cutty Sark's *progress. By 18 October he was halfway to Sydney.*
  Rounding the Cape of Good Hope he was caught up in a storm:

I was rounding the Cape of Good Hope, though well to the south of it, and the weather grew more boisterous. The Forties really were beginning to roar, with strong winds increasing suddenly to gale force. I was bothered still with cramp in my leg, and began to suffer from lack of rest. On the night of 19–20 October at 2.30 a.m. I fell into a sound sleep for what seemed the first time for ages, but just after 4.30 a.m. I had a rude awakening. A dollop of water from a wave coming on board landed on the head of my bunk, and it was followed quickly by a second and a third. It was my own fault, for leaving out the top washboard of the companionway into the cabin, but this did not make it any more pleasant. I got up at once, dressed, dropped the spitfire jib, and turned

dead downwind, because I thought *Gipsy Moth* would run
dead before the wind under bare poles. Conditions were
rugged on deck, with a lot of wind and water, both sea and
heavy rain. I had to make sure of a good grip handy all the
time, because of the rolling, and the seas pitching into the
hull. After dropping the sail I felt seasick, and went below
again to lie down, and try to get some more sleep. It was no
good. No sooner had I undressed from my deck clothes than
Gipsy Moth broached to, and I had to scramble into all my
deck gear again and get back on deck as quickly as I could.
Gipsy Moth had been slewed round broadside on to the
waves, and she refused to answer the helm to take up any
other heading. I noticed that the self-steering vane had
apparently slipped, and was no longer trying to turn the
rudder. I decided to stream a drogue from the stern, in the
hope of bringing the stern to the wind. This I did, after
collecting a shackle, a swivel, some rope from the afterpeak
and the drogue from the forepeak. It didn't work; the yacht
had not enough way on her to give the drogue the power to
haul the stern round.

Gipsy Moth under bare poles in a gale would do nothing
but lie ahull, broadside on to wind and waves. I was
convinced by what had happened that she could not be made
to run downwind under bare poles in a seaway. The rudder
could not control her without a storm jib on the foremast
stay. This was a serious setback; it meant that her slowest
speed running downwind in a gale would be 8 knots. I had
never even considered that such a thing could happen! *Gipsy
Moth III* had steered easily downwind under bare poles, or
even with the wind on the quarter, and the American-
designed *Figaro* had steered lightly and easily when we
brought her up the English Channel one night under bare
poles in a strong gale.

It was damnably uncomfortable. The wind went up to 55
knots, and the yacht was thrown about in all directions.
Water kept forcing its way under the cabin hatch whenever a
wave hit the deck. My sextant, which I stowed for safety in a

cabin berth – fortunately in its box – was thrown out on to the cabin floor. I had one wave come right over me when I was in the cockpit; the water felt oddly warm, and the wave did not seem to strike with much force, I suppose because we were not moving. The air was biting cold with hail.

The self-steering vane was damaged. It had sheared the bolt and pin holding it to its upright mast or shaft, and I thought it remarkable that it had not blown away altogether. I could make no attempt at repair then, because it was impossible to work on it in that high wind and very rough sea. All I could do was to lash it up temporarily.

The storm went on all day. From time to time the wind would seem to ease a little, and I would go on deck to see if I could do anything with the self-steering gear. In one such interval I managed to dismantle the self-steering oar and haul it inboard, because it was getting such a pounding from the waves. It seemed amazing that the vane had not taken off into the air. But always after these lulls the wind came back again, and I could make no start on repairs. The seabirds got very excited about the drogue churning up white water astern. Watching their flight against the strong wind took my mind off my own miseries. They seemed to creep up the sides of the waves uphill, very close to the water. At three o'clock in the afternoon the birds lost whatever entertainment they had had from my drogue, because the warp attached to it parted, and the drogue went.

A big breaking wave struck *Gipsy Moth* and turned her right round, so that she faced north-west. I could do nothing to get her back without setting a sail, and it was too rough for making sail. I felt that it did not matter much which way she was headed because although we were being flung about all over the place, it was hard to tell if *Gipsy Moth* was moving through the water at all.

By that time I had not had anything to eat for twenty-four hours, and still I did not feel hungry. I scribbled in my log: "It is the queasiness which kills appetite, I think. This is not my merriest day, but it might be worse. It is very cold out."

By nightfall I managed to get the yacht going again. At last the wind lulled for long enough to enable me to raise the little spitfire jib, and I gybed round. I contrived a very temporary repair of the self-steering with cordage, but it was not doing a job -the self-steering oar was still on deck. I set the tiller to take advantage of the fact that *Gipsy Moth* liked to lie beam on to the wind, and I left things at that until next morning. It was still appallingly uncomfortable, but we were sailing. The seas were impressive. If I looked up while working on deck I felt that I had to hang on for dear life. It seemed impossible for the monster rolling down on top of us not to submerge boat and all. But always *Gipsy Moth* rode up again. Some waves I called "strikers" – they would slam into the yacht viciously. I think these were waves which started to break about 25 yards from the boat. They looked about 100 feet high, some of them, so I dare say they were about 40 feet. They treated the boat like a cork, slewing it round and rolling it on its side. I would trim the self-steering gear and go below, only to find the heading 40° off what it should have been, so back I would have to go, to retrim the self-steering gear. I decided that the big waves, slewing the boat through an angle of 45–60°, must make things impossible for the self-steering gear.

Gipsy Moth's third vice was taking effect; she could not keep to her heading at the top of a wave face, but whipped round and broached to, lying broadside on to the wind and the waves. Sometimes the self-steering gear could bring her back on to her right heading, but often when the wind vane was suddenly swung 60° across the gale force wind, the pressure on it was too great; if the safety clutch had not given way, the vane must have broken. Broaching-to was the danger that was most dreaded by the clippers. Slewing round, broadside on to a big Southern Ocean storm, they would roll their masts down, and, if the sails went into the water, they were likely to founder, as many did. Leaving the danger aside (which, anyway, I did not consider as great for *Gipsy Moth* as for the clippers because *Gipsy Moth* ought to survive a knock-down which would cause a clipper to founder) those broach-ings seriously threatened the self-steering gear. To cut down the broaching, I was forced to cut down the amount of sail that I would have carried in northern waters. This was a big setback to my plans, because I had reckoned on making long runs in the westerlies down south. I had hoped, before I started the voyage, that a long light boat, which *Gipsy Moth* was designed to be, would knock off runs of 250 miles, day after day. I am not a designer myself; and my opinion as to the cause of this trick of *Gipsy Moth*'s may not be of value, but I did have a long experience of the boat and, in my opinion, her tendency to flip round as easily as a whip is cracked was due to her having too short a forefoot, and no grip on the water there, combined with an unbalance of the hull which required an excessive load on the tiller to activate the rudder.

He was in the southern Indian Ocean in the latitudes known as the Roaring Forties:

Twice I entered the Forties, and was driven out by a gale. A 50-knot squall going through was like the infernal regions, with great white monsters bearing down out of a black void, picking up the boat and dashing it about. I hated the feeling of being out of control. Once a wave broke in the cockpit, not seriously, but the immense power it showed was frightening. I wrote: "It requires a Dr Johnson to describe this life. I should add that the cabin floor is all running wet, and my clothes are beginning to get pretty wet too. *Vive le* yachting!"

On 2 November I could not understand why *Gipsy Moth* nearly gybed time after time. Several times I reached the companion just in time to push the tiller over (leaning out from the cabin) at the gybing point. If she had gybed in that wind with the boom right out, there would have been chaos and damage. Then the boat would come up to wind until the wind was abeam. I began to fear that something had broken in the self-steering gear, so put on a coat and went to investigate. I found that the self-steering gear was not connected to the rudder at all; the link arm between the wind vane and the steering oar had pulled out of its socket after shaking out the safety pin somehow. I was thankful it was no worse. That day my speedometer packed up. At first I was surprised how much I missed it, but as things turned out it did not matter much, for I found that my dead reckoning was as accurate as it had been when the speedometer was working. As a matter of fact, it was more accurate, because the speedometer had been under-registering at low speeds.

Perhaps this was because the little propeller of the speedometer's underwater unit was getting foul with marine growth. After I had got over the feeling of loss when the speedometer failed, it was quite a relief not to have it. There was certainly more peace in not eyeing the speed all the time, wondering if it could be improved.

On 15 November his self-steering gear broke:

I woke to a 40-knot wind – a heavy weight of wind, but no worse than the rough weather over most of the past weeks. The burgee halliard parted, but that was small beer. At 12.15 I went aft to make what I thought would be a minor repair to the self-steering gear, and found that the steel frame holding the top of the steering blade had broken in half. There were two steel plates, one on each side of the top of the blade, to hold the blade and to connect it to the wind vane. Both had fractured. The oar blade was attached to the ship only by a rod used to alter its rake. It was wobbling about in the wake like a dead fish held by a line. I expected it to break away at any moment, and rushed back to the cockpit. I let all the sails drop with a run as fast as I could let the halliards go, so as to stop the ship and take as much strain off the gear as possible. Then I unshipped the blade, and got it aboard as quickly as I could, before the fitting which held the rod broke off and I lost the oar.

The sight of the self-steering gear broken beyond repair

acted like a catalyst. At first I turned cold inside and my feelings, my spirit, seemed to freeze and sink inside me. I had a strange feeling that my personality was split and that I was watching myself drop the sails efficiently and lift out the broken gear coolly. My project was killed. Not only was my plan to race 100 days to Sydney shattered, but to make a non-stop passage there was impossible, too. Then I found out that I was not really crestfallen; it was a relief. I realized that I had been waiting for this to happen for a long time. I went below and stood myself a brandy, hot. Now my thoughts began whirling round in tight circles, as I thought about what had happened, and searched for the best course of action. I went back to the stern and studied the breakage. Two steel plates, 27 inches long, 6 inches wide and a quarter of an inch thick connected the wooden steering oar to the rest of the gear. These had both broken clean across, where a strengthening girder had been welded on to the plates. I considered all the pieces of sheet metal on the boat that I could think of; wondering if I could make a repair. The best bet seemed to be the swinging frame of the Primus stove, but it was not nearly as strong as the original metal that had broken and, besides that, I had no suitable nuts and bolts for bolting it to the broken pieces. The self-steering gear could not be repaired on board – I was well and truly in trouble. If I had had a normal boat I could have trimmed her up to sail herself; but experience so far had convinced me that *Gipsy Moth IV* could never be balanced to sail herself for more than a few minutes. The bald fact was that she could only be sailed from now on while I was at the helm, otherwise she must be hove to while I slept, cooked, ate, navigated or did any of the other many jobs about the ship. I should do well if I could average 10 hours a day at the helm; that would give me 60 miles a day at 6 knots. Taking calms and headwinds into consideration, I should do well to make good, on an average, 50 miles per day. I thought I was 2,758 miles from Sydney which was a long way, only 200 miles less, for example, than the Great Circle distance from Plymouth to New York. It would take an age to reach it, 55 days at 50 miles per day, perhaps 3 months. On top of the 80 days I had spent on the passage so far, it seemed out of the question. The only course open to me was to head for the nearest place where I could get a repair. The nearest suitable place was Fremantle. Even that was 1,160 miles away which would mean a very long time at the helm. I worked out a course for Fremantle.

His improvized adjustments worked well enough to allow him to continue towards Sydney. In the Bass strait between Australia and Tasmania, Gipsy Moth IV *went through a gale.*

I had got stuck with what I had always hoped to avoid, having to enter Bass Strait in a gale with bad visibility and no position check for 12,000 miles. I was on edge about this, for sextant observations of the sun, moon or stars will give an accurate fix only if there is no blunder in working out the sights. I reckon to make some blunders in, I should guess, about one observation in ten or twenty, usually something quite silly, like using the wrong date in the almanac, or copying down the wrong figure from a 6-figure logarithm. Fortunately I nearly always realize when a mistake has been made somewhere; I seem to develop an uncanny instinct for smelling out an error. But, aware of having made these blunders, I could not help feeling nervy when approaching land and relying on astro-navigation for not hitting rocks or an island in the dark when the last positive position check was 12,000 miles back. Suppose there had been some consistent error running through all the astronomical observations, an undetected error in the sextant, or in the time, stop watch, the tables, the almanac . . . I had expected to get a check from the radio beacons in Bass Strait; but when I tuned in to the frequencies listed in the latest Admiralty Signals Manual I could not pick up any of them – I did not know then that all the Australian frequencies had been changed. I searched the whole range of frequencies on my D/F radio set and picked up Mount Gambier airfield beacon on a frequency totally different from the one in the manual. I then began searching the frequency band for the Cape Otway and Cape Wickham beacons. The trouble was that these came on only at intervals of 30 minutes.

To make matters worse it was a head-on gale so that I was having to beat slowly to windward. At 5.30 p.m. I tacked again, and once more was headed for the coast, later in darkness and still a gale with bad visibility. The plunging and pounding of the boat could drive a man crazy and when I called up on the R/T that night I felt it was like trying to use a telephone when standing on a dodgem at a fair.

At 09.40 next morning (December 3) my dead reckoning position should have been within soundings for my little echo sounder, which had a range of 50 fathoms. But the echo sounder recorded no signals, so I assumed I was a couple of miles to the west where the chart showed a depth of over 50 fathoms. If that were right, I was still 9 miles off the lee coast.

An Australian journalist put off to meet him in a rubber boat. He offered him onions and a bottle of whisky. Chichester refused them in case he got into trouble with Australian customs in Sydney. He reached Sydney on 12 December 1966. It had taken him 107 days. He had sailed 14,100 miles.

Nightmare in the Southern Ocean
1967

Francis Chichester stayed in Sydney for over a month. Gipsy Moth IV *was repaired by expert friends. Chichester resumed his solo around the world voyage on 29 January 1967. Chichester:*

I passed Sydney Heads at 12.15, and at 14.30 the last of the accompanying boats left me. I had trouble with the propeller shaft, which I couldn't stop rotating. The brake would not work, so I had to dive down under the cockpit, head first and feet up, to fix the thing. I didn't enjoy these upside-down antics, and I felt horribly seasick. By 18.00 I was becalmed, but the calm didn't last long. There was a dense roll of clouds above the horizon, and wind began coming in from the south, at first lightly, but soon blowing up. By 19.00 it was coming at me in a series of savage bursts. At first I ran off northwards at 8 knots, then I took down all sail and lay ahull – that is, battened down, without sail, to give completely to the sea like a cork-in a great deluge of rain, reducing visibility to about 50 yards. Soon it got dark, and it was very dark – absolutely pitch dark. I was seasick and turned in but didn't get much rest. After about three quarters of an hour I heard the self-steering oar banging about, and went on deck to deal with it. The wind then was about 35 knots, and I thought that *Gipsy Moth* could stand a jib and get moving again. I set a working jib, but it was too much for her. So I replaced it with a storm jib. With this I left her to fight her way slowly east at about 2 knots and turned in again, determined to sleep all night.

I stayed in my bunk until just after 04.00, when the wind began coming still more strongly and I went up to drop the storm jib and lie ahull again. We stayed like this for most of the day; it was too rough for even a storm jib with the wind blowing at 50 knots or more. In the afternoon I did set a storm jib, reefed to only 60 square feet, a mere rag of sail, chiefly to try to cut down thumping in the heavy seas. I hoped that the thumping was due to the self-steering gear, and not to the new false keel.

In spite of the storm, radio conditions were good, and at 8 a.m. I had a good radio talk with Sheila which cheered me up. I was still sick from time to time, but slowly began to feel better, and gave myself some brandy, sugar and lemon, which I managed to keep down. The weather forecasts were bad with renewed cyclone warnings. This was Tropical Cyclone Diana, which was reported to be moving SE at about 20 mph. I tried to work out where it was in relation to me, and I reckoned that the worst of it would pass some 270 miles to the east of my noon position. That was something, but the whole area of the Tasman Sea was violently disturbed with winds from 40 to 60 knots, gusting up to 80 knots in squalls. There was nothing I could do about it. I did not worry over much, but just tried to exist until the storm passed.

That Monday night was as foul and black a night as you could meet at sea. Although it was pitch dark, the white breakers showed in the blackness like monstrous beasts charging down on the yacht. They towered high in the sky; I wouldn't blame anyone for being terrified at the sight. My cross-tree light showed up the breaking water, white in the black darkness, and now and then a wave caught the hull and, breaking against it, sluiced over the decks. As I worked my way along the deck I thought: "Christ! What must it be like in a 120-knot wind!" I dropped the remaining storm sail, furled and tied it down. *Gipsy Moth* had been doing 8 knots with the little sail set, and I thought she would be less liable to damage lying ahull with no forward speed. As I worked my way aft again after finishing the job on the foredeck, I looked at the retaining net amidships, holding the two big genoas bagged up, and the 1,000 feet of warp in several coils. I knew that I ought to pass a couple of ropes over the net between the eye bolts at each side for storm lashings – I had always done this before on the passage out, But these ropes had not been re-rigged in Sydney and I was feeling ghastly, I thought due to sea sickness. (From something which happened later I can only deduce that the chief cause of my trouble was the Australian champagne I had drunk. For some reason this acted like poison on me.) Whatever the cause of my trouble, I weakened, and decided to leave the extra lashing until the morning. When I got below and had stripped off my oilskins I rolled into my bunk and put all the lights out. This was about two hours after dark. The bunk was the only place where one could wait below, for it was difficult to stand up, and I should have been continually thrown off if I had sat on the settee. However, lying on my back in the bunk, I dropped into a fitful sleep after a while.

I think I was awake when the boat began to roll over. If not,

I woke immediately she started to do so. Perhaps when the wave hit her I woke. It was pitch dark. As she started rolling I said to myself, "Over she goes!" I was not frightened, but intensely alert and curious. Then a lot of crashing and banging started, and my head and shoulders were being bombarded with crockery and cutlery and bottles. I had an oppressive feeling of the boat being on top of me. I wondered if she would roll over completely, and what the damage would be; but she came up quietly the same side that she had gone down. I reached up and put my bunk light on. It worked, giving me a curious feeling of something normal in a world of utter chaos. I have only a confused idea of what I did for the next hour or so. I had an absolutely hopeless feeling when I looked at the pile of jumbled up food and gear all along the cabin. Anything that was in my way when I wanted to move I think I put back in its right place, though feeling as I did so that it was a waste of time as she would probably go over again. The cabin was 2 foot deep all along with a jumbled-up pile of hundreds of tins, bottles, tools, shackles, blocks, two sextants and oddments. Every settee locker, the whole starboard bunk, and the three starboard drop lockers had all emptied out when she was upside down. Water was swishing about on the cabin sole beside the chart table, but not much. I looked into the bilge which is 5 feet deep, but it was not quite full, for which I thought, "Thank God."

This made me get cracking with the radio, at forty-five minutes after midnight, and two and a quarter hours after the capsize. I was afraid that the radio telephone would go out of action through water percolating it, and that even if it didn't, if the boat went over again the mass of water in the bilge must inevitably flood the telephone and finish it. I had to try to get a message through to say that I was all right, so that if the telephone went dead people would not think that I had foundered because of that. I called up on the distress frequency 2182 and got Sydney Radio straight away. As usual they were most efficient and co-operative. I asked them to give my wife a message in the morning to say that I had capsized, but that I was all right and that if they got no more messages from me it would only be because the telephone had been swamped and packed up, and not because I had foundered. I asked particularly that they should not wake up Sheila in the middle of the night, but call her at seven o'clock in the morning. I said that I did not need any help.

I am not sure when I discovered that the water was pouring in through the forehatch. What had happened was that when the boat was nearly upside down, the heavy forehatch had swung open, and when the boat righted itself the hatch, instead of falling back in place, fell forwards onto the deck, leaving the hatchway wide open to the seas. It may seem strange that my memory is so confused, but it was a really wild night, the movement was horrible and every step was difficult.

I must have got out on deck to pump the water below the level of the batteries. I found the holding net torn from its lashings. One of my 600-foot genoas had gone, a drogue, and 700 feet of inch-and-a-half plaited warp. The other big genoa was still there in its bag pressed against the leeward lifeline wires. I don't remember how I secured it. I found the forehatch open and closed that. A section of the cockpit coaming and a piece of the side of the cockpit had been torn away. I was extremely puzzled at the time to know how this could have happened. The important thing was that the masts were standing, and the rigging appeared undamaged. I think it was then that I said to myself, "To hell with everything," and decided to have a sleep. I emptied my bunk of plates, cutlery and bottles, etc. One serrated-edged cutting knife was embedded close to where my head had been, and I thought how lucky I was. I had only a slightly cut lip; I do not know what caused that.

My bunk was soaking wet, which was no wonder, considering that in the morning I could see daylight through where the side of the cockpit had been torn away just above the bunk. But I did not give a damn how wet it was, turned in, and was soon fast asleep. I slept soundly till daylight.

His log noted:

Gipsy Moth capsized on the night of Monday, 30 January. My log notes briefly: "About 22.30. Capsize." Heavy weather continued throughout Tuesday 31 January, and I spent the day lying ahull, doing what I could to clear up. The electric bilge pump would not work, so I had to pump by hand, trying to repair the electric pump in the intervals of hand pumping. After I had cleaned the impeller the electric pump worked for a few minutes, but then sucked at an air lock. The bilge was still half-full, but gradually I got the water down. I streamed my remaining green warp in the hope that it would keep the yacht headed down-wind, but without any sails up the warp seemed to have no effect. So I hauled it back inboard and coiled it. The socket for the vane shaft of the self-steering gear was nearly off; so that had to be repaired, a dirty job which put me under water now and again. Thank God the water was warm! As I dealt with these various jobs one after another, my spirits began to pick up. I had been unbelievably lucky. The masts and rigging were all intact, which I attributed largely to Warwick's rigging. I felt a sense of loss that one of the big genoas had gone overboard, but I could get on without it. I was upset at losing one of my drogues and the 700 feet of drogue warp that went with it, for I had intended to stream a drogue at the end of a long warp to slow down *Gipsy Moth* and to keep her stern to the seas in Cape Horner storms. Later, after I had pondered the details of my capsize for many hours, I completely discarded the warp and drogue idea. So the loss of those items was not as serious as I thought at the time.

The weather continued rough, but by Wednesday morning, 1 February, I had the yacht sailing again, under a trysail and working jib. I refastened the foredeck net, rescued the broken pole-stand for my camera, and recovered the boathook from the rigging. There was still a full gale blowing, but the sun was out, and life began to seem more cheerful. But I worked slowly, and was often thrown off balance. I put this down to being weak from lack of food.

As night fell this day I reckoned up my profit and loss account so far since leaving Sydney. The loss was severe. The boat was still in a dreadful mess, and I had sailed only 185 miles since starting. For four days I had been bumped about and thrown, twisted, accelerated and jerked as if in a tiny toy boat in a wild mountain stream, and I was sick of it all. But everything that mattered on *Gipsy Moth* was intact; she had capsized and righted herself. She had been through an experience which few yachts have survived intact and she could still sail. It continued rough, but at last the wind had eased, and even if it was only a lull, it was a relief to be free for a while of that tiring, menacing roar and the whining in the rigging. The Tasman Sea was now much as it was when I had flown it in 1931, on the first solo flight from New Zealand to Australia. There were the same blue-black clouds, and, before darkness came, the same occasional shafts of sunlight slanting from cloud base to the sea.

The fact was, I had been damned lucky.

Chichester was half way from Sydney to Cape Horn when a gale blew up.

That gale lasted off and on-mostly on-for seven days. It was fast going, but rough. From time to time the speedometer needle stuck at its limit of 10 knots for what seemed like long periods, though it was probably only a few seconds. When a steep swell started under-running the ordinary rough sea, *Gipsy Moth* started surfing. Down below I could often tell when there was a big surfing breaker on the way. First there would be a low, quiet roar, and then the wind would increase suddenly by 10–15 knots. Next, the boat would heel sharply to windward, then whip across to the leeward heel, with white water boiling along the lee deck. There was always a biggish swell. The sea was much the same as when *Gipsy Moth* broached to south of Australia. The sun was shining brightly then, and in this equally lonely part of the Southern Ocean there was often sunshine too, giving a brilliant sparkle to the white wave crests, and making the rough sea seem almost unreal. But the roar of the wind, the roll and whiplash heel were reality enough. I was puzzled by the violent roll to windward before the boat went over to leeward, and wondered what caused it. I think a wave must push the bottom of the keel before it affects the top, and then, when the surface caught the top, over she would go in the way one would expect.

Gipsy Moth behaved well, and did not broach to. On the way to Australia I used to wait anxiously for her to broach in these conditions, but after the work done on her in Sydney, she seemed much more stable, and to run more truly. I never ceased to be surprised that Warwick Hood's addition to the keel could make so much difference. All the same, I didn't want to take risks, and I knew I ought to drop the mainsail when the wind reached over 30 knots. I often tried to get photographs of rough seas from the cockpit, but as soon as I was ready with the camera there would be nothing worth snapping and I hated waiting around. As usual, there would be a succession of impressive seas just after I got below.

It was a worrying business as the wind became marginally stronger to decide whether to drop the mainsail or to leave it up. I wanted speed, but these decisions were hard on the nerves, like waiting and wondering in an ocean race if the spinnaker is going to blow out, or if you dare carry it a little longer. Only here the mainsail was much more serious, with the masts at risk if it should go. When I decided to hand the mainsail and got below after doing so it would feel as if the yacht had stopped, but in fact speed did not drop much, from seven and a half to 6 knots, perhaps. And I would be relieved to jog along in comparative peace.

Noon on 25 February finished my fourth week at sea. With a week's run of 1,058 miles *Gipsy Moth* was beginning to make a proper speed at last. I had sailed 3,350 miles from Sydney and by midnight was half way to the Horn.

The night of 26 February was a particularly dirty one, with freshes or squalls up to 40 knots. I sailed under a reduced rig of staysail genoa and working jib, which seemed to meet the circumstances, although the going was rugged at times with heeling. But it was not bumpy, thank God. There was a lull in the early morning, and I set the trysail, wondering as I did so whether it ought to have been the main. However, I distrusted the lull, and decided to bide a while before hoisting the main, for time after time when I had set the main I would have done better to keep to the trysail. It was cold on deck, and below, and I dug out my winter woollies.

This was a grey day, with only a few vistas of pale blue sky, and a watery sun occasionally. It was as well that I had kept to the trysail, for the wind freshened as the day wore on, and by afternoon a storm was getting up fast, with a rapidly falling barometer. I dropped the jib and the trysail, leaving the genoa staysail, but wondering if I ought to change that down while the light was good and before the gale grew worse.

I had to turn out in the night. *Gipsy Moth* was making heavy weather of it, with the genoa staysail up and the wind going up to the limit of 60 knots on the recorder; with a sailing speed of 6 knots downwind, this meant a wind of at least 66 knots. I dropped the genoa staysail. In doing so I lost grip of the halliard tail which blew out to leeward, and it stayed out like a stick in the air. I could only hope that it would suitably jam when the wind dropped so that I could recover it.

I made two mistakes over this operation. Firstly, I should never have left the fore-triangle without a sail. I ought to have set the spitfire [reefed storm jib] when it showed signs of blowing up in the afternoon. I thought that the way on the yacht would keep her sailing downwind under bare poles, but as soon as I dropped the staysail, she broached to, and lay ahull. Secondly, if I did leave the yacht bald-headed I ought first to disconnect the self-steering vane so that it would not be forced when the yacht broached to and the heading suddenly changed by 90° in a wind of more than 60 knots.

I was very hungry when I got below after my struggle in the night, and gave myself some baked beans on toast, with a mug of chocolate. I was still hungry after that, but didn't fancy any of the available foods. A wave washed over the deck and fairly deluged the galley floor through the closed hatch. I caught some of it at the Primus, but luckily not much. It's odd how relative things are! While I was mopping up in the galley I thought that it had suddenly fallen flat calm – the wind had certainly decreased momentarily, but it was still blowing at 35 knots! It was soon gusting at 55 knots again, but in the lulls (relative lulls, that is) there was almost silence. It was very queer.

He continued sailing towards Cape Horn.

The gales of those seven days carried me across 1,115 miles of ocean, and left me with some 3,000 miles to Cape Horn. I began to wonder what I should do if the gale now blew from the opposite quarter as happened to Drake when he ran for three weeks before north-easters after leaving Magellan Strait. What an appalling thought! At one in the morning of March 1 I increased my sail area by 300 per cent. The week of gales had ended. I had finished it with only the little spitfire sail of 60 square feet set. The strongest wind I recorded was 67 knots. The seas were always different. The worst, which rolled up with the last fierce squall, were like steep banks moving on to the boat with a rough turbulent sea on top of them. No wonder the clipper captains ordered their helmsmen not to look astern. Sometimes the seas made me think of valleys; at other times of moving hills. *Gipsy Moth* behaved well, and did not broach. I accepted her flick heeling up to 60° but did not like it. I once thought the crockery would fly out of the vertical holders, but only the gash bucket shot a horrid mess of eggshells, potato skins and tea leaves over the cabin floor. I was using the bucket at the time, and had its locker door open.

I was now convinced that *Gipsy Moth* could do nothing else but run before the wind in very bad seas. There just must not be land ahead! I understood now why the clippers aimed to reach the latitude of the Horn 300 miles west of it.

He noted in his log:

01.30.
Back from a field-day on the foredeck. 1. The inspection lamp, carried forward to the main mast is excellent to work with. 2. Dropped the working jib; the tail I added to the existing halliard tail has made that job easier. 3. Changed twisted shackle on spitfire. 4. Changed over jib sheets. 5. Hoisted spitfire. On return to the cockpit I decided there would certainly be too much sail set in an hour or so's time, and, in fact, there was nearly too much now, so I returned with the lamp and dropped the genoa staysail. *Gipsy Moth* seems to be going nearly as fast and the difference in comfort is amazing. Down below at 6 knots it seems almost as if she is not moving. The extra speed was attractive but reserve of power and everything else should be the motto on this passage. My one-piece suit is a work of art; but it is wetter inside than out. I think a cupful of water condensed inside it. Also my Jersey was wet at the sleeves and, of course, my scarf and shirt wet at the neck. Now for some supper.

07.50
Dropped the trysail and raised the main. I have a much easier drill for this now when downwind; not such a Herculean labour, but still as good as a run in Hyde Park any morning before breakfast.

19.10
It is misty, drizzly weather, nearly fog like the North Atlantic. I have been a busy bee since five o'clock. I had a go at the leak into the foot of my bunk. Then was hard at it with one sail change after another, furling or bagging sails and coaxing the self-steering gear to work. What next with the wind? I hope it does not keep on backing and end up in the east, right in my eye.

22.10

Good R/T contact. Got all messages through. Hard work, though.

22.30

A dark night, black. Nearly becalmed. Wind reads 5 knots, but I expect the true wind is about twenty-two and a half knots.

4 March, 11.55

Took advantage of light airs to slap paint on possible leaks above foot of my bunk and on the deck above the forepeak. Looks horrible with my bad painting, but the leak is the thing. I got plenty of paint on my coat but took it off with paraffin. I reckon that if only I could find these leaks, I should be able to staunch them with enough sloshes of paint on them.

14.13

An albatross is flying up to within 10 feet of the stern; I fed it some gash which it seemed to relish. I have finished my fresh butter. So far my sewing repair of the mizzen stays'l is standing up to usage. Nice sailing with a pretty flat sea and enough breeze. Long may it last.

16.45

What's wrong with me today? I was in the middle of lunch when *Gipsy Moth* went aback. I went out in the long oilskin coat and wore her round on to course again. Trousers and cabin boots pretty wet in heavy rain. Then blowing up and already 30 knots, so I dropped the genoa staysail. Then the boat would not go with only a jib and mizzen, so I dress up and set the storm staysail. Now the wind has dropped to near calm, and *Gipsy Moth* is hobbyhorsing, doing half a knot. She wants all that sail back, of course. However, I'll have another go at finishing my lunch first. I think we are in the eye of a tiny local depression.

17.20

After a calm *Gipsy Moth* is now sailing herself – with the self-steering disconnected – on a heading of due west, at 3 knots. Can you beat it? However, I have finished my spaghetti, and will into the fray yet again.

18.45

This day, or the weather, is playing tricks on me. Just now I hoisted the genny stays'l again in place of the storm stays'l. I was expecting another fresh of wind like this afternoon, but instead, the wind suddenly backed from east to north-west. The boat seemed stuck so I hoisted the main, too. While I was doing so the wind veered 40° before I got back to the cockpit, so now we are sailing beam-on to a north wind (roughly speaking). I seem to have been mucking about with sails all day, and got nowhere at all. Fog and drizzle. Visibility 500 yards. I feel like another drink now, but nothing brings on a shemozzle more surely than my enjoying a drink, and I have had a bellyful of dashing out into the wet for emergencies today. Oh, well, what drink shall I have? The one big want I had then was a quiet night and a good sleep, so I turned in at 8 p.m. and was soon asleep. But the brandy hot must have done it – I was woken up at 9 p.m. by a gale squall, and had to reduce sail quickly. So I dressed again and took care over the oilies, because it was raining heavily – the deck was running rain like a stream. I had quite a job. First, I dropped the mainsail, then the mizzen, then the working jib. After that I hoisted the spitfire and left it with the genny staysail. Then I turned in again to try for some more sleep, but judging by the wave which then hit the boat with a roar of wind in advance of it I thought I was in for a noisy night.

8 March

Gybed at about 04.15. Daybreak about 04.30. Sea more kindly on this gybe, and nearly astern, whereas before it was often nearly abeam. [Later] I was woken up at about 7 o'clock by some big rollings, or rather hurlings, in waves which were near to being dangerous. Most reluctantly I got up and dressed to see if there was anything I should do. But that lot of bad waves seemed to be in a patch, and since I got up we have been in the usual Southern Ocean rough sea that goes with a 35-knot wind. There seems to be a succession of rain squalls, each building up a few big dirty seas. The speed of the boat varies from 4 to 8 knots, and sometimes it is so quiet in the cabin that I look up to see if we have stopped. I seized the opportunity of the sun's coming out bright for a while to get a sun observation. I took 6 shots, but do not feel sure of them because there are big waves only giving occasional glimpses of the distant horizon for perhaps a second or two, which entails snap shooting. I will plot the shots on graph paper which shows pretty clearly how much they are likely to be in error; also shows clearly any 'rogue' shots. Ate my last apple last night and found the first bad grapefruit. I fear the eggs are not going to keep. My beloved wind tell-tale [a thin ribbon of light chiffon] which streams in the wind from the bottom of a monometal rod dangling from the wind vane has carried away. This is a loss because I look at this tell-tale many times in a day.

I can look at it from the cabin without having to go into the cock-pit and it not only gives me the strength and direction of the wind near the sea surface, but also, if it is not streaming in the same direction as the wind vane itself it indicates how much load there is on the self-steering gear.

21.30

I felt it was useless turning in early, and thought of leaving all my clothes on. Sure enough, a fresh of wind, 30 knots, with some fairly hefty waves. Too much for *Gipsy Moth* with that sail area. She heels over to 35°, and when a big breaker strikes abeam, it bashes her too far over. One big wave came along while I was in the cockpit, and I noticed that the wind definitely roared and speeded up before the wave arrived. It must be the displacement of air by the mass of water. I'll be the death of a can of soup and then for some sleep (I hope!).

In changing winds I had to get my sleep in snatches. I had an off-course alarm, which four apprentices at the Kelvin Hughes works rigged up for me. It made a hideous noise above my bunk if the wind changed 45°. The previous night, for instance, it had me jump out of my sleep three times, and each time I had to dress in oilskins and change sail or retrim. The pitch dark night and the grey dawn with misty drizzle reminded me of the North Atlantic.

I was getting used to the wild wind Systems of the Southern Ocean. I could forecast with fair accuracy what the wind was going to do next. For example, on 11 March a log entry reads:

> I have gambled on the wind continuing to veer. I trimmed the sails and the self-steering gear to head 36° to the north of the heading for Cape Horn. I then turned in and had a remarkable sleep till 7 a.m. without having to stir from my bunk. My hunch paid off handsomely and the boat is now headed within 10° of the direction of the Horn after averaging 7.1 knots all night.

When it was calm enough he baked his own bread.

With Cape Horn seas in mind, I took the precaution of fitting wooden strongbacks to the forehatch. Alan Payne had made them up for me in Sydney – I reckon he felt as I did, that a big heavy hatch with light fastenings was a potential danger in trouble.

On Monday, 13 March I had a big day's run. This time it was between good positive sun fixes at each end of the run. Unfortunately I made it a short day of twenty-three hours: that is, I advanced the clocks an hour to compensate for running down the easting through 15° of longitude. The run came out at 191 and a half miles for the twenty-three hours. This was an average speed of 8.326 knots, and at this speed the day's run of twenty-four hours would have amounted to 199.826 miles. So that even if I had not made it a short day

I would still have been nearly one fifth of a mile short of the
200 miles I was always hoping for. That elusive 200 miles!

I was now left with 937 miles to the Horn. Five more days
like that last one would do the trick! I was excited.

The note in the wind, a fierce driving noise, foretold a dirty
night, and I had to face a north-east gale blowing up to 45
knots. At 03.00 I logged that I had had "a fairly serious beam
sea just now". I could expect no relief from the bashing that
the boat was getting, unless I turned and ran south. I
reckoned that I could run for about 150 miles south before
reaching the iceberg area. The wind had shifted, veering 30°
during the past fifteen hours. If it shifted a further 300 in the
next fifteen hours I could, in an emergency, if driven too far
south, gybe and head away from the ice area, even if it meant
sailing away from the Horn. In other words, I could avoid
driving into a trap. Having worked this out, I dropped the
staysail and turned downwind running off to the south.

*On the evening of 16 March he got through to Buenos Aires on the
radio telephone. Chichester described his intentions:*

I aimed to pass between the Diego Ramirez group and the
Ildefonso islands, and to round Cape Horn between 40 and
50 miles south of it. I wanted to give the Horn a good clearance, because it is a bit like Portland Bill in the English
Channel – the closer to the Bill you pass, the more turbulent
the sea, especially with wind against tide. The water diverted
by the Bill has to accelerate to get past it, and, in addition,
the bottom shelves, so that the current is accelerated again
because of the same amount of water having to get through
where there is only half the depth. It is exactly the same case
with the Horn, only the rough water extends 40 miles south
of it instead of 6 miles and where a 40-knot wind would bring
a turbulent, 6-foot sea by the Bill, it will be an 80-knot wind
with a 60-foot sea off the Horn.

At midnight on Saturday–Sunday, 18–19 March, I was
approaching land. I was 134 miles from the Ildefonso Islands

and 157 miles from the Diego Ramirez Islands. The nearest land was at the entrance to the Cockburn Channel, which Joshua Slocum had made famous. That was only 75 miles to the NE by N. The barometer had been dropping steadily for forty hours now. I got up and went into the cockpit, to find out what chance I might have of sighting land ahead. It was raining steadily. The big breaking seas showed up dazzling white with phosphorescence, I would say up to 100 yards away. The falling-off, seething bow waves were brilliant white. The keel was leaving a weaving tail like a comet 50–100 feet long, and under the surface. I thought that one would be lucky to sight land 300 yards ahead. This would pose a nutty problem for me next night if I didn't sight any land during the day. If the weather continued I should be lucky to get a fix, and with the strong currents known to be there, my fix of the day before would not reassure me much. I was uneasy about fixes with no checks since Sydney Heads: suppose I had been making a systematic error in my sights . . . But it was no good thinking like that. I realized that I must trust my navigation as I had done before.

I was lucky, and I got a sun fix at 09.22 next morning. That put me about 40 miles south-west of the nearest rocks off Tierra del Fuego. I was 77 miles due west of the Ildefonso Islands, and one-hundred and forty-eight and a half miles from Cape Horn.

There was a massive bank of cloud, nearly black at the bottom, away to the north, and I supposed that it was lying on the Darwin Mountains of Tierra del Fuego. There was no land in sight, although the nearest land was only 50 miles off. I now had a big problem to solve – where should I head? My then heading of 78° would lead me to Duff Bay and Morton Island, 15 miles north of the Ildefonsos. But I could gybe at any time, because the wind had backed to west by north. My main problem was this: if I kept headed for the Ildefonso Islands and Cape Horn, which was nearly in line with them, I should reach the islands in eleven hours' time, i.e. at 22.00 that night, which was three and a half hours after dark. This was too risky, because if it rained or snowed I should be unable to see the islands close to. The trouble was that if I bore away from the Ildefonsos, I should then have to cope with the Diego Ramirez Group. The bearing of that batch of rocky islets was only 22° (2 points) to starboard of the Ildefonsos. These islands have no lights, and are inhabited only for part of the year.

It was clear that I should not reach the islands until after dark.

The currents were strong here in the neighbourhood of the Horn, running up to 22 miles per day in any direction in fine weather, and up to 50 miles a day in stormy weather. My fix of 09.30 that morning seemed a good one, but at the back of my mind was still the gnawing doubt about my sun navigation, with no check since Sydney Heads, 6,575 miles back. (It was unfortunate that I had made that blunder in my sun fix earlier, on the day before I appeared to have made the big 217 miles day's run.) I could avoid both groups of islands by gybing and heading south-east till dawn; that was safe tactics, but it meant quite a big detour, which I resented. I tried to puzzle out a dog's leg route which would take me between the islands in safety.

At noon the wind shifted, veering suddenly, which put me on a heading of north-east, so I gybed. Then the sun showed through the heavy clouds, and I got a sextant sight. This checked my latitude, for which I was very grateful. I had just finished plotting the result, and had decided on my best heading, when the wind backed in a few seconds from north-west to south. In a matter of minutes it was blowing up to a strong gale, Force 9.1 dropped the mainsail, the jib and the genny staysail in turn. I set the spitfire, and found that was enough sail. "I wish," I logged, "that this famous visibility following a wind shift would prove itself! I should just love to get a glimpse of those islands." Until then I had been heading straight for the Ildefonso Islands, and now I decided that the time had come to change course and head midway between the two groups of islands. This put the wind slightly forward of the beam, so I hoisted a storm staysail with the spitfire jib. The barometer had suddenly risen six and a half millibars in the past hour or two. I hoped that the wind would not go on backing into the south-east, which would make it very awkward for me. By 21.00 that night the wind had eased to 15 knots at times, but with periodic bursts of up to 36 knots. I hoisted a bigger staysail, but with only the two headsails set the speed was down to 4 knots between the squalls. I decided to put up with this until I had got away from the proximity of that rugged land, so notorious for williwaws.

By midnight the barometer had risen nine and a half millibars in the past 7 hours. It was a little less dark out: I could tell the difference between sea and sky.

If my navigation was all right, I should be now passing 18 miles south of the Ildefonso Islands, and at dawn I should be passing 12 miles north of the Diego Ramirez group. It was so dark that I did not think it worth keeping a watch, so I set the off-course alarm to warn me if there was a big wind shift, and I also set an alarm clock to wake me at daybreak. Then I put my trust in my navigation and turned in for a sleep. For a while I lay in the dark with the boat rushing into black night. I used to think I would be better off going head first into danger (in *Gipsy Moth III* I lay feet forward); but I still had the same fear. What would it be like if she hit? Would she crack with a stunning shock and start smashing against the rocks in the breakers? If I could reach the life-raft amidships could I get it untied in the dark, then find the cylinder to inflate it? In the end I slept, and soundly too.

Daybreak was at 05.00. It was a cold, grey morning. The wind had veered right round again to west by south, and the barometer was steady. There was nothing in sight anywhere, which was as it should be. The sea was pretty calm, so I decided to head directly for Cape Horn, instead of passing 40 miles to the south of it as I had planned earlier, in order to avoid the turbulent seas to be expected if closer to the Horn, and if a gale blew up. I decided to hoist the trysail and went on up to do so. I was excited about changing course to east by north after setting the trysail, because changing course northwards there meant changing course for home. I was then 40 miles from the Horn.

When I stepped into the cockpit I was astounded to see a ship near by, about a half-mile off. I had a feeling that if there was one place in the world where I would not see a ship it was off Cape Horn. As soon as I recovered from the shock I realised that because of its drab overall colour it must be a warship, and therefore was likely to be HMS *Protector*. On first sighting it, it had seemed like magic, but on thinking it over I realized that if they had picked up my radio message to Buenos Aires of the night before relating how I was aiming to pass midway between the two groups of islands sailing blind during the night, the warship had only to place herself half-way between the two groups, and if my navigation was correct I should sail straight up to her. I went below and called up HMS *Protector* on 2,182 kcs. She answered immediately. I said I would speak to her again as soon as I had set my trysail.

After setting the trysail I went down below for quite a while. I talked to *Protector*, and that used more time than it should have done, because I had great difficulty in hearing what her operator was saying. This was tantalizing because I could clearly hear some land stations up to 7,000 miles away if I wanted to. After that I had my breakfast, and did not hurry over it, then wrote up the log, studied the chart and decided on my tactics, etc. While I was breakfasting a big wave swept over the boat and filled the cockpit half full. It took more than fifteen minutes to drain. By the time I had finished breakfast the wind had risen to 40 knots. At 09.00 I went on deck, and dropped both the trysail and the genoa staysail, leaving only the spitfire set. As I was finishing the deckwork a big wave took *Gipsy Moth* and slewed her round broadside on; in other words she broached to. It was lucky that I was on deck to free the self-steering gear, and to bring her round on to course again. I stood on the cockpit seat to do this so as to keep my legs out of the water in the cockpit.

I looked round and there was the Horn, quite plain to see. It stood up out of the sea like a black ice-cream cone. Hermite Island, north-west of it, was grey and outlined against the sky.

At 10.43 I logged:

I reckon I am east of Old Horn, but I can't get a bearing without going into the cockpit. Perhaps I had better, as I have kept all my oilskins on. Still gusting over 50 knots.

At 11.15 I took a bearing of the Horn and was then definitely past it. As I had made good 39 miles in the past five and a quarter hours, a speed of 7.4 knots, I must have passed the Horn at 11.07 and a half o'clock. I had no time or inclination at that moment, however, for such niceties of navigation. Before I reached the Horn the familiar quiet roar of wind was beginning; it was blowing up, and the sea was roughing up fast. I dare say that a lot of this was due to being only seven and a half miles south of the Horn when I passed it. I was beginning to feel seasick, and had the usual lethargic reluctance to do anything. I just wanted to be left alone, by things and especially by people. I cursed the *Protector* for hanging about, especially as I noted that she looked steady enough to play a game of billiards on her deck.

He also saw a light aircraft. It was a Piper Apache, carrying Murray Sayle of The Sunday Times. *Sayle had come out to see Francis Chichester at the most dangerous part of his voyage. Sayle described: "It was a flight I am not too anxious to repeat, but the sight of* Gipsy Moth *ploughing bravely into this wilderness of rain and sea was well worth it." The Chilean pilot said: "muy hombre" (which Sayle translated as: "What a man!").*

Ten minutes after noon I logged: "I tried to be too clever (as so often, I regret). I went out to try to coax *Gipsy Moth* to sail more across the wind; the motive being to get north into the lee of land." I thought that if only I could make some northing, I would get protection in the lee of Horn Island, and the islands to the north of it. However, the seas did not like it when I started sailing across them, and a souser filled the cockpit half full when I was in it. As a result, I had to change all my clothes, and also put *Gipsy Moth* back on to her original heading. That kept me just on the edge of the wind shadow from Cape Horn, and that might have made for more turbulence.

However, the wind was backing slowly, so that I steadily approached the heading I wanted to Staten Island. Unfortunately, with the wind shifting into the south-west, I got no protection whatever from the land, and after *Protector* left (one and a half hours after noon) the seas built up to some of the most vicious I had experienced on the voyage.

When *Protector* forged ahead, turned round ahead of *Gipsy Moth* and went away, she left me with a forlorn, empty feeling of desolation. I think it is a far greater strain to have a brief sight of a ship full of people in such conditions than it is to be quite alone: it emphasizes the isolation, because it makes one realise the impossibility of being helped should one require help. The odd thing was that I had not only no feeling of achievement whatever at having passed the Horn, but I had no more feeling about it than if I had been passing landmarks all the way from Australia.

It had certainly been a rough sea before *Protector* left; the cockpit had been filled five times up to then. It was an extra-ordinary sight to see the gear lever throttle control, and instruments of the motor which were placed half-way up the side of the cockpit, all under water. But that sea was kid's stuff compared to what was running three hours later. The biggest wind registered by the anemometer that I noticed was 55 knots. I was doubtful of the accuracy of this instrument in high winds, but even if it was only 55 knots that, added to the 8 knots of speed which *Gipsy Moth* was making, totted up to a 63-knot wind – Force 11. The seas were far more vicious than I should have expected from such a wind and they were frightening.

He expressed his feelings in a radio message on 24 March:

"At last," I reported, "I feel as though I am waking from a nightmare of sailing through that Southern Ocean. There is something nightmarishly frightening about those big breaking seas and screaming wind. They give a feeling of helplessness before their irresistible, remorseless power rolling down on top of one, and it all has ten times the impact when alone. Till yesterday I still felt I was in the wind shadow of the Horn. It was still wet, cold and grey and the wind still blowing hard. The seas were not so threatening but I shall be glad to get north of 50° S. without another big blow."

His average speed for the week in which he rounded Cape Horn was 6.58 knots. He reached Plymouth on 28 May 1967. He was knighted by Queen Elizabeth II. She dubbed him a knight with the same sword Queen Elizabeth I had used to knight Sir Francis Drake.

Adrift for 117 Days
(4 March–30 June 1973)

In 1967–8 Maurice and Maralyn Bailey sold their house, bought a yacht and lived aboard it. In June 1972 they began a voyage to New Zealand. They sailed from the Hamble River, near Southampton to ports in Spain and Portugal, then on to Madeira, the Canary Islands and across the Atlantic Ocean to the West Indies. They were very pleased with the performance of their yacht, Auralyn.

By February 1973 they were in Panama. They laid aboard provisions for nine months for their crossing of the Pacific. Maurice:

We sailed from Panama with what was to be the last of the north-east trade winds on a course that would take us to the

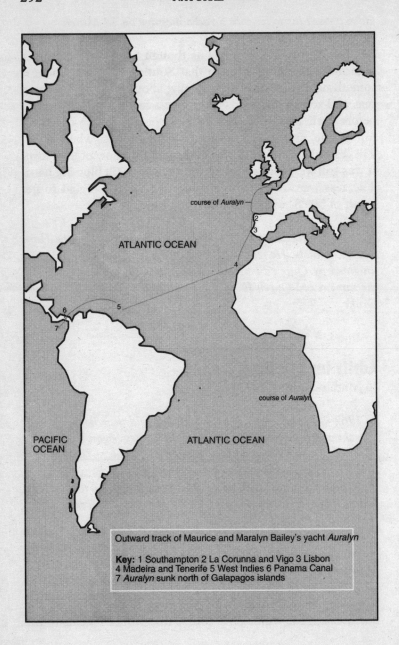

Outward track of Maurice and Maralyn Bailey's yacht *Auralyn*

Key: 1 Southampton 2 La Corunna and Vigo 3 Lisbon
4 Madeira and Tenerife 5 West Indies 6 Panama Canal
7 *Auralyn* sunk north of Galapagos islands

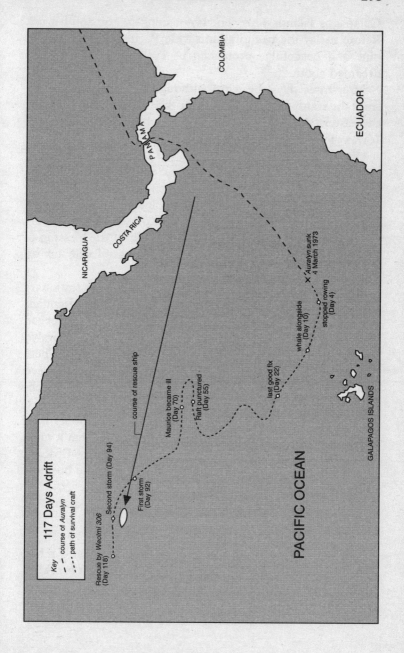

Galapagos Islands only ten days sailing to the south-west. Before us lay the beautiful and wide Pacific Ocean – warm, blue and peaceful – promising us everything that we had dreamed about.

After three days the wind, although light, became steady from the south-east and almost for the first time since leaving the eastern Atlantic we were able to set a full spread of sail. It was glorious sailing over placid seas.

Our sixth day at sea, 4 March 1973, started with one of those perfect nights of light winds, clear skies and calm sea but it was barely seven hours old when disaster struck!

At the change of watch at 0400 I pointed out to Maralyn a light on the horizon just a little to port of our course.

"It's obviously a ship," I said, uncertain of the blessing of meeting our first ship since leaving Panama. "I will stay on deck until we have passed."

As we closed it became clear that it was a large stationary fishing vessel, brilliantly illuminated and with an attendant launch moving rapidly around the parent ship. It began training a powerful searchlight on the sea nearby. Maralyn suggested that we should alter course to miss the ship. There was in fact little danger on our present course but I agreed and sheered off a little. When the ship was abeam its searchlight played for a few moments on our sails and we pondered as to what type of fisherman it was. Only many hours later did we connect our own misfortune with the idea that it must have been a whaler. With the ship well astern of us I turned into my bunk, glad to have relief from the irksome business of trying to stay awake at night.

After what seemed only minutes I became aware of Maralyn shaking me.

"It's your watch," she said. "Seven o'clock."

The sun was just rising above the horizon and Maralyn had already started the stove to begin our usual pleasant breakfast routine. I had barely roused myself when we felt a jolt on the port side which shook the boat with a report like a small explosion. Alarmed, Maralyn dashed on deck whilst I, now fully awake, followed up behind having clambered over the bunk lee-board.

"It's a whale," Maralyn cried, "and it's injured!" I reached the deck to see the monster threshing wildly off our stern leaving a red trail of blood in the water. It was our most terrifying moment: that great tail, at any second, could smash our boat. Maralyn said, "Have we damaged it?", not realizing that it was probably we who were the more seriously hurt. The whale with its tail whipping the surface of the sea into foam suddenly sounded, leaving us alone on a blood-reddened ocean in awesome silence.

"Never mind the whale," I exclaimed. "What damage has it done to us?"

Water was already above the cabin sole, which hindered my search for the damage, but I soon found a hole about eighteen inches long by some twelve inches wide below the water line just abaft the galley on the port side. Almost speechless with shock, I examined the hole and tried to think clearly what to do. Maralyn was already at the bilge pump.

"Get that spare jib sheet with the heavy snap shackle," I shouted.

Maralyn, alive to the danger now, obeyed with promptness. I struggled forward to retrieve a headsail and Maralyn followed.

We trimmed the sails to heel the boat and keep her moving forward at about two to three knots. On the foredeck Maralyn clipped the sheet to the corner of the headsail while I bunched bunched up the luff and lowered the sail over the bow making sure that enough of the sheet had been paid out to clear the keel. We dragged the sail aft to cover the hole and I clipped the luff on to the port life-line whilst Maralyn made the sheet fast to starboard.

We scrambled aft and pumped furiously for ten minutes in an effort to keep down the water level.

"The water isn't going down," gasped Maralyn. "Let's try blankets – push them into the hole!"

Even then we could not believe that the yacht would sink.

We rammed the blankets into the hole, but it was no good. The water was still rising. Perhaps there was more damage elsewhere? Perhaps it was the shape of the hull with its twin keels which was causing our makeshift collision-mat to fail to stem the flow.

Barely forty minutes had passed since we had felt the first shock and we now stared at each other in disbelief.

"We'll have to abandon her."

With the realization that saving *Auralyn* was now beyond our powers we suddenly knew just how much we had come to love that boat. We felt no fear. We had no doubts at all about our chances in the life-raft. We were close to a shipping route; there would be no problem. I set about releasing the Avon life-raft and the small inflatable rubber dinghy whilst Maralyn began to collect together a few essentials of food and gear. She threw as much as she could grab into two sail bags and together with our emergency kit, transferred them to the life-raft. I began to collect all the water containers I could find and tossed them into the dinghy. We worked fast and in silence. There was no panic.

The fifty minutes since the whale attack seemed to us then a lifetime. We left *Auralyn* for the last time. We felt sick at heart and stupefied, watching everything we had worked for sink slowly until the tip of the mast disappeared beneath the waves with fearful finality.

There was no other life we had wanted than to be free to sail our own boat across the oceans of the world. Now it had all gone – our dreams, our great adventure. It was as though life had stopped. Nothing seemed important any more.

But the greatest adventure was yet to come.

Auralyn had finally disappeared and we felt very much alone in that wide ocean. There was nothing left to show her going but the loose equipment that had floated free. Neither of us spoke; each left the other alone with their thoughts. Maralyn kept herself busy by putting the raft in some sort of order, whilst I rowed the dinghy amongst the debris and retrieved four containers of water, one of kerosene and one of methylated spirits (alcohol). Rowing over to the raft I made the dinghy fast with two twenty-five foot lines and then paid out the sea-anchor and made that fast to the raft. My movements were slow and laborious, mentally I was in a state of shock and low spirits.

I rested and looked across at Maralyn. She was weeping. For the first time in my life I felt utter despair, utter helplessness.

"We're near a shipping lane," I said with a confidence I did not feel. "We'll be seen soon."

They were dejected but they were able to analyse the causes of the accident. Maurice Bailey:

After a time we sat and discussed the accident. How did it happen? We thought about the whale, which we identified as a sperm whale of about forty feet or more in length. Although we had not seen the wound, we were certain that it had not been caused by the whale's contact with our hull. The damage to the boat had been caused most probably by its tail. Maralyn, who had the watch, was on deck just before she came below to call me and she had seen nothing of the whale. We were sure that the animal had surfaced almost alongside the boat and had immediately attacked us with its tail. The evidence to support this was the fact that we saw no blood other than in the vicinity of the boat.

What, then, had caused the injury and why should it have attacked us? Our thoughts now turned towards the fishing boat we had passed only four hours previously. We had noted its size, its activity, its use of a searchlight and its attendant launch. Our joint opinion was that it must have been a whaling ship and it did not take us long to associate the whaler with our misfortune. We theorized that the whaler, or its launch, had harpooned the whale just before we had sailed past and by some mischance the whale had escaped, injured and angry. It is possible that it had followed us through the rest of the night and revenged itself on our hull at first light.

Or, it may have come across us by some very unlucky chance.

Although several alternative theories have been suggested to us, none have to date affected our opinion. It is possible that the accident could have been caused by the whale's affinity to the bright red colour of the antifouling. Again, there was the theory that perhaps the whale had associated our boat with another whale. No alternative theory explains the whale's injury. The impact we felt and the resulting damage did not, we are certain, considering the bulk and fat of the creature, inflict any deep wound.

Also, we cannot rid ourselves of the picture of the whaler and its searchlight. It is quite likely that they were searching for a whale that had just escaped. We noticed that just before the ship dipped below the horizon, three miles away, the whaler put out the searchlight and the majority of its deck lights.

Maurice and Maralyn sorted out their gear. Maralyn:

Within an hour all trace of the boat had vanished from the surface of the sea. Maurice arranged the gear in the dinghy as I sorted out the raft. I lashed the sextant in one corner then wedged the polythene bowls containing our tinned food next to it. The bag of clothes was on the other side with a plastic bowl containing our books and diaries and finally by the entrance two one-gallon water containers.

There was nothing else to do and I persuaded Maurice to come into the raft where we had shelter from the sun's direct rays, but not from the heat.

As we sat through that first afternoon we talked quietly for several hours assessing our position. Using a blank page of my diary I made a list of all the food we had. By careful rationing I estimated we could last twenty days and the water would last about the same period. We talked of other shipwrecks and Maurice remembered an incident where the people had been picked up after twenty days and the longest time he could remember people drifting for was approximately ninety days.

I was quite optimistic. I had followed Maurice's plots all the way from Panama and knew we were not that far from the Galapagos Islands. When you have sailed thousands of miles across oceans a mere three hundred miles seems nothing, only three or four days sailing at the most! Maurice was not so optimistic as he had better knowledge of currents and winds and realized the gravity of our position although he didn't let on to me.

We settled into the raft as comfortably as possible and before the sun rose too high we had our breakfast which consisted of four biscuits each spread thickly with margarine and a smear of marmalade. At lunch time we had a small handful of peanuts each and our evening meal was one tin of food between us.

At the last moment as I left the yacht I had grabbed our small "Camping Gaz" butane stove. Unfortunately, the gas canister was part used and we had no spare cartridges, but by careful use I reckoned it would last out our supply of tins. I put the contents of a tin in a small saucepan we had managed to salvage and heated the food for three or four minutes. I took one spoonful then handed the pan to Maurice who also took one spoonful. We shared it like this until the food had gone. At meal times all conversation ceased and we concentrated on our food. When the last mouthful had disappeared we were both still very hungry and occasionally for "afters" we would raid the biscuit tin and have one each, or sometimes a date, and drool over its sweetness.

In our emergency kit I had placed two plastic bottles each holding two pints of water and one of these bottles would be our day's ration. When it was empty we would fill it from the main supply kept in the dinghy. For breakfast we would stir approximately three spoons of Coffee-mate into a cup of water and the rest of the day we would take turns and have sips from the bottle, finishing the rest after our evening meal. We learned later that our thirst might have been better satisfied if we had drunk our ration at one go.

On leaving the yacht I had rescued two books, one was Eric

Hiscock's *Voyaging* which he had kindly autographed for me one day on the Hamble River. The second book was a historical volume, *Richard III* by Paul Kendall Murray. We passed many hours remembering the books we had left behind and usually by starting with the words, "Did you read . . ." we would tell each other the story in minute detail. I remembered one story of the life of Eleanor of Aquitaine; she was imprisoned for sixteen years by her husband and the way in which she kept her mind occupied during that time was fascinating. Another story was of an American soldier captured during the Korean war who was kept in solitary confinement yet retained his sanity by designing and building in his mind his future home. It was this last story that gave us the idea of designing and planning our next boat in every detail.

Maurice:

The sun rose higher and the heat became intense and with it a state of languor pervaded the raft. I opened the chart and plotted our Dead Reckoning position. We were, in fact, quite close to the shipping lane. I estimated our position to be 1° 30' N 85° 47' W, 250 miles north of Ecuador and 300 miles east of the Galapagos Islands, which was too far north to allow the west going current to drift us on to the islands.

The wind blew from the south-east and, although light in strength, would drive us even farther north. Could we, perhaps, row the hundred or so miles south to the latitude of the Galapagos? It would take us about twelve days to reach the longitude of the Galapagos drifting at twenty-five miles per day. We would then have to row ten miles per day south to offset the wind and current and to reach their latitude at the same time as attaining the longitude. These calculations depended a lot on the wind and current remaining constant. Were we capable of rowing the dinghy ten miles each day with the raft in tow? Should we abandon the raft to give ourselves a better chance?

I stopped thinking about this problem and contented myself with the knowledge that in the next few days we should be drifting in a shipping lane. Nevertheless, I would have to mention the possibility of rowing to Maralyn. But later; not now.

We noticed a slight loss of pressure in the raft during the afternoon and I pumped air into the tubes with the pump provided in the raft's emergency kit. This made me aware of the appalling vulnerability of our position; only our two small craft to keep us afloat on that vast ocean.

Maurice described the raft and the dinghy:

The raft consisted principally of two superimposed circular inflated tubes giving four and a half feet internal diameter. A floor was attached around the lower perimeter of the bottom tube. Below the raft was fixed a CO_2 bottle and three stabilizing pockets. A semi-circular inflated tube that bridged the raft was fixed to the top tube and this supported a bright, orange-coloured canopy covering the whole raft.

There was a flap to cover the entrance and opposite this was a ventilation and look-out aperture protected by a skirt. Two non-return topping-up valves were situated just inside the entrance, one for the lower tube, the other for the upper and "bridge" tubes. Life-lines were fixed around the raft on the outside. The raft was made of black natural rubber proofed material. Apart from the pump the raft was equipped with two paddles, a repair kit, a length of orange polythene line and a quoit.

The dinghy, made of heavier grey, rubberized fabric, was boat-shaped, about nine feet overall and was divided into two separate flotation chambers with an inflated seat or thwart attached amid-ships. It had two fixed rubber rowlocks, two oars and a bellows type pump.

They decided to row at night. Their aim was to get to windward of the Galapagos Islands so that they would be carried towards them . . . After three nights they had only covered four miles to the south. Their drift westward had been nearly thirty miles. They discussed this and decided to stop rowing. They improvised a sail from oars and a sail bag. Their hope was to reach a shipping lane and be rescued by a passing ship.

They also noticed that there were many turtles swimming around the raft. Maralyn:

So the first week drew to a close. The days had gone fairly quickly as we had managed to keep ourselves occupied and everything was new and strange.

We had seen many prehistoric-looking turtles and it amazed us how unafraid of us they were. They would swim in a leisurely fashion round the raft and then disappear underneath. They rubbed and bumped the bottom and emerged again on the other side. After our initial surprise and delight at their presence we began to worry about damage to the raft from the barnacles and, in the case of young turtles, the spines on their backs. Surely continual rubbing would chafe and puncture the thin floor of the raft? Next time one approached we turned it round and pushed it off in the opposite direction. But they were very persistent and returned time and time again. Eventually, of course, we became angry and frustrated and we gave them a clout on the head with one of the raft paddles. This treatment surprised them and kept them at bay for a while but ten minutes later they would return, so it turned out to be a constant running battle between us and the turtles.

I mentioned to Maurice the possibility of catching one and eating it, but as we still had a stock of tinned food, albeit very small, Maurice decided to spare them until it was absolutely necessary to kill.

Maurice:

We could not think why turtles should find our raft so congenial. Was it to shelter from the sun, or just to rub themselves on the fabric, ridding themselves of parasites? In the early afternoon when we heard a gasp that invaded the silent world around us, we prepared ourselves for what was usually a very uncomfortable time. Sure enough there was a bump which lifted the sextant case several inches out of place. Followed by another bump towards the centre of the raft, and another. It went on with such frequency that our bodies inevitably received a number of blows. Then there was another gasp as a turtle surfaced to breathe.

Almost simultaneously we both now decided to capture this one for its meat.

Maralyn:

We were having breakfast in the raft when I saw a ship! I shouted excitedly to Maurice; rescue was at hand! It was about two miles away and closing. In the thin light of the early morning it appeared like a dream ship; only eight days and our ordeal was over!

Maurice climbed into the dinghy and shortened the lines between the two craft. As he was doing this I collected all our flares together and laid them out ready for use. The ship appeared to be a small fishing boat or maybe a private yacht, and, on her present course, she would pass about one mile away.

As she drew level with us Maurice asked for the first flare – a smoke flare and with mounting excitement I handed it to him. He tore off the tape and struck the top with the igniter – nothing happened. For long seconds we stared at the useless object and it was with a cry of exasperation that Maurice threw it into the sea. "It's a dud. A bloody dud!" I handed him a second flare and this time we both heaved a sigh of relief as it ignited. As the glow began to diminish I handed him a second red flare. There was no answering signal from the ship and she still maintained her course. A third flare was used – our hopes were fading rapidly.

"How many flares are left?"

"Three, two white and one red."

"Hand me another one – she must see us!" I could see the boat going further and further away. We hadn't been seen. It was pointless using the other two flares.

While Maurice sat dejectedly in the dinghy I began to wave my oilskin jacket although I knew it was no use. After a few minutes Maurice asked me to stop and save my energy and reluctantly I did so. By now the ship's funnel was only visible in the swells on the horizon and before many more minutes had passed the ocean was ours again.

Maurice:

I think for the first time in my life I felt true compassion as I saw the disappointment and sadness in Maralyn's eyes. Our morale at this stage took a further plunge; there was nothing to alleviate our despair. We finished our meal in silence. Our position was becoming daily more critical – our food was running low and, if rain did not come soon, water would have to be restricted to about half a pint each per day.

As we rested during the heat of the day we discussed the ship and the reason why she had not seen us and I came to the conclusion that as it was early (8 a.m.) the crew must have been at breakfast, possibly leaving the vessel on auto-pilot.

Then the subject got round to food and inevitably the turtle we still had in the dinghy. Our gas had run out and I had only just managed to warm the tin the previous night. The remaining tins of food would have to be eaten cold. I suggested using the turtle's meat as bait to catch fish to supplement our diet, but unfortunately we had failed to repack the fish hooks and line into our emergency pack at Panama.

At dawn the following morning Maralyn and I sat in the dinghy and planned the killing. Our instruments were simple – a blunt stainless steel mariner's knife, a mild steel penknife honed to some degree of sharpness on a leather sheath, and a pair of stainless steel scissors.

The reptile lay on the floor of the dinghy in a very docile manner. Both of us felt sick at heart, but we had to kill it if we were to live.

"I'll try knocking it out," I said. If it was unconscious I felt it would not struggle and the slaughter might not be too bad.

I lifted the turtle on to the side tube so that its head protruded over the side. I remember my surprise at discovering that, unlike its shore-based brother, the tortoise, its head did not fully retract into the heart-shaped carapace. The head, ugly yet fascinating, had no teeth. Sadly I wished that it would have been possible to have studied the various tortoise species under better circumstances.

Lifting a paddle over my head I brought it down with a resounding crash on to the turtle's skull. Then again, and again. The turtle ceased its movement, it was unconscious. It had not uttered a sound; to our ears it was mute.

Maralyn:

I knew the only way to kill it was to cut its throat, or decapitate it, and I also knew that I would have to do it as Maurice would have to hold it still. I didn't want to kill it either, it was so friendly and helpless, but we had to be practical and ruthless if we wanted to live. We knew we couldn't put off the deed any longer and I agreed to do the butchery if Maurice could somehow immobilize it.

Maurice had stunned the turtle by hitting it over the head with a paddle. It was then held upside down on the dinghy thwart, its head hanging down over a bowl. I then began the gruesome task of slitting its throat. The first stroke of the knife made no impression at all and it took many minutes to hack a small gash in its throat. I expected its skin to be tough but this thick, rubbery, leathery skin was a surprise and our knife totally inadequate for the job.

It was at this point that the turtle came to life again and

began to struggle, flailing around with its flippers and claws. I felt an unreasonable anger against the creature for making a difficult job more so and Maurice had a hard task to hold it in place. It took a lot of effort to keep the neck stretched and when the head was half severed I dug deep for the arteries and, as the rich blood spurted over my hands, the turtle ceased its struggle.

The bowl filled with thick red blood and, although we had read of people drinking turtle blood, the idea was so revolting that it was emptied into the sea. Immediately, hordes of fish converged on the dinghy and began eating the congealed blood, making loud sucking noises as they greedily devoured the contents of the bowl. I had great difficulty washing my hands as they swarmed towards my fingers as soon as they entered the water.

The next part of the butchery was to remove the lower shell or plastron. After scoring the perimeter deeply, Maurice cut through it with the penknife and eventually we could prise both halves of the shell away, leaving the rich white meat exposed. I hacked about four large steaks from each shoulder blade and we slipped the rest of the carcass over the side, glad to be rid of the bloody mess and relieved it was all over.

Maurice:

Hundreds of fish seized the remaining meat and the blood, and began to devour it all with a terrifying haste.

"We *must* fish," Maralyn said, excited by the sight of so many fish, "and I think I know of a way to do it." She climbed into the raft and, after some little time rummaging about, returned to the dinghy clutching the pliers and several stainless steel safety pins. Without another word she cut away the clip portion of one pin and bent it into a small hook. She then threaded thin cord through the spring hoop and tied it with a single-loop Turle knot.

"There," she said triumphantly. Once more Maralyn had displayed her genius at improvization. I asked, "Where did you find those pins?" She began making another hook, and without looking up answered, "In the first-aid kit. I remembered seeing them when I sorted everything out."

"Do you think they will work?" I asked, immediately regretting the uselessness of the question.

"We'll soon find out," Maralyn replied and began baiting the hook with a small piece of turtle meat. She dropped the line into the water and the meat was immediately seized by several fish who tore it away from the hook. The meat was so soft that it would not stay on. Maralyn tried again but with no more success. "The meat isn't tough enough," she said in an exasperated voice, "Let's look for some tougher steaks." Our search amongst the meat revealed no coarse flesh, but I noticed that several of the steaks were lined with a membrane.

"Try this," I said, handing Maralyn a piece of meat cut with the membrane attached. Maralyn carefully baited the hook once more, ensuring that the membrane was securely pierced. This time, although the fish pounced upon the meat, it stayed on the hook, and in a very short time Maralyn pulled the line on board with a beautiful silver fish firmly attached to it.

I grabbed the wriggling slippery creature and hit it repeatedly on the back of the head with the mariner's knife until it died. The fish were now in fact taking the hook. Maralyn, without stopping, would bait the hook, throw it over the side and land a fish on board. This did not succeed every time, but the fish came in quickly enough to supply us with ample for our morning meal.

The most abundant variety was the flat, somewhat ugly, purple-grey trigger fish, six to nine inches long and oval in shape. Its head occupied nearly half the body, and it had two retractable spines towards the back of the head. The teeth protruded from a relatively small mouth. These fish were to become our main source of food. They were easy to catch and simple to cut up and fillet, although we suffered bites from their teeth and numerous cuts and scratches from their spines. One or two of these scratches caused septic wounds on my thumbs.

While Maralyn fished, I would gut the fish and separate the livers, and hard and soft roes from the females and males respectively. By the time I had finished, Maralyn had started cutting away the heads; then I would slit the underside of each towards the tail. Maralyn followed me by cutting the flesh away from the backbone so that I could strip the fillets away from the skin and tail. Finally only one more thing had to be done. We gouged the eyes out of the head and, sometimes when fish were scarce and we were hungry, we took the heart and anything edible out of the head. For our meal we then had the white-meat steaks, delicacies which we called "sweetmeats", or "poops", as Maralyn would call them, and the eyeballs, which we found full of thirst-satisfying liquid.

To enable us to catch fish for our morning and evening meals we had to make sure several fish steaks were kept from each catch for bait. We therefore seized every opportunity to keep this bait fresh, replacing it whenever we could.

Maralyn:

I chopped the fillets into smallish pieces and placed an equal amount in two bowls. We then returned to the raft and sat facing each other, our raw meal between us, each waiting for the other to begin eating. Maurice was the first to take a bite and tried to encourage me to eat the raw flesh. I ate one fillet but I couldn't face eating any more. I knew I would have to conquer the revulsion I felt.

That evening we used the rest of the turtle meat to catch more fish and this time I managed to eat a little more but not enough to survive on, but gradually my intake of raw fish increased until I could almost match Maurice.

They improvized a way to play dominoes. On 14 March (Day 10) a whale surfaced beside them.

During the first two weeks we observed many whales, both sperm and killer whales. Usually they were in pairs and the sperm whales were always closer to us passing about 20 to 30 feet away. I sat anxiously until they had passed.

Our closest contact with a whale whilst adrift was quite remarkable and I can now look back on the occasion and realize it was a unique meeting that very few people have unintentionally experienced. Strangely enough this time the whale was alone; perhaps it was looking for a mate! A huge sperm whale surfaced about 20 feet behind us. I heard the whoosh of air being expelled and put my head through the vent and shouted to Maurice. We stumbled to the entrance to watch the brute's slow advance. It was not going to pass by like all the others. We could find no words to speak, but sat entranced together, wondering how the monster would react.

Maurice was very calm and said that there was nothing we could do. He sat by the raft doorway whilst I knelt beside him and I gazed in fascinated horror at this huge creature. It was now so very close; within touching distance. The small round blow-hole looked wet and moist like a dog's nose; it opened slowly and a jet of moisture-laden air, so fine it gave the appearance of steam, shot into the air and fell like a shower of rain on the raft.

Maurice tightened his grip on my hand and quietly explained that if the whale tipped the raft over it might be difficult for him to rescue me. He told me to hold on to the dinghy ropes and not to let go. I nodded agreement but I don't think his advice really sank in. I think this was the first time that Maurice was worried about my inability to swim.

We held on to each other as the enormous creature became stationary alongside. I was biting my lip to stop myself crying and I remember hearing Maurice saying quietly – "Why doesn't he go away and leave us in peace?" The portion of its body opposite the doorway was the back and I remember thinking how cow-like it was, jet black shining with moisture, its ribs showing through the skin. The leviathan maintained this position for what seemed to us an incredibly long time;

in fact, it was probably no longer than ten minutes but we expected its fluke to cleave us in two any moment.

At last, as no response was forthcoming to its advances, the whale started moving away from us and began to sink below the surface. "Don't dive now," I whispered in the tenseness of the moment but with a sudden movement its tail was perpendicular and it disappeared below the surface of the sea in a near vertical dive with hardly a splash. Our last view of it was a huge black fan-shaped tail starkly outlined against a brilliant blue sky. Then it was gone deep into the ocean and I was left speechless and trembling with the raft rocking gently as the ripples in the sea subsided.

When whales appeared after this incident I kept a wary eye on them until we knew they had passed. I would not like to have a repeat performance!

They improvized a set of cards by using blank pages from their log book. On 21 March (Day 17) it rained.

Sea water came into the raft from spray and we were kept busy mopping up the floor with sponges. The lower parts of our bodies had become chafed from contact with the rubber, and left sore patches along our legs and bottoms. We also developed numerous blisters which were caused, we assumed, by salt water.

The next day the weather improved and it became very hot with little wind. Not until three days later did we have any respite from the heat. Then the clouds increased and a strong wind from the south turned the sea into steep, dark foam-flecked moving hills. Then it rained . . .

We had to collect this precious liquid and noticed that the water ran freely down through the look-out and ventilation aperture, although we had tied the skirt up tightly. Maralyn placed a bucket beneath the opening and the rain water dripped steadily into it. We then had to turn our attention to mopping up the water as it dripped from the inflated tubes where the canopy was attached. This mopping became an exhausting task, especially when we had heavy rainstorms later. About a pint of water had collected in the bucket and we tasted it. It was dreadful; it had been contaminated with the waterproof rubber coating washed from the canopy. We could not drink it and we threw it away. An hour later the water was better and we collected about a pint and transferred it carefully to a plastic container.

One pint of water seemed very little from a rainstorm lasting two hours, but we found no more efficient way of catching it. Later, in quite different weather, we found that we had too much water. We adopted this procedure whenever it rained and, because the rubber coating was gradually washed off the canopy, the water we collected was always tainted and was never really pleasant.

We caught and killed our second turtle. This time we stripped the carcass and ate as much as we could. We took the steaks from its shoulders and pelvic region, and carefully extracted the liver, heart and kidneys.

We also found a large quantity of fat beneath the shell and in other parts of the body. It was greenish yellow in colour and we thought it delicious and appetizing. Once we had tasted the delicate meat we found it very palatable and looked forward with relish to our next turtle. Perhaps it was our bodies crying out for a particular nourishment that made us crave for more.

Before our next turtle, we had a series of rainstorms. It rained for so long that we were able to collect enough water not only to fill all our empty containers, but also to replace some of our original water which had become tainted through exposure to the sun. When the rain came it would last for several hours, keeping us busy collecting the water in our bucket and transferring it cup by cup to the containers, and mopping up continuously to keep the floor as dry as possible. Despite all our efforts the contents of the raft became thoroughly wet. With very little rest we became very tired, which only deepened our depression.

We settled down to our night routine of regular watches

and an awesome silence settled over our world. I took the first watch. Rarely in our lives had we been able to spend so much of our time gazing at the sky. I looked in wonder at the immensity and clarity of the curtain of stars above me. It was a moment of peace.

The unfamiliar equatorial night sky bewildered me. There was Sirius and Rigel and Capella, but which was Pollux and Kochab? They were lost in the multitude of shining objects, a view unspoilt by any accumulation of haze or cloud. Stretching unobstructed in every direction the boundless sky pivoted slowly around me.

I flashed the torch at my watch. Already it was time to change over, but it seemed a pity to wake Maralyn. I sat a little longer and looked at the sky and watched the meteorites hurry beneath the stars only to burn up in an unexpected moment.

From my meditations came clear resolutions for the future; resolutions that would affect my entire attitude to people. I was conscientiously determined, I told myself, to listen to people's arguments with patience and compassion. Intolerance, although not always a bad thing, must never again colour my criticism. I resolved to improve my selfish approach to our endeavours; to reduce my ego to equable proportions.

It was time to wake Maralyn.

Their health deteriorated. Maralyn:

Although we were eating a fair amount of fish, I noticed Maurice getting thinner almost day by day, his ribs showed plainly and his cheeks were becoming more sunken. His whole face had a gaunt appearance which was not helped by his rapidly growing beard. We were also losing our sun tan as we kept out of the sun as much as possible. It was hard to imagine that less than three weeks ago we had been fit and tanned, yet now we were pale and emaciated.

When we started out from Panama we had no excess fat

and we weighed 118 pounds and 158 pounds respectively. We seemed to lose weight rapidly during the first month and afterwards the rate slowed down. We did not have a mirror, but after much persistent questioning, Maurice told me that my face looked very gaunt. The bruise I had received on my cheek bone had disappeared, but my shins were still bruised and tender from the knocks I had received when leaving the yacht. Our limbs seemed wasted and I thought that our leg muscles probably would not support us for very long.

Water was the main problem at first as we had little rain and it was very hot. Our lips became dry and cracked and the small sips we allowed ourselves from our water flask didn't seem to help very much. Fortunately, we ate fish which helped to alleviate our thirst, but we were getting tired of our fish diet and longed for another turtle to pass by. We had dreamt of the steaks we obtained from the last turtle and they gradually became more and more desirable. We had thought that raw fish would be more palatable than raw turtle meat, but the more fish we ate the less enthusiasm we had for it.

When the next medium-sized female turtle did come along we had none of our previous hesitation. I quickly pushed my head through the vent and, seeing the turtle immediately below me, I caught one of its rear flippers. Maurice, who had in the meantime got into the dinghy, paddled round and, taking hold of the other flipper, he hauled it into the dinghy in record time. We followed the same procedure but this time after taking off the steaks and exposing the intestines.

On 29 March they saw their second ship. They used their second flare but the ship, a tanker, ignored them. They tried to get turtles to tow them towards the Galapagos.

We caught a large male and held him upside down in the water and put two half-hitches round its rear flippers. To our amazement he towed us in the direction of the Galapagos! They must be incredibly strong swimmers as this one towed us fast enough for us to be able to see the ripple of a bow

wave. We reasoned that two or three turtles would tow us
faster. It was with great excitement that we caught another
large male turtle and harnessed him. I had visions of driving
our "team" right into harbour! The vision was quickly
shattered when this turtle began to swim the opposite way!
Just our luck to choose one who had no sense of direction,
but we left him tethered hoping he would follow the good
example of his fellow.

When we turned the large turtles over to harness them, we
found sucker fish nestling in the loose flesh under the rear
flipper. They usually came in pairs, one under each flipper.
We prised them loose and threw them into the dinghy to use
as bait. They made excellent fish bait and often instead of
capturing and killing a turtle we merely tipped him on end
and removed the sucker fish.

*On 10 April (Day 37) they saw their third ship. They had no more
flares. Two days later they saw their fourth ship. On 18 April (Day
45) another ship passed them by. Maralyn described their routine:*

Each day we followed the same routine and worked before
the sun rose too high. After helping Maurice fish I would
return to the raft with our breakfast, top up the raft with air
and make sure everything was tidy. When Maurice had
cleaned the dinghy he would join me for breakfast. We ate
slowly, the meal usually lasting for an hour. After I had
washed up and cleared away we would dream and doze away
the day until our evening fishing time.

Occasionally we still played cards and dominoes but more
often we read our two books and occasionally played a word
game. We talked of our life before and during the voyage and
what it would be like afterwards.

*24 April was Maralyn's birthday. They accidentally punctured
the dinghy while trying to land a large fish. To console each other
Maralyn insisted that they celebrate her birthday. They ate their
only tin of rice pudding with a little treacle. The patch with which*

*they had mended the dinghy came off so they had to pump at least
twice a day.*

*Two days later the raft was punctured by the spines of a Spine
foot fish which had been keeping them company.*

Their health and emotions declined. Maurice described them:

As the days progressed, we became shocked at the physical
decline in each other. Maralyn's brown, smooth skinned and
supple body had now developed into a thin bony frame
motivated by stiff and sore limbs. Her sunken eyes accentu-
ated the gauntness of her face.

My beard, to a large extent, must have disguised the drawn
and angular features of my face but I could feel the bones as
they protruded through my skin. Our muscles were slack and
wasted.

Our emaciated state horrified us. There was all this natural
food around us and yet we were not, apparently, getting
sufficient nourishment.

Day followed day without making any impact on our
minds. We could make no true distinction between different
days of the week. Only the change from day to night and the
fluctuation of the sun's declination, proclaiming the changing
seasons, were obvious to us. The passage of the days was
noted by Maralyn in her diary. She also faithfully marked
each day on the inside of the raft's canopy, putting a circle
round family birthdays, whilst turtle days had a cross and
ship days a plus sign. We could thus work out the average
time between events: four-and-a-half days between turtles,
eleven days between ships.

Maralyn supplemented her diary by starting a letter to her
friend June in England. She always seemed to be writing.
There were times when the diary and her papers would
become wet. Then, with infinite care and patience, she would
dry them out whenever the sun shone.

As more of the area of the canopy was taken up with
Maralyn's markings, the reality of our plight depressed us.
The world around us was indeed our own; it was no longer

inhabited by humans, only sea creatures. Now only our own endeavours could save us.

Our discussions would sometimes revolve round the probable outcome of our misadventure. It was impossible to say that we viewed our seemingly inevitable death with fear but, more correctly, with resignation. We would occasionally think of what we would do when the end was near, and by what means we could quickly die. The gas bottle was empty and suffocation by any other means we thought would be ineffective. Maralyn did not care for the idea of swimming away from the raft.

That left only the knife. I did wonder if nature would settle it for us by sending a poisonous fish into our shoal.

These discussions were fortunately short-lived for Maralyn never lost hope in our survival. She would frequently boost my morale by talking about the food she would cook when we arrived back in England. She had that essential gift of leadership and showed by her own example the will-power needed to keep life going.

Maralyn described early May:

We had been adrift for two months and May brought bad weather. The nylon canopy on our small floating home, having lost its rubber coating and bleached almost white by the sun, was no longer waterproof and each time it rained the whole of the inside became thoroughly sodden. Because of the punctured tube we were that much nearer the water, and waves which normally wouldn't have bothered us, now lapped over the top and into the raft. Sometimes, even on fine days, we were wet through with sea water. We had to bale continuously.

I noticed a split about ten inches long in the tape joining the two circular tubes at the front of the life-raft. The cotton tape had deteriorated in the sun and was now allowing sea water to slop into the raft. This was bad but hardly surprising, the raft having withstood a lot of punishment. If the tape continued to split round the circumference the two tubes would part and we would then have to abandon the raft. It became obvious now that we must be extremely careful and restrict our movements in the raft to a minimum in order to relieve the stresses on the tape.

May also brought bad health. Some of the water had been stored in a white polythene container and had turned very green through the effects of sunlight on it. Not being prepared to throw it away we each drank a cupful. A few hours later we both had violent pains and a mild attack of dysentery. We resolved not to drink any more "bad water" and, when it rained, to throw it away and replace it with fresh. This incident made us decide to check the rest of the water.

They used fishhooks made out of bent safety pins. Because they were not barbed they had to be very careful not to let fish slip off the hook.

On 5 May (Day 62) it rained. They were elated because their water had become tainted. They caught and killed a large turtle. On 8 May (Day 67) a sixth ship passed them by.

Maurice became ill:

Any movement became intolerable for me; even Maralyn's encouraging chatter failed to raise my spirits. The ulcerated sores eating into my flesh were causing a lot of pain. I was never comfortable. Maralyn soothed the wounds as best she could with a cosmetic cream.

Chest pains virtually immobilized me and any excessive movement of my arms only aggravated my distress. A hacking cough that I had developed interfered with any rest Maralyn could get and occasionally I coughed up blood. I was taking very little interest in our survival and Maralyn was bearing an unfair burden in supplying our food, baling out and inflating the raft.

"When we get another spell of sunshine, we can dry everything out and you'll begin to feel much better," she said. "Your sores will be dry and then will soon heal."

I could say nothing, her enthusiasm for life showed in everything she did and she undertook the butchery of our next turtle, our twenty-second, by herself. She would not heed my protest that I must help, that she must not treat me like an invalid.

What was the matter with me? This was no time to develop any serious illness although, I thought, a little rest might help recovery.

Maralyn left the raft after making me as comfortable as possible and started work on the female turtle we had stored in the dinghy which had, fortunately for her, died during the night. She worked alone and was, I suppose, as happy as she could be in the circumstances. It saddened me to think that I felt too ill to anticipate with any real relish the meat that Maralyn was cutting up.

"Whoopee," Maralyn cried. "It's full of eggs, try these." She excitedly passed a dishful of moist, bright golden spheres each about the size of a large marble. I picked one up; it was soft, like a semi-inflated ball. This did not surprise me but I had thought of them as having a white covering. At least, all the illustrations I had seen indicated white eggs.

These were immature eggs, I supposed, but they were so large that they must have been ready for laying in a week or, at the most, ten days. Turtles are, indeed, powerful swimmers to reach the distant islands to lay the eggs in so short a time.

"There are hundreds," Maralyn said. "Have you tried one yet? They must be full of protein."

I put the egg into my mouth and rolled it around. It had a firm membrane. I burst the membrane and a thick, dry-tasting rich yolk spread over my mouth and throat. It clung in glutinous layers to my teeth and tongue and resisted all efforts of my saliva to wash it away.

"They're good," I said bravely. I ate another, then another. "Too many at once will be rather sickly," I went on. "We shall probably drink more water with them."

Maralyn agreed, but she collected every egg. This turtle

proved to be the most rewarding of all up to that time. In future we would look especially for the female turtles, recognized by their short tails, because we found, in addition, that their livers were sweeter and, for their size, bulkier than the male's liver. The male turtles with their long, grotesque tails were generally larger and in plan, of a more oval shape. Apart from the extra meat, the male had little more to offer than the additional roes from above the pelvic bone.

On 1 June (Day 89) they endured squalls and rain. Maurice:

We made ourselves as snug as possible. The biscuit tin which we would use for baling and the sponges were placed ready for the downpour. The sky darkened as though the light had finished for the day and then the onslaught began. It seemed as though the clouds would discharge their complete burden on to us personally. The rain drummed with incredible violence on the canopy and flattened the waves.

We began baling almost immediately, the canopy filtering the rain like a fine spray. We worked hard mopping up water on the side tubes and around ourselves, squeezing the saturated sponges into the biscuit tin. The tin would be full in less than a minute and I would then empty it outside.

Hour after hour the downpour continued. Maralyn would patiently top up our water containers as the bucket filled. When our containers were full she would then pass the bucket to me and I would empty the water over the side.

Nothing could be seen through the rain and we had to shout to make ourselves heard. It poured with increasing ferocity until after many hours a startling flash of lightning followed by the deep resonant boom of thunder proclaimed a slackening of the rain. As the rain decreased the day grew lighter although solid cloud still covered the sky. I left Maralyn to finish baling the raft while I started on the dinghy.

Our fish, hung up to dry, had been reduced to a soggy mess. I threw it away, and settled down to catch some more for our evening meal.

When it rained we wore our oilskin jackets but our bodies were always chilled due to being immersed up to the waist in cold water. We were never dry. Everything we touched was wet and would remain so; our few clothes, our books and the sextant.

With the flooding of the dinghy the water washed dried blood and turtle excreta from hidden corners of the boat and it contaminated our water in the plastic containers because of ill-fitting caps. So this water always needed replacing and it had to be collected in the bucket and painstakingly transferred to the containers a cupful at a time.

We now had rain almost every day. How we longed to see the bright sky again. Never, we told ourselves, would we again complain about the heat of the sun. Conditions were very miserable and we found it impossible to rest. The sky was always overcast and squalls would follow one another across the sky. When one squall passed us by, it would appear to turn and approach us from another direction. The wind and sea tossed the raft and dinghy about like corks. There was no escape. Once started the rainstorms would last several hours and towards the end we would slump in exhaustion, unable to bale any more. Between the rain we were able to fish and prepare our meal, but before we could eat the rain would invariably restart.

It was impossible for us to sit outside in the rain because of the cold. We found what shelter we could under the raft's canopy, the entrance of which had to be firmly closed.

Unfortunately, after several weeks of use the Velcro material used for securing the entrance grew tired and would not stay shut in anything above a light wind. Then I had to sit for most of the day and night holding the cover shut with my hands. Sleep came only during brief respites from the squalls and rainstorms.

To make matters worse I developed a fever during this time and became plagued with diarrhoea. This meant frequent visits to the dinghy to make use of the "outside loo". We had adopted the empty biscuit tin for the calls of nature and, in our weakened state, we found it uncomfortable and painful to crouch over this small tin.

We were now existing at a primeval level where the layers of civilization had been stripped away from us. We found our bodily functions unembarrassing and it was surprisingly easy to stay clean. We would wash in sea water, clean our teeth and comb our hair, and in my case, my beard. It was usually far too cold to sit out in the rain and we did not often take advantage of the frequent downpours for bathing.

On 5 June (Day 93) they had their worst night and day. They had to bale all night and they were very cold.

The wind had increased from the south during the night, bringing big seas which broke with great menace around us. The waves became so large that we doubted the raft's ability to withstand their assault. We appeared to be drifting too fast; the trousers were not working well as a drogue but I could not think of anything else that would help to slow us down. We were reluctant to risk tying any more valuable equipment to our slender drogue line.

Daylight the next morning revealed a wild scene. Heavy cloud covered the sky and the spray from the grey, breaking waves continually soaked us. The raft and dinghy gyrated up the steep walls of the waves and were flung violently against each other. Frequently, the warps had to be freed from the underside of the raft. It seemed to our exhausted minds as though we had always had weather like this.

"I will try and fish," I said balefully after several hours of watching the waves and deciding, inevitably, that our hunger must be satisfied soon and that the seas would not subside.

Maralyn watched my perilous transfer from the raft to the dinghy. "Do be careful," she said, I shouted to reassure her and started to bale out the dinghy with the biscuit tin. Waves would send splashes of water into the nearly empty dinghy frustrating my attempts to drain it completely. The movement was very violent and sitting on the thwart became a trial. The friction between the rubber seat, the salt water and my skin aggravated my sores and any movement became agonizing.

I cut up pieces of fish, baited the hook and trailed it in the water. Few fish were to be seen; they had all disappeared. Only an occasional straggler swam past out of the hundreds that were with us the previous day. No fish seemed to be interested.

The dinghy would collide with the raft, knocking me off my precarious seat and then the two craft would drift quickly apart until the warps pulled up tight with a jerk that would again dislodge me off the thwart. The position was impossible and I told Maralyn so.

"Come into the raft, then," she said. "It looks too dangerous out there."

"If we can't keep replacing this bait we shall have to wait until we find another turtle," I shouted over the wind. "I'll clear up and come in."

This decision came one minute too late. I gazed with horror behind the raft to where an enormous wall of water was building up. The raft was bound to be engulfed. Maralyn could not see the wave and I shouted a warning. In that fractional span of time I could not estimate the height of the wave but I remember being appalled by its size.

Amazingly the raft rode up the side of the wave; it had escaped. The dinghy, however, seemed to be out of phase and I lay low in the boat, gripping the life-lines tightly. The wave broke, pouring its solid mass over the little craft. A chilling blackness covered me, the weight of water pressing me hard to the floor. The world turned dizzily and I found myself sinking to what I imagined was a great depth. As I swam desperately to gain the surface, the discovery of the dinghy upturned above me sent me, for an instant, into a panic.

I broke surface alongside the dinghy; my eyes searched my near surroundings and I saw Maralyn's face peering anxiously from the raft.

That night it was impossible to sleep; waves buffeted the raft and constantly moved our equipment from its various stowed positions. We spent much of our time restowing everything. Occasionally, a wave would strike us hard and water would splash up the canopy and cascade into the raft. Then we would have to bale furiously. This always dismayed us because salt water on the canopy meant that we needed much rain in the future to clean the salt away before it could be used for drinking. Rarely did we manage to get the water below the level of our hips. Our legs, thighs and buttocks were being continually chafed on the black rubber, adding to our discomfort. Because of the deep, ulcer-like sores on my rump and hips and it was impossible to find a comfortable position for my body.

Suddenly, as though we had been struck by some giant's hammer, we found ourselves climbing violently towards the vertical propelled by a blow from a wave that broke right over us. The entrance flap burst open and a mass of water exploded into the raft. After the torrent of water had stopped and we had realized that the raft was still upright we began the tormenting task of emptying the raft once more.

Maralyn and I looked towards each other in the blackness of the night as we sat back, tired out with our efforts.

"What will happen if the raft capsizes?" Maralyn asked. I was angry at this question because I did not know the answer. Surely she can work it out for herself, I thought, but, perhaps, it is just reassurance she needs.

I said, "I don't think it will capsize, but we must prepare ourselves for that to happen. Get what is left of the tinned food, the knives and tin opener and put them all into the haversack."

We groped in the darkness and placed everything we could find inside the haversack we had used for our emergency pack. Then Maralyn found a piece of cord and lashed it to the raft.

"If the raft goes over at least we shall be able to save those few things," I said. "It will be very difficult to right it in these seas."

"I don't feel like dying, not tonight anyway," Maralyn said, feeling for my hand. It was then, I think, that I fully appreciated the extent of Maralyn's tenacity for life; it would not be any failing on her part if we did not survive.

The storm lasted for four days during which time we caught no fish and we had to use our precious supply of canned food. Fresh bait would now be essential before we could start fishing again.

Maralyn described 6 June (Day 94):

Fortune smiled on us next day; the gale had subsided and some hefty bumps underneath us denoted a turtle. I leaned out of the vent hole and waited for the animal to surface. When it did I grabbed a flipper and held on tightly; usually at this stage it didn't struggle very much and we found this was the best routine to adopt. Meanwhile, Maurice got into the dinghy and hauled himself alongside to reach over and take hold of the turtle. As soon as he had a firm grip on it I let go and wriggled back into the raft down the vent chute. I then got into the dinghy and together we heaved the turtle over the side and with a great effort turned it upside down. This procedure was always accompanied with great flapping and clapping of flippers and we usually had several battle scars after the fight. Twice Maurice sustained very nasty bites on his ankle and once as I sat on the thwart getting my breath back I received a hefty nip on my bottom: fortunately the only damage was to my dignity!

We hauled the huge female turtle into the aft section of the dinghy. She was large and we reasoned she could be full of eggs. We decided to keep her until the next day and returned to the raft to drool over the thought of eggs for breakfast. That evening we opened a small, rusty tin of sardines – of all the tinned food on board the yacht, I had to bring tinned fish!

On 10 June (Day 98) they had their first encounter with a booby bird. A booby is a fish-eating bird like a gannet. Maurice:

Single booby birds would settle during the late afternoon on our dinghy and digest their latest catch of fish. Their digestive processes invariably meant a large evacuation and within a short space of time the dinghy and all our water containers would be covered white. This upset us especially when we considered how it might contaminate our drinking water.

When a large blue-faced booby landed one day on the raft we became annoyed at the mess it was making. I hauled the dinghy in close; the bird showed no fear and continued to preen itself. Even then, with the booby in grasping distance, we did not think of it as food. There was no real need as we had ample fish.

I lifted one of the paddles and struck the booby a blow, not to injure it but to make it fly away. With a squawk and an almost surprised look in its eyes it flopped into the water between the raft and the dinghy. It did not fly away but started to regurgitate four whole flying fish in front of us. A fine supplement to our supper, we thought, as we scooped them out of the water.

On 12 June (Day 100) they had a change of diet.

We decided on another celebration day, Tuesday 12 June, we would then have been one hundred days in the raft.

We decided we needed a change of diet and, as the sea was calmer, we began fishing again. The fish were not very enthusiastic and when a large sea bird landed on top of the raft we discussed the possibilities of catching him. Boobies had always been flying around us and often would land on dinghy or raft while we were fishing. Usually we drove them off by giving them a swipe with a paddle; they would flop into the sea with a disconcerted squawk, looking completely perplexed. Often the bird would fly back on to the raft and only after a further swipe would the idea that it wasn't welcome sink in.

This time we tolerated the mess and tried our utmost to make it feel welcome; no wonder it looked so puzzled!

Oblivious of his impending doom, the bird sat serenely on the overhead tube, digesting its meal.

Wrapping part of the towel round my hand, I stretched up and caught its foot. As I dragged it into the raft, Maurice wrapped the other towel round its beak. Muffled squawks came from inside the towel and, as we unwrapped it, the bird lunged forward and caught my thumb in its beak.

Any pity I had for it disappeared. I wrung its neck quickly and then sat back, nursing my injured thumb. The gash was small but very deep and took a long time to heal. We plucked the bird in the dinghy, taking care to make sure that the raft was to windward. Feathers littered the sea and hordes of trigger fish gathered round and nibbled at them.

The trigger fish, showing their usual greediness, grabbed at everything in sight. I twisted off one of the bird's wings and held the slightly bloody end over the side. The fish held on to the shreds of meat and I flipped them into the dinghy before they realized what was happening. I caught several by this method and, of course, it saved the precious hook. The bird's flesh was dark red and very sweet, but such a change from fish or turtle that we thoroughly enjoyed it.

Their captive female turtle died, but when they opened it there were no eggs. The part of the ocean they were in was filled with life; fish swam below them in layers. Spine-foots, trigger fish, milk fish and wolf herrings abounded.

Some days we would catch over one hundred trigger fish. On other days we would catch a dozen or less and on odd days none at all. We have calculated that our average daily catch must have been approximately forty fish and if we caught fish on one hundred days this would make a total of four thousand fish, or more. The catching was the easiest part, the gutting and cutting up was time consuming and exhausting. The softened flesh on our fingers had been chafed to the bone by the continual use of the scissors.

Unfortunately, their eagerness to grab the bait had other detracting features. We would wash our hands over the side and have them seized by the trigger fish, their small mouths biting into our flesh. Sometimes they broke the skin before we could withdraw our hands. At one time we even considered the plan that if we lost all our hooks or required fresh bait we could use our fingers as bait. For their size, we considered the trigger fish more fierce and more aggressive than the much-feared sharks.

In fact, although we realized that sharks have the power to kill men, we did not find them at all ferocious. They would swim contentedly amongst the shoal of fish we had attracted without disturbing our fishing. Care had to be taken to ensure the sharks did not take the bait otherwise we would soon lose a precious hook and, possibly, the line. In tropical waters their food is so abundant that they showed no interest in us at all, nor in any of the turtles' blood and carcasses we jettisoned. Apart from their peculiar desire to buffet our black raft, we had no fear of them; we came to accept them almost as companionable creatures. I really think they are cowards because they would hasten away whenever we splashed the water above them.

Huge white-tipped sharks and much smaller varieties would cruise around us escorted often by gaudy pilot fish. A single whale shark, the largest fish in the world and an extremely rare sighting, we saw below us one day. Its slow, lethargic movement, its broad spotted body and blunt nose made it easily distinguishable from other sharks.

Maralyn:

When we first butchered a turtle during our misadventure I kept a wary lookout for sharks because of the prodigious amount of blood. Blood will send sharks into a frenzy, I had been told. Not once did sharks come close during the killing of fish, turtle or birds. Occasionally an odd one was glimpsed but they usually kept their distance. It was only when they were in large groups that they made themselves offensive: the gang syndrome.

Maurice described the birds:

The days were rare when we did not see a booby bird and, probably, we might encounter two or three species on one day. There were the blue-faced or masked boobies and brown boobies. They are goose-sized birds with heavy streamlined bodies and are of the same family as the northern gannet.

A booby would soar over the sea waiting for flying fish to break cover. It would then plunge into the waves, re-appearing in a moment juggling with a fish in its beak. After swallowing the catch, it would then take up its vigil once more. Although we would invariably remove whole flying fish from their gullets when we killed them, boobies would also feed on the shoals of trigger fish around us.

We would frequently sit fascinated watching frigate birds soaring motionless high above us and watching them chase booby birds, pecking at them until the unfortunate boobies disgorged their fish to escape from their tormentors. The frigate birds would swoop down and pick up the fish in mid-air. This piracy, we felt sure, was not their only means of livelihood.

Dolphins and other large fish would chase shoals of flying fish and the frigate birds would snatch them when they leapt clear of the water. The latter also appeared to pick up anything that floated on the surface; they were attracted to pieces of surplus turtle fat we had discarded.

Despite their partly webbed feet we never saw frigate birds enter the water. I learned later that their feathers would soon become water-logged and they would find difficulty in taking off from the sea. Their long wing span supports a relatively small black-coloured body. We were able to distinguish between the sexes, the male having a distinctive red throat. It surprised us to see them so far from land.

Petrels, truly birds of the sea, came in varying numbers. Although we found them no larger than seven inches in length, they are apparently related to the albatross and shearwater. They flew close to the water with erratic wingbeats, sometimes singly, often in small dispersed flocks. The storm petrels were often attracted to us by the turtle fat we threw over the side, snatching pieces from the sea without alighting.

The petrel's diet is normally drifting plankton. They would hover close to the surface with fluttering wings with their feet moving in the water as though they were walking. After alighting on the water they found little difficulty in becoming airborne again. The storm petrels that we watched were dark-coloured and had square tails and short black legs and feet.

Another bird that sometimes came to us was of a solid grey colour about twelve inches in length. It had webbed feet and we thought that it might have been a noddy of the gull and tern family. We caught one and we found its red meat excellent. Why they should have been so far from land was a mystery to us.

As well as our particular region of plenty, we felt sure that there must also be "desert" areas in which little or no life existed. Fortune smiled upon us; the currents and winds were to keep us in this prolific zone.

From 16 June (Day 104) they endured a four day storm. Maurice:

The thunderstorms came and went with increasing frequency. Then the wind increased and low, dark clouds scudded quickly across the sky, foretelling the coming of another storm. Apprehensively we watched the waves heighten between periods of torrential driving rain. More and more our discomfort grew with the violently increasing motion; rain was now an ever-present facet of our daily routine. It was difficult for us to imagine what it had been like to be warm and dry. My salt water sores were becoming daily more unbearable. The pain from these sapped my spirit and

I found little contentment in living. I was in a state of abject misery. Rest had been a luxury that we had both forgotten. Now all our efforts went towards survival. There was no prospect of fishing in those conditions and we expended our energy ridding the raft of water. Even when it was not raining waves would send water crashing over us and we would start all over again.

Each hour went by slowly and with tedious monotony. I wondered just how we could survive the next hour. Yet Maralyn appeared undaunted, she encouraged me to keep baling with promises of good things when the storm subsided. She spoke of the luxury of sitting there eating meat and the greenish fat from the green turtles. We talked while we worked, describing to each other the relative merits of the male and female turtle. We could no longer talk of the food we would eat had we been rescued, the prospects were too slender at that time and it would have depressed us further. These discussions we referred to as "morale boosters" and our discomfort was tolerable while we dreamed of eating our turtle steaks in warm sunshine.

Reality frequently came upon us as another load of water had to be cleared, or the raft would need inflating again, or the cloths that we had placed in the gaps that had opened up between the tubes would need wringing or replacing. There was no respite.

The storm continued for four more days and we tried to keep warm beneath our oilskin jackets. This was impossible, however, and the jackets chafed our bodies. White blisters appeared on our paunches and arms. We longed to rid ourselves of those jackets, but we feared the cold. Sitting very cramped in the small space of the raft exercise was difficult and, in any case, I became reluctant to move for fear of shifting on to an ulcerated spot.

Nothing was new and our whole existence was as though we belonged to the sea. We could see and feel and hear only the things directly about us. Our association with the sea was no longer detached. It appeared as though we knew no other life. I had stopped dreaming of our life before or after this misadventure.

Our hunger began to increase our distress. We shared our meagre storm rations of one tin a day. Ironically, now that we had ample water our thirst had long since been satisfied. The perverse malignity of fate now adjudged that we discard every drop of water we collected.

On the second day of the storm the dinghy became water-logged and required emptying urgently. I clambered into the dinghy to bale it out, after which I would try to fish to satisfy our hunger. I took with me our last remaining hook. When I had got the dinghy very nearly clear of water, a wave broke across it and, taken by surprise, I was flung clear as the boat capsized. As I surfaced I saw Maralyn at the raft entrance. "Have you got the hook?" she called out anxiously. I lifted my left arm and opened my fist. To my surprise and Maralyn's delight I had gripped our last valuable hook firmly when I had been tipped out.

I swam to the raft and passed Maralyn the hook and then clambered aboard. Then began the struggle to right the dinghy. Once more the combined effect of the wind and the weight of the immersed water containers defied our efforts to turn the dinghy over. We struggled time and again to lift the dinghy and each time the effort sapped at our depleting strength.

"We'll have to untie them all," Maralyn said. The thought of untying the knots securing those containers irritated me. I said, "Let's have one more go." We tried to lift once more without any success. Vexed, I untied the containers and got them into the raft. Our next attempt at lifting the dinghy succeeded. Having replaced all the containers we retreated to the relative peace of the raft. However, our troubles were not yet over.

On the last day of the storm the dinghy turned over again, this time without either of us on board, but righting it was not difficult and we felt for the first time that the wind was easing but our compass and one of the oars had broken loose and disappeared. Although big seas still troubled us we were sure that the storm had passed.

Maralyn:

On the fourth day of the storm we caught a medium-sized female turtle and dropped it in the dinghy with a rope round its rear flipper. We had lost all our bait but this turtle would provide us with food and the means of obtaining other food. It was too rough to kill it but we kept a careful eye on it. The storm was blowing itself out. Once again our dinghy overturned in a welter of foam and this time both of us were concerned for our turtle.

Frantically, we hauled the dinghy close and lifted up one end, the turtle was still there! I began to haul it in and realized the rope was slipping. The turtle was almost within grasp and I reached out for it; my hands passed over its shell but it slipped through my fingers and swam away. I was left holding the rope, the remains of two half-hitches looped in the end.

Once more depression settled on us; we were tired, wet, cold, miserable. In fact, no words are adequate to describe our mood. We had lived in anoraks for days and nights on end and the chafing was adding to our discomfort. My legs were now covered with salt water sores and it was difficult to find a comfortable position. But my discomfort was nothing compared to Maurice's. Although his chest pains had eased the sores on his hips and the base of his spine increased in area and were now open, raw wounds. I had some antiseptic cream and large plasters, but this only helped for a short time, then they would come off because of being soaked in sea water. He couldn't see these sores himself and I kept telling him they were only small spots but, in fact, the sore on his spine was at least three-quarters of an inch across and very deep. If only it could have been kept dry it would heal but there was no chance of that.

The seas were now calmer and the sun occasionally broke

through the covering of cloud to dispense its welcome warmth. To pass the time I knelt by the doorway watching the shoals of fish congregate again; we urgently needed bait so that we could start fishing. During the afternoon a school of sharks kept circling around us, sometimes bumping the raft. Maurice sat and dozed next to me. Several times a small shark swam past just below the surface and about a foot away from me. As he went by I poked him and my finger ran down his rough skin. I waited until he came round again and without thinking grabbed his tail. Maurice was rudely awakened from his doze by my excited shouts, for although I had a firm grip on its tail I couldn't do anything else.

Maurice held a towel ready and asked me to flip it towards him. I did so and within minutes the shark was firmly encased in a towel. Maurice held its biting end tightly while I retained a firm grip on its tail. We were sharing the floor of the raft with a fiercely struggling and voracious shark! To our surprise it soon gave up its struggle for life and after fifteen minutes we carefully unwrapped it and gazed at our catch. It was coloured grey and only about two-and-a-half feet long, but there was a lot of meat on it. Maurice went into the dinghy with the fish and began to gut it. While he worked on I again watched the sharks and when another of similar size went past I couldn't resist the temptation and reached into the water and caught it. Approximately the same size as the other, it threshed around splashing water over both of us until Maurice again caught the head. I didn't dare let go of the tail, so I leaned over into the dinghy and held it tightly whilst Maurice hit it repeatedly with his knife. Eventually Maurice drove the knife through its gills and told me to let go. It still twitched and jumped but Maurice could control it.

"I've got another, I've got another," I shouted a little later. Maurice, hardly able to believe his eyes, repeated the procedure and grabbed this one. With one dead shark in the front of the dinghy, another almost expired shark under his feet and a very much alive one in his hands, Maurice implored me to stop catching them as he had no more hands or feet left! We both burst into gales of merriment at the absurd situation.

I went into the dinghy to help gut our catch, the improving weather and the abundance of food lightening the atmosphere. We were almost gay and discussed the possibility of staying in the dinghy to eat our meal, so much pleasanter than sitting in a drab, soggy raft.

As we threw titbits over the side, one by one the shoal of fish grew larger. After starving for the previous few days the prospect of a good meal was wonderful. I cut the shark meat into small pieces and Maurice prepared for fishing. Before casting the bait a blue-footed booby with a rich brown plumage swooped down and with a great flapping and rustling of wings settled itself on the side of the dinghy only two feet away from Maurice. We looked at each other. "Shall we?" I nodded agreement.

Maurice:

Its lack of fear at our nearness spelt its doom. I edged closer to it until it was well within grasping distance and still it did not move. The gannet-like bird looked directly at me through large ringed eyes which gave it a somewhat idiotic appearance. After examining me carefully for some seconds it went on preening itself, quite unconcerned.

When I reached out and grabbed its neck it gave a cry and struggled to free itself. Maralyn caught hold of its body while I wrung its neck. Its warm, soft body went limp and in less than a minute it was dead.

We laid it down in the dinghy and turned our attention back to the sharks.

Maralyn:

I sat on the dinghy thwart with the bird between my knees ready for plucking when a raucous "Ka-a" made me turn round in time to see a second brown booby settling itself calmly in the same spot on the dinghy as its companion. Quite unconcerned, it began to preen itself.

We were astounded; how could they be so stupid? In reply to Maurice's unasked question, I shrugged my shoulders and said, "Try, but if he goes it doesn't matter." Well, he didn't go and in a few minutes we had a second bird . . . one each, now! We were elated; our feast was growing to mammoth proportions!

Shark meat wasn't very palatable, and now we didn't have to eat it, only the liver and sweetmeats which we enjoyed. We both continued gutting the sharks when we noticed a large white booby diving for food. It circled round and round and when it sighted a particularly luscious fish it would fold back its wings and dive into the sea with a loud splash. The momentum must have carried him a long way down as it was many seconds before the bird reappeared, a fish firmly grasped in its beak.

On 24 June (Day 112) sharks were circling around them. Maralyn:

As they circled round I picked out a couple similar in size to the previous ones I had caught and this time Maurice said he would have a go. Being so stiff and sore, Maurice could only lean over the side of the dinghy and wait for one to swim by. "Small one just disappeared behind the raft – here he is again – now he's under the dinghy – coming up your side – no, he's off the stern – wait, he's turning round and coming back your side – there he is, grab him!"

Maurice leaned over and grabbed. Unfortunately, he grabbed the wrong one, and the threshing monster was half as big again as the ones I had caught. This one was at least four feet long and it took Maurice all his time to hold it. I got the towel ready and when Maurice flipped its head into the bottom of the dinghy I quickly threw the towel over it.

Using his hands and both feet, Maurice held it and transferred the tail into my hands while he reached for the knife.

Its blood ran freely and covered our hands and feet yet still it thrashed and jumped. Blood was everywhere and when it was finally dead and lay still we vowed not to catch any more unless they were really "baby" ones, it was too exhausting.

The shark skin was pearl grey and a very fine texture. It was so beautiful that I wanted to keep it and while Maurice fished I laboriously scraped every bit of flesh away from the skin, intending later to make a purse or some other small object. I rolled it up and stuffed it in a corner of the dinghy, but next day it was dry, crackly, dull and uninteresting so I discarded it.

Larger sharks, which had previously been no trouble, buffeted the bottom of the raft. As the raft deflated our bodies made large protrusions in the floor and were, no doubt, admirable targets. The sharks would approach at high speed but unseen and would hit the raft with a mighty thwack! Often they hit our bodies and jarred our spines until our bones were bruised and tender. Maurice suffered more in these attacks as they hit his open sores and would start them bleeding again. The bangs became agonizing and we dreaded these times. An attack would last up to half an hour before they went away. We could never decide if they were really being vicious or merely playing, but one fact is certain, their aim was good. Nine times out of ten they would hit us! One strange thing we noticed was the way they always buffeted the raft but not the dinghy, even when we were sitting in the dinghy. I wondered if the colour affected them at all, one craft being black and the other grey.

The weather improved but it was damp, depressing and uncomfortable in the raft. They caught two baby turtles which they kept in the dinghy. There was enough water in the dinghy to keep them cool. They were running out of fishhooks. While fishing from the dinghy they improvized a fish trap from a one gallon plastic container with an opening cut. They put some bait inside and hung it in the water. Maralyn:

At first the fish viewed it with suspicion, charging up to the entrance then veering off. But they were voracious by nature and seemed determined to outdo each other. Soon two or three fish had gathered at the opening, gazing longingly at the lump of bait. Suddenly one of them dashed forward into the container and grabbed the bait and dragged it a little way towards the entrance before backing out. I resisted the temptation to scoop it out and explained to Maurice that we had to get them well trained first. Maurice marvelled at my patience. I fed them lump after lump until a large crowd of fish hung around and willingly played my fish trap game. Eventually, I decided to catch a few and it was so easy to wait for the right fish to swim in and to lift the trap out of the water and deposit the fish at Maurice's feet. The fish didn't appear to notice that some of their playmates had disappeared but continued to oblige with renewed vigour.

Maurice was delighted at the trap's efficiency when I caught our breakfast of approximately twenty fish using very little bait and with no danger of losing our hook. Unfortunately this method of fishing only attracted the trigger fish, the golden jacks and silver fish being much more timid and wary. We could only use the trap in reasonably calm weather. A strong wind would make us drift too fast for the fish to swim into the hole, and a disturbed sea made them misjudge distances. Often they would swim in line with the trap and when they had plucked up sufficient courage, dash forward but because of the movement of the sea they would miss the hole completely. They would then turn round and nuzzle the back of the trap, obviously puzzled as to where the bait had gone.

Maralyn had taken over the fishing when Maurice became ill at the beginning of June. Her method was crude but effective. As soon as a fish got close to the bait she gave the line a jerk. Maralyn:

Once I had jerked it away from them they swam fast towards

it and held on tightly to the bait. I would haul them quickly over the side and fling them in the dinghy. My fishing had little style about it but it was fun. Occasionally I got carried away and, jerking the line on board, the fish would whizz through the air attached to the line and land back in the sea on the other side of the dinghy. To me they seemed to enjoy this and there was no lack of contestants for the "high wire" act.

My fishing sessions became known for the "flying trigger fish". As fast as I tossed them in the dinghy Maurice would sort them and throw the smaller ones, "tadpoles", back over the side. There were so many we could pick and choose. At sessions like this we usually contented ourselves with twenty to thirty fish, but I remember, at least, two occasions when we caught fifty.

Using this method we did not have to keep so much bait on hand, as one piece of bait could be used to catch several fish. All we needed was enough bait to catch one fish and then we had fresh bait to start again. It was not unusual to see two fish fly through the air, both hanging on to the same piece of bait.

At other times loud splashes in the distance gradually came closer and closer until we realized the noise was coming from a school of dolphins. Many times we had sat on the foredeck of *Auralyn* as she had ploughed her way across the oceans and watched these graceful creatures gambol alongside us, diving and cavorting in front of the bow. Once, loud squeaking noises had us searching everywhere for the cause only to find we had a school of dolphins alongside talking loudly to each other. Now it seemed these friendly creatures were to visit us once more.

As they came closer we realized they must be catching food and a glance at our shoal of fish cowering in the shade of dinghy and raft made us feel not so well disposed towards them. Suddenly they were amongst us, their black and supple bodies diving in every direction, sending the scurrying fish before them. Both rubber craft were tossed about in the disturbance and dollops of sea water descended on us as they became more and more excited in the chase.

The hullabaloo lasted for almost twenty minutes then suddenly it was still and only an occasional echoing splash in the distance told of their presence. After mopping up and muttering none-too-complimentary things about them, we leaned out and looked at our fish. Only a few bedraggled specimens remained; the rest were dispersed or eaten.

It took many patient hours of feeding and coaxing to get a reasonable-sized shoal about us once more and life would again resume its steady routine. The visits of dolphins came to be looked upon as a time of annoyance and frustration and, although we aimed at them, with our paddles and shouted at them they could not be discouraged. We never managed to hit one, they were far too fast and agile for us, but something had somehow managed to damage them as most of them showed a shattered, chipped or flattened fin.

One morning a plop on the canvas cover turned out to be the one and only squid we saw during our time adrift. It must have been travelling very fast, probably pursued by dolphins or a sperm whale because it hit us with such force. It lay there during the day and by evening the sun had dried it and it had stuck firmly. Squid are related to the octopus and cuttlefish. We didn't feel like eating the creature; it looked like an unappetizing lump of grey jelly. It left a purple ink stain to remind us of its visit.

On several occasions while we sat in the dinghy we had observed sea snakes swimming around. They were deep yellow with black diamond patterns on them. We saw one swimming very close to the surface, its head occasionally breaking water as, like all reptiles, it needed to breathe air. I poked it with the paddle and lifted its gleaming body a few inches out of the sea but its supple and sinuous movements made me drop it quickly back into its element. I didn't want a bite from that!

*On 30 June (Day 118) Maurice was half-asleep in the raft when
Maralyn woke him. Maurice:*

"Get out to the dinghy. A ship is coming," Maralyn's urgent
tone had penetrated my sluggish brain. Cursing, I automati-
cally struggled to a kneeling position and scrambled across to
the dinghy. I sat on the thwart in a dazed condition, trying to
focus my eyes on to different parts of the sea. Maralyn was
standing in the raft waving her jacket. Yet I could see no ship;
Maralyn must be imagining things.

"Wave your jacket, it's there, behind you."

"All right," I said turning round slowly. Then I saw it; a
small white, rust-streaked ship approaching from the east. It
would pass very close and I began to wave my oilskin jacket.
The ship steamed on a course nearly due west and within a
short time it was opposite us, about half a mile away.

"It's a Korean fishing boat," I called to Maralyn.
"Remember seeing them in Tenerife?"

Maralyn answered but did not stop waving. Her vigorous
movements rocked the raft with its nearly deflated lower
section almost under water. The ship went past and I stopped
waving. It was no use, the ship was not going to stop. Why
waste any more energy? I felt ill and slumped to my knees.

I called to Maralyn, "Stop waving, save your strength."
She ignored me and continued to wave as the ship showed its
stern to us. It was the first we had seen for 43 days.

"Please come back," Maralyn shouted. "Please . . ."

I was oblivious now of the ship's movements as I knelt in
the dinghy. Maralyn was still imploring the ship to return.
Let it go on, I thought, this is our world now on the sea,
amongst the birds and the turtles and the fish.

Maralyn had suddenly stopped her entreaties but
continued to wave her jacket quietly. I looked up and stared
for some time at the ship. I looked long and hard at it in
disbelief. Was it returning or was it a trick of my eyes?
Maralyn looked across at me, her eyes moist and gleaming.
"It's coming back," she said.

"You've found us a ship," I said excitedly; then, realizing our nakedness, I went on, "Sort some clothes out, quickly."

She passed over a sodden pair of tennis shorts and a rotting shirt and, while we struggled into our clothes, the fishing boat manoeuvred into the wind to come alongside. I reached down and lifted our two young turtles and lowered them over the side.

A heaving line with a heavy "monkey's fist" on the end descended but it fell short into the sea. Voices shouted from the ship, attracting my attention to a second heaving line now draped across the life-raft and the stern of the dinghy. I wedged the monkey's fist hard into the rowlock and strong hands on the ship began to haul our rubber craft towards a boarding ladder up forward.

A voice came down to us, "Can you speak English?"

"We are English," I replied.

Alongside the ladder, I secured the dinghy with another line and, holding on to the ladder, I began to haul the raft close so that Maralyn could go on board first. A seaman jumped down and stood beside me and indicated that I should board first. "Go on, I'll follow," Maralyn said. I climbed the ladder and over the bulwarks to be greeted by a number of willing arms to support me. I was led across to a blanket laid on deck but, because of my sores, I could not sit. I half knelt taking most of my weight on my arms and thighs.

The ship was Weolmi 306, *a 650-ton tuna fishing boat out of Busan. It was on its way home to South Korea after thirty months' fishing in the Atlantic. The captain was concerned that they might be Russians. It took half an hour to convince him that they did not come from a state with communist affiliations. The captain decided to help them. The crew gave them clothes and food and some medicine for Maurice.*

While the ship was en rote for Busan, Maralyn and Maurice were told they had become a world sensation. The company which owned the ship instructed that they were to be taken to Honolulu to receive medical treatment. They received a tumultuous reception there. They began writing their account while they were aboard the Weolmi. *Their adventure became known as "117 days adrift" from the initial news reports. They had actually spent 118 and a third days adrift.*

Capsized off Kodiak
1989

Spike Walker fished commercially in Alaska for over twenty seasons. He collected exceptional stories of survival and disaster from survivors.

In 1989, Joe Harlan was captain of the 53-foot crab boat, Tidings. *His crew were Bruce Hinman, Chris Rosenthal and George Timpke. They had been out for two weeks when the tanner crab catch fell off dramatically. He and his crew decided to cut their losses and return to port at Kodiak. At that point the seas were moderate but at Narrow Cape they ran into some tide rips. The boat was covered in spray and began making ice heavily. Spike Walker:*

"Guys, we've got to get this ice off of us," he said as he woke the men. With his crew gathered in the wheelhouse, Harlan pointed at the windows surrounding them. They were encased in ice. Only a clear space the size of a quarter in one window remained.

"Knock the windows clear, and then be sure and get the ice that's stuck to our railings," directed the skipper. "But don't let yourself get frostbitten. As soon as you get cold, come on in!" he insisted.

In an amazingly short time, a thick layer of ice had formed on the *Tidings*. Ice covered the boat – except, that is, for the crab pots themselves. Harlan and his crew had wrapped the commonly ice-drawing forms of steel and webbing in a layer of slick plastic, one that drained quickly before the spray from the ocean had time to harden.

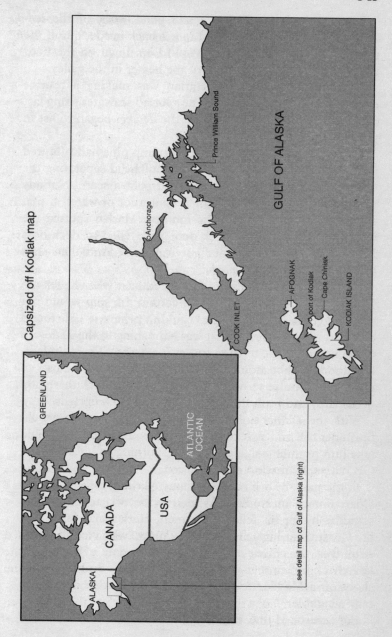

Capsized off Kodiak map

GREENLAND

ATLANTIC OCEAN

CANADA

USA

ALASKA

see detail map of Gulf of Alaska (right)

GULF OF ALASKA

Prince William Sound

Anchorage

COOK INLET

AFOGNAK

port of Kodiak

Cape Chiniak

KODIAK ISLAND

The crew of the *Tidings* made good work of the ice-breaking task. But they longed to get back inside, out of the murderous cold. There they would flop down on the floor and warm themselves in front of the heater in the galley.

Back inside, skipper Joe Harlan was making a routine check of his engine room when he spotted seawater rising fast in the ship's bilge. Seconds later, the *Tidings* began to list to the port side.

Either the crab tank's circulation-pump pipe had ruptured inside the engine room or the steel bulkhead separating the engine room from the crab tank had split a seam. Nobody would ever know for sure. But it "put a lot of water in that engine room right now!" The moment Harlan spotted the water, he rushed to the back door and yelled to deck boss Bruce Hinman, "Grab your survival suits! And then start kicking the pots over the side!"

Joe Harlan was standing in the wheelhouse when he felt the *Tidings* roll. Instinctively, he was certain the ship would not be able to right herself. Yet he "couldn't believe it". He found he was unable to accept what was happening to the *Tidings*, a vessel he had come to trust and even admire. Then a ridiculous thought shot momentarily through his mind: he had an unspoken impulse to order his crew to "run back there hop overboard, and push the thirty-ton vessel back upright."

With the *Tidings* sinking fast, Joe Harlan knew she would finish her roll and sink completely in about the time it would take him to utter a single sentence. Turning to his VHF and GB radios, he made a snap decision.

In the past, he'd listened to many Mayday calls to the US Coast Guard in Kodiak. As glad as he was to have them standing by for his fellow fishermen, Harlan also knew that the Coast Guard usually wanted to know "who your mother's sister was, the colour of your boat," your date of birth, your last check-up, proper spelling, and the like. So rather than shoot off a Mayday to the Coast Guard, Harlan decided to take a gamble.

For much of the night, he'd been listening on VHF

channel 6 to the friendly chatter of the boats traveling ahead of him up the line. He grabbed the GB mike then and yelled, "Mayday! Mayday! Mayday! This is the *Tidings*! We're off Cape Chiniak and we're going down!"

As he spoke, the *Tidings* fell completely over on her starboard side. Below him, Harlan could see batteries breaking loose and flying across the engine room. He felt his heart free-fall into his belly. Before he could unkey his mike, he "lost all power. Everything went dead."

Harlan heard a tremendous crash, and it seemed that all at once everything inside the boat – pots, pans, toasters, even rifles – came flying loose. Then the large hulk of the refrigerator came tumbling from its mounts. Harlan was thrown across the width of the wheelhouse. He struggled to regain his footing, but instead he tumbled backward down into the fo'c'sle.

Then, like a whale sounding, in one continuous motion the stern kicked high, and the *Tidings* sank bow-first, straight for the bottom. She slid toward the ocean floor in one steady motion, burying herself full length in the night sea. And there she paused, floating with only a few feet of her stern showing above the surface, with Joe Harlan still trapped inside.

The crew were on the deck aft when Tidings *sank. Hinman was entangled by a crab pot after he was hurled into the sea. Walker:*

It all happened so quickly. Hinman had been knocked senseless by the sudden shock of the Kodiak waters, ensnared by one of his own crab pots, and was now being dragged along on an unforeseen journey into deepest darkness toward an ocean floor more than a thousand feet below.

He knew instinctively that if he allowed panic to rule him, he would be lost. And he fought to choke back the rising tide of unreasoning fear within himself.

As he descended through the darkness, Hinman gained a measure of composure. He would fight against the building fear by taking action. He was perhaps seventy feet beneath the ocean surface when he managed to jerk his ensnared right arm free. Then he placed both of his stocking feet against the webbing of the crab pot and pushed away violently. The fast-sinking crab pot disappeared quickly, tumbling off into the black body of sea below him.

When Hinman looked up, he was awestruck by what he saw. For a blinding orb of radiant light hovered above him There was something beautiful, even angelic about the vision before him. Brilliant in splendour, it bathed him in spirit-lifting columns of golden light that seemed to beckon him home.

He ascended feverishly then, stroking overhead toward the comforting swathe of inexplicable light like a man with a building hope, a hope tempered by the fear that at any moment another toppling crab pot might very well descend upon him and carry him back down again.

When Hinman reached the surface he saw the stern of Tidings *drifting nearby. She was hanging straight down in the water. Hinman was not wearing his survival suit. These suits not only acted as buoyancy aids, they protected the wearer from the cold. Eventually, the freezing waters would be lethal without one. Hinman trod water and shouted for his crew-mates. Rosenthal and Timpke responded but Harlan was still in the boat. Walker:*

Harlan had been roughed up considerably when the *Tidings* had rolled over. In fact, he had come close to breaking his right arm. He scrambled to gather himself and climb out. Ordinarily, the ladder leading from the engine room to the sleeping quarters stood upright and led down into the engine room. But now the vertical leg of the ladder posed a serious obstacle. With the *Tidings* tilted straight down as she was, the ladder now lay unevenly across the inverted space before him sloping as it stretched between cabins. Scaling it would be a little like trying to climb the underside of a stairway. With his battered right arm, it would be a difficult gymnastic feat.

Now the startled skipper found himself "all the way forward" in the darkest inner reaches of the ship's bow, some fifty feet below the surface of the sea. As the boat continued to leap and roll, he could hear the ongoing crash and clutter of stored parts falling and scattering overhead.

Suddenly, in the grey-black light, a roaring blast of seawater broke through the door to the engine room. The tumultuous white water broke heavily over Harlan, lifting him bodily and washing him out of the fo'c'sle. He gasped for air as the icy flood cascaded over him. As he was carried along through the inverted space of the ship's galley, Harlan reached out and snagged the handle to the wheelhouse door. He tugged frantically but, with the water pressure sealing it shut, he found it immovable.

As the small galley continued to flood, Harlan found himself struggling to remain afloat in the narrowing confines. The galley sink and faucet were now suspended on end below him while beside him, in the claustrophobic space, floated the gyrating hulk of their refrigerator.

Harlan gulped air and dived. He knew he had to think of a way out. He swam down through the watery cubicle of the galley to the sink, grabbed the faucet with both hands, and kicked viciously at the starboard side window behind it. But the leaden cold of the water seemed to drain the power from his blows. This is hopeless! he thought, as he swam numbly back toward the pocket of air above.

The moment his head emerged, he was greeted by a terrifying roar. The flood of gushing seawater into the room seemed to be accelerating. The sound of it echoing in the small sliver of space was deafening. The water sloshed back and forth between walls that rolled and dipped in a dizzying motion around him. Again, the refrigerator drifted into him. And he fought against a building sense of horror.

Treading water, Harlan tilted his head back in the narrow space next to the ceiling and tried to inhale the precious air. But the shocking cold of the seawater continued to make breathing difficult, and his breath came in shallow huffs.

Well, this is it, he thought. This must have been how Jim Miller died on the *George W*.

Harlan considered praying, but it occurred to him that doing so would be an admission that he was going to die. He also made up his mind "not to snivel". He would not pray, and he would not blubber. He would face the outcome, whatever that might be.

Joe Harlan weighed the chances of escaping through the galley door and out onto the back deck. But, with the *Tidings* standing directly on end as she was, he knew the entire 15,000-pound stack of crab pots would be pressing down against the door at that very moment. And, with the refrigerator floating in front of it, he conceded the escape route had been lost.

Yet even at the time, in the midst of all the terror and commotion, Joe Harlan realized that there was something strange about his ongoing ordeal. For he could see virtually everything. With his adrenaline flowing, his senses had somehow become heightened – and now a whole new world seemed to open up before him. When he dived again, he saw, through the blue-green tint of the water, the forms of the faucet and the window behind it, while the blocky brown figure of the refrigerator bobbed above him, suspended in the water overhead.

There was something strange about it all. Harlan knew there were no lights burning on the boat. Everything had gone dead. There was "zero power". Perhaps it was moon-bright up top. But then he recalled that there had been no sign of the moon on such an inclement night. Yet, submerged as he was, Harlan could see clearly through the seawater inside the boat, as well as out into the light green sea space on the other side of the window.

Adrift in the ocean current, the hull of the *Tidings* bounced now in the lumpy winter seas like a floating berg of ice, with barely 10 per cent of her whole self still showing above the surface.

Wild with anger and determination, he sucked in another

brief pull of air and dived again for the sink. He would make another attempt to break out the window. But this time he would try another method. He swam to the sink, then grabbed the faucet tightly again with both hands and began repeatedly ramming his head into the glass.

Suddenly, the window exploded from its mounts. Harlan watched as it tumbled out into the pale green void and fell into the watery oblivion below.

All of a sudden, Harlan felt outside of himself. Imagining himself to be a sea otter, he swam nimbly ahead through one small opening as if it were the most natural thing, arched back, and headed directly for the surface.

In the strange and unexplained illumination that still remained, Harlan was able to see the hull of the *Tidings* as he swam upward. Man, I can't be *that* far from the surface, he thought as he stroked "up and up and up". The moment he broke through the surface, he felt himself return to his old self. It was like breaking into a "completely different world again!"

Harlan gasped wildly for air.

Bruce Hinman was drifting next to the bobbing stern of the *Tidings* when a man's head exploded through the surface, popping up right alongside him.

Choking, thrashing against the water, the man coughed heavily and spun in his direction.

"Hinman! You ugly son of a bitch!" he yelled.

It was none other than his skipper, Joe Harlan.

"Joe! Damn, I thought you were dead!" shot back Hinman, elated to see him.

Hinman's levity at seeing Harlan was quickly tempered, however, by the hopeless realization that there was no way to survive the present predicament. The canister containing the life raft had apparently failed to release when the *Tidings* rolled over, or perhaps it had released, only to get tangled up in the rigging or the crab pots. It didn't matter. Without that life raft, they knew they were all "as good as dead".

"What are we going to do?" shouted Hinman to Joe Harlan. "Did we get off a Mayday call?"

Harlan had tried, but he couldn't be positive that anyone had heard it.

There was nothing the men could do now but tread water and wait. With the wind blowing offshore, there would be no way to try to swim to shore. The deadly effects of hypothermia commonly paralyzed and drowned most men adrift in such seas in a few short minutes, at least those wearing only work clothes. Some began to sink the moment they hit the water. Even if Harlan, and Hinman, and the others could remain afloat, the wind and waves would eventually carry their bodies out to sea, where they would be lost forever.

When one crewman realized how grim things looked, he announced that he might just as well swim back down into the wheelhouse of the *Tidings*, get his pistol, and shoot himself.

Suddenly, an object "as large a dinosaur" exploded out of the water between Hinman and his skipper. It was the fibreglass canister that housed the *Tidings*'s life raft. The canister was about the size and shape of a fifty-five-gallon oil drum.

"Grab that SOB!" yelled Hinman.

The four crewmen converged on it. "Pull the cord!" yelled Joe Harlan.

Unfortunately, it seemed as if the line which activated the ship's life raft was defective. Walker:

Joe Harlan moved in to help. He leaned back in the water, placed both feet on either side of the end of the canister, wrapped the rope line around both of his clumsy, cold-ravaged hands. He reached down all the way then and pulled with everything he had.

The stubborn knot on the other end of the line gave way suddenly. Then came the pop and hiss of the CO_2 cartridge discharging within. In the next instant, the bright orange canister exploded open and the raft began to inflate. But it inflated upside down.

As longtime fishermen, 290-pound Bruce Hinman and 200-pound Joe Harlan continued to work together. They quickly assessed the situation and, without comment, approached the task at hand as if driven by the logic of a single working mind.

Inflated and upright, these rafts are fluorescent orange in colour and round in form, with a diameter of eight feet. Floating, they look like giant inner tubes, or perhaps like those inflatable, backyard pools that small children use, with a dome tent mounted on top.

Swimming to one side of the raft, they crawled atop it. Then, planting their feet (and combined weight of five hundred pounds) on the downwind side of the overturned raft, they reached across, grabbed its upwind edge, and lifted it in unison. When the twenty-five-knot winds caught the exposed upwind edge of the raft, it flipped it upright, scooping more than a foot of icy seawater along with it as it did.

"All right!" yelled one shivering crewman as he breast-stroked nearby.

Drifting in the murderous cold of the ocean currents, the entire crew was thoroughly chilled, their movements sluggish with the steadily advancing effects of hypothermia. Hinman and Harlan decided to drift alongside the raft in the painfully cold seawater and help their crewmates crawl aboard through the narrow doorway of the raft.

Being by far the huskiest of any man in the *Tidings* crew (or in the entire Kodiak crab boat fleet, for that matter), Hinman insisted on going last. It was a wise decision, for when all had been helped aboard, so numbed was he, and so completely had his strength been sucked from his body, that it took not only all of his own failing strength but also the body-wrenching efforts of the entire crew to haul him aboard.

Never in more than a century of brutal Alaskan winter had a storm front this cold struck the Kodiak Island area –

a 40° F reading in Alaska's dry interior country near Anchor or Fairbanks was considered cold, even dangerous, although not unusual. But it was unheard of in the moist marine waters of the Gulf of Alaska.

The storm winds howled incessantly. The unrelenting gusts turned the raft's doorway into a virtual wind tunnel. Caught without a single survival suit among the four of them and constantly awash with more than a foot of icy Gulf Alaska seawater crashing about inside their raft (and with more seawater washing inside all the time), the crew of *Tidings* knew their lives were still in serious jeopardy.

In truth, the record cold front threatened to freeze them where they sat. Packed tightly inside the cramped and drenching confines of the dome-covered raft, the cold-ravaged crew of the fishing vessel *Tidings* huddled together, shivering violently as panting columns of steamy breath jetted from their mouths.

Bruce Hinman rubbed his hands together furiously. He crossed his forearms, folded his hands under his armpits, and turned numbly to his skipper.

As if the record cold and unconfirmed Mayday hadn't been enough to worry the crew of the *Tidings*, they now discovered another unsettling fact: their painter, leading out from the life raft, was still tethered to the sinking hull of the *Tidings*. In theory, the raft was attached this way to keep the crew members in the close vicinity of the boat as long as possible But the status of the inverted *Tidings* was tenuous at best, and they knew she could be heading for the bottom at any moment. If she did, the life raft and all its occupants would likely be pulled down along with her.

The bridle cord attaching the raft to the painter was designed so that it was tethered directly in front of the raft's entrance hole. In any windy conditions, this meant that as long as the raft remained tied to her mother ship, the gaping hole of the doorway would always end up facing directly into the prevailing wind. That wind now drove close-cropped ocean waves against the side of the stationary side of the raft.

And icy walls of sea spray began exploding in through the front door and over those inside. Short of cutting the cord and casting themselves off into the mercy of the night, there was nothing to be done.

In only minutes, the blunt force of the record cold, the knifing edge of the arctic wind, and the drenching blasts of icy sea spray had rendered the men almost unconscious. They prayed then, and waited. And as the murderous cold bore down on them, a heavy silence fell on the crew.

Like the rest of the men, skipper Joe Harlan could no longer feel his fingers. But when he sensed the growing sense of hopelessness in the raft, he turned to his men.

"Look, guys, we're going to make it. Try not to worry about it. We're in the raft. That's the important thing." He paused. "We've just got to keep fighting it," he added. And he set about to keep the men busy. "Now is the time to get things done. And the first thing we need to do is to get that door flap tied shut!"

Their fingers were too numb to open some of the survival equipment in the raft. Walker:

Bruce Hinman furiously rubbed his hands together. He crossed his forearms and folded his hands under his armpits. Then he pulled the door flap a few inches to one side and scanned the late-night seascape all around.

The sinking of the fishing vessel *Tidings* brought with it an especially insistent message. This was the second ship to sink out from under Hinman in the last month. Both had sunk off that very same point of Kodiak Island coastline – Cape Chiniak.

The US Coast Guard squad, flying out of the Kodiak Island base, had been kept hopping all season long. The rescue of Hinman from the sinking *Cape Clear* several weeks before had been performed in huge seas in yet another blinding snow-storm.

The Coast Guard helicopter pilot had descended bravely

out of the night and hovered down over the sinking vessel. But then the helicopter's rotor blades had struck the ship's mast, very nearly killing Hinman as well as the eight men on board the chopper.

Adrift then in the tall seas, Hinman had fought hard to keep from drowning as the torn and flooded suit he wore threatened to sink him. He was completely played out by the time they finally managed to hoist him aboard the Coast Guard chopper.

And now he and his crewmates were waiting to be rescued from yet another crab boat. Hinman was staring out through a silver moonlit haze of ice fog swirling across the lonely black face of the sea, when he spotted a set of approaching mast lights.

"Hey!" he yelled aloud. "Here comes a boat!"

It was another vessel from the Kodiak fishing-fleet. Walker:

The 58-foot fishing vessel *Polar Star* had been under way several miles off Cape Chiniak when the *Tidings* first called for help. The skipper and owner of the *Polar Star*, Pat Pikus, was wrestling with poor visibility himself at the time. He had been standing alone at the helm, moving ahead through a steamy, boiling cloud of ice fog, when the call for help suddenly leapt from his CB radio: "Mayday! Mayday! This is the *Tidings*! We're off Cape Chiniak and we're going down." Then, just as suddenly, the frantic voice fell silent.

Pikus quickly awakened his crew. "Everyone get up right away!" he yelled. "We've got a problem!"

He paused while his crew scrambled to life. Knifing, thirty-knot winds, with a bladelike edge of −26° F, were driving across the face of the sea. More important, Pikus knew there were no charts that could adequately describe the chill factor – nor the utter aloneness a drenched and drifting crew would know on such a night. When crewmen Shannon McCorkle, George Pikus, Gene LeDoux, and William De Hill, Jr., had gathered in the wheelhouse, he turned to them. "Boys," he said, "we've got a boat in real trouble nearby us here. And, cold as it is outside, I'm still going to need one of you men to go climb up on the flying bridge and keep a watch out from there."

The wind was blowing offshore at the time, and Pikus began his search by making passes back and forth across the brackish water between the shoreline of Kodiak Island and an imaginary point several miles offshore. He had no sooner begun his effort when another skipper's voice jumped from the radio.

The skipper claimed that the last time he'd seen the *Tidings*, she'd been cruising several miles offshore. Still another skipper added that he believed he'd seen a tiny blip on his radar screen in the very area where the *Polar Star* was now cruising. But his radar had only fastened upon it once; then it had disappeared, and had never shown again.

After completing several grid-line sweeps, Pikus was about to head back into shore for yet another pass when, squinting through the boiling fog, he thought he saw something dead ahead. It turned out to be the silver flash of a small piece of reflector tape and it was stuck to the side of the dome of a life raft.

Slowing his approach, Pikus and his crew soon spotted the stunning figure of the *Tiding*'s stern bouncing slowly and rhythmically through the choppy black seas. The *Tidings* had somehow managed to remain afloat, standing on end, with almost her full length buried beneath the sea. Only the last few feet of her stern and rudder now showed above the surface.

As he watched, the exposed stern of the wave-slickened hull performed an eerie ballet. What remained to be seen of her rose and fell through a jet-black world of swirling fog and howling wind, a void as cold and oppressive as a journey into the unlit bowels of a walk-in freezer.

Pikus was afraid that, in the strong winds, his vessel would drift right over the top of the life raft. So he swung in downwind of it, then manoeuvred in close.

"Hello! Hello! Is anyone there?" Pat Pikus yelled out his side wheelhouse door.

A muffled cry came back. Then the door flap on the side of the raft's dome flipped out and someone yelled, "*Yah, we're here!*"

The raft was caught in the bleak glare of his sodium lights. When he pulled alongside, Pikus "looked right down into the raft." He had never seen a more pathetic sight. "No one wore survival suits," he recalls. "A couple of them were without shoes. There was a lot of water slopping around in the raft." The entire crew looked as weak and hypothermic as humans can get and still remain alive. "They wouldn't have made it another ten or fifteen minutes," he recalls.

Over the radio, the Coast Guard urged their rescuers to keep the survivors awake. Harlan was saved by one of the Polar Star's *crewmen who kept him warm by stripping and climbing into bed with him. Harlan claimed:*

The real heroes were the crew of the fishing vessel *Polar Star*. There's no doubt in my mind. If we'd been out there another fifteen minutes, we would have died. We were that close to buying it.

Harlan had grown a beard during the bitter cold of the crab season. His one-year-old daughter didn't recognize him. When he came home, she asked him, "Are you Santa Claus?"

Hurricane Roxanne
(1995)

On Tuesday 10 October 1995 Hurricane Roxanne was heading for an oilfield off the coast of Mexico. The pipe-laying barge DLB 269 was anchored in the oilfield laying pipe. It was directly in the path of Hurricane Roxanne. The depth of the water in the area is relatively

Hurricane Roxanne hits Bahia de Campeche 10-15 October 1995

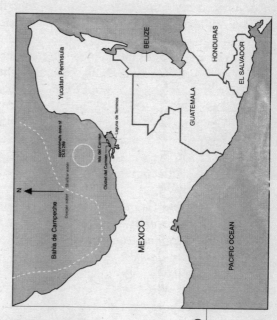

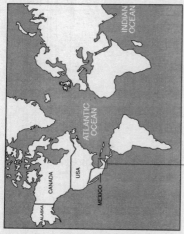

see detail map of Bahia de Campeche (right)

Vessels hit by Hurricane Roxanne 10-15 October 1995

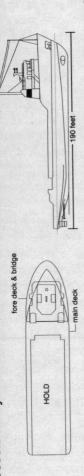

fore deck & bridge

main deck

HOLD

Above: Plan & Side view of the Anchor/supply vessel *North Carolina*; *Ducker Tide* was almost identical. *North Carolina* saved 54 men from *DLB 269*. *Ducker Tide* saved 79 men.

190 feet

11

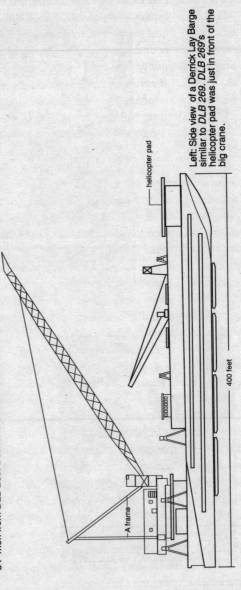

helicopter pad

A frame

400 feet

Left: Side view of a Derrick Lay Barge similar to *DLB 269*. *DLB 269*'s helicopter pad was just in front of the big crane.

*shallow. It is only 70–80 feet deep. This is shallow enough to make
waves both come closer together and mount higher.*

DLB 269 *was a Derrick Laying Barge (DLB). It was 28
years old. It had no form of propulsion and had to be towed. It was
towed by tugs or anchor/supply vessels. A Derrick Laying Barge
dropped sections of pipe from its stern onto the seabed. Divers made
the final connections on the seabed. A jet sled was used to blast a
trench in the seabed. The pipe then dropped into the trench.*

DLB 269 *was working on an oilfield 60 miles North of Isla De
Carmen at the base of the Yucatan peninsula. The oil development
centre was at Ciudad Del Carmen on the Isla De Carmen. The
Isla De Carmen lay at the mouth of the Laguna De Terminus.
This is a shallow salt water bay. It was too shallow for* DLB 269
to enter. DLB 269 *was 400 foot long with a 19 foot draft. It was
equipped with derricks (cranes) to lift the sections of pipe and a
diving bell which weighed 19 tons. The sections of pipe were 40 feet
long and weighed 2 tons each.*

DLB 269 *was owned by a Mexican-American joint venture
company, Corporacion de Construcciones de Campeche (CCC).
CCC was under contract with Penmex, Mexico's national oil
company, to build undersea pipelines connecting offshore oil
drilling platforms in Bahia de Campeche.* DLB 269 *was a small
floating town. It was carrying a crew of 245 including a team of
drivers. To cut down time spent decompressing, the divers stayed in
a pressurized (saturation) chamber between dives.*

*On Tuesday 10 October six divers were in the pressurized
(saturation) chamber. They were in danger of getting the "bends"
if they had to leave the chamber prematurely. CCC decided that*
DLB 269 *would ride out the hurricane under tow. They used
emergency decompression techniques to hasten the divers' decompression. The anchor/supply vessel* North Carolina *and the tug*
Captain John *were standing by to take on the tow. By 0600* DLB
269 *was enduring 80 mph winds and 20-foot waves. Rust in the
bilges was making her pumps clog frequently. But Hurricane
Roxanne passed over to the West.* North Carolina *and* Captain
John *continued towing* DLB 269 *to the north.* DLB 269*'s pumps
were not keeping up with the leaks.*

*By Saturday 14 October weather reports warned that
Hurricane Roxanne was coming back towards* DLB 269. *The
winds and waves were pushing* DLB 269 *and her tugs back
towards the south-east. Conditions aboard were becoming
extremely dangerous:*

The deckhands on the barge rigging the eye on their anchor
line were in almost as much danger as the tug crew. Each
time the *269*'s bow came down the crest of a wave, it
would immediately slam into another wave, and the
following crest would race over the foredeck in a wall of
water. The dozen riggers working on the towline would
leap behind any bit of shelter or try to hold onto something solid. Those who couldn't find shelter within the few
seconds available or who couldn't maintain their hold on
a rail or stanchion were knocked off their feet and swept
down the deck. Sometimes they smashed against an anchor
windlass, a chock, or another piece of deck gear. Other
men were carried in a flood of water to a railing, which
they frantically grabbed to keep from being washed overboard. In spite of near catastrophes and without suffering
more than broken fingers, bruises, and banged heads, they
were finally able to rig an eye in the anchor cable.

Waves now were so high that as the *269* sank into a
trough they would sizzle past the men on the heliodeck
40 feet above the waterline. Each time the heaving line
went out from the bow of the barge and fell into the sea,
and Trosclair would again back his tug just ahead of the
menacing bow, which with one blow could sink his vessel,
just push her right under. In seconds the sea would pour
in and she and her crew would likely be trapped under
the *269*'s hull. The scenario of a tug run over and trapped
under her tow is one with which all experienced towboat
crews are familiar, and the men on the *Captain John* realized only too well that they were just one miscalculation
away from its happening to them.

To compound their problems, Trosclair was having

trouble keeping the *Captain John*'s bow into the wind. As he backed down on the *269*, the wind and seas would push his bow to one side or the other, and the tug would start to go broadside to the barge astern of them Only rapid corrections of heavy throttle and hard rudders saved them. Then, once more, Trosclair would begin backing down toward the behemoth in his wake.

The men on both tug and barge persevered in trying to reconnect the towline. They knew that in the prevailing wind and seas the North Carolina could not keep the *269* in position by herself, nor was her single towline likely to hold for long.

The Captain John *succeeded in passing a new cable. The full force of the hurricane was nearly on top of them. The winds were gusting at 80 mph.*

At 1000 hours, all personnel were ordered to their life-raft stations. If DLB 269 lost her tow she would turn broadside on to the waves. The rising water level was reaching the living quarters on the deck above the machinery level. The pumps were unable to keep up with the flooding on the machinery deck. A bucket chain was organised but after one and a half hours the men were told to go "topside". They were unable to seal the hatch to the machinery level. 269 began listing to starboard. Ray Pepperday was a technician. He remembered:

I started hearing a lot of noises internally, you know, structural creaking and then popping and stuff. The five years I had worked on that barge I had never heard anything like that. Being relatively new compared to some of the other guys like Mr Cobb, he's been in it for years, I'd more or less talk to him. "Well, what do you think the odds are of this thing sinking?" On my part there was a lot of disbelief. I just didn't think that, with the time I'd spent on these vessels, in my mind, it just wasn't gonna sink.

Lee Lloyd was one of the divers who had come out of the

*decompression chamber. He decided not to join the other divers in
their "dive shack":*

I would not go in there or go below deck. (During the day
some of the crew ran below to the galley and grabbed
handfuls of cookies or whatever was there, since no food had
been handed out since breakfast.) "I thought that son of a
bitch [the *269*] might roll over and I was not going to be
trapped inside. So I stayed outside. My whole focus at that
time, and for the whole ten hours that was putting myself in
the best position that I could to give me the best chance to
survive. The whole day I thought that barge was going to roll
over, and I thought, well, if it rolls this way, then I'll go that
way – or if this [piece of equipment] breaks loose, then I'm
going to do that."

Another anchor/supply vessel, the 190-foot Ducker Tide *was sent
from Carmen to assist 269. Captain John's tow line had broken
at the snatch. This was a length of flexible line which absorbed
much of the strain on the tow line. The repaired tow line had no
such absorbent capability. By early afternoon 269 was lower in the
water. This dampened the rolling but made it more vulnerable to
breaking seas. Flotsam and loose equipment made the decks of 269
extremely dangerous. Some life-raft canisters were hit by the
waves. They inflated and were swept away. Ray Pepperday and
a Mexican foreman were watching:*

Ray stood looking over the foreman's shoulder as the *269*
rolled over a wave and sank into the next trough. The
barge seemed to groan, then listed heavily to starboard,
the side the two men were on. Both men saw the next
wave. Even a storey and a half above deck, they watched
it towering over them, and there was nothing between it
and them but one open door. Pepperday turned and ran
for his life down the corridor. It was 15 feet long and 8
feet wide near the doorway but narrowed to 3 feet just
before it turned left. leading to the sat control room. The

last thing Pepperday remembers before he was hit by the water was noticing that somehow the watertight door behind him had closed after the wave hit, sealing and pressurizing the space. The wave bowled him head over heels into the cramped space at the end of the corridor. Picking himself up in the pitch-black hall-way, Pepperday heard the foreman behind him screaming.

Ray waded back to the door. Evidently the foreman had tried to close the door but hadn't managed to close it entirely before the wave hit or been able to retract his hand in time. His hand and most of his forearm were on the outside of the steel door now completely closed. Ray remembers thinking, "He's caught in there and he's comin' completely unglued. I tried to kick the door open. I tried and tried and I couldn't do it. So I ran back through the corridor to where all the guys were. They had been hit pretty good and were still trying to pick themselves up. I shouted for help and headed back to the outside door where the foreman was still stuck. By this time he had gone into shock. He just stared a blank stare."

Ray and Shane Richins tried kicking the door in unison, but something had wedged it shut. Finally, kicking together, they got it to let go. As it went flying open they heard something big go wham, wham, wham, bouncing down the steps leading to the next deck. A 5,000-pound portable hydraulic plant had been picked up from the lower deck by the wave and jammed against the door. Fortunately it was not sitting flat against the door or the two men would never have been able to dislodge it.

Amazingly the foreman had not passed out. He had suffered a compound fracture, and where the skin had not been broken, it immediately started to fill with blood. "We were trying to get him out of there," Ray remembers, "and my Spanish is limited, so I didn't know how to ask him how badly he was hurt. I stuck my hand in his face and I wiggled my fingers, you know, 'Try it.' I'll be damned if this guy didn't look down at his hand and wiggle his fingers. Then we got him the hell out of there – walked him off down to the bow area out of harm's way." Ray figured that losing the use of his arm would cut down on the foreman's chances of coming through alive if they were told to abandon ship. He looked for the foreman later but saw no sign of him again that day, either dead or alive.

They tried anchoring to ease the strain on the towline.

They dropped the two huge bow anchors. The port anchor reached the seabed but the starboard anchor cable was fouled on the bridle of the North Carolina's *towing cable. The towing cable swung to the* North Carolina's *starboard quarter. The cable caught on her starboard bits and she began to roll over. The first mate of* North Carolina *was Eulalio Zapata.*

Zapata was thrown off his feet. He got to his feet and made for the cable-release lever. Before he reached it, the towing cable snapped and the North Carolina *righted itself. The 269 tried dropping her stern anchors. The cables parted the moment the anchors caught on the seabed because she was going astern at six knots. She lost her bow anchor cable and she was adrift. The* Captain John's *repaired tow line had already broken. At 1615 on Sunday 15 October 269 made her final distress call to CCC headquarters. The water level reached her generators and she lost all power before she could make a "Mayday" request. Only emergency lighting remained below decks.*

The Ducker Tide *arrived shortly after 1600. The captains of the* Captain John, North Carolina *and* Ducker Tide *called to ask where to position their vessels but there was no reply. They stayed downwind where men in the water would drift to them. The winds were 80–90 mph and the waves were 35–40 feet high.*

Victor Diaz was a leading dive tender. He described:

There were two men who were next to me and they were nationals and they were talking in Spanish to each other that in case one of them did not make it, to make sure he would tell his family that he loved them and it would go likewise. At the time this thing [the *269*] was almost vertical, and it was extremely dark and the waves are really pounding. I looked at Rick Harris and I said, "Hey, bud, I'll buy you a cold one if we survive this."

I was trying to make my way through the crowd, and all the men, like they didn't want to move, they didn't want to budge. It took a great deal of strength for me to shove a few of them out of the way so I could jump into the water. But before I'd done that I could see the waves as they passed between each crest and the valley, and – the way the barge was – it was a heck of a drop, a heck of a drop. Everybody was so freakin' terrified that nobody wanted to jump. As I jumped into the water I was making sure that I didn't land on top of anybody One of the biggest and the worst things from this whole event is the constant roar of the waves as they passed by. It sounded like – you ever been by the side of the road and you hear an eighteen-wheeler pass by you? That's how loud it was.

There was only one hour of daylight left.

Lee Lloyd and his fellow divers had spotted a raft a few hundred feet to leeward. They jumped together, went under then bobbed back to the surface.

The 269 had hit actually the bottom twice during the last hour. When it did so for the third time most of those left aboard were thrown off their feet.

As dusk fell nearly everyone had abandoned ship.

When Lenn Cobb, the senior diver from Alabama, hit the water, he paddled with determination to reach the closest life raft still tethered to the *269*, about 200 feet to leeward. After a minute of hard swimming, dodging debris in the water and fighting a suction that seemed to be pulling him back toward the sinking barge, he reached the raft and hoisted himself aboard. He slid down the canopy to fall into the raft's water-filled centre. Like nearly all the rafts, Lenn's had landed upside down, and already a sizable pool of water filled the depressed middle of what was now the floor. Lenn climbed back up to the raft's perimeter. Inside huddled Rob Whaley and Rob Boettger and three Mexican crewmen. Within a few minutes they were joined by three more Mexicans and by two other Americans, who hauled themselves over the side. When it appeared that their raft might get dragged down by the sinking barge, someone cut the tether. Immediately they took off, driven by the elements in a wild downwind rush. Their journey was a terrifying one.

Lenn and the other divers just shook their heads in disbelief. Never in their collective decades at sea had they seen anything like this. The waves were vertical walls of water 30 feet, sometimes 40 feet high, and unlike larger ocean swells that a vessel could slide over, these came only a few seconds apart and were so steep that it was impossible to ride them. Their puny raft would try to climb a wave, get halfway up, and then cave in, fold in half, throwing those on the high side on top of those below. Then the whole raft and its human cargo would plunge below the surface as if being driven by a locomotive, and down it would stay for two or three agonizing seconds. It would gradually emerge and begin its rapid ascent of the next wave, where again it would collapse and again be driven back into the trough. Hour after hour the process endlessly repeated itself. The men seemed to be below the surface more than they were above it. If they didn't hold their breaths at just the right moment, they would be choking on seawater and gasping for air as they tried to prepare for the next onslaught – only seconds away.

Everyone became exhausted trying to hang on as the raft continued to cave in. They found it nearly impossible to withstand the force of the waves. Before each collapse of their raft they tried to fend each other off a bit or to blunt the inevitable collisions of one man into another so that they didn't smash heads or break limbs. But that was all they could do, except for trying to sweep out the seawater that nearly filled the raft by using their arms as paddles. That, too, was. useless. Early on they had lost sight of the *269* as well as the other rafts and the rescue vessels. Now it was getting dark and they began to fear that they would not be rescued.

Not all the crew were able to get to rafts so easily. Ray Pepperday, the young sat technician, remembers jumping and hitting the water so hard he felt like he got a saltwater enema. Perhaps his life preserver was one with poor flotation, because he seemed to go far under and then wasn't able to get back to the surface. He began to swim underwater, trying to reach the surface, but, disoriented, he couldn't determine which way was up. Finally he realized he would have to depend on whatever flotation existed in his preserver to save him. Slowly he rose, hoping he would reach the surface before he had to take a breath.

Ray broke water, gasping. He emerged almost under the barge and could feel a current pulling at him, sucking him back beneath the barnacle-covered hull. In desperation he pushed off with his feet and tried to swim away. After about five minutes of furious breast stroking, Ray found that he was getting nowhere. He just couldn't seem to get away from it. Finally alternately side stroking and swimming on his back, he started to put some distance between himself and the barge.

Exhausted, Pepperday stopped to look back at the *269*. It was almost vertical in the water, the bow sticking nearly straight up. In amazement he watched a Mexican crewman scaling a rope, like climbing up a 120 foot cliff, for some reason trying to get back on deck or what was left of it.

He also looked around for the young divers, Phil Richard and Mitch Pheffer. They had found a raft that somehow had been trapped in a calm spot and hadn't been blown away. Ray saw it and began swimming toward them, but he was so tired that it was slow going. And when he finally reached the raft, he had no energy to pull himself out of the water. So he just hung alongside for a while trying to regain some strength.

Using the lines running along the perimeter of the raft, and with a little help from those inside, Ray was soon able to hoist himself aboard. Mitch and Phil were already in the raft along with Chuck Rountree and four or five of the Mexican crew. The 10 foot diameter raft, meant to hold fifteen people, was still not crowded. However, being one of the closest rafts to the barge, it soon filled with weary frightened men. Within twenty minutes of the time Pepperday climbed in, the raft was bulging with twenty-five or thirty people all fighting for space.

By this time the overloaded raft had drifted out from the lee of the barge and was back in the maelstrom, no longer floating much above the sea. It would ride up a big wave crest, but before reaching the top it would fall off and the wave would crash on top of it, burying it in the sea. Three or four men who were hanging on the outside would get swept away and would have to paddle madly to regain the raft. The only saving grace was that the center of gravity was so low that wave after crushing wave couldn't turn it over.

This raft, like all the others that had landed upside down, couldn't be righted easily since its floor had become its top. And the slippery canopy, now the floor, sagged alarmingly with all the bodies kneeling in the middle. Those in the centre had no lines to hold on to, nothing except each other. They jostled for space, fighting to keep their heads above the deep pool that had collected under them.

Rountree, the diving supervisor, was one of those in the centre. A tall, blond athlete, Chuck was in reasonably good shape. Still, he was in his fifties, and during the ordeal, which had worn him down, he had injured his foot. He struggled to keep his head above water, but those he was pushing against were frantic and less than half his age. He started getting shoved beneath other men. Alarmed, Ray, Mitch, and Phil pulled him up between them to a spot along the raft's inner periphery where he hung from a lifeline, gasping for air.

As time passed, the four divers became worried that those in the centre would drown. They tried to convey to their

Mexican comrades that the raft was upside down and that they all needed to climb out so that they could right it. But none of the divers could speak enough Spanish to make themselves understood. The Mexicans, many terrified and nearly all suspicious, were not going back into the sea for anything. Knives appeared, and the attempt to right the raft was abandoned. So they drifted. On top of wave crests they would catch glimpses of the *Captain John*, the *Carolina*, and another boat, but since none of the rescuing craft came anywhere near them or seemed to see them, they just hung on.

The Captain John *was smaller than the two supply vessels. Its after deck was only five feet above the waterline.*

As they waited for Robert Trosclair to guide the tug into position for their attempt to bring aboard the first swimmers, Lorenzo Wilson, the tall, angular Nicaraguan first mate, and the four crew members huddled in the shelter of the big winch drum just aft of the deckhouse. Pedro, Vincent, Wilbert, and Victor Vega, the engineer, looked apprehensively as a wave swept the deck on which they would be working.

"I'm just as scared as you," Lorenzo told them. "We might get washed overboard or this boat might go down, but we aren't gonna worry about that right now. What we gonna do," he continued, fingering a coil of three-eighth-inch nylon line, "is use this so we don't get washed over the side."

The men cut 20-foot lengths, fastened the ends around themselves, and tied off the other ends on deck gear. They had brought all the tug's life rings aft, and as the *Captain John* came up to the first group of a dozen swimmers, they tied the line ends of the preservers to cleats under the bulwarks and tossed the rings to the men in the water. Then two men together would pull a swimmer in over the rail. They were able to get the men on deck, but the safety-line experiment was a disaster. By the time they got the first few men on board the five rescuers were so tangled in each other's safety lines that they could hardly move. They looked at each other in exasperation. Now what?

Lorenzo called his men together. "All right, we gotta take off our lines." Wilbert, the oldest of the deckhands, shook his head. "Come on, Wilbert, take off your line. Nobody gonna be tied. Just be sure that when a wave is coming you pick something to hold on to. All right?" Lorenzo continued looking at his reluctant crew. "I gotta protect you and you gotta protect me. If a wave is coming, you warn the other guys. You hold on and help the guy next to you."

Each time a wave was about to hit, someone would yell out: they dropped to their knees and grabbed the bulwark supports welded to the deck. The waves crashed over them, covering them with white water. In seconds the sea drained out the tug's scuppers and they would get up and again begin pulling people in.

One wave, however, came unnoticed until the last instant. The men turned to see the enormous breaker just before it crashed over the stern. Victor grabbed a support, Lorenzo, one of the bitts, and the others, all except Pedro, at gear next to them. Pedro was caught flat-footed. The wave carried him across the deck, first throwing him against the deckhouse, then into the starboard bulwarks, and finally, all within two or three seconds, it began to wash him back over the stern. Fortunately he grabbed an 8-inch pipe that supported the towing cable tie-down and kept himself from being carried overboard. Afterward he could hardly get up. He thought every bone in his body was broken, though in fact he had suffered no broken bones. Somehow he continued working.

Raul Acosta, the valve technician who had seen his soul crying over his corpse, was fortunate. Not long after he jumped into the sea, a raft floated nearby still attached to the barge. Raul swam to it, and the single occupant, a young

Mexican he didn't know, pulled him in. Once in the raft he took stock of the situation. Their raft had a half-dozen lines, mostly tangled and all leading back to the barge. Each time the 269 rolled or pitched over a wave, their raft followed it with a sickening lurch. Back and forth they went. More sodden men began climbing into the raft until it became crowded. The men already inside looked apprehensive as each newcomer clambered in.

Finally two men began cutting the lines holding them. As they were cutting the last line, Miguel Alvarez Cantu, the acting captain, paddled up looking like a drowned rat. He no longer had the 269's registration, log, and crew manifest. The men dragged him in and he flopped among all the ordinary crewmen. An old American guy was also pulled in.

As soon as the last tether was cut, the overflow-raft headed downwind, more in the water than out of it. The occupants wondered how long the long the bulging raft would be able to withstand the waves that were heaving it skyward and then burying it in their troughs. Everybody inside, besides hanging on each other, seemed to be praying.

Maybe their prayers were answered. After about hour the pitching raft was spotted by Trosclair. As the tug came alongside, he took his engines out of gear. One after another all the men in the raft were grabbed by the *Captain John*'s crew and pulled onboard. Raul Acosta got to his feet on the tug's deck and hurried below, away from the maelstrom.

Marco Polo Ramirez, the diver, had to push his buddy Diego off the barge before he could jump. Diego couldn't swim, and, even with his friend's assurance that he would stay with him and help him, the man refused to budge. Finally Marco threw Diego in and then jumped himself at a point on the starboard side that was only 10 feet above the water. Marco had his eye on an empty raft, still tethered to the barge, that bobbed close by, probably less than 100 feet away. He could certainly pull Diego that far. Once they were in the water Marco struck out for the raft, Diego in tow. With his strong swimmers stroke, and even getting his friend to kick a little, they were able to reach the raft without much trouble. The instant they pull themselves over the side, however they heard a hiss of air and the raft collapsed around them. No wonder there was no one in it. Some rafts had been torn on deck gear even before they were in the water. Some snagged on flotsam in the sea. But the majority of leaky rafts had succumbed to swimmers scrambling in who were still wearing their steel-cleated work boots.

Once more the two men were in the water. Diego wanted to go back to the barge. Marco Polo tried to reason with him. They didn't want to be anywhere near it. With waves breaking over them it was impossible to talk to his friend. Anyway, it didn't make any difference. Diego was incapable of propelling them in any direction. The only trouble was that Marco could no longer tow him against the current, which was now sweeping them back toward the barge. Soon they found themselves being driven under the great dark bow. Even though the 269 was submerged, each wave lifted the bow and then slammed it back into the next trough. The two men were sucked under the hull as if by a giant vacuum. Floating under the 269 was like being in a roaring underwater room whose ceiling kept descending on them. The hull seemed to be smashing down harder and harder. Each time it came down it propelled the swimmers farther underwater, tearing them on its barnacles.

Marco panicked. He had lost control. He was pulled farther under the barge and could not get out. By this time he was totally underwater. With his last lungful of air he swam desperately to escape. He never even felt the barnacles ripping his skin from head to toe. After what seemed like hours he drifted clear of the barge, and this time the current propelled him away from the 269. Marco looked all round for his friend without seeing him. Diego, whom he had lost under the hull, certainly was dead. Unable to save his friend, Marco realised he now had to focus on saving himself.

He began swimming first on his stomach, then on his back. He dodged debris and swallowed some oil which made him retch. While swimming on his back, he bumped into something soft. He turned to see another fellow he knew from the crew. Together they half-drifted and half-swam until they spotted two men in a raft. The guys helped pull them inside, where they collapsed. Gradually other swimmers struggled up to the raft and were helped aboard. Eventually there were nine of them.

Water kept filling the craft. The men tore off their shoes and tried unsuccessfully to sweep it out. Hours passed without seeing anyone. Eventually someone yelled that he saw a rescue boat. Maybe he did and maybe he didn't. Perhaps it was just spindrift blowing in the wind. Suddenly, right in front of them, a ship broke through a wall of spray. It was so big it filled their entire horizon.

Before the men in the raft even had time to become scared, the *Ducker Tide* was between them and the waves, drifting down toward them. Lines were thrown to them by crewmen at a break in the bulwarks amidships. The raft was pulled next to the hull, and at this point the men inside became frightened, because the *Ducker* rose above them on each crest and smashed down next to them in each trough, throwing a wave that threatened to overturn their little raft. Three of the men in the raft grabbed life rings thrown to them and were pulled onboard. The rest could only watch terrified as the *Ducker Tide* rose, then crashed back down a few feet from killing them. Their eyes were riveted on a single man who leaned over the break in the bulwarks. Each time the *Ducker* rolled off a wave, his arm snaked out and grabbed the nearest guy in the raft and in one motion flung him on deck. The arm that grabbed on to each belt or life preserver was like a steel spring. It was the size of most men's thighs, and it yanked one after another of the soaked, helpless men onboard until the raft was nearly empty.

Tim Noble was an experienced diver.

So when Tim hit the water and saw no raft available, he wasn't particularly bothered. John Enrique was nervously trying to swim nearby. Tim floated alongside him, keeping eye contact and getting him settle down and relax. The wind and current swiftly swept them eastward. After a while they were propelled over an especially large wave. When Tim surfaced after being buried in the next trough, he couldn't find John. Nor did searching the surrounding area as he was carried up on succeeding wave crests reveal any sign of the Spanish assistant captain; He cursed himself for losing the man who he knew needed his help.

Besides carrying two dive knives, Tim had equipped himself with a flashlight and a 100-foot quarter-inch line before going over the side of the *269*. Eventually he drifted out of sight of the barge. When, later he came across a small group of survivors, remembering how quickly Enrique had vanished, he offered to use the line to tie himself to the other swimmers. Joining together would increase their chances of being seen and rescued, he thought. It could also help to save someone who otherwise might drown. Even the most inexperienced landlubber instinctively realized that being lashed together was a good idea. So as Tim found others bobbing in the waves, they were added to the little group.

Especially during the first hour they were afloat, the bound stragglers contended with debris from the *269*. These weren't tiny objects, but 55-gallon drums and half-filled grease buckets. When flotsam was driven off a crest, it came hurtling at the men as if it had been thrown off a cliff. Getting hit with a 10-gallon grease can could kill you. So when flotsam came rushing toward them, the men tried frantically to dodge it or fend it off.

Tim and his group had been in the water about two hours when O. P. Chauvin and three crewmen floated by, clinging to a bright orange Norwegian buoy and a big plank. Tim managed to work his way over to Chauvin and tie him onto the line. O. P. would later undergo more hardship than any other survivor of the *269*. But now he just floated with the others, still holding tightly to the buoy. The fellow with the plank presented a special hazard. The young Mexican had been hit by a giant wave while still on the deck of the barge and the front of his life vest had been torn off. When he leaped into the Gulf, he had almost no flotation, but he found a plank to cling to. The problem was that his plank was studded with nails. So Tim fastened him at the opposite end of the line and tried to stay as far away as possible.

Like the survivors in the rafts, the swimmers kept rising up on the great crests, then sliding down the waves' backs until they were covered in the troughs. Each time they headed down, the men held their breath, realizing they would momentarily be stuffed beneath the surface. Sometimes they went under for just a second or two. Other times they were shoved far underwater; and it felt like agonizing minutes, even though it might have been only three or four seconds, before their life jackets brought them back up.

They reached the surface coughing and vomiting, and then with the meagre time allotted them, they sucked in air for the next wave burial. The experience of being on the top of a big wave and looking 40 feet down into the trench and knowing that in a few seconds you were going to be plunged into it was frightening, far worse than riding any engineered roller coaster. And with each near-drowning the men grew weaker.

As they rode up another roller, Tim saw one of the crew – a young Mexican welding inspector, maybe – feet in front of them. He was on his back, kicking furiously looking neither right nor left but straight into the sky. Oblivious to everything around him, at the top of his lungs he screamed his wife's name. "Carmella, Carmella, Carmella," he pleaded to the heavens as he went passing by them at right angles. His body was later found floating in the sea.

Dusk turned into night. As the little group of men rose to the wave tops, they could see the lights of the rescue boats going back and forth, sometimes a half mile from them, sometimes a mile or two. Tim aimed his flashlight at the closer boats as they went by but no one saw them. It grew colder, and with their constant dunkings and the wind screeching over them, the swimmers began to lose heart. Even Tim perhaps the most experienced diver on the *269*, started to have doubts about their survival.

Shane Richins was hanging on to a raft because it was full. He saw the Ducker Tide *coming them towards them. Shane Richins:*

"The bow of that ship would go up on top of a wave, and it seemed like you were looking at the Empire State Building. And then he [the captain] was trying to get as close to us as he could, and the knife-edge of that bow, you know, just seemed like it was gonna come right down on top of us."

As the *Ducker* reached the raft, it was falling down a wave. Its bow just slid by the raft, but Lee, who was still in the water, had become separated from the others. He looked up to see the overwhelming keel of the *Ducker* descending on top of him. Instead being hit by the keel, however, he was pushed by a wall of water ahead of the bow and driven into the depths. The water buffet, a liquid sledgehammer, pounded him into the sea, but it kept him from being crushed by the hull. For an eternity he tumbled underwater. He had no control of his movements, nor did he, nearly unconscious, formulate any plan to save himself. Like a rag doll he rolled and flopped, wondering if he would die.

Lee Lloyd was so scared of being caught in her propellers he tried to wave his rescuers away.

When Lee finally broke the surface, sputtering and coughing, he was amidships, near where the boat deck angled down to the afterdeck. The *Ducker* was still pitching wildly. As another wave came, the bow climbed it and the 2-foot-diameter bow thruster in its transverse tunnel vibrated, making the entire forward section of the ship shudder uncontrollably. He could see half the vessel's keel, still nearly on top of him. Then the *Ducker* plunged into the following trough, and the stern came out of the water, the two giant propellers, each larger than Lee's 6-foot frame, shrieked and the whole vessel shook as if it would break apart. Lee was deafened and he was terrified.

Watching the vessel pitch like a bathtub toy and feeling its roar and vibrations coursing through him, Lee wanted only to get as far away from it as he could. He tried feebly to signal it to go away and leave him alone in the sea, which by comparison now seemed comforting. Then the door of the wheelhouse opened and a tall, dark man came out on the bridge wing. The man, perhaps the first mate looked down directly at Lee, who continued to wave him away. Then, like a tin Jesus, the guy put out his hand toward Lee. "Stay calm, man," he seemed to say. "Just chill out. Everything's going to be OK. We will save your miserable soul."

Though Lee still tried to wave off his rescuers, they paid no attention. "Oh, God, get away from me," he screamed. "Sure as shit you're going to chop me up in your props. Just leave me alone!" But they couldn't hear him over the roar of the engines and the wind, and if they did understand what he was screaming, they ignored it.

By this time Lee had worked his way back to his aft, now floating amidships. But the position of the supply boat had changed relative to the seas. Captain Harold Roche had maneuvered his vessel downwind so that the raft was away from props and bow thruster. In this position the raft would be pushed toward the safest place to board. However, the seas were now coming from abeam, and the *Ducker* was rolling as if she were going to go over right on top of Lee. He couldn't get away, and they wouldn't leave him in peace. So he would have to try to get on board.

A row of tractor tyres serving as fenders hung from chains fastened to welded rings just below the second deck. As the

Ducker rolled away, the tyres were jerked high in the air. When she rolled back toward the men in the raft, the tyres plunged into the water in front of them. Ranging onto the lifeline running around the outside of the raft, Lee watched the movement of the tyre nearest him, and the next time it plummeted, he grabbed the chain above it. Immediately he went soaring 30 feet in the air standing on top of the tyre, then crashed back into the water, but with a steel grip on the chain. Once again he soared skyward, then crashed back down into the sea. He felt like he was being shot out of a gun, first in one direction, then the other. Still, he hung on, and the next time the *Ducker* lofted him into the air, he managed to grab a stanchion at eye level and hoist himself over the railing onto the second deck, where he flopped, exhausted.

After a couple of minutes just holding onto the railing and shaking, Lee climbed down the 8-foot ladder to the after-deck. Hayman Webster, the mate, and another crewman were at a break on the starboard side where the railing had been removed for easy entry. They were trying to snatch men out of the raft in the split second when the *Ducker*'s deck was at water level. Lee took one of the life rings fastened with black polypropylene line to the railing and tossed it to someone in the raft. By taking in slack on the line when the Ducker rolled toward them, the men were able to keep themselves opposite the break in the rail.

Shane was one of the first men to be hauled on. Then he and Lee and Webster began pulling in others. One of them would act as the puller while other two held on to the puller's waist to keep being washed overboard. Clay Horschel and Danny Weidenboener were soon helping them pull other men on board. At each plunge to sea level another man was grabbed, and as the *Ducker* swept to the air, they heaved him on deck. When every soul had been plucked from the water, the men retreated to the galley or to the bridge, and Harold Roche gunned the *Ducker*, swung her around, and headed downwind to look for more survivors.

By coincidence, the three rescue vessels were in a line. The Captain John *continued finding rafts and small groups of swimmers.* Victor *Diaz described his experience after he jumped off* 269:

"As I came back up I opened my eyes; it was dark green. And when I actually came up I felt somebody fall directly behind me. At that moment I swam away because I knew if they would fall right on top of me, I would break my neck and I wouldn't make it. At this moment a lot of the men are just jumping into the sea, like if you would be by a pond and you see the frogs leaping into the pond. They were just flopping in. The tugboat and the supply boat at this time, they were circling the barge like two sharks over a prey and what they wanted to do was to pick up the men once they abandoned ship. They would manoeuvre themselves to pick up the survivors. Getting into the water there were a lot of men. And the waves and everything the way it was working you really had a hard time manoeuvring yourself with so many bodies in the water."

Victor continued with difficulty: "I was in the water and the boat [*North Carolina*] was manoeuvring to pick up some of the men. There was a curtain of men [around the boats]. And the stern [right in front of me] had two giant propellers. A body had gone through the propellers. The poor soul got sucked in. And what landed an arm's length away was the head of the individual. The ocean was saturated with blood. I saw part of the face. It just came hanging from part of the neck itself, so I didn't get a full view of the face. After that happened I just swam away. There was no way I was going to be ground up."

Victor went on to explain that the men on the *Carolina* never even saw the man at the stern. There were so many swimmers around it at that particular time that it was impossible for the captain or the crew to keep track of them all.

Victor just started swimming off by himself. "I figured I'll just take my chances at sea. And [after a while] I just happened to see another man and then another one. So we became a human chain. We basically grabbed each other by the [life] vests. As we were floating, one of the many fears, once blood is in the ocean, the first thing that's attracted are sharks."

Although Victor and his group, which eventually numbered twelve men, never saw sharks, they had all they could do to battle the sea. Victor continued, "At times we were spread out and at times we were in a circle, and it all depended, because sometimes as we would ride a wave up and it would tumble over; we would fall with it and it plunged us underneath. [Then] we broke the chain as we surfaced. We gathered ourselves as much as we could trying to become the human chain again. It was an exhausting process. And as it was happening – we were plunged under – we had no idea which was up or down. When I pushed beneath the surface I swallowed a great deal of salt water. There was a time that I couldn't even taste it any more. It just became regular fresh water in my mouth.

"We drifted a great deal of distance, 'cause I remember looking and the silhouette of the barge was there one minute and it was gone the next. We drifted for quite a distance, and on the horizon every time would rise on top of a swell we could see the search lights of the vessels as they were trying to pick people. The vest that I had was torn on the right-hand side, and the water was saturating it [so] that it kept pulling me forward. So I would grab a man, put him in front of me to hold me upright." Victor and human chain continued to drift through the night.

Eulalio Zapata was singlehandedly pulling men from the water over the bulwarks onto the after deck. He, himself, was tied on by a safety line. He persevered until he was relieved by four rescued men. Exhausted, he retired to the shelter of the wheelhouse.

On the Captain John, *two young divers, Phil Richard and Mitch Pheffer, took over the rescue work from the exhausted crew.*

"Tugboats have huge, huge cleats that you could wrap your

arms and legs around. I would wrap myself around one of those, in the foetal position, and the deck of the tug would go underwater for what seemed like an eternity I would sit there underwater and go 'One-Mississippi, two-Mississippi, three-Mississippi.' I would hold my breath and finally the son of a bitch would pop back out of the water. I was puking up sea water for days after that."

For hours Phil and Mitch kept pulling people in. Some were covered with oil and were nearly impossible to grab. Others were so weary they were unable to help themselves in any way. One of the last people the tug came across was Victor Diaz.

Robert Trosclair, at the helm, saw something – the water reflecting the glare from the tug's search-light. As he brought his vessel closer he could see that it was a group of men – it was Victor's human chain. Victor described it: "Finally after a great deal of just hoping and praying, the tugboat managed to see a reflection off the vests. We were told they spotted us because we were in a group. The searchlight hit the reflectors and they saw that it was a group of us. As it was getting closer and closer, the tugboat was swallowed up, literally, by a wave, just completely, and it's like you would see a submarine piercing through the surface. That's what the tug looked like, and it finally shut its engines off. There were two people, Americans, and they were screaming, 'One at a time, one at a time!' What they had done is taken a rope and they had put knots in it and they had launched it in. our group, and we all managed to be pulled onboard by these guys, who risked themselves being sucked over."

Victor continued, "Once I was on board they had drag me inside the tugboat and I stood there. I wanted to scream. I wanted to laugh. I wanted to cry. But not a word came out of me. I stood there, not even moving. They had a jug of fresh water, and as each individual was rescued and pulled in, they were given the fresh water. As I drank it, the first thing I did, I puked it basically all out, and it was a lot of the salt water that I had ingested that was still in my gut."

Victor was led below. He found a place on the deck in the engine room, squeezed between vomiting, oil-covered survivors. There he collapsed.

Lenn Cobb remembered:

When the *North Carolina* spotted us, they brought the boat alongside. And in those seas it was wild. One minute you're looking at the antennas on the top of the boat and the next minute you're seeing the propellers turning. It didn't look good. I was thinking that our chances would be better if we just hung on in our life raft.

It seemed like we could get swept under the supply boat real easy – but the way the guy [Richard Cassel] did it, he got the boat between us and the seas and then let the seas wash him into us with his engines out of gear. He just drifted into us. He did a hell of a job.

Lenn was last off his raft. He jumped onto of the big airplane tyres used as fenders on the side of the North Carolina.

Tim Noble was tied to eight other crewmen. They had drifted 18 miles to the east of where they abandoned 269.

After four hours in the sea the North Carolina *spotted them with its searchlight; Tim Noble grabbed a tyre but he wouldn't let go of it even when someone on board tried to help him aboard. Eventually he climbed aboard himself Seven of the others in his chain were on deck. The last man was picked up after he failed to get aboard the* Ducker Tide. *Eventually the* North Carolina *threw him a rope with knots in it. He was able to grasp it and was brought aboard.*

Captain Robert Trosclair of the Captain John *was controlling her from the "doghouse". This was a small secondary control position on the stern. The crew and divers on the afterdeck had just gone below when Captain Trosclair left the "doghouse". He had just reached the bridge when a wave smashed the "doghouse" to pieces.*

At 23:00 Captain Roche of the Ducker Tide *and Captain*

Trosclair decided to call off the search. North Carolina *had picked up 54 men. The* Ducker Tide *had picked up 79 men. The* Captain John *had picked up 89 men. The three vessels were filled to overflowing with injured and exhausted men. Both the rescued and their rescuers said that the trip back to Carmen was the worst part of the night. They headed south-west through 20–25 foot seas.*

The North Carolina *stayed out for another hour, looking for survivors. At midnight she turned for port. The fuel line to the port engine ruptured. The engine shut down. On her remaining engine she could only manage three knots.*

Lee Lloyd described the trip back:

"It was the shittiest weather I've ever seen. Oh, man, God, it was just horrific! The waves were just hitting the boat, shaking it. I was concerned about us making it back. I've been sick before at sea, but never like this. I was up in the area behind the wheelhouse and I thought, well, maybe if I go down farther below I might find a lower center of gravity. I went down to the galley and opened the door from the stairway. The floor's covered with vomit. There's probably sixty guys lying there. Also, a dead guy with a sheet over him. Then right beside him they got people just laying there, right beside the dead guy. I said, 'Nooo, I don't believe I can stand this.'"

Lee, throwing up for most of the trip back, added, "It was one of those things, you know, where you're afraid that you'll die, then you're afraid you won't."

The channel into Carmen was shallow and poorly marked. At certain points it only had 14 feet of water. The Ducker Tide *drew 17 feet. At 13:00 on Monday 16 October, the* Ducker Tide *arrived. At 16:00, the* Captain John *arrived.* North Carolina *finally got in at 20:00.*

Officially there were twenty-three dead and missing. Fifteen men never jumped into the sea. When DLB 269 finally sank it settled on the bottom; the A frame of the crane remained above the water. The men still aboard climbed up into the A frame. They tied themselves on and clung to the girders. They were finally rescued on the morning of Wednesday 18 October.

DLB 269 was raised by Smit International. They towed it out to deep water where it would not be a hazard to navigation.

Some of the survivors suffered from Post Traumatic Stress Disorder (PSTD). Victor Diaz was one of them. Ray Pepperday continued to work as a technician but onshore. Lenn Cobb could no longer dive deeper than thirty feet because the accelerated decompression had caused neurological damage. Tim Noble worked on shore. The surviving Mexican employees of CCC were given little more than their wages.

The Dismasting of *Kingfisher 2*
23 February 2003

At 06:48 GMT on 30 January 2003 the racing catamaran, Kingfisher 2, sailed from Ushant. It was attempting to break the record for a continuous round the world voyage. The record was 64 days. This had been made by the same vessel, which was then called Orange. Kingfisher 2 had a crew of 14. The skipper was Ellen MacArthur. At 22:22 GMT on 23 February Kingfisher 2 was sailing under mainsail and spinnaker about 1,000 miles southeast of the Kerguelen islands. Without warning, the 140-foot mast broke in two. MacArthur:

We were surfing with the waves doing 20 knots when I was suddenly thrown forward. I heard a gut-wrenching, ear-piercing, crunching and snapping sound.

I was in the navigation station on our 110-ft catamaran, *Kingfisher 2*, talking on the satellite phone to our weather router. We were 26 days into our round-the-world record attempt, deep in the southern Indian Ocean. I knew instinctively that it was over.

I dropped the phone and hurled myself towards the companionway, looking round my feet to check if water was coming on board from anywhere: nothing. As I reached the

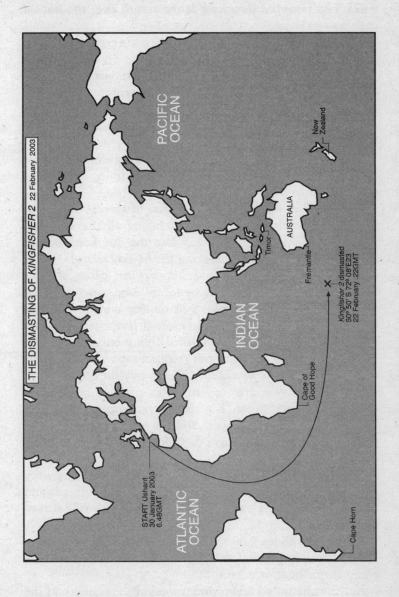

THE DISMASTING OF *KINGFISHER 2*   22 February 2003

PACIFIC OCEAN

New Zealand

AUSTRALIA

Timor

Fremantle

INDIAN OCEAN

Cape of Good Hope

Kingfisher 2 dismasted
50° 50' S 72° 08' E23
22 February .22GMT

ATLANTIC OCEAN

Cape Horn

START Ushant
30 January 2003
6.48GMT

hatch all became clear in a flash of nausea . . . the 140-ft mast which had powered us ahead of the record over the last 24 days was no more.

My first reaction was to make sure everyone was safe. Fortunately, only the on-watch crew were on deck, (watch leader Neal McDonald, Bruno Dubois, Anthony "Youngster" Merrington, with Jason Carriton temporarily below) and everyone was OK. We were lucky. If we had been doing a manoeuvre or changing watch systems it could have been different.

Then we had to get on with cutting away pieces of the mast and sails that were floating in the water, trying to keep as much as we could.

It took about an hour. We managed to save 10 metres of the mast Everything else went, including all the sails and rigging. We saw it all float away into the Southern Ocean, along with our chance of breaking the 64-day record.

Most likely we shall never know the cause of our dismasting, and you just have to accept some cases for what they are. These things happen so quickly and no one was looking at the rig the moment before it happened. It was a brand new rig – the guys had worked on it meticulously – and the issues we had in Plymouth (replacing part of the mast-track the day before we sailed) are certainly unrelated.

It would be wrong to say that this trip has not been a massive challenge so far. But equally nothing, at any stage, has brought tears to my eyes. And the tears right now come with the frustration and anger that I feel at having let so many people down.

So much work has gone into this project, so much energy and commitment, each fitting sealed, each lashing tied, and here we were cutting parts of it over the side. It's so destructive, so final.

Sitting here about 2,000 miles west of our new destination, Perth, I feel empty and sad, but above all relieved that no one, bar our boat, was hurt.

At the same time I feel proud: proud of the strength of the

crew, commitment and proud of their smiles and proud of the way they, too, have handled their frustration. The strange thing is that suddenly, although we are all disappointed, we have shifted our focus on getting ourselves moving and to Australia as fast as we can. With our jury rig we should make landfall in about two weeks.

I glance at my notebook to jot down something and see pages and pages of notes preparing things for this trip. All of a sudden, our challenge feels days away, almost a distant memory. Just three hours ago I was having stitches put in my hand after cutting it open when a rope ripped through it in a manoeuvre. An hour ago I was cutting through rigging as if there was no tomorrow. Now even that seems irrelevant – no longer are we living each day – for our 24-hour distance run or thinking about every aspect of boat-speed. Our attempt to break the 64-day record, the Jules Verne, is over.

It's a funny feeling sitting out here thinking about all that has happened, and wondering what might have been. But "what ifs" will always exist in life. They will never disappear, but you can choose to ignore them . . . what's done is done and, however you want to look at it, you learn from it. We must just get up and on to the next challenge.

When the mast broke, they had sailed 10,254 miles. They had 15,135 to go. They were nearly 23 hours ahead of the record but 53 hours behind a rival attempt. They made and fitted a "jury-rig" from the boom and a salvaged part of the mast. Then they headed towards Fremantle, the port of Perth, on the west coast of Australia, at between 7 and 10 knots. They estimated it would take them two weeks to get there. They reached safety in Australia.

Manmade

Victims of War

Wreck of HMS *Amazon* and *Les Droits de l'Homme*
14 January 1797

In January 1797, Captain Sir Edward Pellew was in command of a squadron consisting of the frigates, HMS Indefatigable, *44 and HMS* Amazon, *36. HMS* Amazon *was commanded by Captain Reynolds. They were patrolling off the west coast of France when they sighted a strange ship. It was the French line of battleship,* Les Droits de l'Homme, *74. Les Droits de l'Homme had been transporting part of a French invasion force to Ireland. Bad weather had prevented them from landing. Les Droits de l'Homme was returning to France carrying soldiers and British prisoners. En razé meant that the ship had been modified by the removal of a deck. HMS* Indefatigable *had been built as a two-decker 64 but was cut down to a single deck in 1795.*

In his report to the Admiralty, Pellew wrote:

Indefatigable, Falmouth. 17 January 1797

Sir, I have the honour to make known to you for the information of the Lords Commissioners of the Admiralty that on Friday last the 13th instant, in latitude 47° 30' N, Ushant

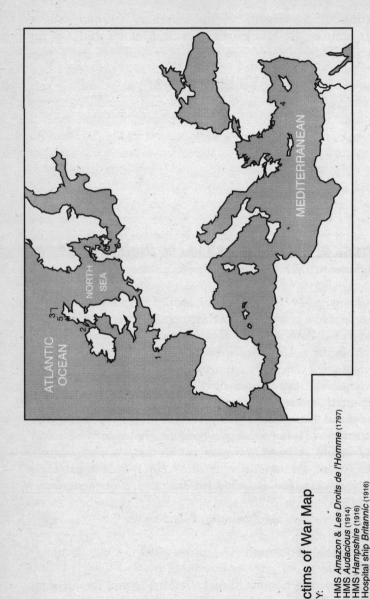

ATLANTIC OCEAN

NORTH SEA

MEDITERRANEAN

Victims of War Map
KEY:

1 HMS *Amazon & Les Droits de l'Homme* (1797)
2 HMS *Audacious* (1914)
3 HMS *Hampshire* (1916)
4 Hospital ship *Britannic* (1916)
5 SS *Athenia* (1939)

bearing NE 50 leagues, we discovered at half-past noon a large ship in the NW quarter, steering under easy sail for France. The wind was then at west, blowing hard, with thick hazy weather. I instantly made the signal to the *Amazon* for a general chase, and follow'd it by the signal that the chase was an enemy. At 4 p.m. the *Indefatigable* had gained sufficiently upon the chase for me to distinguish very clearly that she had two tier of guns, with her lower deck ports shut. She had no poop, and according to my judgement she was a French ship en razé. At a quarter before five I observed with considerable regret that she had carried away her fore and topmasts. The *Indefatigable* at the same instant lost her steering-sail booms. The ship at this time was going 11 or 12 knots, blowing very hard and a great sea. I foresaw from this that the escape of the enemy under her lower masts only in a stormy night of 14 hours continuance, should her defence prove obstinate, was very possible, and I believed as a ship of large force that she would be reduced to persevere in her resistance from the expectation that we should be apprehensive of entangling ourselves upon a lee shore with the wind dead upon it.

The instant she lost her topmasts I reduced my sails to close reef'd topsails, and at 15 minutes before 6 we brought the enemy to close action, which continued to be well supported on both sides near an hour, when we unavoidably shot ahead. At this moment the *Amazon* appeared astern, and gallantly supplied our place, but the eagerness of Captain Reynolds to second his friend had brought him up under a press of sail, and after a well-supported and close fire for a little time, he unavoidably shot ahead also. The enemy, who had nearly effected running me on board, appear'd to be much larger than the *Indefatigable*, and from her very heavy fire of musketry I believe was very full of men. The fire was continued until the end of the action with great vivacity altho' she frequently defended both sides of the ship at once.

As soon as we had replaced some necessary rigging, and the *Amazon* had reduced her sail, we commenced a second attack, placing ourselves after some raking broadsides upon each quarter, and this attack, often within pistol shot, was by both ships unremitted for above 5 hours. Then we sheer'd off to secure our masts. It would be needless to relate to their lordships every effort that we made in an attack which commenced at a quarter before 6 p.m. and ceased not but at intervals until half-past 4 a.m.

Night actions should not be inconsiderably engaged in, but in this instance everything was to be hazarded or the escape of the enemy was absolutely certain, and altho' she was running for her own ports, yet the confidence I felt in my own knowledge of the coast of France forbade me to listen for a moment to any suggestions of danger there from. I placed also some considerable reliance that her commander would not voluntarily sacrifice his ship and his crew by running her for a dangerous part of the coast, and I promised myself to see the day before we should have run down our distance. But in fact every creature was too earnestly and too hardily at work to attend exactly to the run of the ship, and I believe 10 hours or more severe fatigue was scarcely ever experienced. The sea was high, the people on the main deck were up to their middles in water, some guns broke their breechings four times over, and some drew the ring-bolts from the sides, and many of them were repeatedly drawn immediately after loading. All our masts were much wounded, and the maintop mast completely unrigg'd, and saved only by uncommon alacrity.

At about 20 minutes past 4 the moon, opening rather brighter than before, showed to Lieutenant George Bell, who was watchfully looking out on the forecastle, a glimpse of land. He had scarcely reached me to report it when we saw the breakers; we were then close under the enemy's starboard bow, and the *Amazon* as near upon the larboard. Not an instant could be lost, and every life depended upon the prompt execution of my orders, and here it is with heartfelt pleasure I acknowledge the full value of my officers and ship's company who, with incredible alacrity, hauled the tacks on the board, and made sail to the southward. The land could not be ascertained, but we took it to be Ushant, and in the Bay of Brest, crippled as we were, I had no particular fears; but before day we again saw breakers upon the lee bow; the ship was instantly wore to the northward, and myself satisfied that the land we had before seen was not Ushant. The lingering approach of daylight was most anxiously look'd for by all, and soon after it opened we saw the land very close ahead. We again wore to the southward in 20 fathoms water, and in a few minutes after discovered the enemy, who had so bravely defended herself, lying on her broadside, and a tremendous surf beating over her; and the miserable fate of her brave but unhappy crew was perhaps the more sincerely lamented by us from the apprehensions of suffering a similar misfortune. We passed her within a mile in a very bad condition, with 4 feet of water in the hold, a great sea, and the wind dead on the shore; but we ascertained to a certainty our situation to be that of Audierne Bay, and our fate depended upon the possible chance of weathering the Pennmark Rocks. Exhausted as we were with fatigue, every exertion was made, and every inch of canvas set that could be carried, and at 11 a.m. we made the breakers, and by the blessing of God weather'd the Pennmark Rocks about half a mile.

The *Amazon* had haul'd her wind to the northward when we did to the southward; her condition I think was better than ours, and I knew that her activity and exertions were fully equal to them. The judgment with which she was managed during so long an action and the gallantry of her attacks could not but warm the bosom of every spectator, and to the heart of a friend it was particularly delightful. I have full as much reason to speak highly of my own officers and men, to whom I owe infinite obligation, the Lieutenants Thomson, Norway, and Bell, Lieutenants O'Connor and Wilson of the Marines, and Mr Thomson the master, have abundant claims upon my gratitude as well as every inferior officer in the ship.

The sufferings of the *Amazon* are unknown to me. I am singularly happy to say that my own is inconsiderable. The

first lieutenant, Mr Thomson, a brave and worthy officer, is
the only one of that description wounded, with eighteen men,
twelve of which number have wounds of no serious consequence, consisting chiefly of violent contusions from splinters. I have the honour to enclose the minutes of this action
with a state of the damages sustained therein, and shall in a
few days proceed to Plymouth to be ready to receive their
lordships' orders for the repair of the said defects, and am,
with great respect, Sir,
Your most obedient and humble servant
Ed. Pellew

Elias Pipon was one of the English prisonners aboard Les Droits
de l'Homme. *He was a Lieutenant in the 63rd Regiment of Foot
which was stationed in the West Indies.*

On 9 January 1797, returning home on leave of absence for
the recovery of my health, from the West Indies, in the
Cumberland letter of marque, saw a large man of war off the
coast of Ireland, being then within four leagues of the mouth
of the river Shannon. She hoisted English colours and
decoyed us within gun-shot, when she substituted the tri-
coloured flag, and took us. She proved to be *Les Droits de
L'Homme*, of 74 guns, commanded by ci-devant Baron, now
Citoyen La Crosse, and had separated from a fleet of men of
war, on board of which were 20,000 troops intended to
invade Ireland; on board of this ship was General Humbert,
who afterward effected a descent in Ireland, with 900 troops,
and 600 seamen. (Sir Edward Pellew has told me since, that
the official account from France, on which he has received
head-money, amounted to 1,750 souls, at the time of the
shipwreck.)

On 7 January went into Bantry Bay to see if any of the
squadron was still there, and on finding none, the ship
proceeded to the southward; nothing extraordinary occurred
until the evening of the 13th, when two men of war hove in
sight, which proved afterwards to be the *Indefatigable* and

Amazon frigates. It is rather remarkable that the Captain of the ship should inform me that the Squadron which was about to engage him, was Sir Edward Pellew's, and declared, as was afterwards proved by the issue, "that he would not yield to any two English frigates, but would sooner sink his ship with every soul on board"; the ship was cleared for action, and we English prisoners, consisting of three Infantry Officers, two Captains of merchantmen, two women, and forty eight seamen and soldiers, were conducted down to the cable-tier, at the foot of the fore-mast.

The action began with opening the lower-deck ports, which, however, were soon shut again, on account of the great sea (I must here observe that this ship was built on a new construction, considerably longer than men of war of her rate, and her lower-deck, on which she mounted thirty-two pounders, French, equal to forty pounders English, was two feet and a half lower than usual), which occasioned the water to rush in to that degree that we felt it running on the cables. The situation of the ship before she struck on the rocks, has been fully elucidated by Sir Edward Pellew, in his letter of 17 January 1797, to Mr Nepean; the awful task is left for me to relate what ensued.

At about four in the morning, a dreadful convulsion at the foot of the fore-mast, aroused us from a state of anxiety for our fate, to the idea that the ship was sinking! It was the fore-mast that fell over the side; in about a quarter of an hour an awful mandate from above was re-echoed from all parts of the ship, "Pauvres Anglais! Pauvres Anglais! Montes bien vite, tout sommes tout perdues!" Everyone rather flew than climbed up. Though scarcely able before to move, from sickness, I now found an energetic strength in all my frame, and soon gained the upper-deck, but oh, what a sight! dead, wounded, and living, intermingled in a state too shocking to describe, not a mast standing, a dreadful loom of the land, and breakers all around us. The *Indefatigable*, on the starboard quarter, appeared standing off in a most tremendous sea, from the Penmark Rocks, which threatened her with instant destruction. To the great humanity of her Commander those few persons who survived the shipwreck, were indebted for their lives, for had another broadside been fired, the commanding situation of the *Indefatigable* must have swept off at least a thousand men. On the larboard side, was seen the *Amazon*, within two miles, just struck on the shore – our own fate drew near. The ship struck, and immediately sunk! Shrieks, horror, and dismay were heard from all quarters, whilst the merciless waves tore from the wreck many early victims. Daylight appeared, and we beheld the shore lined with people who could render us no assistance. At low water, rafts were constructed and the boats got in readiness to be hoisted out. The dusk arrived, and an awful night ensued. The dawn of the second day brought with it still severer miseries than the first, for the wants of nature could hardly be endured any longer, having been already near thirty hours without any means of subsistence, and no possibility of procuring them. At low water a small boat was hoisted out, and an English captain and eight sailors succeeded in getting to the shore. Elated at the success of these men, all thought their deliverance at hand, and many launched out on their rafts, but ah! death soon ended their hopes.

Another night renewed our afflictions. The morn of the third day, fraught with greater evils than ever, appeared, our continued sufferings made us exert the last effort, and we English prisoners, tried every means to save as many fellow-creatures as laid in our power. Larger rafts were constructed, and the largest boat was got over the side. The first consideration was to lay the surviving wounded, the women, and helpless men, in the boat, but the idea of equality, so fatally promulgated among the French, lost them all subordination, and nearly 120 jumped into the boat, in defiance of their officers, and sunk it. The most dreadful sea that I ever saw, seemed at that fatal moment to add to the calamity, nothing of the boat was seen for a quarter of an hour, when the bodies floated in all directions; then appeared, in all the horrors of sight, the wreck, the shores, the dying, and the drowned! Indefatigable in acts of humanity, an Adjutant-General (Renier) launched himself into the sea, to obtain succours from the shore, and was drowned in the attempt.

Already near one-half of the people had perished, when the fourth night renewed in its horrors, all our miseries. Weak, distracted, and wanting everything, we envied the fate of those whose lifeless corpses no longer wanted sustenance. The sense of hunger was already lost, but a parching thirst consumed our vitals. Recourse was had to urine and salt water, which only increased the want; half a hogshead of vinegar indeed floated up, and each had half a wine glass, which gave a momentary relief, yet soon left us again in the same state of dreadful thirst. Almost at the last gasp! Everyone was dying with misery, and the ship, which was now one-third shattered away from the stern, scarcely afforded a grasp to hold by, to the exhausted and helpless survivors.

The fourth day brought with it a more serene sky, and the sea seemed to subside, but to behold from fore to aft, the dying in all directions, was a sight too shocking for the feeling mind to endure. Almost lost to a sense of humanity, we no longer looked with pity on those who were the speedy forerunners of our own fate, and a consultation took place, to sacrifice some one to be food for the remainder. The die was going to be cast, when the welcome sight of a man-of-war brig renewed our hopes. A cutter speedily followed, and both anchored at a short distance from the wreck. They then sent their boats to us, and by means of large rafts about 150, of near 400 who attempted it, were saved by the brig that evening. Three hundred and eighty were left to endure another night's misery, when, dreadful to relate, above one-half were found dead next morning.

I was saved at about ten o'clock on the morning of the 18th, with my two brother officers, the captain of the ship, and General Humbert. They treated us with great humanity on board the cutter, by giving us a little weak brandy and water every five or six minutes, after which a bason of good soup. I fell on the locker in a kind of trance for near thirty hours, swelled to that degreee, as to require medical aid to restore my decayed faculties. We were taken to Brest almost naked, having lost all our baggage, where they gave us a rough shift of clothes, and in consequence of our sufferings, and the help we afforded in saving many lives, a cartel was fitted out by order of the French Government, to send us home without ransom or exchange. We arrived at Plymouth on 7 March following.

To that Providence, whose great workings I have experienced on this most awful trial of human afflictions, be ever offered the tribute of my praise and thanksgivings!

Elias Pipon,
Lieutenant 63rd Reg.

The Sinking of HMS *Audacious*
27 October 1914

On 27 October 1914 the new battleship, HMS Audacious, *struck a German moored mine on her port side. It happened a short distance from the entrance of Lough Swilly in North West Ireland. Sea conditions were rough and the battleship began to fill with water. The White Star liner RMS* Olympic *was nearby and went to assist her. Violet Jessop, a* Titanic *survivor, was a stewardess aboard Royal Mail Ship* Olympic. *The* Olympic *was the elder sister of the* Titanic. *The* Olympic *had been on its way to Scotland. Jessop:*

The smell of land on a beautiful autumn mornlng brought us that satisfying odour of peat-fires as we skirted the coast of Northern Ireland on our way to Scotland.

We had noticed at a distance grey shapes that proved to be some cruisers out for target practice, we thought. Suddenly there was a dispersal and change of tactics indicating that something was amiss. Putting on speed, we soon found one of the largest cruisers had been struck. As we hurried to the scene, all our lifeboats, with voluntary crews including a great many stewards, stood ready to lower.

On the swell of enormous waves, the huge battleship rhythmically rose and dipped. Serrated ranks of men in blue lined her decks, watching groups of their comrades being swept over as monster waves washed the decks. The next wave, however, brought them back again and not one man lost his life through drowning.

As our lifeboats laboriously made the crossing, appearing at times to be completely submerged in the trough of the sea, we held our breaths. Then as they came and went, transferring groups of those extraordinarily well-disciplined men with their cheery, grateful faces, the whole ship began to smile as one man. We watched those somewhat embarrassed men being rendered still more tongue-tied by the warmth of welcome they found as willing hands pulled them aboard *Olympic*. Their eyes lit up at the sight of comrades already brought to safety. I was touched by their eager, simple wonder as they made comparisons between the appointments of a luxury liner and their own austere surroundings.

All day we laboured frantically to take that huge hulk in tow. Everybody not otherwise engaged, including passengers, helped transfer the large steel hawser from one part of the ship to another, after our first cable had snapped. It seemed a superhuman effort to move its unwieldy end on to the waiting tugs and destroyers standing by, waiting to connect it to the distressed ship.

But it was all hopeless. It snapped again. As evening drew near we left the *Audacious* a wounded and tired giant, heaving herself up every now and then, only to sink lower and lower in the restless sea with the setting sun's rays illuminating her doom. We steamed for Lough Swilly, near those Donegal hills where the lights and shadows of indigo and purple always wove a different picture. Here and there, tiny spirals of smoke from the cottagers' peat-fires curled heavenward like incense at evening prayer, filling the crystal clear air with its unforgettable odour. The only sound was the tinkling church bells echoing faintly through the valleys, calling the faithful to early mass.

A fairy-tale setting discovered by accident, it was a most realistic place in which to be "interned". It was hoped by this internment to avoid the publicity about this latest disaster. The news would doubtless leak out once the passengers – some of them most important – were free to go their different ways; many, moreover, stood to be great losers by the enforced delay.

I am afraid all the precautions to keep the news from leaking were in vain, for while we were still living in that pool of peace, Lough Swilly, the news was already being yelled abroad by newsboys in the capitals of Europe.

With regret, we weighed anchor from that beautiful spot where we had got familiar with jolly Royal Navy men, who had the entire freedom of our ship when duty permitted. I noticed that they never lost an opportunity to take advantage of our hospitality, accepting things that sailors appreciate.

The Sinking of HMS *Hampshire*
5 June 1916

The Battle of Jutland was fought on 31 May 1916. On 5 June 1916 the cruiser HMS Hampshire, *sailed from Scapa Flow. She was carrying Lord Kitchener, the secretary of state for war, to Archangel. He was due to meet Great Britain's Russian allies. The commander of the Grand Fleet, Admiral Jellicoe, reported in a despatch to the Admiralty:*

I have to report with deep regret that HMS *Hampshire* (Captain Herbert J. Savill, RN), with Lord Kitchener and his staff on board, was sunk last night about 8 p.m. to the west of the Orkneys, either by a mine or torpedo. Four boats were seen by observers to leave the ship. The wind was N.N.E. and heavy seas were running. Patrol vessels and destroyers at once proceeded to the spot, and a party was sent along the coast to search, but only some bodies and a capsized boat have been found up to the present. As the whole shore has been searched from the seaward I greatly fear that there is little hope of there being any survivors. No report has yet been received from the search party on shore. H.M.S. *Hampshire* was on her way to Russia.

On the day HMS Hampshire *sailed, Lord Kitchener had eaten lunch with Admiral Jellicoe.*

Jellicoe:

During the day, the weather at Scapa, which had been bad in the morning, gradually became worse, and by the afternoon it was blowing a gale from the north-eastward. It had been orginally intended that the *Hampshire* should take the route which passed up the eastern side of the Orkneys, following the channel ordinarily searched by mine-sweeping vessels as a routine measure; but as the north-easterly gale was causing a heavy sea on that side, mine-sweeping was out of the question, and it was also obvious that the escorting destroyers could not face the sea at high speed. I discussed with my Staff which route on the west, or lee, side would be the safest, and finally decided that the *Hampshire* should pass close in shore, and not take the alternative route passing farther to the westward.

There were twelve survivors from HMS Hampshire. *One of them was First Class Petty Officer Wilfred Wesson:*

At 8 p.m. while the watch below were standing by their hammocks ready to turn in, an explosion occurred. I was on the mess deck at the time. When the explosion happened all lights immediately went out and a terrible draught came rushing along the mess deck, blowing all the men's caps off . . . While I was waiting with the others on the half-deck an officer came with Lord Kitchener from the Captain's cabin. He called out, "Make room for Lord Kitchener," and the men opened out to let Lord Kitchener pass. He went on deck and I did not see any more of him after that.

Leading Seaman Charles Rogerson added:

I was the last of the survivors to see Lord Kitchener before leaving the ship. In the papers I notice that his Lordship is said to have been drowned by the overturning of a boat, but this is not correct. Lord Kitchener went down with the ship. He did not leave her. I saw Captain Savill helping his boat's crew to clear a way to the galley. The captain at this time was calling to Lord Kitchener to go to the boat, but owing to the noise of the wind and the sea Lord Kitchener apparently could not hear him. When the explosion occurred Lord Kitchener walked calmly from the captain's cabin, went up the ladder and on to the quarter-deck . . . Although I do not really know what happened, my belief is that the *Hampshire* struck a mine which exploded under her fore-part. It could not have been a submarine in such weather.

Another survivor also saw Lord Kitchener standing on the quarter-deck:

I won't say, he did not feel the strain of the perilous situation like the rest of us, but he gave no outward sign of nervousness, and from the little time that elapsed between my leaving the ship and her sinking I feel certain that Lord Kitchener went down with her, standing on the deck at the time.

After the war, the German commander in chief, Admiral Sheer, confirmed:

Besides this, one of our minelayers, occupied in laying mines west of the Orkney Islands, achieved an important success. The English armoured cruiser *Hampshire* (11,000 tons) struck one of these mines on 5 June and sank; with her perished Field Marshal Lord Kitchener and all his staff.

The cruiser *Hampshire*, on which Lord Kitchener went down, was sent to sea in a heavy storm in the belief that in such weather little danger was to be apprehended west of the Orkneys from mines or U-boats; and yet one of our boats (Lieutenant-Commander Curt Beitzen) had been at work, and had made use of the opportunity provided by the bad weather to lay the mines to which this ship was to fall a victim.

The British Admiralty concluded that:

[The mine] was laid by the German submarine U.75 as part of Admiral Scheer's preliminary dispositions prior to the Battle of Jutland . . . It is quite certain that the mines were laid solely for this purpose and that the Germans had no information from any source which enabled them to lay mines in the *Hampshire*'s path.

The Sinking of the Hospital Ship, *Britannic*
21 November 1916

The Britannic *was being built at the time of the* Titanic *inquiry. As a result of the* Titanic *inquiry, a number of improvements were made to the* Britannic. *Unlike the* Titanic, *the bulkheads which separated* Britannic's *watertight compartments were built all the way up to the deck. Water should have been unable to flow over the top of her bulkheads. She should have been able to stay afloat even if six compartments became flooded. She was well equipped with lifeboats which could be launched quickly by new improved davits.*

After the sinking of HMS Audacious *in 1914, Violet Jessop enlisted in the Voluntary Aid Detachment, as a junior nurse. She was assigned to the* Titanic's *sister ship,* Britannic, *which had been fitted out as a hospital ship.*

On 21 November, 1916 Britannic *was in the Mediterranean, heading for Moudros to embark wounded. Jessop:*

It was the feast of Our Lady, 21 November 1916. The early sun was shining through the windows of the lounge, across the faces of khaki-clad figures of officers and men as they knelt at early mass, fingering their rosary beads.

The padre was a big man with a face like a rough mountain crag. His eyes were both child-like and humorous, eyes that seemed always to be asking the world to be kinder, though their owner was far too shy to ask anything. Now he addressed his congregation. As he raised that rich Irish brogue, you could see by the unconsciously rapt expressions around him that this man knew just how to reach the side of men's hearts that is very simple and very human. He had spent many months in the trenches and, rumour had it, still longed to be back there.

Mass over, everyone rolled out amid laughter and jollity in the wake of the padre. The men had adopted him as their chum and counsellor. He was the most popular man on the ship except for Major Priestley. The major, a modest, quiet man whom anyone could approach, had escaped and helped others to escape from Ruhleban, that notorious prison. He was a hero to the troops.

Everybody scrambled down to breakfast, talking and joking, for breakfast time was quite the nicest, friendliest time aboard. And this day the animation of good spirits, coupled with the prospect of hard work ahead – we were to embark wounded that afternoon at Moudros – was noticeable everywhere. Banter was rife, even at the austere commanding officer's table, I noticed as I passed through the saloon to get breakfast for a sick sister I was looking after.

Suddenly, there was a dull, deafening roar. *Britannic* gave a shiver, a long drawn out shudder from stem to stern, shaking crockery on the tables, breaking things till it subsided as she slowly continued on her way. We all knew she had been struck.

As one man, the whole saloon rose from their seats. Doctors and nurses vanished to their posts in a trice. The pantry where I stood holding a teapot in one hand and a pat of butter in the other, was cleared too, as men dropped what they were doing and jumped over presses with the agility of deer. In seconds, not a soul was to be seen and not a sound had been uttered.

This contrasted so forcibly with my recollections, not so far distant, of *Titanic*'s night of doom. The unhurried calmness with which we then confronted the unexpected left an impression that has remained with me vividly ever since. But this was different. War, with its anticipated horrors and ghastly possibilities, filled the imagination of those who feared and yet had not foreseen danger.

Fascinated, I watched the movement about me. My own fears, never absent from me for one moment of my sea life, were now, strangely, forgotten. Then I suddenly remembered I must go to the nurse in sick bay, help her to dress and send her to the lifeboats.

There was a hubbub of conversation on the decks below. Doors stood ajar, revealing sisters and nurses hurriedly collecting any little treasures, commenting with relief at the fortunate absence of wounded on board, while they tried hard to smother their feelings of concern at Matron's command for haste.

Two of them thanked me in passing for having made them go up early for mass. But for that they would have gone to breakfast, they invariably did, wearing pajamas under their uniform because the could never manage to get out of bed till the breakfast bell went.

I found my own special charge trying to dress herself with fingers shaking with weakness from her recent illness, dropping more garments than she put on. We made a pretence of chattering and joking, we completed her toilet and I sent her with a companion to join others on the boat deck.

The babble was stilled as the last nurse made her way up. The alleyways were almost deserted as I went to my own cabin. There the breakfast my roommate had assembled for us both lay temptingly before me. I was very hungry, for not a bite had passed my lips since the previous evening, as I had taken communion at mass.

My companion had already taken her coat and lifebelt and was gone. I sorted out things to take, the things I treasured most, Ned's ring and my clock, of course. The clock was a precious gift from a friend whose simple philosophy had helped me in many dark moments. Then there was my prayer book and my toothbrush. This latter because there had always been much fun at my expense after the *Titanic*, when I complained of my inability to get a toothbrush on the *Carpathia*. I recalled Patrick's joking advice: "Never undertake another disaster without first making sure of your toothbrush." Additionally, I stuffed all sorts of things into my pockets, even a roll from the breakfast table.

I donned the new coat for which I had saved so long, brought especially because I wanted to be so smart when I met dear old William. Carelessly, I put my lifebelt over the coat, contradicting my own admonishments to others when assisting at lifeboat drill, to always put on a lifebelt under the coat, so that in moments of emergency the weight of a coat could be easily discarded. I did not bother to change, however, as I felt reassured that this time there would be room in the lifeboats for all and I did not expect to be in the water.

Our comfortable cabin, which, if the ship had been used as a passenger liner, would have been the doctor's cabin, looked very cozy as I put out the lights and went up on deck, a little self-conscious at the incongruous mixture of a smart coat and a uniform cap, though being on board and on duty it never would have occurred to me to remove that cap.

The blaze of sunshine that met me out on the boat deck

was both warming and reassuring. But I was taken aback by the look of surprise on an officer's face as I emerged in the midst of a crowd of soldiers and sailors. When I asked, "Where are the others?" I was told they had all gone in the first two boats. Indeed, I could see boats slowly drawing away clear of the ship. *Britannic* was still steaming ahead, making the lowering of lifeboats a ticklish job. I gave that foolish, nervous laugh, as people sometimes do when faced with an unpleasant discovery and a doubtful alternative.

An officer came up and told me hastily that as all the women had left, I must take my place in the boat assigned to me by the official boat-muster list. Number four happened to be mine. Nicely I reflected, away from that churning water aft, where the propellers were having their little joke with anything in their way. Just at that moment, a lifeboat caught my eye. It had been lowered safely to the water but then drifted with sudden impetus, resisting the efforts of the unskilled oarsmen, right into those cruel, swirling blades.

Number four boat filled rapidly, but everybody was focusing fascinatedly on those blades aft. Though hands were lowering boats mechanically, eyes were looking with unexpected horror at the debris and the red streaks all over the water. The falls of the lowered lifeboat left hanging, could now be seen with human beings clinging to them, like flies on flypaper, holding on for dear life, with a growing fear of the certain death that awaited them if they let go.

The ship started gradually listing to starboard as our boat prepared to lower. The little sea scout near me took a deep breath as he got in; it was a long way down to the water, even in sunshine, and he was only a kid, despite his manly bearing.

He got his first shock when our lifeboat, hooking itself on an open porthole, whose circular, brass-rimmed glass jutted out, tilted us considerably; then, righting itself, started gliding down rapidly, scraping the ship's sides, splintering the glass in our faces from the boxes, which formed, when lighted, the green lighted band around a hospital ship's middle, and making a terrible impact as we landed on the water.

The boy's eye caught the struggling people in the water, left in the wake of the churning propellers, again reducing the poor little fellow to a frightened child. He had been hanging on for dear life to one of the boat falls and nothing would induce him to let it go. He kept giving me reassuring smiles every now and then, as if to say, "I'm not really afraid, I'm only doing this to keep the boat steady."

After we had touched the water, I looked round to see how my small friend took the impact, only to find him hanging halfway up the ship's side now, still attached to the rope! It took the forceful persuasion of a boatload of men to get that youngster to let go and drop back into the boat.

Meanwhile, we were not making much headway getting free from the ship's side; the boats clustered together in a hopeless group, fumbling hands struggling unsuccessfully to get control.

Britannic was still proceeding under her own steam. A few minutes after the lifeboat first touched the water, every man jack in the group of surrounding boats took a flying leap into the sea. They came thudding from behind and all around me, taking to the water like a vast army of rats.

Not a word, not a shout was heard, just hundreds of men fleeing into the sea as if from an enemy in pursuit. It was extraordinary to find myself in the space of a few minutes almost the only occupant of the boat; I say almost, for one man, a doctor, was still standing in silence beside me. I turned around to see the reason for this exodus and, to my horror, saw *Britannic*'s huge propellers churning and mincing up everything near them – men, boats and everything were just one ghastly whirl.

I turned in consternation to the man beside me to find he, too, had slipped silently away. In another moment I would be under those glittering, relentless blades, unless . . . I looked at the equally inexorable sea and, for a fraction of a second, hesitated, for I have always been afraid of water. Drowning was my one irrational fear all my life; I had not been able to learn to swim because of the loss of part of one lung in those far-off Argentine days.

Then suddenly I was no longer conscious of fear. I knew I must go into the sea and had to make that decision alone. I just jumped overboard, leaving everything that was solid, not even wondering why I did so, going down and down into what seemed bottomless depths, clutching desperately at my lifebelt which was something tangible though it had become loose and was bothering my chin.

Why had I put my belt over my coat was my one thought, as I felt its weight drag me down deeper. I kept my eyes tightly closed and held my breath instinctively, though it was the first time in my life I had been under water.

I felt myself rising and my head came into violent contact with something solid, something that prevented me from reaching the surface. Then again, there was another terrific crash above me and something very solid struck the back of my head a resounding blow, but happily on that part where my plentiful hair was thickest.

My brain shook like a solid body in a bottle of liquid. It was a very unpleasant feeling and at the third repetition I imagined the next time would be the last.

Suddenly some twist of fancy made me see even then, under water, the humour of my situation, and I chuckled – that was very nearly my undoing for I swallowed what seemed gallons of water and everything that was in it.

Panic seized me then and I remember making frantic efforts under whatever was keeping me down to catch on to something. Reaching out in despair, I groped blindly in that water that was now a thundering centre of noise, every sound magnified a hundredfold.

Suddenly, joy of joys, I touched something – an arm – that moved as mine moved! My fingers gripped it like a vice, but only for a second, until my almost senseless head remembered what is said of people drowning, that they retain their hold after death, bringing death to another. With that cheering thought, I let go.

Just as life seemed nothing but a whirling, choking ache, I rose to the light of day, my nose barely above the little lapping waves. I opened my eyes on an indescribable scene of slaughter, which made me shut them again to keep it out. In that moment I felt I was sinking; my lifejacket was loose and not sufficient to support me. Just then another went floating by so I grabbed at it and felt a little more confident; at last I had something to hold on to.

The first thing my smarting eyes beheld was a head near me, a head split open, like a sheep's head served by the butcher, the poor brains trickling over on to the khaki shoulders. All around were heart-breaking scenes of agony, poor limbs wrenched out as if some giant had torn them in his rage. The dead floated by so peacefully now, men coming up only to go down again for the last time, a look of frightful horror on their faces.

Wreckage of every sort was everywhere and, at a distance, stricken *Britannic* slowly ploughed her way ahead, the white pride of the ocean's medical world. She dipped her head a little, then a little lower and still lower. All the deck machinery fell into the sea like a child's toys. Then she took a fearful plunge, her stern rearing hundreds of feet into the air until with a final roar, she disappeared into the depths, the noise of her going resounding through the water with undreamt-of violence.

Violet Jessop had come to the surface under an upturned lifeboat. This saved her from the lethal propeller blades.

Despite the improvements made as a result of the Titanic *enquiry, the* Britannic *sank 50 minutes after the underwater explosion. 28 lives were lost in the sinking. All those who died had been in the lifeboats. The new equipment launched them so fast that the captain was unaware that they were clustered under her stern.*

The most likely cause of the underwater explosion was a moored mine. It is thought that it was laid by a U-boat. In 2003 divers discovered several reasons why she sank so fast. They were able to get inside the wreck and reached the engine rooms where they made some surprising discoveries. The watertight doors between the engine room compartments were open. This may have been because the watch was changing at the time of the explosion. In addition numerous portholes were open. This was against regulations but may have been tolerated because it would have been very hot in a coal-fired ship in the Mediterranean. The Britannic *had been designed for the cold temperatures of the North Atlantic. The divers also discovered that many of the rivets in her hull had popped out. This is thought to have been because they were cold rivetted (drilled but not welded). In salt water rivets and plates made of different metals are much more likely to separate unless they are hot rivetted (welded together).*

The suction of the Olympic *class ships' enormous propellers was so strong that they sucked large ships towards them. The ships' enormous size and displacement added to this effect. On 20 September 1911, the* Titanic's *elder sister, RMS* Olympic, *was involved in a collision with the cruiser HMS* Hawke *in the Solent. 1911. An enquiry into the collision the* Olympic *was found to blame as its speed and size had sucked the* Hawke *off course. Ironically Violet Jessop was aboard at the time.*

34-foot lifeboats had no chance anywhere near the Britannic's *enormous propellers. Violet Jessop was saved because the lifeboat she jumped out of turned over and protected her from being struck directly by a propeller.*

The Britannic *was listing when her lifeboats were sucked into her propellers. The propeller which did the damage was the one which was out of the water.*

The captain of the Britannic *was trying to get to shallower waters to run her aground. He was unaware of the casualties the propellers were inflicting at the stern.*

Violet Jessop retired in 1950 aged 63. She died in 1971.

The Sinking of SS *Athenia*
3 September 1939

The Second World War began on 3 September 1939. That day James Goodson, an American, was sailing back to the United States from Glasgow, aboard the British liner SS Athenia. *In the evening they were off the Hebrides when the* Athenia *was torpedoed. Goodson:*

I had just mounted the staircase and was moving forward to the dining room when it struck. It was a powerful explosion quickly followed by a loud crack and whistle. The ship shuddered under the blow. The lights went out. There were women's screams. The movement of the ship changed strangely as she slewed to a stop. People were running in all directions, calling desperately to one another.

We all knew the ship was mortally stricken; she was beginning to list.

The emergency lights were turned on. I went back to the companionway I had just come up. I gazed down at a sort of Dante's Inferno, a gaping hole at the bottom of which was a churning mass of water on which there were broken bits of wooden stairway, flooring and furniture. Terrified people were clinging to this flotsam, and to the wreckage of the rest of the stairway which was cascading down the side of the gaping hole. The blast must have come up through here from the engine room below, past the cabin decks, and the third-class restaurant and galley. I clambered and slithered down to the level of the restaurant. I started by reaching for the outstretched arms and pulling the weeping shaking, frightened women to safety; but I soon saw that the most urgent danger was to those who were floundering in the water, or clinging to the wreckage lower down. Many were screaming that they couldn't swim. Some were already close to drowning.

I slithered down the shattered stairway, slipped off my jacket and shoes, and plunged into the surging water. One by one, I dragged them to the foot of the broken companionway, and left them to clamber up to the other rescuers above.

When there were no more bodies floundering in the water, I turned to those who were cowering in the openings of the corridors which led from the cabins to what had been the landing at the foot of the stairs and which was now a seething, lurching mass of water. Most of them were women, many were children and some were men. I went first to the children. They left their mothers, put their small arms around my neck and clung to me.

They clung as we slipped into the water; they clung as I swam to the foot of the dangling steps; they clung as I climbed the slippery wreckage; and they clung as I prised their little arms from around me and passed them to those at the top. These were members of the crew. A few stewards and stewardesses, and even some seamen. The *Athenia* was a Glasgow ship and so was her crew. They knew their jobs, they rose to the challenge and, above all, they kept their heads. One seaman had climbed half-way down to take the women and children from me and pass them on to those waiting above. With a strong Glasgow accent, he soothed and comforted the mothers and children, and shouted praise and encouragement to me.

"Bloody guid, mon! Keep 'em coming!"

I looked up out of the water.

"I could do with some help down here."

The seaman shook his head sadly.

"Ah wish the hell ah cuid, but ah canna swum!"

I looked up at the others. They shook their heads too. It had never occurred to me that members of a ship's crew would not be able to swim. Finally there were no more left either in the water, or waiting at the openings of the corridors. I was at the base of the broken stairs. For the first time, I was able to pause and look around. By now, the ship had listed much more. The water had slopped into the corridors on the down side until it was waist high. The corridors on the upper side were out of the water. Two seamen were crawling down to help.

"We've got to make sure there's no one left in the cabins. We'll take this upper passageway. Can you swim to the lower one? There's not many of them. The emergency watertight doors have been closed at the next bulkhead, so we just have to check the ones in this section."

I pushed off into the lurching water and swam to the opening of one of the half flooded gangways. I was able to swim right to it, get to my feet and splash my way into darkness, walking half on the floor and half on the bulkheads. The water in most of the cabins was too deep and the light was too dim to conduct any kind of a search. What was worse as I stumbled through the water and darkness, there was a movement of the ship as it listed further. The water sloshed higher, and there were deep rumblings in the bowels of the sinking ship.

I yelled out through the dark, ghostly gangways and cabins. "Anyone there? Anyone there?"

There wasn't. The feeling grew in me that this deck was already at the bottom of the sea, as it would be for hundreds of years.

As I felt my way through the flooded, dark cabins and gangways, I stumbled across mysterious objects moving under the shifting water. I stumbled into what seemed to be a half-submerged bundle of clothing. It seemed to follow me as I returned towards the open shaft. In the dim light, I turned it over. Then I saw the innocent face, gashed and bloodied, and the dark, curly hair, and the blue eyes, which would never weep again for the bonnie banks of Loch Lomond. Now other lips would be asking where their highland laddie had gone.

I realized it was useless to search any longer. I strugsled back to the light, and left the lower decks to the dead, the darkness and the sea.

The crew members were waiting to help me up the wreckage, up past the smashed dining-rooms to the upper decks.

"Thanks!" I said when we got to the top. I shook both seamen by the hand.

The ship was listing quite a bit now. We headed up the sloping deck to the higher side. We found them launching one of the last lifeboats. It was crowded. Members of the crew were holding back those for whom there was no more room and telling them to go to another boat. Meanwhile, the two seamen fore and aft in the boat were desperately trying to lower it. But as the heavy boat lurched unevenly down as the ropes slid through the pulleys of the davits, a problem arose which was apparently not foreseen by the designers of lifeboat launching systems. Because of the listing of the ship, when the lifeboat was lowered from its davits, and, as it swayed with the slight rolling, it fouled the side. Although the seamen were playing out their ropes as evenly as possible, the forward part got caught against the side of the ship. The seaman continued to play out his rope. Suddenly it slid free and dropped. But the after rope hadn't played out as much as the one forward. The front of the boat dropped, but the rear was caught by its rope. Soon the boat was hanging by the after rope. The screaming passengers were tumbling out of the boat like rag dolls, and falling down to the surface of the sea far below.

There was nothing we could do. I helped the crew to shepherd the remaining group of passengers to the other side of the ship.

We made our way to what seemed to be the last lifeboat, at least on that deck. Here there was another problem caused by the same list and the same swell; the boat was hanging on its davits, but swinging in and out. On its outer swing, there was a yawning between the lifeboat and the ship. Most of the passengers were women or elderly, or both. The responsible crew members were trying to persuade them to make their leap into the boat when it was close to the ship, but many of them waited too long, and the boat swung out again.

We pushed our way through the waiting crowd to help. As I reached the boat, the seaman in the bow shouted to an elderly lady: "Jump! Now!"

But she hesitated. Perhaps she was pushed and the push

badly timed. As the boat swung away, she lurched out towards it, the gap was already too wide. Her arms reached the gunwale, but her body fell through the space between lifeboat and ship, wrenching her arms away from the boat and those who were trying to drag her into it. I gazed after the falling body, dazed and speechless, until it hit the waves far below.

Finally the lifeboat could take no more passengers, and was lowered away, leaving a small group of us on the deserted, sloping deck. One of the ship's officers took command.

"That was the last of the boats, but the Captain's launch will be back for us soon; it's distributing the passengers evenly between the boats. Some of the ones that got away weren't quite full!"

"Aye, but how much time do we have before she goes?"

"There's no immediate danger. There was only one torpedo which hit midships and blew up through that compartment. The watertight doors were closed before other compartments were flooded, so they should keep her afloat awhile."

Now that there was nothing to do, I felt depressed. Suddenly I thought of my money and papers I'd left with the Purser. I ran back to the companionway, and made my way to the Purser's office. There was the large safe still firmly locked shut. The state of the papers on the desk indicated a hurried departure. I tried in vain to open the safe, then turned and clambered back to the upper deck. Somehow I didn't feel like waiting for the Captain's launch; I wanted to be doing something, anything.

I went to the higher side of the ship and looked down the sloping side to the dark, rolling sea. There, just about 100 yards from the ship, I saw a lifeboat. Hanging from the davits, and making down the steel side of the ship were the ropes which had launched the boats.

In the dark, I couldn't see if they reached all the way to the sea, but they went far enough for me. Soon I was going down a rope hand over hand, fending myself off the side with my feet as the ship rolled. It was further than I had thought. Halfway down, my arms were aching. Long before I reached the bottom, I couldn't hold on any longer. As the rope slipped through my hands, I kicked away from the side and fell. It seemed a long time before I hit the water. I went in feet first; I started to struggle to the surface right away, but it seemed to take a long time. I thought I was a good underwater swimmer, but soon I desperately needed to breathe. In the darkness, there was no sign of the surface. For the first time I wished I'd been able to get to my life-jacket. If I passed out, it would at least have brought me to the surface. Just as I felt I could hold out no longer, I got to the surface. I gasped for breath. The sea was choppy, and I got a mouthful of water. It was colder, rougher and more brutal than I had expected. I looked for the lifeboat I had seen from the deck. I could only see it when I was lifted by a wave, and it looked much further away now.

I struck out in the direction of the boat, but it was a struggle. At times I felt I was making no headway at all. Eventually I got close enough to see one of the reasons. They had a few oars out, and were trying to row away from the ship. I knew that was in line with instructions, because of the danger of being sucked down with the ship when she sank; but, as I struggled to keep going, I did feel they could at least stop rowing until I caught up with them.

Fortunately, their efforts were badly co-ordinated and I finally reached them, and grabbed the gunwale. I tried to pull myself up, expecting helping hands to lift me into the boat; instead a dark young man, screaming in a foreign language, put his hand in my face to push me away. A frantic middle-aged woman was prising my fingers off the side of the boat and banging on my knuckles. Dimly I realized they were panicking because they felt the boat was already overcrowded. I heard the voices of the seaman in charge down in the stern, yelling to them to stop, but help came from another direction, and it was much more effective. The diminutive figure of a girl appeared. In a flash, she had

landed a sharp right to the face of the young man, and sent
him sprawling back off his seat. In the next second, my other
tormentor was hauled away, and the strong young arms were
reaching down to me. Other hands helped to haul me over
the gunwale.

I collapsed in a wet heap on the bottom of the boat and
gasped my thanks to my rescuers.

Amid peals of young female laughter I heard: "Hey! You're
an American!"

"So are you!" I mumbled in surprise.

"My God! You're half drowned and freezing cold! Here!"

A blanket was being wrapped around my shoulders. I
struggled to sit up, and opened my eyes to look at my
guardian angel. She was a small, slim brunette, about
nineteen or twenty, with an elfin face, full of life and humour.
She was wearing a bra and pants and nothing else. I realized
she had been wrapped in the blanket she was now trying to
put around me.

"No! No! You need it more than I do," and I took it off my
shoulders and put it around hers.

"OK. We'll share it. That way we'll keep each other
warm!" and she snuggled into my arms as I wrapped the
blanket around us.

"What happened to the rest of your clothes?" I asked.

"We were dressing for dinner when the torpedo struck. We
grabbed what we could and ran."

I looked around and saw we were surrounded by young
girls in various stages of undress. Some had borrowed
sweaters and jackets from members of the crew. Others were
huddled in blankets. At least most of them had life jackets. As
they snuggled together around us, I showed my surprise.

"Who are you?"

The little brunette laughed. "We're college kids. We've
been touring Europe after graduation. I guess our timing
could have been better. I'm Jenny. This is Kay. That's
Dodie."

They were a wonderful, cheery bunch, cracking jokes and

singing songs. We were an oasis of fun in the lifeboat. Most of the others were frightened or seasick or both. Many were refugees mostly from Poland. Many were Jewish, but by no means all.

I was surprised at how large the boat seemed, even as it rolled and pitched on the North Atlantic swells. Up in the bow was a member of the ship's crew, and another in the stern. In spite of the crowd in the boat, they had been able to get some of the oars out, and had got some of the men to start rowing. After getting warmed up, I felt guilty at not pulling my weight. I got up and picked my way carefully to within shouting distance of the seaman in the stern.

"Do you want me to help out on the oars?"

He was surprised to find a volunteer. "Aye! These two here are having a struggle. Maybe you could help them out. All we need to do is to keep away from the *Athenia* and head into the waves."

I took the place of a young Jewish boy who was more of a hindrance than a help to his partner on the oar. He didn't speak English, but was delighted to find I spoke German, which meant he could communicate with me in Yiddish. He was even happier to be relieved of his task. The other man on the oar was also young. He didn't speak Yiddish or German, but he spoke a little English. He seemed to be somewhat handicapped by something hanging out of his mouth. At first I thought it was saliva or spittle, but when he saw me looking at it, he took it out of his mouth, and I saw that it was a St Christopher medallion on a silver chain around his neck.

"He save us!" he said and put the medal back in his mouth, clamped between his teeth.

I nodded, but I sincerely hoped that St Christopher was being helped by the last messages of the *Athenia*'s wireless operator. I knew that the crack of the second explosion had been a shell from the U-Boat, but I had seen that although it had killed a few people on the upper deck, it hadn't hit the radio mast or superstructure.

After an hour or so on the oars I suggested that we could

stop rowing. We were far enough from the ship to be out of danger, but shouldn't get too far from her, because the rescue ships would be heading for her last reported position.

I went back to Jenny and my friendly college girls. Through he night, we clung together, chatted, sang and slept fitfully. At one point, I remember the Jews joining in singing that beautiful plaintive dirge which became the hymn of the Jewish refugees, oppressed, and martyred throughout the world.

Occasionally we looked across to the stricken *Athenia*. We were amazed at how long she was staying afloat; she was sinking lower in the water, and listing further, but during most of the night, she was still there. It was about 1.30 a.m. when everyone in our boat woke out of their fitful sleep and looked across at the dark hulk. There had probably been a noise of some kind; or perhaps a shift in her position, although I don't remember either. Anyway, we were all watching when the stern began to sink lower. Soon it seemed to me that most of the near half of the ship was under water. Everything was in slow motion. Gradually, as the stern disappeared, the bow began to rise. We could see the water cascading off as the great ship reared up; slowly, and with enormous dignity. It was frightening, unbelievable, awesome. Finally the entire forward half of the ship was towering above us. When it was absolutely vertical, it paused. Then she started her final dive; imperceptibly at first, but gaining in momentum until she plunged to her death. A column of water came up as she disappeared, then there was only a great turbulence, and then nothing but the rolling sea and some floating debris. We felt lonelier and sadder. There was no singing now. We were tired and shivering with cold.

It was 4.30 when I saw it looming up through the dark. It was a ship. It was even carrying lights. We were too numbed to cheer.

There was just a stirring in the boat; a grateful murmuring. The rowers picked up their oars and started rowing slowly towards the ship.

Other lifeboats were doing the same. Soon we found

ourselves close to the big rescue ship, surrounded by five or six other boats. The big ship had stopped as soon as she was close to the boats. Rope ladders were dropped over the side near the stern of the ship. She was a tanker and must have been empty. She towered above us and we could see the blades of her big propeller as we came around to her stern. I looked up and saw her name and home port: "Knute Nelson – CHRISTIANSAND"; a Norwegian tanker.

As we came close, I called on the seaman on the tiller of our boat to keep us away from the menacing propeller. It was not moving, but I knew it could windmill, or the Captain might call for some weigh, unaware of the boats under his stern. One lifeboat was being tossed by the waves ever closer to the propeller. I yelled across to them, but apparently there were not enough rowers to stop the drift. Then the great propeller started to turn, churning up the water, and sucking the lifeboat in under the stern. As we watched, they were drawn into the whirlpool. We saw one big propeller blade slash through the boat; but as the shattered bow went down, the rest of the boat was lifted by the next blade coming up. The rearing, shattered boat spilled its human cargo into the churning water.

I called to the man on our tiller and on the rowers to make for the spot where the survivors were floundering in the water. The screw was no longer turning, and the ship had moved forward slightly. Some of the strong swimmers were already making for the bottom of the rope and wooden ladder dangling down the side of the ship dose to the stern; some were pulled into our boat; others clung to the gunwales or oars for the short distance to the ladder; but many just disappeared under the foaming water.

We got the survivors from the broken lifeboat onto the ladder first. Then it was the turn of the weakest from our own boat. It wasn't easy. The boat was rising and falling on the waves, smashing against the steel sides of the tanker. Sometimes we got someone onto the ladder only to have them fall back into the boat as the ladder swung, or the boat dropped away too soon. We had to get them to get onto the ladder when the boat was at the top of its rise.

Finally there was no one left in the boat but the two seamen, the American college girls and myself. One by one, the girls started up the twisting, writhing ladder. Even for lithe, young, athletic teenagers, clambering up the tricky rope ladder took all their strength and concentration. There was no way they could keep the blankets wrapped around them; even those who had huddled into seamen's jackets which were far too big for them wriggled out of them before attempting to scale the towering side of the tanker.

When I finally reached the top of the ladder and was hauled over the rail by two large Norwegian sailors onto the deck, I saw the incredulous Captain of the *Knute Nelson* staring at a group of shivering girls, mostly dressed in pants and bras, and nothing else. He hurried them to a companionway.

"Go down! Down! Any door! Any room! Warm! You must have warm!"

I followed them down the iron stairs until we came to a lower deck, and into the first door. The cabin was dark, but warm! It smelt cosily of human sleep; there was the sound of heavy breathing.

The light came on. We saw a series of bunks, one above the other. In each bunk was a large Norwegian seaman. The girls had only one thing in mind: to get warm. They didn't hesitate. The seamen, who had been at sea for weeks, and didn't even know that war had been declared, awoke to find half-naked girls clambering into their bunks and snuggling up to their warm bodies under the rough blankets. I'll never forget the expressions on the faces of those big Norwegians. They knew they must be dreaming.

When we had explained what had happened to those who understood English, and they had translated it to the others, those magnificent gentle giants turned out of their bunks, made us coffee, served out hard-tack biscuits, lent us their sweaters, and blankets, showed us the way to the head, and made us feel that, in spite of what we had been through, life was good!

We slept the sleep of the exhausted for many hours. When we came to, we learned that, as a ship of a neutral country, the *Knute Nelson* was taking us to the nearest neutral port: Galway on the west coast of Eire. We heard that other rescue ships, including British destroyers, had picked up other survivors.

James Goodson was taken back to Glasgow where he volunteered to join the Royal Air Force. He became a fighter pilot. He was transferred to the United States Army Air Force in September 1942. By the end of the war he had become a squadron commander and shot down 32 enemy aircaft.

Fire

The Burning of the *Elizabeth*
c. 1762

William Spavens was an English seaman. In 1762 he sailed to the East Indies aboard the East Indiaman, Elizabeth. *He was away from the ship when she caught fire.*

Spavens:

Of this gentleman I learned the fate of my ship, *Elizabeth*, and afterwards obtained a more accurate account of her catastrophe from Mr John Ogelby, a Midshipman on board of her at that time, whom I met with at the Cape of Good Hope, and who then belonged to an outward-bound ship commanded by Mr Henry Gardener, late our purser. He said, the ship having completed her cargo at Wampoa, had dropped down and joined the homeward bound ships at Macoa, and while she lay there, a Dutchman, who was her sail-maker, having got drunk, after the crew was gone to sleep let a candle fall amongst some oakum, which taking fire, communicated to the pitch of the seams which were caulked and payed, but not scraped, and ran along them to the cables, the smoke of which suffocating the men who slept in the cable tiers, their cries alarmed those that lay on the gun-deck, who used their utmost efforts to extricate them from their dreadful situation, and save the ship from destruction, but without effect; and several who were exerting themselves in a fruitless endeavour to rescue their fellows from death, shared the same fate. Amongst these heroes were Mr Bearsley and Mr Gillow, two fine young fellows who perished from a pure principle of philanthropy. At length the flames rapidly spreading fore and aft, the ship became an entire conflagration; and burning down to the water's edge, the bottom sunk. Thus perished one of the finest ships that ever crossed the Indian ocean, with a cargo worth near half a million, and thirty-six precious lives (including Captain Stuart, who refused to quit her), through the carelessness and stupidity of an individual, who instead of giving the necessary alarm, had secretly escaped from the ship to secure himself, without shewing any concern for the rest.

How dear is life! A man whose name was Andrew Seaton, during the awful scene got over-board and caught hold of the rudder-rings where he supported himself till several holes were burnt in his head, before a boat came to take him away, not daring to quit his hold because he could not swim.

HMS *Boyne*
1795

On 1 May 1795, HMS Boyne, *98, lay at anchor at Spithead. She was the flagship of Admiral Peyton. Her captain was the Hon. George Grey. W. O. S. Gilly compiled this account from the official Admiralty documents:*

The origin of the fire has never been correctly ascertained; but it is supposed that some of lighted paper from the cartridges of the marines, as they were exercising and firing on the windward side of the poop, flew through the quarter-gallery into the admiral's cabin, and set fire to the papers or other inflammable materials that were lying there. Be this as it may, the flames burst through the poop before the fire was discovered, and not withstanding the united efforts of both officers and men they soon wrapt the vessel in a blaze fore and aft.

Upon the discovery of the fire, all the boats from the different ships put out to the *Boyne*'s assistance, and the crew, with the exception of eleven were saved.

The *Boyne*'s guns being loaded, went off as they became heated, and much injury would have been done to the shipping and those on board, had not the Port-Admiral, Sir William Parker, made the signal for the vessels most in danger to get under weigh. As it was, two men were killed, and one wounded on board the *Queen Charlotte*.

About half-past one in the afternoon, the burning ship parted from her cables, and blew up with a dreadful explosion. At the time of the accident Admiral Peyton and Captain Grey were attending a court-martial in Portsmouth Harbour, on Captain A. J. P. Molloy.

The Blowing Up of HMS *Amphion*
1796

HMS Amphion, *a frigate, had put into Plymouth for repairs. On 22 September 1796, she was lying alongside of a sheer-hulk taking in her bowsprit, within a few yards of the dockyard jetty. W. O. S. Gilly compiled this account from the official Admiralty documents:*

The ship, being on the eve of sailing, was crowded with more than an hundred men, women, and children, above her usual complement. It was four o'clock in the afternoon that a violent shock, like an earthquake, was felt at Stonehouse and Plymouth. The sky towards the dock appeared as if from fire, and in a moment the streets were crowded with the inhabitants, each asking his neighbour what had occurred. When the confusion had somewhat abated, it was announced that the *Amphion* had blown up, and then every one hastened to the dock, where a most heart-rending scene presented itself. Strewed in all directions were pieces of broken timber, spars, and rigging, whilst the deck of the hulk to which the frigate had been lashed was red with blood, and covered with mangled limbs and lifeless trunks, all blackened with powder.

The frigate had been originally manned from Plymouth; and as the mutilated forms were collected together and carried to the hospital, fathers, mothers, brothers, and sisters, flocked to the gates, in their anxiety to discover if their relatives were numbered amongst the dying or the dead.

From the suddenness of the catastrophe, no accurate account can of course be given; but the following particulars were collected from the survivors.

The captain, Israel Pellew, was at dinner in his cabin with Captain Swaffield of the *Overyssel*, a Dutch 64, and the first lieutenant of the *Amphion*, when in an instant they were all violently thrown against the carlings of the upper deck. Captain Pellew had sufficient presence of mind to rush to the cabin window before a second explosion followed, by which he was blown into the water; he was soon, however, picked up by a boat, and was found to have sustained but little injury.

The first lieutenant, who followed his example escaped in a similar manner. Unfortunately, Captain Swaffield perished, in all probability having been stunned either by the first blow he received against the carlings, or by coming in contact with some part of the hulk. His body was found a month afterwards, with the skull fractured, apparently crushed between the sides of the two vessels.

At the moment of the explosion, the sentinel at the cabin door was looking at his watch, which was dashed from his hands and he was stunned; he knew nothing more until he found himself safe on shore, and comparatively unhurt. The escape of the boatswain was also very remarkable; he was standing on the cathead, directing the men in rigging out the jib-boom, when he felt himself suddenly carried off his feet into the air; he then fell into the sea senseless; and on recovering his consciousness, he found that he bad got entangled amongst the rigging, and that his arm was broken. He contrived to extricate himself, though with some difficulty, and he was soon picked up by a boat without further injury.

The preservation of a child was no less singular: in the terror of the moment, the mother had grasped it in her arms, but, horrible to relate, the lower part of her body was blown to pieces, whilst the upper part remained unhurt, and it was discovered with the arms still clasping the living child to the lifeless bosom.

The exact complement of of the Amphion was 215, but from the the crowded state of her decks at the time of the accident, it is supposed that 300, out of 310 or 312 persons, perished with the ship.

The captain, two lieutenants, a boatswain, three men, a marine, one woman, and the child, were all that were saved.

The cause of this unfortunate event was never clearly known; but it was conjectured that the gunner might have let fall some powder near the fore-magazine, which accidentally igniting, had communicated with the magazine itself. The gunner had been suspected of stealing the powder, and on that day he is said to have been intoxicated, and was probably less careful than usual. He was amongst the numbers who perished.

HMS *Resistance* is Struck by Lightning
24 July 1798

A survivors' account of how HMS Resistance *blew up after being struck by lightning was related by W. O. S. Gilly:*

It appears that the *Resistance*, of 44 guns, Captain Edward Pakenham, had anchored in the Straits of Banca, on the 23 July 1798. Between three and four o'clock in the morning of the 24th, the ship was struck by lightning: the electric fluid must have penetrated and set fire to some part of the vessel near to the magazine, as she blew up with a fearful violence a few moments after the flash.

Thomas Scott, a seaman, one of the few survivors, stated that he was lying asleep on the starboard side of the quarter-deck, when, being suddenly awakened by a bright blaze, and the sensation of scorching heat, he found his hair and clothes were on fire. A tremendous explosion immediately followed, and he became insensible. He supposed that some minutes might have elapsed before he recovered, when he found himself, with many comrades, struggling in the waves amongst pieces of the wreck. The *Resistance* had sunk, but the hammock netting was just above water on the starboard side, and with much difficulty Scott and the other survivors contrived to reach it. When they were able to look around them, they found that only twelve men alone remained of a crew of three hundred, including the marines. The calmness of the weather enabled the unfortunate sufferers to construct a raft with the pieces of timber that were floating about; but most of the men were so much bruised and burnt as to be unable to assist in the work. The raft was finished about one o'clock, p.m., but in a very rough and insecure manner. Part of the mainsail attached to the mast of the jolly-boat served them for a sail and they committed themselves to the care of Providence upon this frail raft, and made for the nearest shore, which was the low land of Sumatra, about three leagues distant.

About seven o'clock in the evening, a gale sprung up, the sea ran high, and the lashings of the raft began to give way, the planks which formed the platform were washed off; and in a short time the mast and sail were also carried away. An anchor-stock which formed part of the raft had separated and was floating away; but although it was at some distance, Scott proposed to swim for it, encouraging three others to follow his example, they all reached it in safety. In about an hour afterwards they lost sight of their companions on the raft, and never saw them more. The four men upon the anchor-stock gained the shore, and they then fell into the hands of the Malays.

Thomas Scott was twice sold as a slave, but was at length released, at the request of Major Taylor, the governor of Malacca, who, hearing that four British seamen were captives at Lingan, sent to the sultan to beg his assistance in procuring their liberty. Thomas Scott returned with Major Taylor's messenger to Malacca, from whence he sailed to England: the other three men had been previously released by the Sultan's orders, and conveyed to Penang.

Error

The Sinking of HMS *Victoria*
22 June 1893

On 22 June 1893 the Mediterranean squadron of the Royal Navy was en route from Beirut to Tripoli. It was exercising in two columns about six cables (1,200 yards) apart. The commander in chief was Vice-Admiral Sir George Tryon. He was leading the starboard column in his flagship, HMS Victoria. The port column was led by HMS Camperdown, commanded by Rear-Admiral Markham. Sir George Tryon gave a strange order. He signalled that the squadron should reverse its course by turning inwards in succession. The ships were evidently too close to avoid collision if they obeyed the order. His officers warned him but he insisted and signalled:

Second division alter course in succession sixteen points to starboard, preserving the order of the fleet; and the first division alter course in succession sixteen points to port, preserving the order of the fleet.

Rear-Admiral Markham signalled that he had not understood. After conferring with the captain of HMS Camperdown, they signalled back that the order was understood and the Victoria and the Camperdown began to turn.

At the subsequent court martial, the captain of HMS Victoria,
the Honourable Maurice Bourke, gave the following evidence:

Directly the signal came down and the helm was put over, the
ship having swung about two points with the helm extreme, I
said to the Admiral, "We shall be very close to that ship,"
meaning the *Camperdown*. I then turned to Mr Lanyon,
midshipman, who was my aide-de-camp, and told him to
take the distance to the *Camperdown*. To the best of my recollection, when I spoke to the Admiral he looked aft, but made
no answer at all. After I spoke to Mr Lanyon I again said,
"We had better do something. We shall be very close to the
Camperdown." All this time we were turning. I then said to
the Admiral, receiving no answer, "May I go astern full speed
with the port screw?" I asked this question to the best of my
belief twice or three times quickly, one after the other. At last
he said, "Yes." The port telegraph was immediately put full
speed, and, without further orders, very shortly after I
ordered both screws to be put full speed astern.

Aboard HMS *Camperdown* they tried the same maneouvre.
But it was too late. The *Camperdown* crashed into the bows
of the *Victoria*. Her steel ram burst into the hull of the
Victoria. The *Victoria* heeled over and began to sink. She
turned over as she did so. As she sank there were several
explosions as her boilers burst. The crew maintained their
discipline as they abandoned ship. The other ships sent boats
to their assistance. Vice-Admiral Sir George Tryon refused to
put on a lifebelt and stayed with the ship. He drowned.

The court martial blamed Vice-Admiral Sir George Tryon for the
disaster.

The *Torrey Canyon*
18 March 1967

Timetable of events of the Torrey Canyon *disaster:*

Saturday 18 March 1967: *Torrey Canyon* aground on Seven Stones. Tug *Utrecht* arrived and her owners, the Dutch firm of Wijsmuller, agreed to undertake salvage. Royal Naval vessels began spraying detergent on oil leaking from tanker.

Sunday 19 March: near gale from north-west. Thirty-two members of tanker's crew taken off, leaving only captain and three officers aboard. Oil slick covering area 18 by 2 miles.

Monday 20 March: weather fine. Salvage preparations begin. Fourteen ships spraying oil slick, now 30 by 8 miles.

Tuesday 21 March: an explosion in engine-room killed a Dutch salvage expert, blew a hole in deck. The ship was abandoned. Oil slick, 35 by 20 miles.

Wednesday 22 March: preparations began for renewal of salvage work. Nineteen ships fighting oil, now 12 miles from Cornish coast.

Thursday 23 March: salvage operations resumed. Weather still holding good. Oil breaking up into large patches.

Friday 24 March: wind backing from north-west to south-west, freshening. List of ship being corrected; high hopes of tow off during big spring tides over the week-end. Oil nears coast; troops are called out.

Saturday 25 March: wind increasing to near gale force. Tugs move ship to starboard, but she is apparently only pivoting on rocks amidships. First oil reaches beaches of Whitesand Bay.

Location of the *Torrey Canyon* disaster 18 March 1967

Below: detail of the channel between the Scilly Isles & Land's End

Land's End

Wolf Rock

Seven Stones Reef
(Lightship)

Scilly Isles

Milford Haven

North

intended
position

actual
position

Sunday 26 March: wind gusting to gale force. Four tugs heave at ship without success. Torrey Canyon breaks her back just abaft the bridge, and is now lying in two sections at an angle to each other, both awash. Oil fills Mounts Bay.

Monday 27 March: wind moderating but rough seas and heavy swell. Broken sections moving further apart and sinking. Forward section breaks, leaving wreck in three parts. Oil round Cornish coast from Newquay to the Lizard.

Tuesday 28 March: Wijsmuller end salvage contract. *Seven Stones* lightship towed into Penzance, shipping and aircraft warned off. *Torrey Canyon* bombed and set on fire from the air. Oil in St Ives Bay, Mounts Bay now clear.

Wednesday 29 March: more bombing and fires. Big explosion. Slicks of oil at sea from Hartland Point to Start Point.

Thursday 30 March: bombing resumed but increasingly difficult to start fires. Ship finally declared free from oil, and the battered wreck left to the sea. *Seven Stones* lightship towed back on station. Oil 35 miles from Channel Islands.

Friday 31 March: many Cornish beaches cleared of oil.

Wednesday 5 April: 1,600 troops working on oil clearance. Big landings of fish at Newlyn in good condition.

Friday 7 April: Britain estimates expenditure of £2m on fighting oil. Oil reaches Guernsey beaches.

Monday 10 April: oil fight moving to smaller Cornish coves. Many main beaches clear. Oil now on north coast of Brittany.

Tuesday 11 April: 90 miles of Brittany coast polluted. Oyster beds hit.

Wednesday 12 April: France posted 3,000 troops to fight oil. Made first credit of £1m for oil clearance.

Saturday 15 April: French Government ordered another 6,000 troops to join those already on the beaches. 290 naval ships ordered to the area and 400 fishing boats chartered to spread sawdust on oil slicks off Brittany coast. Floating dams ordered to protect estuaries. Minister of the Interior took command of operations.

Wednesday 26 April: Fresh pollution of Cornish beaches.

Wednesday 3 May: Liberian court of inquiry into stranding published their report. The captain was held solely responsible.

Thursday 4 May: Inter-Governmental Marine Consultative Organization met in London to study action needed to prevent similar disasters.

On 18 March 1967 the oil tanker Torrey Canyon *struck Pollard's Rock in the Seven Stones reef between the Scilly Isles and Land's End, England. She belonged to the first generation of supertankers. She was carrying a cargo of 120,000 tons of oil.*

The Torrey Canyon *was originally built in the USA, in 1959, with a cargo capacity of 60,000 tons. Later, she was expanded to twice that capacity in Japan; 63,000 tonnes for the ship and 120,000 for the cargo. She was owned by a subsidiary of Union Oil. She was registered in Liberia. She had an Italian crew. Her captain was Pastrengo Rugiati.*

Because of her size she was almost unmanoeuverable. At her cruising speed of 17 knots she took 5 miles to stop. She took about 1 minute to turn through 20 degrees. She was equipped with a Sperry autopilot. When the autopilot was engaged, the ship's officers could still change course plus or minus 3 degrees. The autopilot clicked for every degree of change, in both automatic and manual modes. At sea, the clicking autopilot was the best way to tell that the ship was turning, because the turn rate was so slow. The Torrey Canyon *was equipped with radar which had a range of 40 miles.*

The Torrey Canyon *left Kuwait on 19 February 1967 with full cargo of oil, bound for the Atlantic ocean. She reached the Canary Isles on 14 March 1967. Here the captain was informed of her destination. This was Milford Haven, which he had to reach by 18 March. Due to the oil market, it was best for business to be able to choose the final destination of the cargo as late as possible. This meant that the ship had to have a full set of navigation charts for wherever it might be sent, before it left harbour.*

Because of the size of the ship, they had to catch the high tide at 11 p.m., or wait another six days. They had five days to steam nearly 2,000 miles. Navigation was by autopilot, using classical navigation techniques. GPS satellites had not yet been introduced. Their first landfall was the Scilly Isles. This was standard practice. They had only one chart of the Scilly Isles and Land's End, with insufficient detail for close navigation. However, the captain had sailed through those waters eighteen times before, so he had some experience for interpreting the chart.

At 6.30 a.m, the Scilly Isles appeared on the radar. This revealed that the ship was further east than her intended position. Her course should have allowed her to pass the west side of the Scillies. Her captain ordered "continue course". This meant going through the gap between the Scilly Isles and the Seven Stones Reef. The deep-water channel in this gap was only about 7 miles wide.

At 7 a.m., the Captain came onto the bridge.

At 8 a.m., the watch changed over. The captain, a junior officer (on his first trip) and an experienced helmsman were now in charge on the bridge. The junior officer was assigned the navigation duties.

At 8.15 a.m. Torrey Canyon *was passing the Scilly Isles. Captain ordered a change of direction while on autopilot (clicks).*

The captain moved the ship to the right of channel (closer to the "Seven Stones" reef) to avoid the nets of some fishing boats.

At 8.40 a.m. they discovered a plotting error. When they re-plotted their position they discovered they were only 2.8 miles from the edge of the reef. The ship was still moving at 17 knots; it could not stop in time. They attempted to change course. Neither the helmsman nor the captain could hear the clicks of the autopilot. By the time they had worked out what was wrong, it was too late. The Torrey Canyon *hit Pollard's Rock in the Seven Stones reef at 17 knots. 6 tanks were ripped open.*

A member of the crew made a statement to a reporter from the Western Morning News:

We were proceeding at full speed when, just before the collision, we saw the lightship signalling to us with an Aldis lamp. The captain said "What's going on?" and a moment later the ship struck.

When members of the crew were landed ashore they made various statements to reporters:

An engineer, Giobbe Salvatore, explained that when the ship struck the captain ordered full astern on the engines but that "the sea pushed her further on". He thought that the ship had been blown off course. Another engineer, Antonio Zaccardi, said that he was in the engine-room when the ship struck. There was a grinding noise along the length of the hull, which lasted for some time before the ship was brought up short, throwing everyone off their feet.

According to The Sunday Times *of 26 March, the young second mate, Pierpaulo Fontana, had finished a four-hour watch at 4 am that morning. He is reported as saying:*

As far as I am concerned we were on a safe, steady course when I went to bed. I can't tell you anything about the automatic steering. All I know is that I was awakened by the shudder as the ship hit something. But the man on watch had no reason to believe anything would go wrong.

From conversation among the crew when they returned to Genoa, The Times *Milan correspondent gathered that the ship had been on automatic steering at the time of the stranding, but that the officer on watch at the time, Coccio, had not set the course. The captain was on the bridge.* The Sunday Times *of 26 March recorded an engineer on duty at the time of the impact as saying, "None of us knew what had happened and we had had no instructions from anybody before the accident." He also said that he looked at the clock when the crash came, it was 8.45 a.m. The lightship said 9.23 a.m., and later the Government White Paper put the time at 9.11 a.m.*

The Torrey Canyon *came to rest with her bows pointing to the north-west and her stern to the south-east, on the western side of the Pollard Rock, biggest of all the Seven Stones. At low water its tip was just abeam of the tanker's bridge, on the starboard side. If Captain Rugiati had altered course to port when he saw the lightship then he had almost succeeded in clearing the rocks; the last north-westerly projection had been his undoing.*

The Torrey Canyon *made a radio call asking for immediate assistance. Several powerful Dutch tugs were standing by ready for salvage calls. The* Utrecht *replied immediately, saying she was "proceeding". A lifeboat from St Mary's in the Scillies and helicopters were scrambled from the Naval Air Station at the Lizard.*

Captain Rugiati made a radio signal at 11.05 a.m.:

Cancel distress for the moment, and treat it as urgency.

By this time, two lifeboats were alongside and two helicopters were overhead. Numerous other vessels were in the vicinity.

Dutch salvage tugs were racing to win the salvage contract. The Utrecht *of the Wijsmuller Bureau got there first. The plan was to pull the* Torrey Canyon *off the reef on the evening tide. The crew began pumping the oil out to lighten the ship.*

The weather was deteriorating. The wind was North-west at 25 to 30 mph. The sea was moderate to rough. The Torrey Canyon *was "rolling and pounding". They knew that she was badly holed between bulkheads 10 to 18. Oil was streaming out downwind. During the afternoon it had reached six miles downwind. By the evening it stretched for eight miles to the South East.*

It was pollution on a scale never known before. The Royal

Navy was alerted. They began spraying the oil with detergent as it became available.

Water was coming over part of the tanker's foredeck at high tide, and she was listing about eight degrees to starboard. There were six feet of water in the engine-room and the boilers had been closed down. The crew had emergency power, but were unable to use the ship's pumps. No attempt to refloat would be made until the next day. St Mary's lifeboat was standing by, the tugs Utrecht, Albatross *(which had heard the original "Mayday" call when in Torbay), and* Praia da Adraga *were in attendance. The tug* Stentor *had also left Avonmouth at 5 p.m. with large air compressors aboard.*

The crew had a sleepless night. The stench of crude oil was appalling. Captain Summerlee of the BEA helicopter, who first saw the wreck, said he smelt it three miles downwind. A week later when the oil had spread far and wide it was smelt, on the Saturday night with a south-west wind, as far away as the western slopes of Dartmoor, at Ipplepen, near Newton Abbot, and in Torquay. For those living on top of it that first night, it was an added horror. The tanker moved with every sea. First officer Silvano Bonefiglio said later:

The sound was terrible, crunching and scraping all through the night.

Soon after dawn on Sunday 19 March Matt Lethbridge reported from the St Mary's lifeboat that the Torrey Canyon *"does not look so good". Her starboard rail on the foredeck was awash. A north-west gale was forecast and there were serious fears for the safety of the crew. The lifeboat went alongside and took off fourteen members of the crew and all their baggage. These were transferred to the Trinity House ship* Stella. *The* Stella *was based at Penzance and acted as tender to the Seven Stones lightship and all the lighthouses in the area.*

At 9.02 a.m. St Just Coastguard suggested to the master of the Torrey Canyon *that the rest of the crew should be taken off in view of the deteriorating weather and the difficulty of operating*

helicopters in high winds. There was no reply. Captain Rugiati
was too busy with the morning's salvage attempt. With the oil that
had escaped, and the amount pumped out, it was reckoned that
the ship had been lightened by some 20,000 tons. All the tugs
standing by had lines aboard, but all their heaving was of no
avail. The Utrecht parted her heavy wire hawser under the
strain, but the Torrey Canyon stayed firmly on the rocks.

The wind was becoming a decisive element. The morning's
weather forecast had been: wind north-west to north, Force 4 to 6,
gusting to Force 8 (gale force) at times, sea rough to very rough,
visibility good. It was the wind, rather than the tides, which was
affecting the oil as it leaked from the ship. There was a heavy
concentration all round the ship for about a thousand yards, but
the slick stretched for twelve miles away to the south, and was up
to six miles in width. The heaviest contamination was along the
eastern edge and in the southeastern corner. A destroyer, HMS
Barossa, and a minesweeper, HMS Clarbeston, were spraying,
both steaming up and down through the mass so that their propel-
lors churned the detergent well into the oil, and their progress cut
channels through the great mass.

At 11.30 a.m. the lifeboat repeated the earlier coastguard signal
recommending the transfer of the remainder of the crew. Captain
Rugiati replied that he was awaiting compressors and that the crew
would stay. He quickly changed his mind. Two minutes later he
made a signal that three crew and the two salvage experts from the
Utrecht were staying aboard, but the rest of the crew were leaving.
Matt Lethbridge took the lifeboat alongside again but the wind
had got up and, with the falling tide, the Torrey Canyon was
higher out of the water. The men had to jump for it. Eight men
managed it successfully, but the ninth went into the sea. He was
quickly rescued but conditions were clearly deteriorating rapidly.
The lifeboat had been as close in as she dared, already her
starboard quarter had crashed against the tanker's side and been
badly damaged. So, one minute before noon, the Torrey Canyon
asked that helicopters be sent, explaining that there was too much
swell for the lifeboat to take the men off, and danger of their falling
into the water.

By 1.11 p.m. this had been accomplished. Fourteen men were in the Stella, *nine in the St Mary's lifeboat, still standing by, and another nine had been lifted by helicopter and flown to St Mary's. Four members of the ship's company, the captain and his principal officers, remained aboard, with two salvage officers from the* Utrecht. *The* Stella *moved off eastwards to land her men at Penzance. Penlee lifeboat was called out to take over watch from St Mary's lifeboat and, when relieved, she turned her bows south-west for the islands. The lifeboat arrived alongside the pier in Hughtown harbour at 6 p.m., having been at sea continuously for over 32 hours. It was the longest continuous spell of duty ever for an Isles of Scilly lifeboat. The* Utrecht *managed to get a five-inch steel hawser to the wreck that evening, but there was little easing in the weather. One of the last radio messages before darkness set in was the laconic:*

Torrey Canyon settling down, taking heavy seas.

Frans van Rixel, from Belgium, was a member of the salvage team:

I was a young engineer (21) working for Wijsmuller, the salvage company, and onboard the *Torrey Canyon* attempting to salvage it when the engine room exploded, blowing open the aft castle. Myself and others ended up in oil-filled sea and we had to be rescued ourselves.

Nightmarish experience. Never had any good pictures as all my gear was left onboard and is now on the bottom of the ocean. We witnessed the breaking up and RAF attempts to fire the vessel.

One of our colleagues, Captain Stal, was blown overboard by the explosion. He was taken from the water onboard the tug but in spite of immediate action by RAF or Coast Guard [who dropped a doctor by helicopter] he died an hour later and he was the only victim of this disaster.

We were all taken by tug to Falmouth where an inquiry was held. Later we returned to the site but too much damage was done to the vessel and it was than decided to destroy it.

I myself was in the engine room at about 10:00 looking for bolts when the fumes hit me. I decided to get out then. As the vessel was still being rocked by the heavy swells something must have fallen and created a spark which caused the explosion. I remember the swimming pool, which was located on top of the engine room, completely being blown out at around noon.

At this time we were all on the bridge having a lunch break, but we immediately donned our lifejackets and jumped into the sea as this was the only thing we could do.

The Salvage Association had a surveyor aboard the wreck. On that Tuesday the Salvage Association received a report from their staff surveyor aboard the tanker and for the first time the full extent of the damage became known. The message recorded that the Torrey Canyon *was wrecked on the west side of the Seven Stones, and was lying approximately fifteen feet down by the head and with a five degree list to starboard. No apparent twist or deformation of the hull could be noted. Nos 4 and 5 port wing and No. 5 centre were the only tanks not leaking. The remaining fourteen cargo tanks and five bunker tanks, together with the forepeak and fore and aft pump-rooms, were all holed. There was approximately ten feet of water in the engine-room, through a leakage from the after pump-room bulkhead. The rudder and the after end of the vessel abaft the after pump-room appeared to be free from the rocks. Fifteen salvage crew with the master and three seamen were aboard. Four portable air compressors were pressurising the starboard forward tanks to increase buoyancy and submersible pumps were being used to pump out the engine-room. Four tugs were standing by to pull on each high tide, the first attempt to be made that evening.*

Four tugs were waiting to try to haul her off the reef. They were the Utrecht *(638 tons) and the smaller* Titan *(245 tons) and* Stentor *(200 tons), all owned by Wijsmuller, and the Portuguese* Praia da Adraga *(516 tons).*

Lloyd's List recorded a whole series of radio messages:

12.13 p.m. the Seven Stones lightship reported: "After end *Torrey Canyon* now on fire."

At 12.20 p.m. Tug *Titan* requested: "Require medical assistance. Require doctor by helicopter. Explosion in engine-room of *Torrey Canyon*, one man injured, burned."

At 12.35 p.m. the St Mary's lifeboat was launched with a doctor on board. A helicopter was scrambled.

Tug *Titan*, 12.43 p.m. reported: "All salvage crew taken off. Arrange ambulance and hospital Newlyn. Estimated time of arrival there by *Titan*, 2.45 pm."

To Rescue Co-ordination Centre, Plymouth, 2 p.m.: "Explosion but no sign of fire."

Salvage Association, via Southampton, 2 p.m.: "Vessel now abandoned due to explosion. Gas condition now very dangerous. Stern settled further since explosion."

Tug *Utrecht*, 2.03 p.m.: "Cannot see any fire or smoke. Man lowered on board from helicopter and taken off again. Hope to get aboard in an hour."

Compressed air was being pumped into confined spaces which contained gases from the oil. The petrol-driven engines of the compressors and the emergency generators were capable of igniting an explosion. At 9.30 a.m. the men aboard became aware of the build-up of gas in the engine room. They told The Times:

We shut down the emergency generator and lighting, and took all precautions to prevent an explosion.

Just after mid day, a salvage engineer went to the engine-room to make an inspection. He opened the door, and there was an explosion. Pieces of metal flew everywhere. Two men were blown clean overboard into the sea. Seven other men were injured. The explosion cut a hole eighteen feet square right through the three decks above the engine-room. The explosion completely removed living quarters and the swimming pool on deck.

The uninjured moved to help at once. Fortunately crude oil is uninflammable. Salvage chief Captain Hans Barend Stahl was rescued from the sea by men from the tug.

The tug Titan *took all the salvage crew off. Captain Stahl died before the tug reached Newlyn.*

The wreck had been officially abandoned. The Salvage Association made a report on 22 March:

The engine-room was flooded to a depth of twenty feet now, with the turbines submerged. The superstructure above the engine-room, including accommodation, had been destroyed by blast, the engine-room itself was gutted, and the boiler-room bulkhead was probably affected. Tests for gas were to be made that day and, in the meantime, the compressors had been stopped as pumping air was an explosive risk. Before the explosion the ship had been pivoting in the region of No. 4 tank, with bow and stern movement, and pounding. Since the explosion, the ship had settled further aft, and the leakage of oil had increased.

It was estimated that 80,000 tons of oil remained in the wreck, 20–25,000 tons had washed out. On 25 March they finally made their first attempt to haul her off. It moved her but could not drag her off. She remained firmly jammed amidships. She seemed to be pivoted on the rocks. The attempt was abandoned after a fifty-minute pull.

On 26 March they tried again at 5 p.m. on the afternoon tide. At 7.45 p.m., under the strain of the waves pounding her on the rocks as she half floated with the new buoyancy, and the stresses four powerful tugs were inflicting on her hull, the Torrey Canyon *broke in two. She had survived for eight and a half days on the Seven Stones, suffered two gales, one explosion, and three previous attempts to tow her off.*

Her back was broken just behind the bridge, her sides split open across No. 3 cargo tanks (No. 3 port wing tank had been one of the three unfractured in the original disaster) and oil began to pour out. The stern section swung to a ten degree angle to the bows, and both parts of the ship were listing four or five degrees to port. Captain H. Post of the Utrecht made a signal to his owners in Holland that the ship had broken up in the stormy conditions, that she was split in two, was gradually sinking, and must be considered a total loss.

At high water the next morning, soon after 7 a.m., the coastguard at St Mary's said that the ship was awash, except for the forecastle, the bridge and a small part of the stern, and that heavy seas were breaking over her. The wind was moderating, down to Force 4 to 5, but there were still moderate to rough seas over a heavy swell. This delayed the naval spraying force, but they were tackling the new oil menace in strength as soon as weather permitted. The first aerial reconnaissance on Easter Monday showed that the two parts were now nearly at right angles to each other. The bow section was above water, but was rolling and pitching every time the huge waves broke across it. The stern was partly submerged. By the afternoon, St Mary's coastguards said that the two sections were gradually drawing apart. A photographer who flew over the wreck said that the stern was well separated from the bow, which was actually rocking as though pivoted on the rocks, and that every time it lifted oil sprayed out from the fractured tanks. A Salvage Association surveyor who, with other officers, inspected her from a helicopter at low water on Easter Monday afternoon, said the two parts were about thirty feet distant from each other and thirty degrees out of line, with the stern settled and the poop deck awash. The forward section was hogged and the sides fractured at Nos 1 and 2 tanks, with a large volume of oil washing out.

Experiments had shown that crude oil could be burnt on water but it had to be spilt from the wreck. Bombing the wreck could be the solution.

The British Government decided to bomb the wreck to limit the damage and burn off the oil.

The Stella *moved out to the Seven Stones lightship and towed her away into Penzance. Ships were warned to keep clear of a danger zone of twenty miles radius round the* Torrey Canyon. *Four destroyers and two frigates patrolled the ring to see that the area was kept clear, two minesweepers and two naval tugs stood by. The* Scillonian *altered her course to the southward, as did the regular helicopter service between Penzance and St Mary's. In Hughtown, the capital of the island, the one-legged town crier, Wilfred Tonkin, was out with his bell warning people to keep off the beaches. But all the islanders and all the holidaymakers, the Prime Minister and his family among them, climbed to vantage points where they could see the show, and similar crowds congregated on the cliffs at Land's End.*

At 4 p.m. on Tuesday 28 March, eight Royal Navy "Buccaneer" strike aircraft roared in from the air station at Lossiemouth in Scotland, circled the target once, and then swept in singly from the direction of the Islands. They were flying at 500 miles an hour, 2,500 feet up. The commanding officer of the squadron, Lieutenant Commander David Howard, dropped two 1,000-lb bombs but his one hit failed to explode. Behind him came Lieutenant Commander David Mears whose two bombs hit the after section plumb amidships. Fire started at once. After the first four hits, the flame and smoke spread so fast that on the second run the pilots had difficulty in even seeing the stern of the ship, and there was a circle of flames about 150 yards round the wreck. The pilots estimated that the black, dense smoke rose to 8,000 feet and the line of attack had to be varied to avoid it. Altogether, about thirty of the forty bombs they dropped scored hits before the "Buccaneers" flew back to Brawdy in Pembrokeshire.

Then, to keep the fires burning, twenty-six "Hunter" fighter jets from the Royal Air Force station at Chivenor in North Devon came in, two at a time, jettisoning under-wing fuel tanks, each containing 100 gallons of kerosene. Altogether 5,400 gallons of this jet fuel were dropped, just up-wind of the blazing sea, so that as the tanks split on hitting the sea their contents were drifted into the blaze. The fire blazed for four and a half hours.

On Wednesday 29 March it was clear that the Torrey Canyon

had been badly battered, but the coastguard at St Mary's could still see part of the bows, half the midships hull, two derrick posts and the funnel. Oil was still coming away. So was wreckage from the tanker. A lifeboat was later washed up on Sennen beach, and the research ship Sarsia from the Marine Biological Association station at Plymouth, which was investigating the damage to marine life in the area, reported floating wreckage from the Torrey Canyon on the Tuesday, which the Utrecht went to investigate. It was the last message from the Dutch tug; she steamed away to a towing job on the French coast.

At 12.20 p.m. three "Hunter" jets from the RAF station at West Raynham in Norfolk went in at fifty feet with napalm bombs which started fires, though they were seen to be dying down within ten minutes. At 1.30 p.m. two more "Hunters" opened up the wreck with rockets and set the stern ablaze. At 2 p.m. the "Buccaneers" were back again with 1,000-lb bombs, and later both the "Hunters" and naval "Sea Vixens" from Yeovilton in Somerset used more napalm, still with no great success. A swoop of twenty-seven "Hunters" jettisoning their wing-tanks set the sea alight and at 4 pm three "Buccaneers" returned with more 1,000-lb bombs. One produced an enormous explosion which sent a solid core of flame 500 feet into the air. The coastguards at St Mary's, watching from their tall tower at Telegraph, reported three separate explosions in the stern section. The ship was now burning over her full length. The last strike of the day was by three "Buccaneers" at 7 p.m. with high-explosive, but though direct hits were scored again, the bombs did not start fires. Smoke was still coming from the wreck and the sea, but there was no fire that evening.

A reconnaissance on Friday morning showed no trace of oil within five miles of the ship, and none issuing from her. But the pattern of the previous days was repeated, with Fleet Air Arm "Sea Vixens" and "Buccaneers", and Royal Air Force "Hunters" putting in high-explosives and napalm throughout the afternoon. A strike by the "Buccaneers" at 3 p.m. was specifically aimed at what was believed to be the last full oil-tank. As the day wore on the reports were of hits being scored but no significant fires being started. There was nothing left to burn. Service chiefs who watched

*the bombing from a helicopter described the final attacks as an
insurance. Air Vice-Marshal John Lapsley said, "We are satisfied
beyond reasonable doubt that the source of oil on the ship is now
destroyed". The Seven Stones lightship was towed back to her
station, the cliff-top crowds, who had cheered the hits, disappeared.*

*It has been estimated that 161 1,000-lb bombs, 11,000 gallons
of kerosene, 3,000 gallons of napalm and 16 rockets were aimed
at the wreck. The oil had been destroyed but the ship was still
there, battered, broken, but still recognizable. She was a menace
no longer. A month after the stranding, the bow section disappeared. Early on Friday 21 April the stern went. A coastguard
said:*

One minute it was there, the next it was not. I don't think it
has gone down very far; we can still see the sea breaking
where the submerged part of the hull is.

*David Axford was a communicator aboard the destroyer, HMS
Daring. HMS Daring was sent to the scene.*

Axford:

HMS *Daring* was in the middle of her work-up at Portland.
This is when the ship and the men are put through every
eventuality conceived, to test whether the men and the ship
are proficient to become part of the operational fleet.

Given that the following dates of the bombing are accurate,
we sailed in the early hours of Monday morning, that must
have been the Easter Monday 27 March 1967.
Approximately seven sailors had just got off a coach at 04:00
from weekend leave and, realizing what was happening they
quickly ducked behind one of the buildings on the pier, not
wanting to go to sea that day. The First Lieutenant had
spotted them from the *Daring*'s bridge wing and shouted at
them to get on board. As soon as they were onboard the
gangway was raised and the ship sailed. The ship had been at

8 hours notice for steam and yet achieved the impossible by being ready for sea within just 3 hours!

There were quite a few ships' company left behind, as leave didn't finish until 07:30 that morning. Only half the ship's cooks were onboard. The communicators onboard worked watches of six hours on and six hours off for the three days we were required to be on station.

Daring's presence was required as a range safety ship to keep all unwanted shipping well away from the *Torrey Canyon* wreck. There were a large number of Russian trawlers (bristling with aerials) all jockeying for a good position to view the bombing, presumably.

On Tuesday 28 March 1967 the Fleet Air Arm sent Buccaneers from Lossiemouth to drop forty-two 1,000-lb bombs on the wreck. This was followed by the Royal Air Force in sending Hunter jets to drop cans of aviation fuel to make the oil blaze. Seventy-five per cent of the bombs were on target and both sections of the wreck were on fire.

However, exceptionally high tides had put the blaze out and it took further attacks by Sea Vixens from the Naval Air Station at Yeovilton and Buccaneers from the Naval Air Station at Brawdy as well as more RAF Hunters with napalm to ignite the oil until the wreck was free from oil.

Crowds of holidaymakers were watching the spectacle from the shoreline at Lands End. Though the bombing was declared a success, the Press made much of the twenty-five per cent of misses on a stationary target.

After *Daring* had completed her Guard ship duties we then sailed back to Portland to continue with our work-up.

On 26 March, one week after the tanker ran aground, oil hit the beaches of West Cornwall. It was an unprecedented pollution problem. They used a kerosene based detergent. The bombing had disposed of about half the cargo. Emulsifying by detergent proved to be the most successful way of breaking up the oil at sea and cleaning the beaches.

Soldiers and civilians struggled to repel the tide of oil.

Under the headline "Oil winning on the beaches", the
Guardian's *correspondent Dennis Barker wrote:*

. . . the results seem puny and almost pathetic. Trying to
track down and sink with detergents the sinuous slabs of oil
nearly two feet thick which are now forming on this coast is
like trying to pick up quicksilver with boxing gloves – and
moreover without practice. The attempts at dealing with the
oil already landed, in the few cases where the efforts have
been made, have been even more chaotic and unsuccessful.

Barker described soldiers trying to clear a beach:

At one point the sea-sprays – 15-ft long tubes flung out over
the sides of ships – were so useless that the men began
emptying the 45-gallon drums of detergent straight over the
side.

Barker continued:

It is all a deadly serious business, but there is bound to be
something of the Heath Robinson about it. The people
whose livelihoods are theatened are not slow to point this out.
One cannot reassure them.

*The wind that had brought the oil also took it away. A north wind
drove it south towards the French coast. It began to come ashore
on the Cherbourg peninsula from 5 April. The pollution was most
serious on the Channel Island of Guernsey.*

*The incident prompted the British Government to take the
initiative in organizing an early meeting of the Intergovernmental
Maritime Consultative Organization to consider necessary
changes in international maritime law and practice. Relevant
maritime laws were considered to be too complex and out of date in
many respects.*

An estimated 25,000 birds died as a result of the Torrey
Canyon *spill because the incident coincided with their northerly*

migration. The coasts of southern England and Brittany are nesting beaches for a variety of seabirds such as guillemots, razor-bills, shags, puffins, and Great Northern divers. Thousands of oiled birds were picked up from the beaches for treatment, but the survival rate was only around one per cent due to ingestion of oil, pneumonia, and improper handling and cleaning.

It was the first disaster of this type. All sorts of emergency measures were attempted. Some of the emergency measures made matters worse. In particular, some of the chemical dispersants sprayed onto the oil slicks were more lethal for life than the original oil.

It was the first incident to draw attention to the dangers of dispersants. Contamination by oil mixed with dispersants was worse than contamination by just the oil. Many herbivores, such as limpets and barnacles, were killed due to the toxicity of the dispersant.

Exxon Valdez
24 March 1989

On 24 March 1989 the oil tanker, Exxon Valdez, ran aground on Bligh Reef in Prince William Sound, Alaska. Millions of gallons of crude oil spilt into Prince William Sound. The state of Alaska set up a commission to investigate the accident. Oil had flowed through the trans-Alaska pipeline for over ten years. During that time there had been few serious incidents. This experience gave little reason to suspect impending disaster. The industry was therefore largely self-regulated. The Final Report of the Alaska Oil Spill Commission stated:

No one anticipated any unusual problems as the *Exxon Valdez* left the Alyeska Pipeline Terminal at 9.12 p.m., Alaska Standard Time, on 23 March 1989. The 987-foot ship, second newest in Exxon Shipping Company's 20-tanker fleet, was loaded with 53,094,510 gallons (1,264,155 barrels)

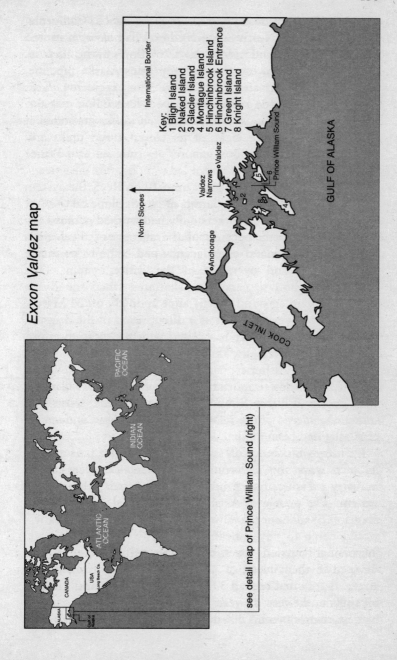

Exxon Valdez map

see detail map of Prince William Sound (right)

Key:
1 Bligh Island
2 Naked Island
3 Glacier Island
4 Montague Island
5 Hinchinbrook Island
6 Hinchinbrook Entrance
7 Green Island
8 Knight Island

International Border

North Slopes

Valdez Narrows

Valdez

Anchorage

Prince William Sound

GULF OF ALASKA

COOK INLET

PACIFIC OCEAN

INDIAN OCEAN

ATLANTIC OCEAN

CANADA

USA

ALASKA

of North Slope crude oil bound for Long Beach, California. Tankers carrying North Slope crude oil had safely transited Prince William Sound more than 8,700 times in the 12 years since oil began flowing through the trans-Alaska pipeline, with no major disasters and few serious incidents. This experience gave little reason to suspect impending disaster. Yet less than three hours later, the *Exxon Valdez* grounded at Bligh Reef, rupturing eight of its eleven cargo tanks and spewing some 10.8 million gallons of crude oil into Prince William Sound.

Until the *Exxon Valdez* piled onto Bligh Reef, the system designed to carry 2 million barrels of North Slope oil to West Coast and Gulf Coast markets daily had worked perhaps too well. At least partly because of the success of the Valdez tanker trade, a general complacency had come to permeate the operation and oversight of the entire system. That complacency and success were shattered when the *Exxon Valdez* ran hard aground shortly after midnight on 24 March.

No human lives were lost as a direct result of the disaster, though four deaths were associated with the cleanup effort. Indirectly, however, the human and natural losses were immense – to fisheries, subsistence livelihoods, tourism, wildlife. The most important loss for many who will never visit Prince William Sound was the aesthetic sense that something sacred in the relatively unspoiled land and waters of Alaska had been defiled.

Industry's insistence on regulating the Valdez tanker trade its own way, and government's incremental accession to industry pressure, had produced a disastrous failure of the system. The people of Alaska's Southcentral coast – not to mention Exxon and the Alyeska Pipeline Service Company – would come to pay a heavy price. The American people, increasingly anxious over environmental degradation and devoted to their image of Alaska's wilderness, reacted with anger. A spill that ranked 34th on a list of the world's largest oil spills in the past 25 years came to be seen as the nation's biggest environmental disaster since Three Mile Island.

The *Exxon Valdez* had reached the Alyeska Marine Terminal at 11.30 p.m. on March 22 to take on cargo. It carried a crew of 19 plus the captain. Third Mate Gregory Cousins, who became a central figure in the grounding, was relieved of watch duty at 11.50 p.m. Ship and terminal crews began loading crude oil onto the tanker at 5.05 a.m. on 23 March and increased loading to its full rate of 100,000 barrels an hour by 5.30 a.m. Chief Mate James R. Kunkel supervised the loading.

23 March 1989 was a rest day of sorts for some members of the *Exxon Valdez* crew. Capt. Joseph Hazelwood, chief engineer Jerry Glowacki and radio officer Joel Roberson left the *Exxon Valdez* about 11.00 a.m., driven from the Alyeska terminal into the town of Valdez by marine pilot William Murphy, who had piloted the *Exxon Valdez* into port the previous night and would take it back out through Valdez Narrows on its fateful trip to Bligh Reef. When the three ship's officers left the terminal that day, they expected the *Exxon Valdez*'s sailing time to be 10 p.m. that evening. The posted sailing time was changed, however, during the day, and when the party arrived back at the ship at 8.24 p.m., they learned the sailing time had been fixed at 9 p.m.

Hazelwood spent most of the day conducting ship's business, shopping and, according to testimony before the National Transportation Safety Board (NTSB), drinking alcoholic beverages with the other ship's officers in at least two Valdez bars. Testimony indicated Hazelwood drank non-alcoholic beverages that day at lunch, a number of alcoholic drinks late that afternoon while relaxing in a Valdez bar, and at least one more drink at a bar while the party waited for pizza to take with them back to the ship.

Loading of the *Exxon Valdez* had been completed for an hour by the time the group returned to the ship. They left Valdez by taxi cab at about 7.30 p.m., got through Alyeska terminal gate security at 8.24 p.m. and boarded ship. Radio officer Roberson, who commenced prevoyage tests and checks in the radio room soon after arriving at the ship, later

said no one in the group going ashore had expected the ship
to be ready to leave as soon as they returned.

Both the cab driver and the gate security guard later testi-
fied that no one in the party appeared to be intoxicated. A
ship's agent who met with Hazelwood after he got back on
the ship said it appeared the captain may have been drinking
because his eyes were watery, but she did not smell alcohol
on his breath. Ship's pilot Murphy, however later indicated
that he did detect the odour of alcohol on Hazelwood's
breath.

Hazelwood's activities in town that day and on the ship
that night would become a key focus of accident inquiries,
the cause of a state criminal prosecution, and the basis of
widespread media sensation. Without intending to minimize
the impact of Hazelwood's actions, however, one basic
conclusion of this report is that the grounding at Bligh Reef
represents much more than the error of a possibly drunken
skipper: it was the result of the gradual degradation of
oversight and safety practices that had been intended, 12
years before, to safeguard and backstop the inevitable
mistakes of human beings.

Third Mate Cousins performed required tests of navigational, mechanical and safety gear at 7.48 p.m., and all
systems were found to be in working order. The *Exxon Valdez*
slipped its last mooring line at 9.12 p.m. and, with the
assistance of two tugboats, began manoeuvring away from
the berth. The tanker's deck log shows it was clear of the
dock at 9.21 p.m.

The ship was under the direction of pilot Murphy and
accompanied by a single tug for the passage through Valdez
Narrows, the constricted harbour entrance about 7 miles
from the berth. According to Murphy, Hazelwood left the
bridge at 9.35 p.m. and did not return until about 11.10
p.m., even though Exxon company policy requires two ship's
officers on the bridge during transit of Valdez Narrows.

The passage through Valdez Narrows proceeded unevent-
fully. At 10.49 p.m. the ship reported to the Valdez Vessel

Traffic Centre that it had passed out of the narrows and was increasing speed. At 11:05 p.m. Murphy asked that Hazelwood be called to the bridge in anticipation of his disembarking from the ship, and at 11.10 p.m. Hazelwood returned. Murphy disembarked at 11.24 p.m., with assistance from Third Mate Cousins. While Cousins was helping Murphy and then helping stow the pilot ladder, Hazelwood was the only officer on the bridge and there was no lookout even though one was required, according to an NTSB report.

At 11.25 p.m. Hazelwood informed the Vessel Traffic Centre that the pilot had departed and that he was increasing speed to sea speed. He also reported that "judging, ah, by our radar, we'll probably divert from the TSS [traffic separation scheme] and end up in the inbound lane if there is no conflicting traffic." The traffic centre indicated concurrence, stating there was no reported traffic in the inbound lane.

The traffic separation scheme is designed to do just that – separate incoming and outgoing tankers in Prince William Sound and keep them in clear, deep waters during their transit. It consists of inbound and outbound lanes, with a half-mile-wide separation zone between them. Small icebergs from nearby Columbia Glacier occasionally enter the traffic lanes. Captains had the choice of slowing down to push through them safely or deviating from their lanes if traffic permitted. Hazelwood's report, and the Valdez traffic centre's concurrence, meant the ship would change course to leave the western outbound lane, cross the separation zone and, if necessary, enter the eastern inbound lane to avoid floating ice. At no time did the *Exxon Valdez* report or seek permission to depart farther east from the inbound traffic lane; but that is exactly what it did.

At 11.30 p.m. Hazelwood informed the Valdez traffic centre that he was turning the ship toward the east on a heading of 200 degrees and reducing speed to "wind my way through the ice" (engine logs, however, show the vessel's speed continued to increase). At 11.39 Cousins plotted a fix that showed the ship in the middle of the traffic separation scheme. Hazelwood ordered a further course change to a heading of 180 degrees (due south) and, according to the helmsman, directed that the ship be placed on autopilot. The second course change was not reported to the Valdez traffic center. For a total of 19 or 20 minutes the ship sailed south-through the inbound traffic lane, then across its easterly boundary and on toward its peril at Bligh Reef. Traveling at approximately 12 knots, the *Exxon Valdez* crossed the traffic lanes' easterly boundary at 11.47 p.m.

At 11.52 p.m. the command was given to place the ship's engine on "load program up" – a computer program that, over a span of 43 minutes, would increase engine speed from 55 RPM to sea speed full ahead at 78.7 RPM. After conferring with Cousins about where and how to return the ship to its designated traffic lane, Hazelwood left the bridge. The time, according to NTSB testimony, was approximately 11.53 p.m.

By this time Third Mate Cousins had been on duty for six hours and was scheduled to be relieved by Second Mate Lloyd LeCain. But Cousins, knowing LeCain had worked long hours during loading operations during the day, had told the second mate he could take his time in relieving him. Cousins did not call LeCain to awaken him for the midnight-to-4-a.m. watch, instead remaining on duty himself.

Cousins was the only officer on the bridge – a situation that violated company policy and perhaps contributed to the accident. A second officer on the bridge might have been more alert to the danger in the ship's position, the failure of its efforts to turn, the autopilot steering status, and the threat of ice in the tanker lane.

Cousins' duty hours and rest periods became an issue in subsequent investigations. Exxon Shipping Company has said the third mate slept between 1 a.m. and 7.20 a.m. the morning of March 23 and again between 1.30 p.m. and 5 p.m., for a total of nearly 10 hours sleep in the 24 hours preceding the accident. But testimony before the NTSB suggests that Cousins "pounded the deck" that afternoon, that he did paperwork in his cabin, and that he ate dinner starting at 4:30 p.m. before relieving the chief mate at 5 p.m. An NTSB report shows that Cousins' customary in-port watches were scheduled from 5.50 a.m. to 11.50 a.m. and again from 5.50 p.m. to 11.50 p.m. Testimony before the NTSB suggests that Cousins may have been awake and generally at work for up to 18 hours preceding the accident.

The report continued:

It is conceivable, that excessive work hours (sleep deprivation) contributed to an overall impact of fatigue, which in turn contributed to the *Exxon Valdez* grounding.

Manning policies also may have affected crew fatigue. Tankers in the 1950s used to carry a crew of 40 to 42 to manage about 6.3 million gallons of oil. By comparison, the *Exxon Valdez* carried a crew of 19 to transport 53 million gallons of oil.

Minimum vessel manning limits are set by the US Coast Guard, but without any agencywide standard for policy. The Coast Guard has certified Exxon tankers for a minimum of 15 persons (14 if the radio officer is not required). Frank Iarossi, president of Exxon Shipping Company, has stated that his company's policy is to reduce its standard crew complement to 16 on fully automated, diesel-powered vessels by 1990. "While Exxon has defended their actions as an economic decision," the manning report says, "criticism has been levelled against them for manipulating overtime records to better justify reduced manning levels."

Iarossi and Exxon maintain that modern automated vessel technology permits reduced manning without compromise of safety or function. "Yet the literature on the subject suggests that automation does not replace humans in systems, rather, it places the human in a different, more demanding role. Automation typically reduces manual workload but increases mental workload."

Whatever the NTSB or the courts may finally determine

concerning Cousins' work hours that day, manning limits
and crew fatigue have received considerable attention as
contributing factors to the accident. The Alaska Oil Spill
Commission recommends that crew levels be set high enough
not only to permit safe operations during ordinary conditions
– which, in the Gulf of Alaska, can be highly demanding – but
also to provide enough crew backups and rest periods that
crisis situations can be confronted by a fresh, well-supported
crew.

Accounts and interpretations differ as to events on the
bridge from the time Hazelwood left his post to the moment
the *Exxon Valdez* struck Bligh Reef. NTSB testimony by crew
members and interpretations of evidence by the State of
Alaska conflict in key areas, leaving the precise timing of
events still a mystery. But the rough outlines are discernible:

Some time during the critical period before the grounding
during the first few minutes of Good Friday, 24 March,
Cousins plotted a fix indicating it was time to turn the vessel
back toward the traffic lanes. About the same time, lookout
Maureen Jones reported that Bligh Reef light appeared broad
off the starboard bow – i.e., off the bow at an angle of about
45 degrees. The light should have been seen off the port side
(the left side of a ship, facing forward); its position off the
starboard side indicated great peril for a supertanker that was
out of its lanes and accelerating through close waters.
Cousins gave right rudder commands to cause the desired
course change and took the ship off autopilot. He also
phoned Hazelwood in his cabin to inform him the ship was
turning back toward the traffic lanes and that, in the process,
it would be getting into ice. When the vessel did not turn
swiftly enough, Cousins ordered further right rudder with
increasing urgency. Finally, realizing the ship was in serious
trouble, Cousins phoned Hazelwood again to report the
danger – and at the end of the conversation, felt an initial
shock to the vessel. The grounding, described by helmsman
Robert Kagan as "a bumpy ride" and by Cousins as six "very
sharp jolts", occurred at 12.04 a.m.

The vessel came to rest facing roughly southwest, perched across its middle on a pinnacle of Bligh Reef. Eight of eleven cargo tanks were punctured. Computations aboard the *Exxon Valdez* showed that 5.8 million gallons had gushed out of the tanker in the first three and a quarter hours. Weather conditions at the site were, reported to be 33 degrees F, slight drizzle rain/snow mixed, north winds at 10 knots and visibility 10 miles at the time of the grounding.

The *Exxon Valdez* nightmare had begun. Hazelwood – perhaps drunk, certainly facing a position of great difficulty and confusion – would struggle vainly to power the ship off its perch on Bligh Reef. The response capabilities of Alyeska Pipeline Service Company to deal with the spreading sea of oil would be tested and found to be both unexpectedly slow and woefully inadequate. The worldwide capabilities of Exxon Corp. would mobilize huge quantities of equipment and personnel to respond to the spill – but not in the crucial first few hours and days when containment and cleanup efforts are at a premium. The US Coast Guard would demonstrate its prowess at ship salvage, protecting crews and lightering operations, but prove utterly incapable of oil spill containment and response. State and federal agencies would show differing levels of preparedness and command capability. And the waters of Prince William Sound – and eventually more than 1,000 miles of beach in Southcentral Alaska – would be fouled by 10.8 million gallons of crude oil.

After feeling the grounding Hazelwood rushed to the bridge, arriving as the ship came to rest. He immediately gave a series of rudder orders in an attempt to free the vessel, and power to the ship's engine remained in the "load program up" condition for about 15 minutes after impact. Chief Mate Kunkel went to the engine control room and determined that eight cargo tanks and two ballast tanks had been ruptured; he concluded the cargo tanks had lost an average of 10 feet of cargo, with approximately 67 feet of cargo remaining in each. He informed Hazelwood of his initial damage assessment and was instructed to perform stability and stress analysis. At

12.19 a.m. Hazelwood ordered that the vessel's engine be reduced to idle speed.

At 12.26 a.m., Hazelwood radioed the Valdez traffic center and reported his predicament to Bruce Blandford, a civilian employee of the Coast Guard who was on duty:

> We've fetched up, ah, hard aground, north of Goose Island, off Bligh Reef and, ah, evidently leaking some oil and we're gonna be here for a while and, ah, if you want, ah, so you're notified.

That report triggered a nightlong cascade of phone calls reaching from Valdez to Anchorage to Houston and eventually around the world as the magnitude of the spill became known and Alyeska and Exxon searched for clean-up machinery and materials.

Hazelwood, meanwhile, was not finished with efforts to power the *Exxon Valdez* off the reef. At approximately 12.30 am, Chief Mate Kunkel used a computer program to determine that though stress on the vessel exceeded acceptable limits, the ship still had required stability. He went to the bridge to advise Hazelwood that the vessel should not go to sea or leave the area. The skipper directed him to return to the control room to continue assessing the damage and to determine available options. At 12.35 pm, Hazelwood ordered the engine back on-and eventually to "full ahead" and began another series of rudder commands in an effort to free the vessel. After running his computer program again another way, Kunkel concluded that the ship did not have acceptable stability without being supported by the reef. The chief mate relayed his new analysis to the captain at I a.m. and again recommended that the ship not leave the area. Nonetheless, Hazelwood kept the engine running until 1.41 a.m., when he finally abandoned efforts to get the vessel off the reef.

Oil was transferred from the *Exxon Valdez* to another tanker, the *Exxon Baton Rouge*, in a successful effort to keep the oil remaining on the *Exxon Valdez* from spilling into Prince William Sound. Only about one-fifth of the oil carried by the *Exxon Valdez* was spilled; the remaining 42 million gallons of oil was safely transferred to the *Baton Rouge*. As the spilled oil moved across the waters of Prince William Sound, recue workers tried to protect especially sensitive locations by surrounding them with protective booms. These booms floated on the surface and were designed to act as a barrier to the oil. It was estimated that 11 million gallons of crude oil spilt across 1,300 miles of coastline.

After the remaining cargo was offloaded, the *Exxon Valdez* was refloated. The vessel was moved to Outside Bay, south-west of Naked Island, where temporary repairs were made. The Exxon Shipping Company was renamed Sea River Shipping Company. Eventually, the *Exxon Valdez* itself was fully repaired and renamed the *Sea River Mediterranean*. It is still used to carry oil across the Atlantic. The ship is now prohibited by law from returning to Prince William Sound.

The National Transportation Safety Board investigated the accident. It decided that the probable causes of the grounding were:

1. The failure of the third mate to properly manoeuvre the vessel, possibly due to fatigue and excessive workload;
2. The failure of the master to provide a proper navigation watch, possibly due to impairment from alcohol;
3. The failure of Exxon Shipping Company to supervise the master and provide a rested and sufficient crew for the *Exxon Valdez*;
4. The failure of the US Coast Guard to provide an effective vessel traffic system;
5. The lack of effective pilot and escort services.

Efforts were made to clean up the area and monitor the damage. The *Exxon Valdez* Oil Spill (EVOS) Trustee Council was established. This was funded by the legal settlement between the State of Alaska, the Federal

Government and Exxon. Its purpose was to develop research, restoration and habitat conservation plans for the affected area.

Clean-up crews found the carcasses of more than 35,000 birds and 1,000 sea otters. The *Exxon Valdez* Oil Spill Trustee Council concluded that most of the animals' remains would have sunk. Therefore, the council estimated the dead wildlife at 250,000 seabirds, 2,800 sea otters, 300 harbour seals, 250 bald eagles, around 22 killer whales, and billions of salmon and herring eggs.

The three-year clean up effort cost Exxon $2.1bn. It is thought that ocean waves cleaned more oil away from Alaska's beaches than the clean up-effort.

Evidence of the oil spill can still be found but much of the shoreline has proved remarkably resilient. Some beaches lost all their plants and animals due to the toxic effects of the oil and the clean-up operations. These beaches have now been recolonized and look similar to those unaffected by the disaster.

Following the disaster, the US Congress enacted the Oil Pollution Act of 1990. This Act called for a ban on single-hull tankers in US waters by 2015. In 1991 the National Research Council produced a report on tanker designs. The report suggested that double-hull ships would prevent oil leaks and operate more safely.

Following the Act and the Report, a UN body, the International Maritime Organization, agreed that most single hull oil tankers should be phased out by 2015. Double-hull rather than single-hull tankers became the industry standard, and nearly all ships in the world maritime oil transportation fleet were expected to have double hulls by about 2020.

But by 2002, single-hull tankers were still much more common than double-hull ships. Two recent oil spills involved single-hull tankers. These were the Erika *in 1999 and the* Prestige *in 2002.*

The *Kursk* Disaster
12 August 2000

The SSGN Kursk, *designated* K141, *was the largest nuclear and most modern submarine in the Russian Northern fleet. She displaced 18k tons. At over 150 metres, she was longer than a 747 jumbo jet. She set sail from her home port of Viajaevo, to take part in manoeuvres in the Arctic/Barents sea. She may have intended to continue on a "base related voyage", a type of "round the world" voyage. 28-year-old Dmitri Kolesnikov was Lieutenant in command.*

At 8.51 a.m. on 12 August 2000 the submarine requested permission to proceed with a torpedo firing exercise and received "Dobro" ("Good").

A Norwegian listening post heard two underwater explosions. NORSAR (Norwegian seismic array) reported two explosions detected at approximately 69°38' N 37°1' E. The first explosion was at 11.29 (Moscow time) and had magnitude of 1.5 on the Richter scale (corresponding to about 100 kg of explosives), and second was at 11.31.

Two American submarines (USS Memphis *and USS* Toledo*) and a British submarine (HMS* Splendid*) were shadowing the exercises; all three submarines registered two underwater explosions.*

Later video film showed massive damage to the front and one side of the Kursk.

A Russian submarine and the Russian cruiser Petr Velikiy *also detected these explosions. At 17.30 Northern Fleet Headquarters sent a radio message to* Kursk*: "Report your co-ordinates and operations." By 23.30, the time allowed for reply had elapsed. Fleet Headquarters declared a state of alarm. Search forces were sent to the area of the submarine's disappearance.*

Two IL-38 search aircraft detected oil at the Kursk's *last known position.*

On 13 August a Russian Deep Sea Rescue Vehicle discovered the submarine lying on the seabed. Russian rescue attempts continued without success on 14 and 15 August.

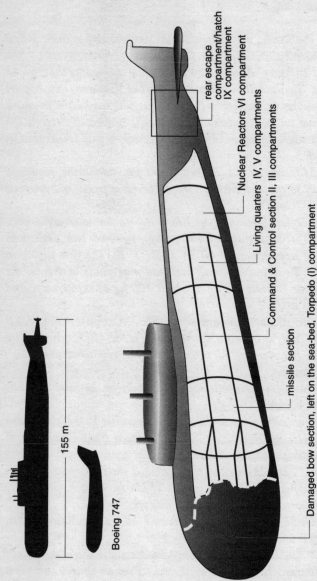

rear escape compartment/hatch IX compartment

Nuclear Reactors VI compartment

Living quarters IV, V compartments

Command & Control section II, III compartments

missile section

Damaged bow section, left on the sea-bed, Torpedo (I) compartment

SSGN *Kursk*, K-141, sunk 12 April 2000

155 m

Boeing 747

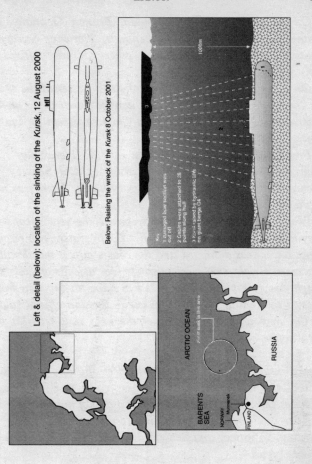

Left & detail (below): location of the sinking of the *Kursk*, 12 August 2000

Below: Raising the wreck of the *Kursk* 8 October 2001

Key
1 damaged bow section was cut off
2 Cables were attached to 26 points along hull
3 *Kursk* raised by hydraulic jacks on giant barge GI4

100m

BARENTS
SEA

ARCTIC OCEAN

Kursk sank in this area

NORWAY

Murmansk

FINLAND

RUSSIA

On 14 and 15 August, Canada, France, Germany, Great Britain, Israel, Italy, the Netherlands, Norway, Sweden, the United States of America and other countries offered their assistance.

On 17 August President Putin of Russia assessed the situation as "heavy, critical". Putin, as Supreme Commander-in-Chief, ordered the Navy Commander-in-Chief to accept foreign assistance.

Finally on Monday, 21 August at 7.45 Norwegian rescuers from the rescue ships Normand Pioneer and Seaway Eagle opened the upper door of the emergency hatch. There was nobody in the air lock.

When the rescuers eventually opened the rear escape hatch they found the whole vessel had filled with water. The reconnaissance tower was damaged and the covers of two missile tubes on the vessel's right side were missing. UK defence officials said a "high energy explosion" appeared to have hit an area from the nose to the central fin of the vessel. A Russian official said most of the crew were in the part of the boat that was hit by the catastrophe.

The Military Council of Northern Fleet officially recognized the fact of the loss of all crew and expressed their condolence to relatives. 23 August was declared as a day of national mourning.

After an on-board mourning ceremony the rescue ships Normand Pioneer and Seaway Eagle left the scene of the wreck on 22 August.

On 22 August the Minister of Defence and the Commander of the Northern Fleet offered to resign. President Putin did not accept their resignations.

On 26 October Norwegian divers started to cut a new opening in the outer hull. This gave them access to the VII compartment. They found a note in the pocket of the dead captain Lieutenant Dmitriy Kolesnikov. Kolesnikov's note was written between 13.34 and 15.45 and was addressed to his relatives. It said:

13.15. All crew of VI, VII and VIII compartments has gone to

IX-th. There are 23 men of us there. We've taken this decision due to accident. Nobody of us can to lift upward . . .

On the reverse side of the note, it said:

15.45. It is dark here, but I'll try to write to the touch. It looks that there are no chances. Percents 10–20. Let us try, that anyone at all will read. There are lists of compartments' crew here, some are in IX-th and will try to escape. Greetings to all. Don't despair.

His wife, Olga, was later told what he had written to her:

I am writing blindly, Olga, my greetings, I love you, don't take it to heart too much.

On 19 August, Olga Kolesnikov had realized that her husband was dead. She said:

I knew all of a sudden that he was no longer alive.

In 2001 the Russians employed a Dutch company to salvage the Kursk. *The Dutch company subcontracted some of the diving work to a British company.*
    On 28 September 2001 Gabor Szabo reported:

Operations to raise the sunken *Kursk* nuclear submarine from the ocean floor were under threat . . . from fresh storms in the Barents Sea.

The lifting of the submarine – which lies 108 metres below the surface with torpedoes, two nuclear reactors and the bodies of 106 sailors – was scheduled to take place Tuesday, but technical delays and rough waters forced the multinational team to scrub the attempt. It is unclear when the lift may take place, though Deputy Prime Minister Ilya Klebanov told journalists that it would happen no earlier than 29 September.

Igor Spassky was head of the Rubin Marine Design Bureau, which had built the Kursk. *He said:*

Why fix a date? We don't control the weather. In making such operations, we shouldn't rush. Everything should be done reliably and consistently, so that we don't regret our haste in the future.

Deep-sea divers ran into problems clearing the holes in the submarine's seventh compartment, to which the lifting cables were to be attached. Pipes and other equipment got in the way. But all 26 of the lifting holes along the hull were cleared. Navy official Igor Dygalo stated:

Early winter storms began in the seas off Murmansk. Winds reached 16 metres per second, whipping up 5-force waves. Divers and other workers on the project had already made adjustments for bad weather but are only prepared to work in waves 4-force or below.

RIA-Novosti reported:

The worsening weather made it impossible for the *Giant 4* barge – which arrived Monday night to raise the *Kursk* and tow it to shore – to position over the wreckage site until Thursday.

The operation is being managed by the Russian Navy, the Rubin Marine Design Bureau and Holland's Mamoet-Smit International, co-ordinating a total of 20 subcontractors and 1,500 workers.

Officials on all sides remain confident, though, that as soon as the weather clears the lifting operation can begin, although Spassky warned journalists as late as 21 September that there could be no certainty that the first compartment – containing unexploded torpedoes – had been completely severed.

After lifting begins, it will take 10 to 12 hours to raise the submarine to the surface and tether it to the *Giant 4*, Spassky said. Once the *Kursk* is secured, it will be towed to dry dock at Roslyakovo, a trip that will take three days.

Once the *Kursk* is in dock, it will be handed over to investigators and technical experts from the federal prosecutor general's office, who will begin work to determine the cause of the accident, according to a statement posted on President Vladimir Putin's Website. Investigators are concentrating on three theories, RIA-Novosti reported: a torpedo malfunction, a collision with another ship and a collision with a World War II-era mine.

Later, the salvage teams will return for the first compartment, the wreckage of which should hold the answers as to exactly why the *Kursk* went down.

Klebanov told RIA-Novosti:

A torpedo exploded on the submarine, but no one knows the reason for that explosion.

Bob Gardiner, an oil industry consultant from Kirkbymoorside, Scotland, was involved with the raising of the submarine Kursk. *He described the salvage operation:*

DSND Subsea Ltd began work on the operation on 3 July 2001, having been appointed by Dutch salvage company Smit-Mammoet. The dive vessel, the DSND *Mayo*, set sail for the Barents Sea on 6 July 2001, picking up Russian divers for saturation training and exercises en route in Kirkenes, Norway and began work at the *Kursk* site on 15 July.

The operation on *Kursk* took a total of 85 days and involved first clearing the seabed around the devastated bow and cutting into the submarine's hull. Having cut into *Kursk* and removed its periscopes, the bow section was removed and gripper guides fitted and installed to the hull to enable the 10,000 tonne submarine to be lifted by *Giant 4* barge, using Mammoet Heavy Lift Technology.

On 8 October 2001, Kursk was successfully raised from the seabed.

DSND had to employ many innovative engineering solutions to the problems of cutting into a huge, tangled mass of steel and debris at a depth of 120 metres. This was achieved by operating the hull cutting grit system at 1500 bar which could then cut through the 2-inch thick, specially hardened steel pressure hull of the Kursk.

Holes were carefully cut into the hull section and gripper mechanisms latched into them to enable the lifting to take place.

Bob Gardiner explained:

Like any big event, it doesn't happen without significant preparation. Before the divers could get into the final stage of fitting the grippers – the mechanism used to secure the lifting equipment to the wreck – dozens of detailed surveys and assessments had to be performed, hundreds of accurate measurements were made, tonnes of steel structures had to be removed and guides had to be precisely fitted before the grippers could be inserted into their respective holes.

Sean Pople, Offshore Project Manager, said:

We were [also] governed by a very tight schedule which had the Arctic winter looming just around the corner.

Despite all of this, the crew never forgot that the *Kursk* was a grave, where many men had perished. Three memorial services were held on *Mayo* and our deepest sympathies were always with their relatives.

Ilya Klebanov was the Russian trade, science and technology minister. He presided over the inquiry into the disaster. On 19 June 2002 he said:

The commission has discounted a collision and a mine. There remains only one version – a torpedo blast.

The *Prestige* Disaster
19 November 2002

The Prestige *left Riga, in Latvia. She was bound for Singapore. She was a 26-year-old, single-hull oil tanker, registered in the Bahamas. She was carrying 70,000 tons of heavy fuel oil. By 13 November, she was off Finistere. She was being battered by Force 8 gales, gusting to Force 9, with 6-metre waves. She sent SOS messages. Spanish Air Sea Rescue helicopters from Vigo lifted off 24 of her crew. Her Greek captain, Apostolos Mangouras, and two other sailors stayed aboard. Later, he was accused of failing to co-operate with the maritime authorities after making a distress call.*

51 km from the coast, her hull was breached by a 15-metre crack. The Spanish authorities subsequently blamed metal fatigue and the poor condition of the 26-year-old ship. The ship drifted to 15 km off the coast, trailing a long oil slick. By 18 November the Smit Tak salvage company was using four tugs in an attempt to turn the ship to prevent it from splitting. Both Portugal and Spain had banned it from their entering their ports. The tugs could only tow it south-west. Oil was already coming ashore from Finistere to La Coruna. The ship was lying low in the water, listing at 45° and being battered by waves. The breach in the hull widened. Fierce seas ripped off part of the upper deck. At 07:00 on 19 November the Prestige *broke apart. The rear section which contained six oil tanks sank in 3,600 metres of water. The bow section slowly turned and pointed vertically at the sky before it, too, sank. 1.3–2.6 million tons of heavy oil was released while the ship was still afloat. The Spanish government was hoping that the increased pressure and lower temperatures on the seabed would solidify the remaining oil.*

A cable news reporter commented:

The estimates are that about 75 per cent of the cargo went down. We do not know how much of that has floated to the surface. Everybody is worried about the second phase.

Location of the *Prestige* and *Erika* disasters

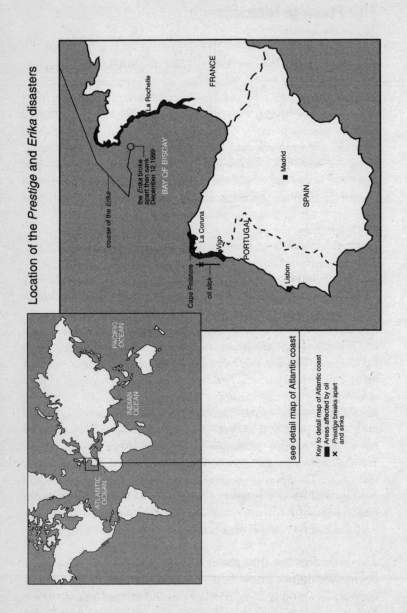

the *Erika* broke
apart then sank
December 12 1999

course of the *Erika*

La Rochelle

FRANCE

BAY OF BISCAY

Madrid

SPAIN

La Coruna

Vigo

PORTUGAL

Cape Finistère

oil slick

Lisbon

PACIFIC
OCEAN

INDIAN
OCEAN

ATLANTIC
OCEAN

see detail map of Atlantic coast

Key to detail map of Atlantic coast

■ Areas affected by oil

✖ *Prestige* breaks apart
and sinks

A Greenpeace spokesperson said:

Every evidence shows that the oil could be leaking from the wreck. The ship has sunk to a depth of 3,000 metres so it is impossible to do anything now.

Maria José Caballero, of Greenpeace's coastal protection project, asserted:

It's a time bomb at the bottom of the sea . . . There's nothing that makes us believe it won't finally burst and leak all its oil . . . It's insoluble, viscous and sticky, which makes it difficult for the clean-up operations.

Another News Agency added:

Ecologists have been trying to cope with the dozens of birds being washed up smothered in tar, while hundreds of soldiers and volunteers attempted to clean the beaches. Retired fisherman Jose Camano said: "This is going to take 10 years to recover. They try and clean it up but the sea brings in more. This means complete ruin for us. Who will buy our fish now?"

On 10 December the Spanish government finally admitted that the tanker was still leaking 125 tonnes of fuel oil a day from some 14 separate cracks. José Manuel Martinez, head fisherman in the Galician town of Finisterre, said:

The Portuguese had said it all before and the moment came when [the Spanish government] just couldn't hide it any more. They had to say it, they knew they were losing.

The Spanish government was heavily criticized for its handling of the Prestige *affair. 200,000 people demonstrated in La Coruna against the Spanish government. When the captain, Apostolos Mangouras, was released on bail, he was hailed as a hero by his fellow sailors. It was the Spanish government who were regarded as the villains for their reluctance to assist his damaged vessel.*

The clean up operation used a series of techniques:

1. Detergents were sprayed from the air offshore.
2. Skimmers were deployed offshore.
3. Booms were deployed offshore to catch and collect the oil before it came ashore.
4. Volunteers scraped the oil off the sand onshore.
5. Sand and shingle coated with oil were lifted off the shore for washing and decontamination elsewhere.
6. High pressure hoses were used to blast oil off rocks onshore.

By 9 December 2002, clean-up operations had collected more than 12,000 tonnes of oil from the sea, plus around 3,000 tonnes from local beaches. Blobs of oil had also appeared hundreds of kilometres away in the regions of Asturias, Cantabria and the Basque country, blackening the coastline.

By July 2003, the Spanish government were considering various options for removing the remaining oil from the wreck. A major offshore clean-up operation was being carried out using vessels from Spain and nine other European countries. The oil from the Prestige *was affecting the Atlantic coast from Vigo in Spain to La Rochelle in France. On-shore clean-up operations had been carried out along about 1,000 km of shoreline. Around 117,000 tonnes of oil waste had been collected in Spain and some 16,500 tonnes in France.*

The *Tricolor*
14 December 2002

The Tricolor *was a 50,000-tonne, 200-metre vehicle carrier. It was built in 1987 and sailed under the Norwegian flag. On 14 December 2002, the* Tricolor *was carrying 2,862 cars through the English channel. During the early morning, in thick fog, it was collided with the* Kariba *20 miles north of Dunkirk. The* Tricolor *sank as a result of the impact. The* Kariba *was a container ship, built in 1982, which sailed under the Bahamian flag. The* Kariba *was badly damaged but made its way safely to Antwerp.*

The Tricolor *went down within 90 minutes. The 24 crewmen of the* Tricolor *scrambled into lifeboats. The* Tricolor *was declared a total loss.*

Salvage work began on 15 December. The wreck lay in 25 m of water. A team of Dutch divers was sent down to investigate it. The wreck was an immediate hazard to other vessels because the waters in which she sank were so shallow. A beacon was placed on top of the sunken vessel.

Despite this, on 16 December, between 2 a.m. and 3 a.m., another ship, collided with the wreck of the Tricolor. *This was the* Nicola, *a 3,000-tonne cargo ship registered in the Dutch Antilles. The* Nicola *stuck fast on top of the wreck while authorities waited for the next tide to help float it off. Two tugboats pulled the* Nicola *clear before high tide. Its crew were not hurt.*

On 2 January 2003 the Scotsman *newspaper reported that another ship had collided with the wreck of the* Tricolor. *The* Scotsman:

A ship carrying 70,000 tonnes of highly flammable gas oil last night collided with the submerged car transporter which sank in the English Channel two weeks ago.

The Dover coastguard said the Turkish-registered *Vicky* hit the *Tricolor* at about 7:30 p.m. last night and became stuck on top of it. French officials were co-ordinating an emergency operation following the accident, which happened in one of the world's busiest shipping lanes.

The master of the *Vicky* said he did not believe the 24 crew members needed to be evacuated from the ship, which was listing 10 degrees to its port side. There were no reported injuries.

The *Vicky* floated off the *Tricolor* during high tide just after 10 p.m. and was last night anchored one mile north of the wreck where a damage inspection was being carried out.

Three tug boats, including one which is English, and a warship from the French navy were on standby nearby.

The *Vicky* is the second vessel to strike the submerged *Tricolor*, which was carrying 2,862 BMWs, Volvos and Saabs worth an estimated £30 million when it sank off the French port of Dunkirk on 14 December.

The *Vicky* was built in 1981. It is a single-hulled, double-bottomed vessel, meaning it has an extra layer of metal around the base of the hull.

It was not yet known how badly damaged the hull was, or whether the vessel was leaking its load of kerosene. But eyewitnesses described a smell of fuel in the air.

The coastguard said it was not yet known if there was any imminent danger of the *Vicky*'s highly flammable oil igniting, or whether the ship was sinking.

Andrew Linington, a spokesman for the maritime union NUMAST, said he was "appalled" to hear of the latest accident. "About 90 per cent of accidents like this are the result of the human factor," he said. "People are the key to shipping safety and it's time attention was drawn to the people on board ships and the conditions they work under. There is a constant drive to reduce crewing levels and people can be working 80 to 90 hours a week on busy waterways like these."

The 243-metre-long, 43,000-tonne tanker was sailing from Antwerp in Belgium to New York when it struck the ship.

The French authorities have been accused of not doing enough to warn other ships about the *Tricolor*'s whereabouts.

The Dutch firm Smit Salvage, which was overseeing the recovery of *Tricolor*, believed adequate warnings were given.

The French maritime prefecture has defended its actions regarding the recovery operation, saying the position of the *Tricolor* had already been marked by two buoys.

A salvage consortium, Combinatie Salvage Tricolor, *was formed to remove the wreck of the* Tricolor. *On 31 July 2003 the salvage consortium reported:*

It is with pleasure that the "Combinatie Salvage *Tricolor*" can report that the first cut of the *Tricolor* has been completed. This morning at 10.55 a.m. the specially designed cutting wire sliced through the last centimetres, completing a cut exceeding 30 metres. This cut was probably the most difficult cut of the entire cutting operation. This was due the fact that the wire had to go through parts of the engine room and the very thick propeller shaft.

At this stage the sheerlegs (floating cranes) *Asian Hercules II* and *Rambiz* are being positioned alongside the first section. Later today and tomorrow they will be connected to this section. Weather permitting, the tandem-lift of this section will be executed during the course of the weekend. The sheerlegs will place the section, weighing approximately 3,000 tonnes, on top of the semi-submersible barge *Giant 4*.

The barge will transport the section to specially prepared sites in Zeebrugge where the cargo will be disposed. At those sites, any materials that may have a detrimental environmental impact will be removed. The cargo will then be dismantled and destroyed.

Unexplained

Jonah

The story of Jonah is taken from the Authorized (King James) version of the Holy Bible.

Chapter 1
1. Now the word of the LORD came unto Jonah the son of Amittai, saying
2. Arise, go to Nineveh, that great city, and cry against it; for their wickedness is come up before me.
3. But Jonah rose up to flee unto Tarshish from the presence of the LORD and went down to Joppa; and he found a ship going to Tarshish: so he paid the fare thereof, and went down into it, to go with them unto Tarshish from the presence of the LORD.
4. But the LORD sent out a great wind into the sea, and there was a mighty tempest in the sea, so that the ship was like to be broken.
5. Then the mariners were afraid, and cried every man unto his god, and cast forth the wares that were in the ship into the sea, to lighten it of them. But Jonah was gone down into the sides of the ship; and he lay and was fast asleep.
6. So the shipmaster came to him, and said unto him What

meanest thou, O sleeper? arise, call upon thy God, if so be that God will think upon us, that we perish not.

7. And they said every one to his fellow, Come, and let us cast lots, that we may know for whose cause this evil is upon us. So they cast lots, and the lot fell upon Jonah.

8. Then said they unto him, Tell us, we pray thee, for whose cause this evil it upon us; What it thine occupation? and whence comest thou? what is thy country? and of what people art thou?

9. And he said unto them I am an Hebrew; and I fear the LORD, the God of heaven, which hath made the sea and the dry land.

10. Then were the men exceedingly afraid, and said unto him, Why hast thou done this? For the men knew that he fled from the presence of the LORD, because he had told them.

11. Then said they unto him, What shall we do unto thee, that the sea may he calm unto us? for the sea wrought, and was tempestuous.

12. And he said unto them, Take me up, and cast me forth into the sea; so shall the sea be calm unto you: for I know that for my sake this great tempest is upon you.

13. Nevertheless the men rowed hard to bring it to the land; but they could not: for the sea wrought and was tempestuous against them.

14. Wherefore they cried unto the LORD, and said, We beseech thee, O LORD, we beseech thee, let us not perish for this man's life, and lay not upon us innocent blood: for thou, O LORD, hast done as it pleased thee.

15. So they took up Jonah, and cast him forth into the sea: and the sea ceased from her raging.

16. Then the men feared the LORD exceedingly, and offered a sacrifice unto the LORD, and made vows.

17. Now the LORD had prepared a great fish to swallow up Jonah. And Jonah was in the belly of the fish three day and three nights.

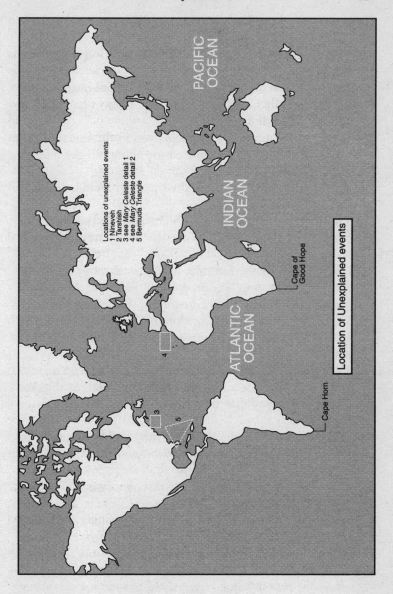

Locations of unexplained events
1 Nineveh
2 Tarshish
3 see *Mary Celeste* detail 1
4 see *Mary Celeste* detail 2
5 Bermuda Triangle

PACIFIC OCEAN

INDIAN OCEAN

ATLANTIC OCEAN

Cape of Good Hope

Cape Horn

Location of Unexplained events

Chapter 2

1. Then Jonah prayed unto the LORD his God out of the fish's belly.
2. And said, I cried by reason of mine affliction unto the LORD, and he heard me; and of the belly of hell cried I, and thou heardest my voice.
3. For thou hadst cast me into the deep in the midst of the seas; and the floods compassed me about: all thy billows and thy waves passed over me.
4. Then I said I am cast out of thy sight; yet I will look again toward thy holy temple.
5. The waters compassed me about, even to the soul: the depth closed me round about, the weeds were wrapped about my head.
6. I went down to the bottoms of the mountains; the earth with her bars was about me for ever: yet hast thou brought up my life from corruption, O Lord my God.
7. When my Soul fainted within me I remembered the LORD: and my prayer came in unto thee, into thine holy temple.
8. They that observe lying vanities forsake their own mercy.
9. But I will sacrifice unto thee with the voice of thanksgiving; I will pay that that I have vowed. Salvation is of the LORD.
10. And the LORD spake unto the fish, and it vomited out Jonah upon the dry land.

Jonah preached to the Ninevites and they repented. God spared them. Jonah was not pleased. This was why he had been reluctant to go to Nineveh in the first place. While Jonah waited to see what would happen to the city, he enjoyed the shade of a gourd tree. So God sent a worm to eat the tree so Jonah had no shade. He prayed that he might die.

God replied that if Jonah regretted the tree but not the city of Nineveh. why shouldn't He have pity on the people of Nineveh.

The Flying Dutchman
1821

The original story of the Flying Dutchman comes from Jal's Scènes de la Vie Maritime:

Once upon a time, a good many years ago, there was a ship's captain who feared neither God nor His Saints. He is said to have been a Dutchman, but I do not know, nor does it greatly matter, from what town he came. He happened once to be making a voyage to the South. All went well until he came near to the Cape of Good Hope, where he ran into a head wind strong enough to blow the horns off a bull. The ship was in great danger, and everyone began to say to the Captain: "Captain, we must turn back. If you insist on continuing to try to round the Cape we shall be lost. We shall inevitably perish, and there is no priest on board to give us absolution."

But the Captain laughed at the fears of his crew and passengers, and began to sing songs so horrible and blasphemous that they might well have attracted the lightning to his mast a hundred times over. Then he calmly smoked his pipe and drank his beer as though he was seated in a tavern at home. His people renewed their entreaties to him to turn back, but the more they implored him the more obstinate he became. His masts were broken, his sails had been carried away, but he merely laughed as a man might who has had a piece of good news.

So the Captain continued to treat with equal contempt the violence of the storm, the protests of the crew and the fears of the passengers, and when his men attempted to force him to make for the shelter of a bay near by, he flung the ringleader overboard, But even as he did so the clouds opened and a Form alighted on the quarterdeck of the ship. This Form is said to have been the Almighty Himself. The crew and passengers were stricken with fear, but the Captain went on smoking his pipe, and did not even touch his cap when the Form addressed him.

"Captain" said the Form, "you are very stubborn."

"And you're a rascal," cried the Captain. "Who wants a peaceful passage? I don't. I'm asking nothing from you, so clear out of this unless you want your brains blown out."

The Form gave no other answer than a shrug of the shoulders. The Captain then snatched up a pistol, cocked it and fired; but the bullet, instead of reaching its target, pierced his hand. His fury knew no bounds. He leaped up to strike the Form in the face with his fist, but his arm dropped limply to his side, as though paralysed. In his impotent rage he cursed and blasphemed and called the good God all sorts of impious names.

But the Form said to him: "Henceforth you are accursed, condemned to sail on for ever without rest or anchorage or port of any kind. You shall have neither beer nor tobacco. Gall shall be your drink and red-hot iron your meat. Of your crew your cabin-boy alone shall remain with you; horns shall grow out of his forehead, and he shall have the muzzle of a tiger and skin rougher than that of a dog-fish."

The Captain groaned, but the Form continued: "It shall ever be your watch, and when you wish, you will not be able to sleep, for directly you close your eyes a sword shall pierce your body. And since it is your delight to torment sailors, you shall torment them."

The Captain smiled. "For you shall be the evil spirit of the sea. You shall traverse all latitudes without respite or repose, and your ship shall bring misfortune to all who sight it."

"Amen to that! " cried the Captain with a shout of laughter. "And on the Day of Judgment Satan shall claim you."

"A fig for Satan!" was all the Captain answered.

The Almighty disappeared, and the Dutchman found himself alone with his cabin-boy, who was already changed as had been predicted. The rest of his crew had vanished.

From that day forward the Flying Dutchman has sailed the seas, and it is his pleasure to plague poor mariners. He casts away their ship on an uncharted shoal, sets them on a false course and then shipwrecks them. He turns their wine sour and all their food into beans. Sometimes he will send letters on board the ships he meets, and if the Captain tries to read them he is lost. Or an empty boat will draw alongside the Phantom Ship and disappear, a sure sign of ill-fortune. He can change at will the appearance of his ship, so as not to be recognized; and round him he has collected a crew as cursed as himself, all the criminals, pirates and cowards of the sea.

In 1821 a small squadron, including the Barracouta *brig, was sent to explore the coasts of Arabia, Africa and Madagascar. In the course of the voyage the squadron separated. Captain Owen, who was in HMS* Severn, *recorded the following episode:*

In the evening 6 April, when off Port Danger, the *Barracouta* was seen about two miles to leeward. Struck with the singularity of her being so soon after us, we at first concluded that it could not be she; but the peculiarity of her rigging and other circumstances convinced us that we were not mistaken. Nay, so distinctly was she seen that many well-known faces could be observed on deck, looking towards our ship.

After keeping thus for some time, we became surprised that she made no effort to join us, but on the contrary stood away. But being so near to the port to which we were both destined, Captain Owen did not attach much importance to this proceeding, and we accordingly continued our course. At sunset it was observed that she hove to and sent a boat away, apparently for the purpose of picking up a man overboard. During the night we could not perceive any light or other indication of her locality. The next morning we anchored in Simon's Bay, where for a whole week we were in anxious expectation of her arrival; but it afterwards appeared that at this very period the *Barracouta* must have been above 300 miles from us, and no other vessel of the same class was ever seen about the Cape.

The Mystery of the *Mary Celeste*
5 December 1872

The Mary Celeste *was launched in Nova Scotia in 1860. Her original name was* Amazon. *She was 103-ft overall displacing 280 tons and listed as a half-brig. Until 1870 she was involved in several accidents at sea and had several owners. She was purchased for $3,000 at a New York salvage auction. After extensive repairs she was put under American registry and renamed* Mary Celeste.

The new captain of Mary Celeste *was Benjamin Briggs, 37, a master with three previous commands. On 7 November 1872 the ship departed New York with Captain Briggs, his wife, young daughter and a crew of eight. The ship was carrying 1,700 barrels of raw American alcohol bound for Genoa, Italy. The captain, his family and crew were never seen again.*

On 5 December 1872 the Dei Gratia, *a barque sailing from New York to Gibraltar sighted a brig 300 miles from Gibraltar. The* Dei Gratia *received no reply to her hails or signals. The brig appeared to be deserted. The* Dei Gratia *lowered a boat and her captain, second mate and two men pulled across. They saw the name* Mary Celeste, New York *painted on the stern of the brig. They searched the brig but found no one. The ship was in good condition but was derelict. The last recording in the ship's log had been 24 November but the slate log showed that the ship had passed north of the island of St Mary's in the Azores on the morning of 25 November. The* Dei Gratia *towed the derelict brig into Gibraltar.*

Her Majesty's Advocate-General and Proctor for the Queen in her Office of Admiralty, and Attorney-General for Gibraltar, Mr Solly Flood, sent in a report to the British Board of Trade which stated:

I have the honour to acquaint you, for the information of the Privy Council of Trade, that early on the morning of December 13th, part of the crew of the British vessel *Dei Gratia*, bound from New York to Gibraltar for orders,

Approximate courses sailed by the *Mary Celeste* and *Dei Gratia*, 7 Nov. – 5 Dec. 1872

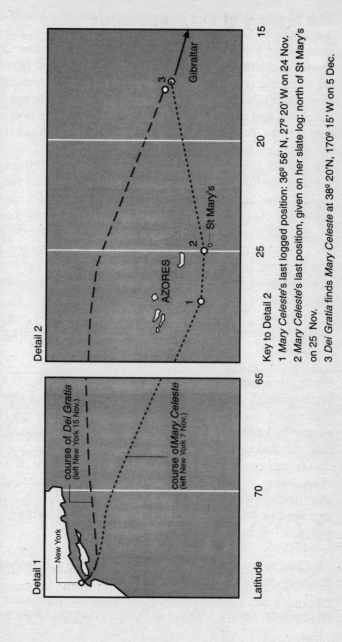

Key to Detail 2

1 *Mary Celeste*'s last logged position: 36° 56' N, 27° 20' W on 24 Nov.

2 *Mary Celeste*'s last position, given on her slate log: north of St Mary's on 25 Nov.

3 *Dei Gratia* finds *Mary Celeste* at 38° 20'N, 170° 15' W on 5 Dec.

brought into this port a brigantine, which they stated they had found on the 5th of that month, in latitude 38 degrees 20 minutes N., longitude 170 15' W., at 3 p.m. sea time, totally abandoned and derelict, and which they supposed from the log to be the American brigantine *Mary Celeste*, bound from New York to Genoa. They stated that the wind being from the north, and the *Dei Gratia*, consequently, on the port tack, they met the derelict with her jib and foremast staysail set on the starboard tack.

I caused the derelict to be arrested in the customary manner upon her arrival, whereupon the Master of the *Dei Gratia*, who had arrived on the evening of 12 December, made his claim for salvage. The second mate of the *Dei Gratia*, and those of her crew who had boarded the derelict, were examined in support of the claim to salvage on the 20th and 21st ult. But the account which they gave of the soundness and good condition of the derelict was so extraordinary that I found it necessary to apply for a survey.

After giving some particulars of the Board appointed, Mr Flood continued:

From that survey it appears that both bows of the derelict had been recently cut by a sharp instrument, but that she was thoroughly sound, staunch, strong and in every way seaworthy and well found; that. she was well provisioned, and that she had encountered no seriously heavy weather; and that no appearance of fire or explosion, or of alarm of fire or of explosion, or any other assignable cause for abandonment was discoverable. A sword, however, was found, which appeared to me to exhibit traces of blood, and to have been wiped before being returned into its scabbard.

Mr Flood goes on to describe how he arranged for a second examination of the ship by a new Board:

all of whom agreed with me in opinion that the injury to the bows had been effected intentionally by a sharp instrument. On examining the starboard top-gallant rail, marks were discovered, apparently of blood, and a mark of a blow, apparently of a sharp axe. On descending through the fore hatch, a barrel, ostensibly of alcohol, appeared to have been tampered with. The vessel's Register, Manifest, and Bills of Lading have not been found, neither has any sextant or chronometer been found. On the other hand, almost the whole personal effects of the master, and, as I believe, of his wife and child, and of the crew, have been found in good order and condition. They are of considerable value.

In 1884 Arthur Conan Doyle, writing under a pseudonym, published a story about a derelict ship which he called Marie Celeste. *It was entitled "J. Habakuk Jephson's Statement". This tale captured the public interest. It recounted the some of the actual events of the* Mary Celeste *with added fictional and provocative details.*

The Mary Celeste *struck a coral reef off Haiti and sank in 1885. It is thought that her captain was trying to collect on the insurance policy. The wreck has been found and identified.*

The Bermuda Triangle
1945

The US Board of Geographic Names does not recognize the Bermuda Triangle as an official name.

The "Bermuda or Devil's Triangle" is an imaginary area located off the southeastern Atlantic coast of the United States. The area is noted for a high incidence of unexplained losses of ships, small boats, and aircraft. The apexes of the triangle are generally accepted to be Bermuda, Miami, Florida, and San Juan, Puerto Rico.

The "Devil's Triangle" is one of the two places on earth that a magnetic compass actually points towards true north. Normally it points toward magnetic north. The difference between the two is known as compass variation. The compass variation varies by as much as 20 degrees in different locations.

The other place where a magnetic compass points towards true north is an area off the east coast of Japan. It is called the "Devil's Sea" by Japanese and Filipino seamen. It is also known for mysterious disappearances.

Much of the interest in the "Bermuda Triangle" can be traced back to an article by Vincent Gaddis, "The Deadly Bermuda Triangle". The article appeared in the February 1964 edition of Argosy *magazine. The article included details of the disappearance of Flight 19.*

At 2.10 in the afternoon, on 5 December 1945, five Avenger aircraft took off from the Naval Air Station at Fort Lauderdale, Florida. The Grumman Avenger was a single-engine torpedo bomber which usually carried a crew of three. It was a routine practice mission and the flight was composed entirely of students except for the officer in command, a Lieutenant Charles Taylor.

The mission required Taylor and his students to fly due east 56 miles to Hens and Chicken Shoals to make practice bombing runs. When they had completed their bombing runs, they were to fly an additional 67 miles east, then turn north for 73 miles and finally straight back to base, a distance of 120 miles. This course would take them on a triangular path over the sea.

About an hour and a half after the flight had left, a Lt Robert Cox picked up a radio transmission from Taylor. Taylor indicated that his compasses were not working, but he believed himself to be somewhere over the Florida Keys (south of the Florida mainland). Cox urged him to fly north, toward Miami, if Taylor was sure the flight was over the Keys.

Taylor was an experienced pilot, but may have become confused at some point during the flight. He was unused to flying east toward the Bahamas. For some reason Taylor apparently thought the flight had started out in the wrong direction and had headed south toward the Keys, instead of east. This thought was to colour his decisions throughout the rest of the flight with deadly results.

The more Taylor took his flight north to try to get out of the Keys, the further out to sea the Avengers were actually travelling. Snatches of transmissions were picked up on the mainland indicating the other Flight 19 pilots were trying to get Taylor to change course. "If we would just fly west," one student told another, "we would get home."

By 4.45 p.m. it was obvious to the people on the ground that Taylor was lost. He was urged to turn control of the flight over to one of his students, but apparently he didn't. As it grew dark, communications deteriorated. From the few words that did get through it was apparent Taylor was still flying north and east, the wrong directions.

At 5.50 p.m. the ComGulf Sea Frontier Evaluation Centre managed get a fix on Flight 19's weakening signals. It was apparently east of New Smyrna Beach, Florida. By then communications were so poor that this information could not be passed to the lost planes.

At 6:20 a Dumbo Flying Boat was dispatched to try and find Flight 19 and guide it back. Within the hour two more planes, Martin Mariners, joined the search. By then, hope was rapidly fading for Flight 19. The weather was getting rough and the Avengers were very low on fuel.

The two Martin Mariners were supposed to rendezvous at the search zone. The second one, designated Training 49, never showed up.

The crew of the SS Gaines Mill observed an explosion over the water shortly after Training 49 had taken off. They headed toward the site. They saw what looked like oil and airplane debris floating on the surface. They were unable to recover any of it because of the bad weather. There was little doubt it was the remains of Training 49.

The last transmission from Flight 19 was heard at 7.04 p.m. Planes searched the area through the night and the next day. There was no sign of the Avengers.

The authorities didn't really expect to find much. The Avengers, crashing when their fuel was exhausted, would have been sent to the bottom in seconds by the 50-foot waves of the storm. As one of

Taylor's colleagues noted:

. . . they didn't call those planes "Iron Birds" for nothing. They weighed 14,000 pounds empty. So when they ditched, they went down pretty fast.

The US Navy's original investigation concluded the accident had been caused by Taylor's confusion. Taylor's mother refused to accept this. Finally the Navy changed the report to read that the disaster was for: "causes or reasons unknown."

In April 1952, another pilot, Gerald Hawkes, had a strange experience while flying from Idlewild Airport to Bermuda. Hawkes began his trip on a clear-skied, windless late afternoon. Suddenly, his plane dropped 200 ft, then shot up again. This pattern began again. To make matters worse, he and his crew were experiencing instrumentation problems. Consequently he was unable to make radio contact with either Florida or Bermuda, and had no idea where they were. They were finally able to get their bearings after they finally made contact with a radio ship. Hawkes thought that perhaps he was: "caught in an area where time and space seem to disappear".

Bibliography and Sources

Introduction – extracts from:
Letters of English Seamen, ed EH Moorhouse (Chapman & Hall, 1910)
Stove by a Whale, T. F. Heffernan (Wesleyan University Press, 1981)
Narratives of Shipwrecks of the Royal Navy between 1793 and 1857 compiled from official documents in the Admiralty by W. O. S. Gilly (Longman, 1864)

Natural – extracts from:
The Holy Bible, Oxford, 1830
Narratives of Shipwrecks of the Royal Navy between 1793 and 1857 compiled from official documents in the Admiralty by W. O. S. Gilly (Longman, 1864)
Report on the loss of the *Titanic* originally published 1912 (facsimile edition Alan Sutton Publishing, 1990)
The narratives of William Spavens first published in Louth, Lincolnshire in 1796. Published as *Memories of a Seafaring Life*, W. S. Spavens Folio Society (2000)
The Golden Wreck, A. McKee (New English Library, 1961)
The Uncommercial Traveller, Charles Dickens (London, Chapman & Hall, 1860)

Survivors of the Armada, E. Hardy (Constable, 1966)

Stove by a Whale, T. F. Heffernan (Wesleyan University Press, 1981)

The Wreck of the Serica, Thomas Cubbin (facsimile ed.) (Dropmore Press, London, 1950)

Report on the Loss of the Titanic, (Alan Sutton Publishing, 1990), originally published 1912

Titanic Survivor, The Memoirs of Violet Jessop Stewardess, (Sutton Publishing, 1998) © Sheridan House Inc.

The Last Voyage of the Schooner Rosamond Haakon Chevalier (Andre Deutsch, 1970)

Three Corvettes, Nicholas Monsarrat (Cassell & Co., 1945)

Gipsy Moth Circles the World, F. Chichester (Hodder & Stoughton, 1967)

117 Days Adrift, Maurice & Maralyn Bailey (Adlard Coles Nautical, 1974)

Nights of Ice Spike, Walker (St Martin's Griffin, New York, 1997)

All the Men in the Sea, Michael Krieger (Pocket Books, 2002)

Man-made – extracts from:

Pellew's Report to the Admiralty (Public Records office, Kew)

Titanic Survivor, The Memoirs of Violet Jessop Stewardess, (Sutton Publishing, 1998) © Sheridan House Inc.

Mysteries of the Sea, J. G. Lockhart (London, Philip Allan, 1924)

Tumult in the Clouds, J. A. Goodson (Arrow, 1986)

The Narratives of William Spavens, first published in Louth, Lincolnshire in 1796. Published as *Memories of a Seafaring Life*, W. S. Spavens Folio Society (2000)

Narratives of Shipwrecks of the Royal Navy between 1793 and 1857 compiled from official documents in the Admiralty by W. O. S. Gilly (Longman, 1864)

Mysteries of the Sea, J. G. Lockhart (London, Philip Allan, 1924)

The Wreck of the Torrey Canyon, C. Gill, F. Booker & A.

Soper (David & Charles, 1967)
Final Report of the Alaska Oil Spill Commission published in February 1990 by the State of Alaska
The Scotsman, 2 January 2003

Unexplained – extracts from:
The Holy Bible, Oxford, 1830
Mysteries of the Sea, J. G. Lockhart (London, Philip Allan, 1924)